ORALITY AND LITERACY IN THE MIDDLE AGES

UTRECHT STUDIES IN MEDIEVAL LITERACY

12

UTRECHT STUDIES IN MEDIEVAL LITERACY

ORALITY AND LITERACY IN THE MIDDLE AGES

ESSAYS ON A CONJUNCTION AND ITS CONSEQUENCES IN HONOUR OF D.H. GREEN

Edited by
Mark Chinca *and* Christopher Young

BREPOLS

British Library Cataloguing in Publication Data

Orality and literacy in the Middle Ages : essays on a conjunction and its consquences in honour of D.H. Green. – (Utrecht studies in medieval literacy ; 12)
1.Oral tradition – Europe – History – To 1500 2.Literature, Medieval – History and criticism 3.Oral tradition in literature 4.Literacy – Europe – History – To 1500
I.Chinca, Mark, 1959- II.Young, Christopher, 1967- III.Green, Dennis Howard, 1922-
302.2'242'094'0902

ISBN 2503514510

D/2005/0095/17

ISBN 2-503-51451-0

Printed in the E.U. on acid-free paper

With this volume in the series Utrecht Studies in Medieval Literacy the editors and contributors pay tribute to D.H. Green. If, for them, medieval literacy is now simply unthinkable except in its intricate relations with orality, this is thanks to his pioneering work, which – the disciplinary affiliations of the authors prove it – has resounded and provided inspiration far beyond its home in German studies.

Contents

Abbreviations

ABäG	*Amsterdamer Beiträge zur älteren Germanistik*
ANTS	*Anglo-Norman Text Society*
ASPR	*Anglo-Saxon Poetic Records*
ATB	*Altdeutsche Textbibliothek*
CCM	*Cahiers de Civilisation Médiévale*
CCSL	*Corpus Christianorum Series Latina*
DOE	*Dictionary of Old English*
EEMF	*Early English Manuscripts in Facsimile*
EETS	*Early English Text Society*
OS	*Original Series*
SS	*Supplementary Series*
GAG	*Göppinger Arbeiten zur Germanistik*
GRM	*Germanisch-Romanische Monatsschrift*
LiLi	*Zeitschrift für Literaturwissenschaft und Linguistik*
LMA	*Lexikon des Mittelalters*
Mfrk. Jb	*Mittelfränkisches Jahrbuch*
MGH	*Monumenta Germaniae Historica*
SS	*Scriptores*
MIGNE, *PL*	*Patrologiae Cursus Completus, Series Latina*, ed. J.-P. MIGNE
MLR	*Modern Language Review*
MTU	*Münchener Texte und Untersuchungen*
PBB	*Beiträge zur Geschichte der deutschen Sprache und Literatur*
(T)	Tübingen series
PhStQu	*Philologische Studien und Quellen*
RUB	*Reclams Universal-Bibliothek*
²*VL*	*Die deutsche Literatur des Mittelalters. Verfasserlexikon,* second, completely revised edition, ed. K. RUH, 10 volumes (Berlin, 1977-1999)

WSB	*Sitzungsberichte der [Kaiserlichen] Akademie der Wissenschaften [in Wien]. Philosophisch-historische Klasse*
ZfdA	*Zeitschrift für deutsches Altertum*
ZfdPh	*Zeitschrift für deutsche Philologie*

Orality and Literacy in the Middle Ages: A Conjunction and its Consequences

MARK CHINCA and CHRISTOPHER YOUNG

D.H. Green concludes his monumental study *Medieval Listening and Reading* with the statement that "the most important part of the title of this book is the word 'and'".[1] The conjunction does indeed encapsulate the premise underlying his entire argument, namely that medieval literacy and medieval orality must not be considered as two separate and largely unrelated cultures or modes of communication, but in their interpenetration, interplay and symbiosis. This is, of course, the premise of what has come to be called the 'weak' theory of the relationship between literacy and orality. Unlike its competitor, the 'strong' theory, this approach avoids polar oppositions and grandiose claims about the 'cognitive revolution' supposedly entailed by the advent of literacy;[2] it favours instead an emphasis on coexistence and interaction coupled with a more modest, non-determinist view of literacy as a facilita-

[1] D.H. GREEN, *Medieval Listening and Reading: The Primary Reception of German Literature 800-1300* (Cambridge, 1994), p. 315.

[2] The often-cited progenitors of the 'strong' approach are J. GOODY and I. WATT, "The Consequences of Literacy", *Comparative Studies in History and Society* 5 (1963), pp. 304-345 (repr. in: *Literacy in Traditional Societies*, ed. J. GOODY (Cambridge, 1968), pp. 27-68). In that essay, the authors highlighted what they consider to be intellectual differences between oral societies and literate societies: the former are characterized by homeostasis, the latter by a capacity for sceptical and logical thought. In his many subsequent publications on the social and cognitive consequences of literacy, however, Goody insists that, contrary to the opinion of his critics, he has never argued for any kind of hard-and-fast or polar opposition. See, for example, J. GOODY, *The Domestication of the Savage Mind* (Cambridge, 1977), pp. 3, 19, 37, 50, 165 n. 5 to c. 3; ID., *The Logic of Writing and the Organization of Society* (Cambridge, 1986), pp. XIII, XV, XVII, 182; ID., *The Interface between the Written and the Oral* (Cambridge, 1987), pp. 105-106.

tor of cognitive change. Since its explicit formulation by Ruth Finnegan,[3] the 'weak' theory has steadily gained ground in ethnography, history and sociology;[4] Green was the first scholar, however, to harness it to the production of a large-scale account of an entire medieval literature (understood here in a broad sense to include pragmatic as well as belletristic genres) over a long span of time.[5] Since the publication of his book, the approach has been extended to take in other textual cultures of the Middle Ages, for example English and French literature of the late Middle Ages,[6] Celtic society,[7] ninth-century Latin historiography,[8] and French literature of the twelfth and thirteenth centuries;[9] the appearance of studies like these in rapid succession indicates that a fundamental reorientation has taken place in medieval studies, with far-reaching consequences for our conceptions of the production, communication and reception of texts in the Middle Ages.

Of the several areas opened up by Green's work as ripe for further investigation, the contributors to this present volume have chosen to focus on two, which are central to the problem of orality and literacy in the Middle Ages: (1) the scope, content and interplay of medieval orality and literacy; (2) the status of the written word and the nature of reading in an 'aural' culture.[10]

[3] R. FINNEGAN, *Literacy and Orality: Studies in the Technology of Communication* (Oxford, 1988), pp. 141, 160.

[4] See M. INNES, "Memory, Orality and Literacy in an Early Medieval Society", *Past and Present* 158 (1998), pp. 3-36, at pp. 3-4.

[5] An important precursor is R. MCKITTERICK, *The Carolingians and the Written Word* (Cambridge, 1989), although her concern is not so much to examine literacy and orality in their interaction as to establish the importance of writing in what were no longer "purely oral societies" (p. 1). The relationship between writing and other means of communication is highlighted rather more in: *The Uses of Literacy in Early Medieval Europe*, ed. R. MCKITTERICK (Cambridge, 1990); see especially the editor's introduction and conclusion at pp. 6, 320-321.

[6] J. COLEMAN, *Public Reading and the Reading Public in Late Medieval England and France* (Cambridge, 1996: *Cambridge Studies in Medieval Literature* 26).

[7] *Literacy in Medieval Celtic Societies*, ed. H. PRYCE (Cambridge, 1998: *Cambridge Studies in Medieval Literature* 33). See especially the editor's introduction, pp. 10-11, and the essays by D.E. THORNTON, "Orality, Literacy and Genealogy in Early Medieval Ireland and Wales", pp. 83-98, and S. DAVIES, "Written Text as Performance: The Implications for Middle Welsh Narratives", pp. 133-148.

[8] INNES, "Memory, Orality and Literacy"; ID., "Trojans or Teutons? The Carolingians and the Germanic Past", in: *The Uses of the Past in Early Medieval Europe*, ed. Y. HEN and M. INNES (Cambridge, 2000), pp. 227-249.

[9] S. GAUNT, *Retelling the Tale: An Introduction to Medieval French Literature* (London, 2001).

[10] A third important area raised by Green, which would require a volume all of its own in order to do it justice, is the relationship between the rise of vernacular literacy and the emergence

Scope, Content and Interplay of Orality and Literacy

Although our understanding of culture and communication in the Middle Ages may now have put behind it the assumption of a 'Great Divide' between orality and literacy,[11] Green has pointed out that our basic terminology – word-pairs like 'orality' and 'literacy', 'listening' and 'reading' – continues to be freighted by assumptions of a polar opposition.[12] If we are to avoid giving an anachronistic picture of the Middle Ages, then both our definitions of these key terms and our conception of their interrelation are in need of reconsideration

of literary fiction. The notion that fiction is 'rediscovered' in the twelfth century is not new, and there has long existed a sense that, in the vernacular, this rediscovery is somehow related to the meeting of oral tradition and literate modes in the romance genre (see for example H.-R. JAUSS, "Epos und Roman – eine vergleichende Betrachtung an Texten des XII. Jahrhunderts", *Nachrichten der Gießener Hochschulgesellschaft* 31 (1962), pp. 76-92). Yet it has proved difficult to get any real purchase on the problem so long as the key terms ('orality', 'literacy', 'fiction') remain only vaguely or anachronistically defined. Green's work has put the discussion on a new footing. According to him, it was precisely the encounter and interplay of literacy and orality at secular courts that gave rise to the most significant innovation in vernacular literature of the twelfth and thirteenth centuries, namely fictionality. A simplified account of a complex process must suffice here (see *Medieval Listening*, pp. 249-264). The encounter at court of the written Latin culture of clerics on the one hand and the oral vernacular culture of lay aristocrats on the other led to a forcing of the issue of truth and falsehood (clerics disparage oral tradition as unverifiable and mendacious) and concomitantly to an equation of *res scripta* with *res facta*. When oral traditions are treated in writing, there are consequently two possible outcomes. One is the assimilation of the oral 'history' of laymen to the norms of the written historiography of clerics. The other is the emergence of a concept of truth whose basis is not factual or historical. This occurs when oral traditions are committed to writing but continue to attract criticism for falsehood (for example Arthurian stories); here we have an alliance of *res scripta* (connoting truth) with *res falsa* (connoting non-factuality) which develops into the self-conscious fictionality of vernacular written romance of the late twelfth and early thirteenth centuries. For recent discussion and development of this suggestive line of thinking, see K. RIDDER, "Fiktionalität und Medialität. Der höfische Roman zwischen Mündlichkeit und Schriftlichkeit", *Poetica* 34 (2002), pp. 29-40.

[11] The phrase 'Great Divide' originates with R. FINNEGAN, "Literacy versus Non-Literacy: The Great Divide? Some Comments on the Significance of 'Literature' in Non-Literate Cultures", in: *Modes of Thought: Essays on Thinking in Western and Non-Western Societies*, ed. R. HORTON and R. FINNEGAN (London, 1973), pp. 112-144. One of the most determined and cogent assaults on the notion of a 'Great Divide' in relation to medieval culture is mounted by COLEMAN, *Public Reading*, pp. 1-33.

[12] See his most recent statement on this question: D.H. GREEN, "Terminologische Überlegungen zum Hören und Lesen im Mittelalter", in: *Eine Epoche im Umbruch: Volkssprachliche Literalität 1200-1300. Cambridger Symposium 2001*, ed. C. BERTELSMEIER-KIERST and C. YOUNG (Tübingen, 2003), pp. 1-22, at pp. 1-3.

and refinement. Already a fair amount of terminology is available for distinguishing between different kinds of literacy and different levels of literate competence in medieval and earlier cultures,[13] but Green argues that our conception of medieval literacy must also be refined in a further important respect. Literacy in the Middle Ages cannot be defined adequately without taking into account the many ways in which the written word was embedded in orality. Written texts might be dictated, communicated and discussed orally; even reading to oneself could involve vocalizing the words on the page.[14] Acknowledging the spoken and aural dimensions of the written word also has repercussions for our definition of orality, for if it is true that the written word was spoken and heard as well as seen, it was also the case that the spoken word was implicated in the 'literate' domains of writing and visual apperception. The spoken word prompted its addressees to see as well as hear; this seeing might be physical, as when a scribe to whom another dictates sees the words he has been listening to, or when a listening audience observe the deictic gestures with which a reciter might accompany his reading from a book; on the other hand it might involve imaginary envisioning – 'seeing with the mind's eye' – of what is recited.[15] The spoken word is implicated in literacy in a further sense. Not all oral culture of the Middle Ages was illiterate culture, and illiterate culture was not exclusively oral. Centres of literacy such as monasteries and schools sustained an oral culture of their own, and as literacy spread out of its monastic and clerical bases into the domains of secular law, administration and literature, knowledge of at least the existence of the written word became a component of the oral culture of the laity.[16] There is, then, no pure literacy and no pure orality in the Middle Ages. Emphasizing this opens the way for fresh research whose basic assumption is the interplay, rather than the polar opposition, between the written word and oral networks of communication, in both clerical and lay contexts.

[13] For example M.B. PARKES, "The Literacy of the Laity", in: *Literature and Western Civilisation*, ed. D. DAICHES and A. THORLBY, vol. 2: *The Medieval World* (London, 1973), pp. 555-577, at pp. 555-560; E.A. HAVELOCK, *The Literate Revolution in Greece and its Cultural Consequences* (Princeton, 1982), pp. 59, 188, 339.

[14] GREEN, *Medieval Listening*, pp. 15-17, 30-35. See also (although the author's concern is to trace the rise of silent reading from the seventh century, rather than demonstrate the persistence of reading aloud): P. SAENGER, *Space between Words: The Origins of Silent Reading* (Stanford, 1997).

[15] GREEN, "Terminologische Überlegungen", pp. 7-11.

[16] GREEN, *Medieval Listening*, pp. 17, 273-293; cf. INNES, "Memory, Orality and Literacy", pp. 8-9.

Trying to define the scope and content of medieval orality and literacy leads on to consideration whether these categories are completely appropriate for the Middle Ages. Indeed, a striking feature of research in the field over the past twenty or so years has been the sometimes bewildering proliferation of new terminology intended to supplant, or at least supplement, the traditional vocabulary of orality and literacy. In 1983 Paul Zumthor sought to capture the interaction of the spoken and written word in medieval communication by introducing the term *vocalité*; it was intended as an overarching replacement for both 'orality', which suggests a culture totally uninfluenced by writing, as well as 'literacy', which fails to highlight the regular conversion of written marks into speech.[17] Because it tries to do justice to the specific complexities of medieval communication, the term has acquired a degree of currency;[18] its limitation however lies in its foregrounding of the voice, thus covering up again precisely the phenomenon to which it was intended to draw attention, namely the interaction of orality and literacy, of hearing, speaking and seeing.[19] Awareness of this interaction also motivates the terminological creativity of Joachim Bumke; arguing that the term 'orality' obscures the fact that in oral performance the voice is not the sole channel of communication, but is accompanied by facial expression, gesture and posture, he suggests that the truly operative distinction in medieval culture is not between orality and literacy, but between literacy and 'corporeality' (*Körperlichkeit*).[20] Although this term serves a useful purpose by provoking us to a keener appreciation of the ways in which communication in the Middle Ages was 'embodied',[21] the distinction between 'corporeality' and literacy is difficult to sustain, because, as Green reminds us, the activities of writing and reading also involve the body.[22]

[17] P. ZUMTHOR, *La Poésie et la voix dans la littérature médiévale* (Paris, 1987).

[18] See for example U. SCHAEFER, *Vokalität. Altenglische Dichtung zwischen Mündlichkeit und Schriftlichkeit* (Tübingen, 1992: *ScriptOralia* 39); J.-D. MÜLLER, *Spielregeln für den Untergang. Die Welt des Nibelungenliedes* (Tübingen, 1998), pp. 25-38.

[19] GREEN, "Terminologische Überlegungen", pp. 12-13.

[20] J. BUMKE, "Höfischer Körper – Höfische Kultur", in: *Modernes Mittelalter: Neue Bilder einer populären Epoche*, ed. J. HEINZLE (Frankfurt, 1994), pp. 67-102, at pp. 97-98; cf. H.-U. GUMBRECHT, "Beginn von 'Literatur'/Abschied vom Körper?", in: *Der Ursprung von Literatur: Medien, Rollen, Kommunikationsformen zwischen 1450 und 1550*, ed. G. SMOLKA-KOERDT, P.M. SPANGENBERG and D. TILLMANN-BARTYLLA (Munich, 1988), pp. 15-50.

[21] Cf. M. CARRUTHERS, *The Book of Memory: A Study of Memory in Medieval Culture* (Cambridge 1990: *Cambridge Studies in Medieval Literature* 10), pp. 54, 57; H. WENZEL, *Hören und Sehen, Schrift und Bild: Kultur und Gedächtnis im Mittelalter* (Munich, 1995).

[22] GREEN, "Terminologische Überlegungen", pp. 11-12.

Common to both the traditional terms and these newcomers is their isolation of what one might call the instrumental aspect of communication: the materials deployed, the organs of the body that are brought into play, and the senses involved in the production and reception of discourse. These aspects, though certainly important, do not, however, exhaust the nature of communication; the desire for an approach that also takes into account contextual and strategic as well as instrumental aspects of communication lies behind a recent trend to re-express the opposition between orality and literacy in terms of proximity and distance. The distinction between *Sprache der Nähe* and *Sprache der Distanz* was first formulated by the Romance linguists Peter Koch and Wulf Oesterreicher. For them proximity and distance represent two different conceptions of communication: immediacy, intimacy and open-endedness on the one hand, detachment, abstractness and finality on the other.[23] Although these conceptions frequently correlate with the media of speech and writing, so that the language of proximity is characteristic of oral face-to-face communication, whereas distance is typical of writing and reading, they are neither identical with nor completely tied to orality and literacy. Oral discourse may deploy the language of distance (for instance in the case of a formal speech, which may even be based on a text composed beforehand) and, conversely, written language can affect spontaneity and immediacy, feigning the directness of face-to-face communication. Of the numerous attractions and opportunities offered to medievalists by this approach,[24] the most important is the distinction it makes between communicative medium and communicative concept, together with the recognition that there is no fixed and straightforward correlation between them. This is stimulating a reappraisal of what have frequently been described as 'oral' or 'oral-formulaic' features of medieval texts. Rather than interpret these features as residues of an original or 'primary' orality that supposedly preceded the transmission of these texts in writing and which we can – at least dimly – glimpse, we are encouraged to consider whether we are not in fact dealing with the communicative strategy of a literate author, who is deploying the 'language of proximity' for rhetorical ends.[25] This 'conceptual', or 'fictive', orality there-

[23] P. KOCH and W. OESTERREICHER, "Sprache der Nähe – Sprache der Distanz. Mündlichkeit und Schriftlichkeit im Spannungsfeld von Sprachtheorie und Sprachgeschichte", *Romanistisches Jahrbuch* 36 (1986), pp. 15-43.

[24] See GREEN, "Terminologische Überlegungen", pp. 17-21.

[25] For an example of how the literate authors of Tristan romances could choose between languages of proximity and distance, see M. SCHAUSTEN, *Erzählwelten der Tristangeschichte im hohen Mittelalter. Untersuchungen zu den deutschsprachigen Tristanfassungen des 12. und 13. Jahrhunderts* (Munich, 1999: *Forschungen zur Geschichte der älteren deutschen Literatur* 24),

fore tells us nothing about the origins of written texts in orality, but much about the strategies of communication available to literate authors who work in a culture where the written word most usually reached its addressees through being read aloud.[26]

The Status of the Written Word and the Nature of Reading in an 'Aural' Culture

Green draws attention to the importance of what he calls the "intermediate mode of reception" for vernacular German literature.[27] There were few books destined for an exclusively reading or an exclusively listening public; rather vernacular books were written both for a reading public (which was very small, consisting typically of court clerics and noblewomen) and for reading aloud to a listening public. Recital – or, to use Joyce Coleman's term, 'aurality'[28] – was the predominant reception format, not just because allowance had to be made for the many lay people who could not read, but also because even those members of the public who had literate training would only occasionally possess or have direct access to a manuscript. A related point is that authors anticipated this double reception and included in their works features that were calculated to appeal both to listeners and to readers; some authors even appear to have felt a special bond of affinity with readers, who would be better able to work out and appreciate the more demanding aspects of the work.[29] Bringing the 'aurality' of book culture into view opens up two possible lines of further inquiry. First, it encourages a fresh examination of manuscripts in the light of their status as books intended for reading aloud; palaeographical and codicological evidence can be expected to yield new insights here. Second, it will be interesting to see whether this intermediate (or 'aural') mode, whose rise in Germany Green dates to the decades around 1200,[30] is equally important for the reception of literature in other European vernaculars, and if it is, what are the local and

pp. 91-106, 185-200.

[26] The term 'fictive orality' must therefore be used judiciously, because even written 'language of proximity', when read aloud, has a real medial orality; see D.H. GREEN, "Fictive Orality: A Restriction on the Use of the Concept", in: *Blütezeit. Festschrift für L. Peter Johnson zum 70. Geburtstag*, ed. M. CHINCA, J. HEINZLE and C. YOUNG (Tübingen, 2000), pp. 161-174.

[27] GREEN, *Medieval Listening*, pp. 169-230.

[28] COLEMAN, *Public Reading*, pp. 27-32.

[29] GREEN, *Medieval Listening*, pp. 171-172, 196.

[30] GREEN, *Medieval Listening*, pp. 299-300.

temporal variations. For French and English literature of the fourteenth and fifteenth centuries Coleman has argued that public recital from a manuscript to a group of listeners was still the most usual reception format; yet whereas Green brings out the difference between readers and listeners in thirteenth-century Germany, and emphasizes how readers probably had a keener appreciation of all the author's subtleties, Coleman tends to play down this contrast for France and England in the period she covers. According to her, even educated people preferred recital to private reading because they valued the companionability of a shared literary experience; those who read books closely and carefully were typically writers culling material for their next production.[31]

The Present Volume

The essays in this volume between them cover the whole of the Middle Ages, from the ninth to fifteenth centuries; they cover texts in several languages (English, Latin, French, Occitan, German) and range across the disciplines of literature, palaeography and art history. All the chapters, however, have a shared engagement with one or both of the themes described above.

The precocious literary cultures of Anglo-Saxon England and Carolingian Germany are the concern of Katherine O'Brien O'Keeffe and Wolfgang Haubrichs respectively. In both of these cultural spheres orality and literacy interact in historically specific forms of aurality. O'Brien O'Keeffe examines scenes of reading either described or envisaged by texts emanating from King Alfred and his circle. All of these sources provide evidence for what she terms 'corporate reading', a reading scene which corresponds to the 'intermediate' or 'aural' reception format outlined above in a number of respects. Unlike private reading (which was not unknown in the period – O'Brien O'Keeffe notes that Alfred's books reckon with educated users who read them in solitude), corporate reading involves more people than the individual holding the book in his or her hands. There are also listeners and discussants, who are not all necessarily literate and yet must be considered as *within* literate culture, in virtue of their exposure to and involvement in book-learning; this is the class of people who will later be termed *quasi litterati*.[32] Corporate reading also brings more human faculties and

[31] COLEMAN, *Public Reading*, pp. 88-108.

[32] The phrase is used by Lambert of Ardres to describe Count Baldwin II of Guines (d. 1206) who, although unable to read himself, listened so attentively to theological arguments and took such an interest in them that he was able to hold his own in learned discussions "*quasi literatus*"

senses into play than sight alone: speech (the book is read aloud), hearing (it is listened to), intellection (the book's contents are absorbed or learned); all these dimensions are comprised in the contemporary usage of the verb *legere*. The book one sees as a reader can also be imagined as talking to one; the metaphor of the 'talking book' is conceivable only in the context of a culture where books are regularly read aloud. O'Brien O'Keeffe further highlights a dimension of recital that has hitherto not been noticed: she suggests that the social and interactive nature of corporate reading draws in individuals who might, if they studied books in solitude, fall victim to self-regarding delusions about the extent of their knowledge and understanding. This ethical consideration is an interesting addition to other motivations that have been adduced for the popularity of recital – the scarcity of books, the desire for sociability, the opportunity for fostering group solidarity or for disseminating propaganda – and it will surely stimulate further investigations into whether it is more widespread in medieval culture.

Wolfgang Haubrichs is concerned with ways in which the oral culture of lay elites is present in written works intended for them. His chapter focuses on the two longest poetic works of the early Middle Ages – the anonymous *Heliand* and Otfrid von Weissenburg's *Evangelienbuch*, vernacular Bible epics composed in Old Saxon and Old High German respectively for the religious instruction of members of the lay nobility. Despite their tendency towards summary and synopsis, both texts swell up with narrative detail that goes beyond the pithiness of their biblical sources and contains elements that reflect the authors' contemporary mores and milieu. By taking a wide variety of examples, Haubrichs argues for a renewed engagement with these texts as sources for a wider appreciation of the cultural models and rituals of early medieval lay society. The colourful padding out of King Herod's birthday celebrations in the *Heliand* resonates with other sources of the period, and thus, despite literary refraction, lays bare the contemporary cultural habitus. The familiar heroic topoi that adorn the depiction of Peter cutting off the High Priest's servant's ear show, however, that the texts do not operate a simple 'germanification' of biblical matter. Rather, Christ's reaction to his disciple's violence negates well-known models of heroic behaviour in a manner that renders the latter obsolete. Against this general background, Haubrichs turns to the depiction of linguistic activity itself within the texts. The expansive portrayal of the naming of John the Baptist in both works shows the importance of such acts for dynastic pur-

(*Historia comitum Ghisnensium*, ed. J. HELLER [Hanover, 1879: *MGH SS* 24], p. 598).

poses within the lay nobility. The way in which Mary is addressed first by the angel Gabriel and later by her son Jesus at the wedding in Cana allows a rare glimpse of the way politeness was articulated in an early medieval vernacular.

The following four chapters, by Palmer, Hunt, Gaunt, Wolf, cover the period of the high Middle Ages. The position of the book in aurality, in particular the relation between its material layout and the ways in which its users may have read it, is the topic of Nigel F. Palmer's chapter on manuscripts containing verse narrative in Middle High German. Assumptions about how the verses written on the page were read or performed have frequently been based on arguments from analogy. The deployment, for example, in vernacular works of concluding formulae drawn from the liturgy (*Amen*, *Tu autem*) has been taken as an indication that these works were also intoned in the manner of liturgical recitative. Palmer places our ideas about the ways in which the written word was performed on the firmer ground of the palaeographical evidence of the manuscripts themselves. In this first-ever systematic analysis of punctuation and layout conventions in Middle High German manuscripts from the period 1100-1250, Palmer highlights a marked change that made itself felt around 1220/1230. Up until then, the convention – derived from Latin religious verse in a manner that remains to be clarified – was for verse to be written continuously, with the metrical structure (verses and couplets) marked by various combinations of *punctus*, *positurae* and *litterae notabiliores* which sometimes also provide the reader with hints about the syntactic or rhetorical structure of the text; these forms of material presentation can be related to a conception of vernacular narrative poetry – extending from religious poetry, through historiography to courtly literature based on French models – as intended for performance (whether intoned or not). The new layout conventions, which are copied from French and Anglo-Norman models, involve the setting out of verse in lines, so that what could previously only be heard in performance (the verse form) is now also visible to the reader on the page. Palmer cautiously relates this change to a shift in the cultural practice of reading and the related conceptualization of the text, from a dominant focus on performance to a new additional awareness of the verse as a literary form, to be seen in individual reading as well as heard in public recital.

The problem of 'manuscripts for reading' is also the focus of Tony Hunt's examination of one particular example, the early thirteenth-century Anglo-Norman *Life of St Modwenna*. The text contains both formal and stylistic features apparently suggestive of oral performance: a stanzaic form, originating in hymns, indicating the narrative might have been sung; direct appeals by the reciting narrator to a listening audience in the form of *audite/attendite* formulae; the orchestration of an immediate, emotive reaction to narrated events; the segmentation of narrative episodes by means of formulae of transition. Against this appearance of orality, however, Hunt marshals evidence for written composition and reading reception of the *Life*: the stanzaic form is handled in a 'writerly' manner, with frequent enjambment, suggesting that the text was not sung; initials, layout, and *scedulae* in the Campsey Manuscript are all evidence for individual reading (which does not of course exclude the possibility of reading aloud); the narrative units segmented by 'oral' formulae are highly variable in their length, and hence seem not to be units of original oral composition or performance. We are more likely therefore to be dealing with the textual imitation, or simulacra, of oral recitation techniques; in the terminology of Koch and Oesterreicher, we are confronted with a literate use of the language of proximity or *Sprache der Nähe*. The *Life* as it is transmitted is a written composition whose reception was realized in the spectrum from individual reading to public reading. Thus Hunt confirms for Anglo-Norman too the importance attached by Green to the 'intermediate mode', and reminds us once more of the usefulness of the distinction between medial and conceptual orality.

This distinction is elaborated theoretically by Simon Gaunt, in his chapter on troubadour lyric. Gaunt is less concerned with orality and writing in their medial sense than with 'conceptual' orality and literacy – the notions of presence and absence, immediacy and distance, often associated with these communication modes. Furthermore, Gaunt does not formulate the interplay between orality and literacy in terms of a written word that is subsidiary to, and englobed within, a primary context of orality. On the contrary, conceptual orality is the secondary and fictive product of a 'literate mentality' which is full of nostalgia for those features of oral communication that supposedly were disturbed by the advent of writing technology: immediacy, directness and presence. In the case of troubadour lyric, Gaunt argues that performance – often posited by scholars as the originary *Sitz im Leben* of the songs – was already enmeshed in communication networks marked by writing. He means this not just (or even primarily) in the sense that troubadours may have composed their own lyrics in writing, but also and especially in the sense that they composed as 'conceptual literates', that is, with an awareness of language as broken, distanced, alienated. (Here Gaunt highlights the similarity between Marcabru's conception of 'woven' and 'braided' discourse and Derrida's notions of *différance* and supplement.) This awareness is however obscured by the *chansonniers*, which are assiduous in their promotion of 'fictions of orality'.

The *vidas* and *razos* that accompany the lyrics, and which conjure up an *Urszene* for the songs of pure oral performance, are interpreted by Gaunt as secondary phenomena motivated by literate nostalgia for the immediacy and plenitude of the word sung or spoken in the co-presence of speaker and audience. Hence, when modern critics posit the 'primary orality' of medieval texts, they are uncritically buying into the nostalgic fictions of presence and immediacy that we find in the medieval sources themselves, and which a careful reading of these same sources often exposes as a secondary product of literateness. The actual oral-performative dimensions of medieval texts cannot be made present again via this kind of fictive construct, indeed probably elude our imaginative grasp altogether.

In his chapter, too, Jürgen Wolf interrogates commonly held notions about vernacular court culture in the thirteenth century by turning his attention to the relationship between Latin and the vernacular in psalters and prayer books. While such texts enjoyed an obviously important role in the clerical sphere, they seemed to occupy an equally significant place within the culture of the lay nobility, especially among literate women. The frequency with which these books are portrayed, both in German literary sources from the earliest stages (e.g. Otfrid) to the court narratives of the thirteenth century, and in sculpture on tombs and in churches, clearly points in this direction. Empirical facts bear out the evidence of these sources; the large number of extant psalter manuscripts indicates that the text-type belonged to the standard inventory of court life. Its popularity in the private devotional as well as the public representational sphere increased with the growth of lay piety from the second half of the twelfth century onwards. Gradually, the limited use of the vernacular in these books underwent a conceptual change. Whereas German instructions (what Psalm to read on which occasion), prayers and translations etc. had often been incorporated into already existing Latin books, these eventually became a part of the original design. Yet, it was not until the late thirteenth century that the German elements even came close to balancing out the Latin. Wolf's extensive knowledge of the manuscript base (the article concludes with a long appendix of Latin-German psalters from the twelfth and thirteenth centuries) allows him to draw authoritative conclusions. The contexts in which the vernacular is used clearly show not only that these books were intended to be *read*, but also that their Latin content would have been *actively* received. The calendar function of the psalter confirms this finding: dates recording the death of relatives were incorporated into the books, which were handed on from generation to generation. In the late twelfth and thirteenth centuries, therefore, lay courts had a deep sense of religiosity which was founded on writing. This climate meant that even before the explosion in the production of vernacular writing in the second half of the thirteenth century, central elements of court culture were anchored in writing. The high degree to which such writing was established in the lay milieu is exemplified by its simultaneous appropriation – key courtly literature manuscripts adopt psalter layout conventions – and rejection: critical voices (which portray a growing cynicism on the part of the clergy?) are raised against treating the psalter as a mere courtly accessory.

Each of the three late medieval contributions, by Monika Schausten, Sylvia Huot and Joyce Coleman, is concerned with the role of pictures in reading practices. Monika Schausten stays within the bounds of the written text itself, focusing on the function and significance of *ekphrasis* in the late medieval German romance. Much recent work has drawn attention to the ways in which key features of oral communication are assimilated by the medium of writing, where non-verbal signs are often highlighted in a gesture towards the importance of (audio-)visual modes of perception in oral culture.[33] Schausten moves the debate about such features on one stage by posing questions about their rhetorical and poetological functions, and their interaction with important thematic discourses, such as love. She does this by focusing on an ekphrastic episode in Johann von Würzburg's early fourteenth-century *Wilhelm von Österreich*, a text whose peculiar configuration is ideally suited to a problematization of the relation between visual and linguistic arts: the author expends far more energy on portraying the creative process than on producing a major *ekphrasis*; the protagonist asks artists to produce an image of his beloved without telling them what she looks like. Schausten's analysis uncovers a layering of effects: the ekphrastic passage forces the recipient to reflect on the narratability of the story; to recognize the position of the linguistic above the pictorial in the hierarchy of artistic skills; to appreciate the extremity of the protagonist's emotional state; and to reflect on the author's own handling of the literary process. In so doing, she paves the way for a more nuanced interpretation of the visual within media-historical approaches to medieval texts.

Sylvia Huot describes a mode of lay reading practice whereby the text on the page before the reader's eyes is associated with other 'virtual' texts to which it alludes or with which the reader connects it through mental processes of memory, association, meditation, imagination. This kind of 'polytextual' reading has its origins in the monastic practice of *lectio* coupled with *meditatio*

[33] For example WENZEL, *Hören und Sehen*; H. WANDHOFF, *Der epische Blick. Eine mediengeschichtliche Studie zur höfischen Literatur* (Berlin, 1996: *PhStQu* 141).

and *oratio*; the cultivation of reading as a spiritual exercise carries over into devotional and didactic books written in the vernacular and intended for a lay audience. Devotional books of the thirteenth and fourteenth centuries envisage their reception in terms of a shuttling between the physical book on the one hand and the metaphorical books of conscience, knowledge and wisdom on the other – books that the reader carried in himself or herself. Although these metaphorics often feature explicitly in the texts, the actual cognitive processes involved in what Huot terms a 'freewheeling' process of meaning-construction can only be speculatively recovered. Huot discusses illustrated psalters and Books of Hours made for lay readers in the fourteenth and fifteenth centuries, suggesting ways in which illuminations, marginalia, and bas-de-page illustrations (the latter often not obviously illustrating the text) could have sparked off trains of meditative association and reflection in readers of the text. Although in one respect the reading practice excavated by Huot resembles the modern experience (this is individual reading, and the primary sense engaged is sight), in its feeding off pictorial stimulus-material and the intertexts and countertexts stored in the book of one's memory it is quite different

The final chapter returns to the continued importance of public reading in late medieval vernacular culture. Joyce Coleman extends her pathbreaking work on this topic to discuss how even illuminations may have functioned within the aural reception format. The widespread assumption that illustrated codices were destined solely for visual reception, through individual reading and viewing, is called into question by the existence of what Coleman terms 'prelection pictures': illuminations, often frontispieces, depicting a public reading of the book in question to an audience of listeners. Coleman concentrates on one prominent example, the frontispieces to the two-volume Latin-French *City of God* made for Bishop Jean Chevrot ca. 1445. Through a close examination of the codicological and iconographic information in its interrelation with the political context, Coleman uncovers the ideological import of these pictures and links them to the aural reception format. The frontispiece to volume 1 is an illumination *of* aurality, in the sense that it depicts a scene of public reading; its politico-ideological message consists in the portrayal of the diffusion of ecclesiastical doctrine down lines of authority and hierarchy (Augustine – divines, who translate Latin – laity) that completely bypass and exclude temporal power. Both frontispieces are however also illuminations *in* aurality: their statements about the priority of church over state, and of clergy over laity, could have formed part of a listening public's 'horizon of expectation', shaping their understanding of what they heard, if we allow for the possibility of their seeing the picture before, during, or after a recital. The written and the spoken, the textual and the pictorial, past and present are all illuminated in their conjunction – testimony to the gain in understanding that comes with the willingness to dwell on the word ‘and’.

Listening to the Scenes of Reading: King Alfred's Talking Prefaces

KATHERINE O'BRIEN O'KEEFFE

In his fundamental study, *Medieval Listening and Reading*, Dennis Green taught us to think imaginatively and precisely about the multiple styles of interaction between the 'oral' and the 'written' in the early and central Middle Ages. His tests for the interaction of reading and listening across a range of early written texts guard against easy assumptions about trans-historical literacy when interpreting the evidence for listeners, readers and books before the advent of print.[1] The following essay hopes to follow where he has led by attending to evidence for multiple interactions between listening and reading at a particular moment in the history of English literacy. The three sets of prefaces examined here were written to accompany translations associated with King Alfred's project of vernacular literacy. These brief works offer useful evidence for reception of the translations by listeners, readers, or both.

King Alfred (later to be known as 'the great') is remembered in history for an unlikely pair of accomplishments: success in the field in securing Wessex against Viking invaders and a no less remarkable undertaking to revive and secure learning in the kingdom through a project of vernacular literacy. The rationale for this project – which ultimately encompassed four translations done by the king and his helpers as well as the introduction to his laws,[2] three other

[1] D.H. GREEN, *Medieval Listening and Reading: The Primary Reception of German Literature 800-1300* (Cambridge, 1994), pp. 169-202.

[2] *King Alfred's West Saxon Version of Gregory's Pastoral Care*, ed. H. SWEET (Oxford, 1871; repr. London, 1958: *EETS OS* 45, 50); *King Alfred's Old English Version of Boethius, De Consolatione Philosophiae*, ed. W.J. SEDGEFIELD (Oxford, 1899); *King Alfred's Version of St. Augustine's "Soliloquies"*, ed. T.A. CARNICELLI (Cambridge, MA, 1969); *King Alfred's Old English Prose Translation of the First Fifty Psalms*, ed. P. O'NEILL (Cambridge, MA, 2001); *Die*

translations undertaken perhaps at the king's instigation,[3] and possibly as well the 'Common Stock' of the Anglo-Saxon Chronicle[4] – is laid out in the much-studied Preface to the first of his translation projects.[5] The prose Preface that accompanied and introduced the king's translation of Gregory's *Regula pastoralis* assesses the state of learning in England amid the wreckage of decades of Viking depredations. If the king's repeated use of "*ða ic ða ðis eall gemunde*" ("when I remembered all this") and "*ða gemunde ic*" ("then I remembered") suggests a nostalgic construction of a brilliant culture of Latin learning in the Anglo-Saxon past, it is a rhetorical nostalgia immediately in the service of his present, for the king's radical project to translate into Old English those books "*niedbeðearfosta ... eallum monnum to wiotonne*" ("most necessary for all men to know") imagined a culture of readers, clerical and lay, religious and bureaucratic, with literacy in Old English as its centrepiece.

As part of his plan for a culture of readers, the king envisions "*sio giogúð*" (i.e. young, free men) set to learning how to read the vernacular. The most talented of these would proceed to study Latin and enter the clergy. Alfred does not spell out in the Preface how this training would be accomplished, but the Preface's switch from "*ic*" to "*ge*" to "*we*" at this point suggests that the king

Gesetze der Angelsachsen, ed. F. LIEBERMANN, 3 vols. (Halle, 1903-16; repr. Aalen, 1960).

[3] *The Old English Orosius*, ed. J.M. BATELY (London, 1980: *EETS SS* 6); *The Old English Version of Bede's Ecclesiastical History of the English People*, ed. T. MILLER, 2 vols. (London, 1890-98; repr. London, 1959: *EETS OS* 95, 96, 110, 111); *Bischof Wærferths von Worcester Übersetzung der Dialoge Gregors des Grossen*, ed. H. HECHT (Leipzig 1900; repr. Darmstadt, 1965: *Bibliothek der angelsächsischen Prosa* 5). For an assessment of the Old English prose texts written in the thirty years prior to 900 see J.M. BATELY, "Old English Prose Before and During the Reign of Alfred", *Anglo-Saxon England* 17 (1988), pp. 93-138, at p. 118 and n. 145.

[4] *Two of the Saxon Chronicles Parallel*, ed. C. PLUMMER, 2 vols. (Oxford, 1892-98; reissued with a bibliographical note by D. WHITELOCK, Oxford, 1952). For the earliest representative of the 'Common Stock', MS A, see now *The Anglo-Saxon Chronicle, A Collaborative Edition*, vol. 3: *MS A*, ed. J.M. BATELY (Cambridge, 1986).

[5] Although the 'Preface' was actually a circular letter (see below, p. 25 and n. 25). I use its conventional title. On the basis of surviving ninth-century manuscripts and other evidence, Jennifer Morrish evaluates Alfred's exaggeration in "King Alfred's Letter as a Source on Learning in England in the Ninth Century", in: *Studies in Earlier Old English Prose*, ed. P.E. SZARMACH (Albany, 1986), pp. 87-107, at p. 90. On 'pragmatic literacy', see M.B. PARKES, "The Literacy of the Laity", in: *Literature and Western Civilisation*, ed. D. DAICHES and A. THORLBY, vol. 2: *The Medieval World* (London, 1973), pp. 555-577, at pp. 555-556. On the king's vernacular project as a building of 'national' identity see S. FOOT, "The Making of *Angelcynn*: English Identity Before the Norman Conquest", *Transactions of the Royal Historical Society*, 6th ser. vol. 6 (1996), pp. 25-49; K. DAVIS, "National Writing in the Ninth Century: A Reminder for Postcolonial Thinking about the Nation", *Journal of Medieval and Early Modern Studies* 28 (1998), pp. 611-637.

imagines an active collaboration with the bishops who receive this letter along with the *Pastoral Care*: "*& gedon swæ we swiðe eaðe magon mid Godes fultume ... ðæt*[*te*] *eall sio gioguð ... sien to liornunga oðfæste ... oð ðone first ðe hie wel cunnen Englisc gewrit arædan*" ("and bring about as we may very easily with God's help ... that all the youth ... be put to learning ... until the time that they know well how to read English writings").[6] Such a project, then, required collaboration not only between the king and his helpers to produce the translations and their copies but also collaboration between the king and the bishops to produce the readers who would learn to read these texts. What scenes of reading are imagined for the texts in the king's project? While Alfred is explicit in the Preface about assessing the contemporary state of literacy in terms of the relative dearth of Latin and English readers, he tells us little directly about the actual process of reading, that is, the precise set of activities implied in his phrase "*Englisc gewrit arædan*" ("to read English writings") or indeed "*Læden gewrit arædan*" ("to read Latin writings").[7]

Three of the texts that the king either translated or had translated have prefaces in prose and in verse that tell us much in their own voices about the scenes of reading imagined for these works by Alfred and his helpers, if we are willing to listen attentively. To understand what these prefatory texts tell us, however, we must first look at the circumstances of the king's own reading as Asser portrays it in his biography as well as the ways in which the king himself refers to the process. Only then will it be possible to understand the functions of voice, listening and reading in the prose and verse prefaces and the evidence they offer for the imagined reception of Alfred's works.

Alfred's Corporate Reading

The beginning and conclusion of Asser's famous account of Alfred's journey into literacy are marked, appropriately enough, by the king's holding a book.[8] In the first of these scenes (c. 23), when he is seven or younger, all he can do with the book in his hand is convey it to his teacher. Any further interac-

[6] *King Alfred's West Saxon Version of Gregory's Pastoral Care*, p. 7, ll. 8-12. Sweet's text prints "*ge don*" instead of "*gedon*".

[7] Alfred hints at the process when he talks in the preface about his own learning from his teacher/helpers.

[8] *Asser's Life of King Alfred Together with the Annals of Saint Neots Erroneously Ascribed to Asser*, ed. W.H. STEVENSON (Oxford, 1906; repr. with an introductory article by D. WHITELOCK, Oxford, 1959).

tion with the book requires the mediation of a reader, through whose voice Alfred hears and learns. By contrast, in the final scene of his reading, the account of his undertaking to read Latin, the book the king holds in his hand is one of his own making (though written by another or others). This book, containing Latin passages he had caused to be recorded from what he heard aloud from the reading of his helpers, grew, Asser says, to the size of a psalter (c. 89). From this book Alfred hoped to read, translate, and teach.

Asser's early portrait of Alfred as the illiterate prince thirsting for knowledge (c. 22) presents an Alfred for whom books are ciphers, but whose eagerness to learn is indexed by his easily trained memory. The meeting of illiterate and book culture is famously staged in c. 23 where his mother, Osburh, offers a book of Old English poetry to whichever of her sons could learn it first. Though the youngest of the brothers, Alfred is "*pulchritudine principalis litterae illius libri illectus*" ("attracted by the beauty of the book's first letter"), an illiterate's visual response to an object otherwise unintelligible to him.[9] To gain the book, Alfred applies his skills at learning vernacular poetry *memoriter*, but the significant difference in c. 23 from the preceding scene of learning vernacular poetry is that Asser has inserted a book into the scene of Alfred's learning. Alfred is still an *auditor* in the process of learning verse, and his teacher, functioning as *lector*, substitutes for the performer of verse.[10] What is interesting about this scene, however, is the degree to which *intellegere, legere*, and *recitare* are interrelated. In translating "*magistrum adiit et legit*" as "[he] went to his teacher and learnt it", Keynes and Lapidge point out that Alfred's undoubted illiteracy at this point strains the meaning of "*legit*". They suggest that either the text's "*et*" is an error for "*qui*" (i.e. Alfred took it to his teacher *who* read it) or that "*legit* means 'absorbed its contents' or 'learnt'", as they have translated it.[11] I would suggest that the nexus of 'learning', 'reading', and 'hearing' in the text as it stands, shows us how vital the presence of the voice is in the scene of reading and how social that scene is in Alfred's experience. For the teacher to read is for Alfred to hear and learn. In fact, at this point in the narrative, for

[9] S. LERER, *Literacy and Power in Anglo-Saxon Literature* (Lincoln, 1991), pp. 68 and 215, n. 12, would interpret "*illectus*" as 'seduced' rather than 'attracted'. While he is correct to point to the range of meanings of *illicere, illectare*, which he also cites, could not produce the participle in question. Given the operation of divine inspiration in the episode, 'attracted' is the more likely meaning.

[10] Though concentrating on the central Middle Ages, M.T. CLANCHY, *From Memory to Written Record: England 1066-1307* (second edition; Oxford, 1993), p. 270, illustrates vividly the amount of hearing in *lectio*.

[11] *Alfred the Great: Asser's Life of King Alfred and Other Contemporary Sources*, trans. S. KEYNES and M. LAPIDGE (New York, 1983), p. 239, n. 48.

Alfred, *legere* is 'to hear' as part of a corporate process of using books. "*Quo lecto*" (here "when the book had been read" means with reference to Alfred, "when the book had been learned"), Alfred returns to his mother and recites the contents as proof of the process. These two instances of *legere* make reading a corporate activity that is not solely owned by the one who pronounces the words inked on the page. Though not, at this point in his life, a reader in our sense of the term, Alfred is, nonetheless, *within* reading in the extended sense of learning from a book by listening.[12]

To understand what reading Alfred himself performs in c. 89, the climax in Asser's portrayal of his literacy, we must inflect that description with Asser's characterization of his association with the king on his second visit in 886 (c. 81), where the bishop describes his main activity at court as reading aloud to the king:[13]

> *et cum eo illa vice octo mensibus in curto mansi, in quibus recitavi illi libros quoscunque ille vellet, et quos ad manum haberemus. Nam haec est propria et usitatissima illius consuetudo ... aut per se ipsum libros recitare, aut aliis recitantibus audire.*

> and on that occasion I remained with him at court for eight months, during which time I read aloud to him whatever books he wished and which we had to hand. For it is his peculiar and most characteristic habit either to read books aloud himself or to listen to others doing so.[14]

Whatever books Asser may have read to the king, and in whichever language, at this point in Asser's narrative of the king's developing literacy, "read books aloud himself" must refer to the king's reading books in English, since Asser dates the king's miraculous ability to read Latin to 11 Nov. 887.[15] It is equally clear, however, that the king listened to books in Latin read by others, although here, "read" may mean read to him and translated into English. The king's first reading in Latin is, significantly, Scripture, and later the passages that Asser copied for him (cc. 87, 89). But these later passages were first read aloud by Asser and then entered into the 'enchiridion' at the king's direction. In Asser's climax to the narrative of the king's reading, the last stop in the royal progress toward reading is the king's entrance into reading and translating Latin. Even

[12] At this point Alfred may be described as *quasi litteratus*. See GREEN, *Medieval Listening and Reading*, p. 288.

[13] *Alfred the Great*, p. 27; see also pp. 213-214, n. 24 on the chronology of Asser's visit.

[14] *Asser's Life of King Alfred*, p. 67, c. 81, ll. 9-15; *Alfred the Great*, pp. 96-97.

[15] *Alfred the Great*, pp. 213-214, n. 24.

this was almost certainly a scene of reading aloud, since the king required an amanuensis for writing what he read and translated.

The corporate model of reading implicit here is that laid out in cc. 77 and 88, where reflection takes place not in solitude, but in a scene of reading where books are heard:

> *Nam die noctuque, quandocunque aliquam licentiam haberet, libros ante se recitare talibus imperabat – non enim unquam sine aliquo eorum se esse pateretur – quapropter pene omnium librorum notitiam habebat, quamvis per se ipsum aliquid adhuc de libris intelligere non posset. Non enim adhuc aliquid legere inceperat.*

> For day and night, whenever he had any free time, he would order them to read books aloud in his presence – nor could he bear ever to be without some one of them – in which fashion he had knowledge of almost all books, although at this point he was not able by himself [= "*per se ipsum*"] to understand anything from books. For he had not yet begun to read anything.[16]

Elsewhere I have considered the implications of this passage (and of c. 88) for Alfred's history of learning to read and his inability to write.[17] In the present argument, however, of primary interest is the evidence for the interaction of learned listening with reading in Alfred's circle and the incorporation of both modes of reception in the contemporary vocabulary of literacy. The meaning of *legere* in this chapter is extended beyond the meaning of the word in c. 23. There, in the context of Alfred's total illiteracy, the king was an actor in the scene of reading by his active listening and evident learning. Here Asser has raised the stakes, for *legere* in the context of c. 77 (where Alfred is assembling his learned helpers Wærferth, Plegmund, Athelstan, Werwulf, Grimbald and Asser) clearly means to read Latin. Asser distinguishes between being able to read on one's own ("*per se ipsum*"), which the king is unable to do, and reading/learning from books with the help of teachers who read aloud ("*recitare*"), which is the king's regular practice.

A modification that Alfred makes in Augustine's *Soliloquies* (perhaps with an attendant error) suggests how dominant the corporate scene of reading was in Alfred's experience of literacy. When Augustine admits to Ratio that it would be impossible for him to hold everything in his memory, Ratio observes that writing offers the solution but poses a further problem:

[16] *Asser's Life of King Alfred*, p. 63, c. 77, ll. 20-26.

[17] K. O'Brien O'Keeffe, *Visible Song: Transitional Literacy in Old English Verse* (Cambridge, 1990), pp. 81-84.

> R[*atio*]. *Ergo scribendum est. Sed quid agis, quod valetudo tua scribendi laborem recusat? Nec ista dictari debent; nam solitudinem meram desiderant. A*[*ugustinus*]. *Verum dicis. Itaque prorsus nescio quid agam. R. Ora salutem et auxilium quo ad concupita pervenias, et hoc ipsum litteris manda, ut prole tua fias animosior. Deinde quod invenis paucis conclusiunculis breviter collige. Nec modo cures invitationem turbae legentium; paucis ista sat erunt civibus tuis. A. Ita faciam.*
>
> Ratio: Therefore, it must be written down. But how will you do this, when your illness prevents the exertion of writing? Nor should such things be dictated, for they require pure solitude. Augustine: You are right. And I certainly do not know what I should do. Ratio: Pray for health and for the help by which you may arrive at what you are striving for, and to this end commit it to writing, that you may become the stronger by your progeny. Then what you discover collect briefly in a few short conclusions. Do not worry about attracting a crowd of readers; these things will be sufficient for a few of your fellow countrymen. Augustine: I will do so.[18]

As Keynes and Lapidge point out, the Old English translation reverses the sense of the Latin text, which makes "pure solitude" ("*solitudo mera*") the requirement for learned composition.[19]

> *Þa cwæð heo: befæste hit þonne bocstafum and awrit hit. ac me þincð þath þeah, þæt þu si to unhal þæt ðu ne mage hit æall awritan; and þeah þu æall hal were, þu beþorftest þæt ðu hæfdest digele stoge and æmanne ælces oðres þinges, and fæawa cuðe men and creftige mid þe, ðe nan wiht ne amyrdan, ac fultmoden to þinum crefte.*
>
> Then she said: secure it with letters and write it down. But it seems to me, however, that you are too unwell to write it entirely, and even if you were completely well, you require a private place and solitude from all other affairs, and a few men learned and knowledgeable with you, who would not bother you at all, but assist you in your work.[20]

Alfred's revision, however, does not so much misunderstand Augustine's description of his own process of reflection as represent it in terms of the king's experience of reading and learning. By replacing Augustine's "*solitudo mera*" with a scene busy with helpers, Alfred effectively reconceives Augustine's

[18] Augustine, *Soliloquiorum libri duo*, MIGNE, *PL* 32 (1841), col. 869: "*Ecce, fac te invenisse aliquid; cui commendabis, ut pergas ad alia? A. Memoriae scilicet. R. Tantane illa est ut excogitata omnia bene servet? A. Difficile est, imo non potest*".

[19] *Alfred the Great*, p. 300, n. 6.

[20] *King Alfred's Version of St. Augustine's "Soliloquies"*, p. 49, ll. 17-21.

fruits of mental reflection as the gathering of discrete pieces of knowledge from books. Just such a process is imagined allegorically in the preface to the *Soliloquies*. In the extended image of gathering building timber from the forest of Augustine's, Gregory's, and Jerome's works in order to "enlighten the eyes of my mind" ("*mines modes eagan to þam ongelihte*"),[21] Alfred makes spiritual enlightenment the end point of a process of gathering things from books. In this process far from solitary reflection, a "few" well-known and learned ("*cræftige*") men assist the king to pursue his "*cræfte*", here to be understood as reflection and learning from books. Although I have claimed that this revision of Augustine's description is less misunderstanding than cultural translation, one clause may well be a result of misprision. Ratio's advice against seeking a readership ("*Nec modo cures invitationem turbae legentium*") is deleted from Alfred's translation. However, a proleptic, defensive response to (and, I suggest, a misunderstanding of) the deleted phrase is inserted into the description of Alfred's ideal scene of reading. Interpreting "*legentium*" as 'readers aloud' rather than the 'reading public' of Augustine's text, Alfred's translation has the *Soliloquies*' interlocutor qualify his helpers as those "*ðe nan wiht ne amyrdan*" – that is, readers in the corporate scene of literacy who would not disturb him, but rather would assist his work of thinking and learning. This transformation also suggests the degree to which Alfred understood reading as a corporate activity.

Asser's narratives and the testimony of Alfred's revision in the *Soliloquies* offer concrete evidence of Alfred's corporate and aural style of literacy. We may turn, now, to the evidence that the publication of three translations associated with Alfred's program of English literacy offers for imagining reading and hearing in the reception of these texts.

The Speaking Prefaces

Three of the translations emerging from Alfred's circle were furnished with verse and prose 'prefaces' early in the history of their publication. The evidence offered by these varied introductory texts is complicated by the differing generic expectations of prose and verse. The metaphorics of the verse texts particularly require careful reading to distinguish among the different voices that claim an audience's ear. Read together, these prefaces, authored variously by Alfred or members of his wider circle, situate their accompanying text within

[21] *King Alfred's Version of St. Augustine's "Soliloquies"*, p. 48, l. 1.

Alfred's vernacular project and attest, in different registers, to the circumstances of reception imagined for each text.

The first of Alfred's translations, his Old English version of Gregory's *Regula pastoralis*, was accompanied by two prefatory texts, one prose and the other verse. Alfred's authorship of the prose text is unquestioned; his authorship of the verse preface, the "Metrical Preface to the Pastoral Care", is generally accepted. Even so, the structure and hands of Oxford, Bodleian Library, Hatton 20, a 'headquarters' copy of Alfred's translation, show that the prefatory material was not integral to the translation. The prose Preface, written separately on a bifolium in a hand other than those of the two main scribes of the translation, was added to the completed copy of the translation, after which its inscription was written.[22] Afterwards, the "Metrical Preface to the Pastoral Care" was copied onto the back page of the bifolium (f. 2v, ll. 14-23) by another hand, probably that of the main scribe of the translation.[23] The format of the book and the sequence of its copying indicate that Alfred's circular letter, now universally referred to as "the prose Preface", was an afterthought.[24] The change of hands between the prose and verse prefaces and the location of the "Metrical Preface" in the empty space after the end of the prose Preface together suggest that there was no intrinsic relationship between the prose Preface (actually simply Alfred's circular letter) and the following "Metrical Preface".[25] Nonetheless, their inclusion in the 'headquarters' copy of the text by hands dateable to the period 890-97 should give us confidence that their evidence speaks clearly to early expectations for the circumstances of the text's reception.

Alfred's circular letter (the prose Preface), in laying out the case for vernacular literacy, addresses the bishops who have received the translation. These episcopal recipients comprise an unusually well-defined group of users for the text. The prose Preface does not state directly the mode of reception Alfred imagined for the book, though his graceful compliment to the bishops ("*uncuð hu longe ðær swæ gelærede biscepas sien*" ["It is unknown how long there will

[22] *The Pastoral Care: King Alfred's Translation of St. Gregory's Regula Pastoralis*, ed. N.R. KER (Copenhagen, 1956: *EEMF* 6), pp. 19-22. N.R. KER, *Catalogue of Manuscripts Containing Anglo-Saxon* (Oxford, 1957; reissued 1990), p. 385.

[23] *The Pastoral Care*, p. 22. *Anglo-Saxon Minor Poems*, ed. E.V.K. DOBBIE, *Anglo-Saxon Poetic Records* vol. 6 (New York, 1942), p. 110.

[24] As argued by K. SISAM, *Studies in the History of Old English Literature* (Oxford, 1953), p. 145.

[25] On the difference between 'Preface' and circular letter see F.P. MAGOUN, "King Alfred's Letter on Educational Policy According to the Cambridge Manuscripts", *Mediaeval Studies* 11 (1947), pp. 113-122, and MORRISH, "King Alfred's Letter", p. 87.

be such learned bishops"]), implies that he expected the bishops to read the book themselves, much as any of his learned teachers was able to read "*per se ipsum*".[26] The conceit of the talking book in the following verse preface makes that inference a likelihood. There the voice given to the book speaks the text's history from Gregory's evangelization to Alfred's promulgation of it in English.[27] The voice speaks directly of itself as a translation, as one in a set of copies produced from the exemplar ("*bi ðære bisene*"). The writing of this poem in Hatton 20 identifies the object upon which it is inscribed as "*þis ærendgewrit*" ("this message"), suggesting an identity between 'text' and book – even in the face of a multiplicity of copies – that runs counter to our own textual sensibilities.[28] Thus when the talking book speaks, it is always as an object being looked at. "Me" and "my words" are themselves objects inviting and expecting the gaze of readers, here imagined as the bishops of the circular letter, less learned successors, or copyists. The voice of the "Metrical Preface" speaks, paradoxically, to the eyes of a reader imagined to read "*per se ipsum*". Together the two prefaces imagine a scene of individual reading.

The conceit of the talking book is similarly used in a prefatory poem coming from Alfred's extended circle. From Asser (c. 77) we learn that Alfred commissioned Wærferth, the bishop of Worcester, to translate Gregory's *Dialogi* into Old English. Asser is complimentary about Wærferth's skills, pronouncing the translation to have been done "*elucabratim* [*sic*] *et elegantissime*" ("intelligently and in a very polished style"),[29] though recent evaluation has been considerably cooler.[30] Although Wærferth's translation rejoices as well in a prose preface speaking in Alfred's voice, neither is likely to be the king's own composition, and the Old English translation of the *Dialogi* appears to have been sent out initially with out any preface at all.[31] The "Metrical Preface to Wærferth's Translation of Gregory's Dialogues" begins at the top of London,

[26] *King Alfred's West Saxon Version of Gregory's Pastoral Care*, p. 9, ll. 3-4.

[27] On the speaking book within the genre of talking object riddles see *Alfred the Great*, p. 333, n. 1. J.W. EARL, "King Alfred's Talking Poems", *Pacific Coast Philology* 24.1-2 (1989), pp. 49-61, at p. 58, suggests that these poems are closer in genre to colophons. This essay is reprinted with minor revisions in his *Thinking About "Beowulf"* (Stanford, 1994), pp. 87-99.

[28] EARL, "King Alfred's Talking Poems", p. 51 argues that the text is speaking, and offers as analogy the portrait of St. John in the Book of Kells.

[29] *Alfred the Great*, p. 92.

[30] M. Godden suggests that Asser was more enthusiastic than discerning about Wærferth's abilities as a translator. See his "Wærferth and King Alfred: the Fate of the Old English *Dialogues*", in: *Alfred the Wise: Studies in Honour of Janet Bately on the Occasion of her Sixty-Fifth Birthday*, ed. J. ROBERTS and J.L. NELSON with M. GODDEN (Cambridge, 1997), pp. 35-51, at pp. 44-47.

[31] GODDEN, "Wærferth and King Alfred", p. 40.

British Library, Otho C. i, vol. 2, f. 1r (=Hecht's O).[32] Although the MS was damaged in the 1731 Cotton fire and its leaves are now mounted separately, there was no loss of leaves at the beginning,[33] and it appears that the *Dialogues* in Otho C. i were copied without the prose preface that appears in the other two manuscripts.[34] It is likely, therefore, that the ninth-century ancestor of Otho C. i, sent by Alfred to Wulfsige, bishop of Sherborne, also lacked the prose preface. In the single copy of the "Metrical Preface" as we now have it, the last three letters of 'Wulfstan', the bishop's name currently in l. 12b, are written over an erasure made to change the name 'Wulfsige' to the name of a bishop of Worcester, where the later part of the manuscript was copied.[35] Thus the "Metrical Preface" seems to have been added in Sherborne, perhaps by Wulfsige himself.

The textual difficulties with this poem are compounded by the fire damage to the first page. Yerkes reconstructs the first line as: "*Se ðe me rædan ðencð teonð mid rihtum geðance*" and translates "he who thinks to read me troubles himself with a good intention".[36] Keynes and Lapidge reasonably find his translation of "*teonð*" wanting. Their alternative, which takes "*teonð*" to mean 'close' (from *tynan*), leads them to translate: "He who sets out to read me

[32] *The Anglo-Saxon Minor Poems*, pp. 112-113. For a facsimile see *Old English Verse Texts From Many Sources: A Comprehensive Collection*, ed. F.C. ROBINSON and E.G. STANLEY (Copenhagen, 1991: *EEMF* 23), Pl. 7.

[33] KER, *Catalogue*, item 182, p. 236.

[34] Cambridge, Corpus Christi College, 322 (= C) and Oxford, Bodleian Library, Hatton 76 (= H). Although referred to as a verse preface, the complete prefatory material as copied in Otho C. i, vol. 2 includes as well a short prose introduction that appears only in this manuscript: "*Her ongynneð se æresða stream ... on liues weg*". SISAM, *Studies*, p. 229, believes that this brief prose statement is proper to the translation, rather than the preface, since it is very much in the manner of the brief introductory statements that introduce each book in the translation. The palaeography of the manuscript is complex and a full discussion is beyond the scope of the present paper. KER, *Catalogue*, item 182, p. 237, states that ff. 1-61 are in "a late type of square Anglo-Saxon minuscule which looks about 40 years older than the rest of the manuscript". H. GNEUSS, *Handlist of Anglo-Saxon Manuscripts: A List of Manuscripts and Manuscript Fragments Written or Owned in England up to 1100* (Tempe, AZ, 2001), item 359, tentatively locates the first 61 folios in "SW England?" in s. XI^{in}. Godden discusses the implications of the current state of the manuscript for the origin of its first two books of the Dialogues at Sherborne in "Wærferth and King Alfred", p. 41.

[35] K. SISAM, "Addendum: The Verses Prefixed to Gregory's 'Dialogues'", in: ID., *Studies*, pp. 225-231; D. YERKES, "The Translation of Gregory's Dialogues and its Revision: Textual History, Provenance, Authorship", in: *Studies in Earlier Old English Prose*, ed. P.E. SZARMACH (Albany, 1986), pp. 335-343, at pp. 340-341, attributes the prose portion of the preface in Otho C. i to Wulfsige not Wærferth.

[36] D. YERKES, "The Full Text of the Metrical Preface to Wærferth's Translation of Gregory", *Speculum* 55 (1980), pp. 505-513, at p. 510 and p. 512.

through will close me with appropriate recompense".[37] This sense of 'close' is supported by the description of St. Chad in the OE translation of Bede's *Historia ecclesiastica* (IV.3) where the saint is said to have closed his books and prayed when bad weather approached: "*Gif þonne swiðra wind aras, þonne tynde he his bec & forþleat in his ondwlitan & geornlice in his gebede hleoðrade ...* ".[38] In this reading, the reader addressed directly in line one is imagined to be holding the book. Beyond that, the poem's further deployment of the conceit makes the book appeal directly for prayers from a user who holds it: "*þu [ðas boc] on þinum handum nu hafast 7 sceawast*" ("you [who] now have and look at this book in your hands"). If the implied "you" of this poem is the one who opens and closes the book in reading, and while holding the book, by implication, reads its inscribed verse, Wulfsige's "Metrical Preface" imagines a scene of individual reading similar to that imagined for the translation of the *Regula pastoralis*.

By contrast, the separately supplied prose Preface to Wærferth's *Dialogues* (in C and H), contains a number of double gestures about books and hearing: in ventriloquizing the king, the prose Preface has Alfred claim to have acquired materials for spiritual reflection by *hearing* the discourse of holy books ("*þurh haligra boca gesægene oft gehyred*").[39] The eleventh-century revision in the H-Preface "often heard through the *reading* of holy books" ("*þurh haligra boca* rædinge *oft gehyred*", emphasis added), while clearly imagining a combination of reading and listening, speaks most likely to a generic notion of reception by hearing imagined for the eleventh rather than the ninth century. Despite the apparently conflicting information in the verse and prose prefaces, all versions have one piece of information in common, for they begin the translation proper with a statement suggesting a listening audience: "*Forþon nu æt ærestan we magon gehyran*" ("therefore at the beginning we may now hear"; H has variants). The difficulty with these teasing strands of evidence, however, is that they cannot simply be combined. Only Otho C. i, vol. 2 contains the verse preface; the Corpus and Hatton MSS contain the prose Preface only, and it is likely that the exemplar ("*bisene*") that Alfred sent Wulfsige had no preface at all. The prefaces to the translation of Gregory's *Dialogues* suggest, but cannot confirm, the double expectation of reading and hearing for this text in the ninth century.

The evidence for reception by reading, hearing or both is even more complex for Alfred's translation of Boethius's *De consolatione Philosophiae*. The

[37] *Alfred the Great*, p. 187 and p. 333, n. 2.

[38] *The Old English Version of Bede's Ecclesiastical History*, I, p. 268, ll. 18-19.

[39] *Bischof Wærferths von Worcester Übersetzung der Dialoge Gregors des Grossen*, p. 1.

text survives in two versions. Oxford, Bodleian Library, Bodley 180 (s. XII^{1}) preserves a prose translation, generally accepted to be the earlier version of the work.[40] The earlier manuscript, London, Cotton Otho A. vi (s. X$^{med.}$) transmits the later state of the translation, in which the prose renditions of Boethius' meters are revised into Old English verse.[41] The version in this manuscript had, effectively, two 'prefaces', the first, in prose (shared by the version in Bodley 180) and a following preface in verse, the otherwise untitled "Proem" to the prosimetrical version of the Old English *Consolation.*[42] We are at a distinct disadvantage, however, in understanding the interrelationships among the prose Preface, the "Proem" and the opening of the translation proper, because they survive only in early modern transcriptions. The prose Preface in Bodley 180 begins at the top of f. 1r/1-15 with two lines of capitals, and at its conclusion the chapter headings begin immediately on the following line. The text proper begins at the top of f. 3v. This mid-twelfth-century manuscript tells us little about the make-up or layout of the text in the late ninth century, and for this reason the absence of visual information for the first leaves of Otho A. vi is particularly regrettable. If Malcolm Godden is correct in his surmise that the prose Preface was written for the text in its later state (as preserved in Otho A. vi), it would be useful to know the order of composition for these prefaces as well as their relationship to the text proper.

[40] KER, *Catalogue*, item 305. K. SISAM, "The Authorship of the Verse Translation of Boethius's Metra", in: ID., *Studies*, pp. 293-297; M. GODDEN, "Editing Old English and the Problem of Alfred's Boethius", in: *The Editing of Old English*, ed. D.G. SCRAGG and P.E. SZARMACH (Cambridge, 1994), pp. 163-176, at p. 165 suggests that the prose preface in both manuscripts was written by Alfred for the second state of the text and subsequently copied into the twelfth-century manuscript. On the inadequacy of Sedgefield's edition see now P.E. SZARMACH, "Editions of Alfred: The Wages of Un-influence", in: *Early Medieval English Texts and Interpretations: Studies Presented to Donald G. Scragg*, ed. E. TREHARNE and S. ROSSER (Tempe, AZ, 2002), pp. 135-149. N.G. DISCENZA, "Alfred the Poet and the Proems to the Boethius", in a paper delivered at the December 2002 meeting of the MLA, made a strong case against Alfred's authorship of the prose preface to the Boethius.

[41] GNEUSS, *Handlist*, item 346. *The Paris Psalter and the Meters of Boethius*, ed. G.P. KRAPP (New York, 1933: *ASPR* 5). GODDEN, "Editing and the Problem of Alfred's Boethius", p. 169, accepts the prosimetrical version as representing Alfred's final intention.

[42] This "Proem" destroyed in the burnt early leaves of Otho A. vi is preserved in Junius's transcript (Oxford, Bodleian Library Junius 12, f. iiibr). Junius notes that Otho had a prose preface which he collated against the Bodley version, but it lacked chapter headings. An image of Junius's headnote and transcription of the poem is printed in *Old English Verse Texts From Many Sources*, Pl. 5.1. For an image of the full page see K. KIERNAN *et al.*, *Alfred the Great's Boethius: An Electronic Edition*, http://beowulf.engl.uky.edu/~kiernan/eBoethius, accessed 3 June 2003.

The prose Preface to the *Consolation* would appear to expect reception by individual reading. In its conventional request for prayers, it addresses "*ælcne þara þe þas boc rædan lyste*" ("each of those who desires to read this book"). The verse "Proem" offers considerably more complex evidence, and requires detailed consideration. This "Proem" has generally been accepted as Alfred's composition; indeed Malcolm Godden has pointed out how closely tied the "Proem" is to the first metrum of the revised translation.[43] This prefatory poem makes two claims: that Alfred is the author of the translation, and that he furnished the translation with verse to provide "*myrgen*" ("pleasure") to men. In marked contrast to the previous prefatory poems we have considered, the "Proem" does not refer to itself as an object and makes no appeal to the gaze of a reader. Indeed, the voice of the "Proem" does not come from a talking book at all, but emerges from the scene of reading itself.

Ðus Ælfred us ealdspell reahte,
cyning Westsexna, cræft meldode,
leoðwyrhta<n> list. Him wæs lust micel
ðæt he ðiossum leodum leoð spellode,
monnum myrgen, mislice cwidas,
þy læs ælinge ut adrife
selflicne secg, þonne he swelces lyt
gymð for his gilpe. Ic sceal giet sprecan,
fon on fitte, folcuðne ræd
hæleðum secgean. Hliste se þe wille!

Thus Alfred, king of the West-Saxons, interpreted old stories for us, made known his ability, the skill of a poet. He had a great desire to proclaim poetry to this people, pleasure for men, various speeches, lest weariness drive away the self-regarding man, when he values such a thing little for his arrogance. I must yet speak, endeavour in poetry, speak to men wisdom known to the people.[44]

The "Proem" combines within itself the lexicon of traditional poetry and the learned vocabulary of Alfred's prose translations. It gestures to the oral world in its first-person narration and invitation to listen, but its preoccupation is the king's project of vernacular (book) learning. To describe Alfred's role in the production of the translation – his "*cræft*" and his "*list*" – the poem uses three verbs of speaking: "*reahte*" < *reccan* ('tell, explain, interpret'), "*meldode*"

[43] "Editing and the Problem of Alfred's Boethius", pp. 166-167; see also SISAM, "Authorship", p. 297.
[44] *The Meters of Boethius*, p. 153. I emend to "*leoðwyrhta<n>*" at 3a.

< *meldian* ('announce, declare, reveal'), and "*spellode*" < *spellian* ('speak, proclaim, relate').[45] A further three, "*sprecan*" ('speak, say'), "*fon on fitte*" ('undertake in a poem'), and "*secgean*" ('say, recite'), characterize what the voice of the poem itself claims to be doing. Vocabulary from the world of verse – "*leoð*", "*leoðwyrhta*[*n*]", "*fitte*", and the poetic word "*hæleþum*" – should not surprise given their context in the revision of the prose translation into prosimetrical form. What might initially surprise, however, given the "Proem"'s explicit reference to the world of verse, are particular lexical items clearly taken from the language of Alfred's prose translations: "*ælinge*", "*gymð*", "*selflicne*" and "*gilpe*". The unusual combination of the two associate the poem strongly with Alfred's scene of corporate reading.

The first of these words, *ælenge*, is as rare in the corpus as *gieman* ('care for, regard') is frequent in Alfred's translation of the *Regula pastoralis*.[46] The noun *ælenge* is only attested in the "Proem", and the *DOE* glosses "tedium, weariness" as its possible meanings.[47] The related adjective *ælenge* ('lengthy' or 'tedious') occurs once in the *Pastoral Care* and once in *Boethius* where it is used in a highly suggestive context.[48] In *Boethius* c. XXXIX.iv Wisdom tells Boethius how time-consuming it is to explain the philosophical concepts he wishes to know:

> *Forðæm hit is neah þære tide þe ic getiohhod hæfde on oðer weorc to fonne, 7 get næbbe þis gedon; 7 me þincð eac þ<æt> þu sadige hwæthwugununges, 7 þe ðyncen to ælenge þas langan spell, swelce þe nu lyste lioða. Ic wat eac þ<æt> þe hiora lyst, ac ðu scealt þeah geþolian sume hwile; ic ne mæg hit nu swa hraðe*

[45] On the semantic range of *cræft* in Alfred's translation of the *Consolation* and its political ramifications see N.G. DISCENZA, "Power, Skill and Virtue in the Old English Boethius", *Anglo-Saxon England* 26 (1997), pp. 81-108, at pp. 104-105.

[46] *King Alfred's West Saxon Version of Gregory's Pastoral Care* (= CP). The verb *gieman* in its various forms occurs in CP 26 times, though not at all, apparently, in the translation of the *Consolation*.

[47] *DOE*, under 'æ', p. 279. The *DOE* also cites an adjective, *ælenge* (= 'lengthy, tedious', p. 279) and a related noun *ælengness* (= 'tedium, weariness', p. 280).

[48] *King Alfred's West Saxon Version of Gregory's Pastoral Care*, p. 41, ll. 15-16 ("*Feorðe is ðæt hi beoð on ælengum ðingum & ælcre longunge geðyldige*" ["Fourth is that they be patient in tedious things and in each delay"]); *ælenge* probably was in the *Soliloquies*, although the MS reads "*ælegge*" (*King Alfred's Version of St. Augustines's "Soliloquies"*, p. 86, l. 21: "*Ac me þincð nu þæt to lang æall to rimande and ðe to ælenge to gehyranne*" ["but it seems to me now to long to recount entirely and to you to tedious to hear"]). K. DEKKER, "Francis Junius (1591-1677): Copyist or Editor?", *Anglo-Saxon-England* 29 (2000), pp. 279-296, at pp. 294-295 and n. 91, warns against overconfidence in interpreting a word whose only occurrence is in a transcription made by Junius.

asingan, ne æmettan næbbe, forðæm hit is swiðe long spell. Ða cwæð ic: Do swæðer ðu wolde.

For that reason [i.e. what Boethius must learn takes a long time to teach] it is near the time that I had intended for other work and I have not yet completed this one; and it also seems to me that you are somewhat tired, and these long discourses seem *ælenge* [wearisome] to you, and thus you would now prefer poems. I also understand that you like them [poems], but you must however persevere for a while. I may not sing it now so readily, and I do not have the leisure, because it is a very long argument. Then I said, Do whatever you wish.[49]

This passage considerably expands the Latin, which only comments that time is short and that Boethius must put aside the pleasure of verse while Philosophy marshals her arguments.[50] By contrast, Alfred's translation emphasizes how difficult it is for Wisdom to explain Providence, fate, and freedom. While poetry is usually referred to in both Latin and OE texts as a healing antidote to Boethius's dejection – indeed, at the end of OE prosa 6, Wisdom calls poetry "*se læcedom 7 se drenc þe þu lange wilnodest*" ("the medicine and antidote that you have long desired")[51] – in this passage we see not the patient's but the teacher's point of view. Glossing difficult ideas consumes Wisdom's time. Just such an explanatory gloss, added to explain "*Hydra*" in the Latin, occurs some fifteen lines earlier in the passage, and with it another rare word from the "Proem". "*Ealdspell*", the "old stories" that Alfred is said to recount in the first line of the "Proem", makes its only other appearance here (XXXIX.iv, l. 8). In this passage, "*on ealdspellum*" refers to the sources of information that Alfred's translation taps to explain Boethius's compressed simile by sketching Hercules' second Labour. The "*ealdspell*" in the "Proem" are indeed "old stories", but they appear in the translation as narrative glosses taken from the scene of the king's own reading and pressed into the service of explaining the unfamiliar references of a difficult Latin text.

The other difficult word in the "Proem" is the adjective *selflice*, occurring only here and in the *Pastoral Care*, where it is used in analysing different preaching strategies required for the rich and the poor.[52] Alfred translates the

[49] *King Alfred's Old English Version of Boethius*, c. XXXIX.iv, p. 127, ll. 26-32. (= Bo.)

[50] *Anicii Manlii Severini Boethii Philosophiae Consolatio*, ed. L. BIELER (Turnhout, 1957: *CCSL* 94.1), p. 79 (IV pr. 6. 5-6): "*Sed quoniam haec quoque te nosse quaedam medicinae tuae portio est, quamquam angusto limite temporis saepti tamen aliquid deliberare conabimur. Quodsi te musici carminis oblectamenta delectant, hanc oportet paulisper differas uoluptatem dum nexas sibi ordine contexo rationes – Vt libet, inquam*".

[51] *King Alfred's Old English Version of Boethius*, c. XXXIX.xii, p. 135, ll. 18-21.

[52] *King Alfred's West Saxon Version of Gregory's Pastoral Care*, p. 183, l. 11. The adjec-

final clause of Gregory's observation "*Plerumque tamen personarum ordinem permutat qualitas morum, ut sit diues humilis, sit pauper elatus*"[53] as "*& se wædla bið upahæfen & selflice*" ("and the poor man is proud and *selflice*"). Here, "*upahæfen*" translates "*elatus*",[54] and the term "*selflice*" in the doublet appears as value added. To understand the sense of "*selflice*" here and in the "Proem" we must look further at the noun form, found only in Alfred's translations, seven times in *Pastoral Care* and once in *Boethius*. The word translates a narrow range of phrases in the *Regula pastoralis*: e.g. "*tumor elationis*" (RP 126.23-26; CP 25.5-7); "*in cogitatione se animus elevat*" (RP 142.20-24; CP 39.10); "*quo se apud se per arrogantiam exaltat*" (RP 170.80; CP 69.22-71.1); "*amor proprius*" (RP 232.12-15; CP 143.5); "*in superbiam*" (RP 234.56; CP 145.24-147.3); and is used in conjunction with an approximate translation for: "*quod se sapientes arbitrantur*" (RP, 286.7; CP 203.8) and an elaboration without parallel in the Latin (CP 203.16-19).[55]

Most striking about *selflice* as a noun, with its range from 'pride' to 'self-regard', is that it regularly refers to a process of self-deception, at times hypocritical, but always internal, where the individual misjudges his own worth, ability, or intention. *Selflice* is a failure of (self-)knowledge accompanied by an inappropriate reliance on one's own abilities. It is a state to be avoided in the ruler and to be corrected in those he rules. The closest contextual match to the sense of "*selflicne*" in the "Proem" may be found in Gregory's observation about what happens when understanding deludes itself about its own wisdom: " ... *gif he* [= *ongiett*] *ðonne self wenð ðæt he sie wis & gescadwislice ryhtwis ... micle ðy læs he ongiet ða bierhto ðæs soðan leohtes ðonne he upahefeð on his mode on suelc gielp & on suelc selflice*" ("If [his understanding] then deems itself wise and prudently righteous ... it perceives that much less the brightness of the true light, when it puffs itself up in the mind with such pride and *selflice*").[56] Alfred's translation here has "*gielp*" approximate "*arrogantiam*",[57]

tive occurs only three times – in OE glosses – in each case glossing either the adjectives, *spontaneus*, *ultroneus*, *voluntarius*, or their adverb forms.

[53] *Grégoire le Grand: Règle Pastorale*, ed. and trans. B. JUDIC, F. ROMMEL and C. MOREL, 2 vols. (Paris, 1992: *Sources Chrétiennes* 381-382), II.270.38-39.

[54] *Upahæfen* (in various spellings and inflections) is the overwhelming lexical equivalent for *elevatus* (and its inflected forms) in OE glosses.

[55] The single instance of *selflice* in Boethius has no equivalent in the Latin version: *King Alfred's Old English Version of Boethius*, III.iv (= p. 9, ll. 24-27).

[56] *King Alfred's West Saxon Version of Gregory's Pastoral Care*, pp. 69, l. 22-71, l. 1.

[57] STRYKER, "The Latin-Old English Glossary in MS Cotton Cleopatra A. iii" (Ph.D. Diss. Stanford University, cited in *DOE* Corpus), p. 21: *arroganter* gilplice; p. 32: *arrogantiæ* gilpes; and R.T. OLIPHANT, *The Harley Latin-Old English Glossary* (The Hague, 1966: *Janua Linguarum, Series Practica* 20), F1: "*Fastus .i. felix benignus uel contemptus elatio demens superbus*

once again inflecting a word for intellectual presumption with "*selflice*". This co-occurrence of *gilp* and *selflice* in a context of internal self-deception is very close to that in the "Proem", and tracks closely with the effective gloss to "*selflice*" further on in *Pastoral Care*: "*ðæm lytegan is æresð to beleanne hiera selflice, ðæt hie ne wenen ðæt hie sien wiese*" ("First, the cunning [Lat. "*illis*" referring to "*sapientes huius saeculi*"] should be reproved for their *selflice*, so that they do not think that they are wise"). Here, "*selflice*" marks a form of self-delusion about an individual's intellectual or spiritual achievement in the larger context of his correction. It characterizes an individual whose self-regard keeps him ignorant of his need for correction and learning. In using these learned words, the speaking voice of the "Proem" thus situates doubly Alfred's desire to make poetry: within the thought-world of the *Boethius*, where verse is both the antidote for distress of spirit and relief from the weariness produced by difficult argument, and within the ethics of Gregory's discourse on preaching, where the appeals of the ruler/teacher are chosen to match the needs of the audience. The combination folds aesthetics onto ethics to attract the self-regarding individual into a scene of corporate intellectual pleasure where 'we' enjoy instructive verse.

We must look at the difficulty presented by a further word, not rare, but puzzling all the same. Arguing that the "Proem" speaks through the conceit of the talking book, Earl has made the ingenious argument that "*us*" in the first half-line is not a dative plural (= "for us") but rather an accusative plural, that is, "*us*" refers to the speaking book. He then translates "Thus Alfred recounted us, old-spells".[58] In this interpretive manoeuvre, he sees the Meters speaking in the plural and the book itself speaking in the singular at the end of the poem (= ll. 8b-10b). In offering this solution, Earl wished to counter Krapp's reading, where Alfred speaks of himself in the text in the third person ("Alfred has recounted to us old stories") only to switch to the first person at the end of the poem. Unfortunately, Earl's argument is almost certainly mistaken for the simple reason that the Meters (to which he would have the "*us*" refer) do not themselves constitute a book, even in Krapp's edition of them as "The Meters of Boethius", and certainly not in Otho A. vi. Rather, upon translation the Meters were carefully integrated into the earlier prose translation and published by Alfred in prosimetrical form.[59] In the "Proem", then, "*us*" is used proleptically for the subsequent reference to the West-Saxons, "this people" ("*ðiossum leo-*

uel liber consulatus uel geþþungennes *uel arrogantia uel* gelp".

[58] EARL, "King Alfred's Talking Poems", p. 52: "There is little if any discontinuity in the switch of person; a book of poems can speak comfortably in the singular or plural or both".

[59] GODDEN, "Editing and the Problem of Alfred's Boethius", p. 168.

dum", l. 4a), whom Alfred imagined as the target of his ambitious project of vernacular learning and literacy. But the interpretive difficulty Earl points out remains: how do we understand the awkward switch between the third person reference to Alfred and the speaking "*ic*" at the end of the poem. The answer requires reassigning the speaking voice. I suggest that in this "Proem" we have neither speaking book nor speaking author, but the voice of Alfred's scene of corporate reading, where the authoritative voice of the reader identifies Alfred as author, reveals his intention, makes an ethical appeal to the 'reader/user' of the book, and calls for attention from his listeners. If the prose Preface points to a single reader, the "Proem" inserts the voice of the reader/teacher into the text and points to a scene of corporate reading familiar from Asser's detailing of it in Alfred's *Life*.

Although the combined prefaces to Otho A. vi can only suggest to us mixed reception by reading and listening, a later reader of Alfred's *Consolation* attests the expectation of the two forms of reception in the late tenth century. In his Latin translation of the Anglo-Saxon Chronicle, Æthelweard (d. 998), ealdorman and patron of Ælfric, writes warmly about the excellence of Alfred's translation:

> *Denique in eodem anno magnanimus transiit de mundo Ælfredus, rex Saxonum, immobilis occidentalium postis, uir iustitia plenus, acer in armis, sermone doctus, diuinis quippe super omnia documentis imbutus. Nam ex Latino rhetorico fasmate in propriam uerterat linguam uolumina, numero ignoto, ita uarie, ita præopime, ut non tantum expertioribus sed et audientibus liber Boetii lachrymosus quodammodo suscitaretur motus.*

> Then in the same year, there passed from the world Ælfred, king of the Saxons, unshakable pillar of the people of the west, a man full of justice, active in war, learned in speech, steeped in sacred literature above all things, for from the ornate Latin tongue he turned unknown numbers of books into his own language with such variety and richness, that not only for scholars, but for any who might hear it read, the tearful passion of the book of Boethius would be in a measure brought to life.[60]

[60] *The Chronicle of Æthelweard*, ed. A. CAMPBELL (London, 1962), pp. 51, his translation. Because Æthelweard's addressee, Matilda of Essen was a lineal descendant of Alfred, and Æthelweard was himself a descendant of Alfred's older brother, Æthelred I) we may be tempted to discount Æthelweard's warmth as a compliment to their shared ancestor. The compliment would only work, however, if the description of reading in which he frames it fitted contemporary practice.

In contrasting "*expertiores*" with "*audientes*" Æthelweard imagines two sets of users for the translation of the *Consolation* and two scenes of reading. That the scholars of the first set are readers with unmediated access to the text is reasonably inferred from the contrast with the 'listeners' of the second set. The listeners, by contrast, are moved by hearing the excellence of Alfred's language as it is animated by reading aloud. In this doubled reception, Æthelweard's comment on Alfred's translation, written almost a century after the king's death, realizes for his own time the imagined speaker of the "Proem" as one who read to others who heard. The speaking voice of the ninth-century "Proem" was more historically specific. Voicing the concerns of the *Pastoral Care* and the *Boethius*, borrowing Wisdom's words and Gregory's, the voice recalls Alfred's own scenes of corporate reading, once as listener and later as reader/teacher. If the prefaces of the *Pastoral Care* suggest an individual, episcopal reader for that translation, the prefaces of *Boethius* imagine corporate reading in a wider context for "*ðiossum leodum*".

Rituale, Feste, Sprechhandlungen: Spuren oraler und laikaler Kultur in den Bibelepen des *Heliand* und Otfrids von Weißenburg

WOLFGANG HAUBRICHS

Es mag vielleicht immer noch überraschen, doch die beiden umfangreichsten poetischen Texte, die beiden längsten Epen des frühen Mittelalters, sind nicht – wie man erwarten könnte – in der Buch-, Kirchen- und Gelehrtensprache Latein verfasst, welche die Textproduktion der Zeit sonst weitaus dominiert, sondern in zwei Volkssprachen des frühen Mittelalters, in Altsächsisch und in Althochdeutsch. Es sind Bibelepen, welche die Evangelien in heimischer Form, das eine in der germanischen Epenform des Stabreims, das andere in der kaum lange vorher entwickelten Form des Endreims aufnehmen, harmonisieren und interpretieren. Auch als Bibelepen übertreffen sie die spätantiken, im vergilischen Hexameter gehaltenen Vorbilder der Arator, Juvencus, Prudentius und Sedulius an Länge.[1] Das altsächsische Epos des *Heliand* (as. Bezeichnung für 'Heiland, *salvator*'), Fragment geblieben und um 840 von einem "*non ignobilis vates*" (einem "nicht unedlen oder unberühmten Sänger") in engem Kontakt mit dem königlichen Hofe verfasst, umfasst 5983 Langzeilen.[2] Der *liber evangeliorum*, das *Evangelienbuch* des Mönchs und *magister*

[1] Vgl. zur spätantiken Bibeldichtung D. KARTSCHOKE, *Bibeldichtung. Studien zur Geschichte der epischen Bibelparaphrase von Juvencus bis Otfrid von Weißenburg* (München, 1975), S. 30 ff.; zur volkssprachigen Bibeldichtung der Karolingerzeit ebd., S. 130 ff.; 271 ff.; DERS., *Altdeutsche Bibeldichtung* (Stuttgart, 1975: *Sammlung Metzler* 135).

[2] *Heliand und Genesis*, hg. v. O. BEHAGHEL und B. TAEGER (Tübingen, ^{10}1996: *ATB* 4). Vgl. dazu zusammenfassend: B. TAEGER, "Heliand", ^{2}*VL* 3 (1981), Sp. 958-971; W. HAUBRICHS, *Die Anfänge. Versuche volkssprachiger Schriftlichkeit im frühen Mittelalter* (ca. 700-1050/60), (Tübingen, ^{2}1995), S. 271 ff.; DERS., "Heliand und Altsächsische Genesis", *Reallexikon der Germanischen Altertumskunde*, Bd. 14 (Berlin, ^{2}1999), S. 297-308.

Otfrid von Weißenburg, einem südlich von Speyer (im heutigen Dép. Bas-Rhin, nicht im historischen Elsaß) gelegenen bedeutenden Kloster, entstand zwischen 863 und 871, ist König Ludwig 'dem Deutschen' gewidmet und umfasst insgesamt 7104 binnengereimte Langverse.[3]

Warum sind diese Texte, welche teils kürzend, teils die unterschiedlichen Evangelien (der *Heliand* nach dem Vorbild der Evangelienharmonie des *Tatian*) synoptisch zusammenfassend, doch eine nicht allzu umfangreiche Geschichte von Geburt, Leben und Sterben des 'Erlösers' erzählen, warum sind diese Texte so lang geraten?

Die Antwort ist nicht so schwer: Sie sind so extensiv ausgearbeitet, weil sie, weit über die biblischen Texte hinaus, aber auch in einem gesteigertem Maße über die spätantiken Bibelepen hinaus, Erzählung sind. Sie sind Epen, wozu beim Theologen Otfrid von Weißenburg noch eine wohldosierte und wohlseparierte Portion geistlicher Deutung hinzukommt. Das Epos muss Welt schaffen, muss den Sinn des Erzählten im äußeren Anschein erfahren lassen. Die farbige Welthaltigkeit beider karolingischer Bibelepen ist natürlich nicht verborgen geblieben. Besonders für den *Heliand*-Autor war es sicherlich eine Hauptintention, dem evangelischen Stoff die Stil- und Denkformen der ererbten Standesdichtung zu adaptieren. Dazu gehörte zweifellos die Umsetzung mancher biblischer Strukturen und Begriffe in die Terminologie und Muster des heimischen Epos; dazu gehörte manches formelhafte Dekor der heroischen Lieder, der Heldenlieder, die in der oralen Kultur des frühen Mittelalters eine bedeutsame Rolle spielten, auch wenn sie selten (und nur fragmentarisch) aufs Pergament gelangten. Dazu gehörte die Breite des Erzählens und schließlich gehörte dazu die Übernahme von Wertvorstellungen eines adligen Publikums, als da waren: genealogisch verankertes Standesethos, Gefolgschaftstreue im Personenverband, Herrschaftsdenken, kriegerische Mentalität (auch wo sie dementiert wird), Ostentation und Repräsentation.

Dass unter anderem, neben der monastischen Schicht von *conversi*, späteingetretener, lateinunkundiger Brüder in den Klöstern auch adliges Publikum angezielt wurde, wissen wir. Für den *Heliand* sagt die lateinische Praefatio des

[3] *Otfrids Evangelienbuch*, hg. v. O. ERDMANN und L. WOLFF (Tübingen, [4]1962: *ATB* 49). Vgl. dazu zusammenfassend W. SCHRÖDER, "Otfrid von Weißenburg", [2]*VL* 7 (1987), Sp. 172-193. HAUBRICHS, *Die Anfänge*, S. 292 ff.; DERS., "Otfrid von Weißenburg", *Theologische Realenzyklopädie*, Bd. 25 (Berlin und New York, 1995), S. 541-544. Zu den Bindungen an Ludwig den Deutschen vgl. C. STAITI, "Otfrid von Weißenburg e la biografia impossibile di Ludovico il Germanico", in: *Scripturus vitam. Lateinische Biographie von der Antike bis in die Gegenwart. Festgabe Walter Berschin*, hg. v. D. WALZ (Heidelberg. 2002), S. 755-768; W. HAUBRICHS, "Ludwig der Deutsche und die volkssprachige Literatur", in: *Ludwig der Deutsche und seine Zeit*, hg. v. W. HARTMANN (Darmstadt, 2004), S. 203-232.

Werks ausdrücklich, dass es die Absicht des Herrschers ist, "allem seiner Herrschaft unterworfenen Volk, das die *theodiske* Sprache spricht", auch den Latein- und Leseunkundigen, "nichts Geringeres als die Kenntnis der göttlichen Schriften zu verschaffen".[4] Ein handschriftengeschichtliches Indiz weist ebenfalls in diese Richtung: Die berühmte Münchner Handschrift des *Heliand*, in der zweiten Hälfte des neunten Jahrhunderts im ottonischen Hauskloster Corvey geschrieben, dürfte wie viele andere Bamberger Codices aus ottonischem Besitz in die Bibliothek der ostfränkischen Bistums-Neugründung des letzten Ottonen Heinrich II. um 1009 gelangt sein, wo sie sprachlich eigentlich ziemlich nutzlos war. Bei Otfrid von Weißenburg befindet sich unter den Anregern der Dichtung eine *matrona veneranda* Judith, die ihrem respektvollen Titel nach von adliger Abkunft sein muss; den bewidmeten König Ludwig den Deutschen bittet der Weißenburger *magister* um Verbreitung des Werks und auch hier trägt eine Handschrift, die Heidelberger (P), Indizien dafür, dass sie einer hochgestellten alemannischen Adelsfamilie gehörte.[5] Ein Lesereintrag findet sich auf Fol. 90r von einer Hand des 10. Jahrhunderts – "*Kicila diu scona mîn filu las*" ("Die angesehene und gut anzusehende Gisela las mich oft"). Es spricht hier übrigens das Buch![6]

Gerade beim *Heliand* (aber auch in manchen Passagen Otfrids) verleihen das Kolorit der heimischen Adelskultur, die Farben aus der Welt der Grundherrschaften der Dichtung an vielen Stellen einen in eigentümlichem Kontrast zur Welt des Evangeliums stehenden archaischen Reiz, so wenn das der Geburt Christi in Bethlehem vorangehende Census-Gebot des Augustus mit einer Rechtsformel als "*ban endi bodskepi*" ('Bann und Gebot') verkündet wird, wenn die Betroffenen sich zu ihrem "*ôdil*" ('Heimsitz') und "*hantmahal*" ('Erb-

[4] Vgl. W. HAUBRICHS, "Die Praefatio des 'Heliand'", in: *Der Heliand*, hg. v. J. EICHHOFF und I. RAUCH (Darmstadt, 1973), S. 400-435; DERS., "Heliand und Altsächsische Genesis", S. 297 ff. [mit Lit.]; DERS., "Ludwig der Deutsche", S. 217 ff.

[5] Vgl. W. HAUBRICHS, "Die alemannische Herzogsfamilie des 10. Jahrhunderts als Rezipient von Otfrids Evangelienbuch? Das Spendenverzeichnis im Codex Heidelberg Palatinus lat. 52", in: *Festschrift für Eduard Hlawitschka*, hg. v. K.R. SCHNITH und R. PAULER (Kallmünz, 1993), S. 165-211.

[6] Vgl. R. SCHÜTZEICHEL, *Codex Pal. Lat. 52. Studien zur Heidelberger Otfridhandschrift. Zum Kicila-Vers und zum Georgslied* (Göttingen, 1982: *Abh. der Akademie der Wissenschaften in Göttingen, phil.-hist. Kl.* 3. Folge, Nr. 130), S. 48 ff.; V. SCHUPP, "KICILA DIU SCONA MIN FILO LAS. Bemerkungen zur Georgsliedforschung", *ZfdA* 120 (1991), S. 452 ff.; dazu HAUBRICHS, "Die alemannische Herzogsfamilie", S. 197. Zur Rezeption des *Evangelienbuche*s vgl. allgemein D.H. GREEN, "Zur primären Rezeption von Otfrids Evangelienbuch", in: *Althochdeutsch*, hg. v. R. BERGMANN, H. TIEFENBACH und L. VOETZ (Heidelberg, 1987), I, S. 737-771; DERS., *Medieval Listening and Reading. The Primary Reception of German Literature* 800-1300. (Cambridge, 1994), S. 47 ff., 179 ff.

sitz') aufmachen, zu den "Burgen" ihrer Heimat wandern und Schreiber eine "Zinsliste" anlegen, in der sie "sämtliche Namen, Land und Leute" verzeichnen (v. 339 ff.). Auch die entsprechende Szene bei Otfrid (I, 11) ist auf das intensivste von Rechts- und Herrschaftsformeln durchzogen. Wie selbstverständlich erscheinen in beiden Epen die Jünger Jesu als 'Gefolgsleute', wenn auch eines himmlischen Königs. Christus hält sich – wie ein Einsiedler der Karolingerzeit – vor seinem öffentlichen Auftreten nicht in der Wüste, sondern im Urwald, in der "*wuostwaldi*" ('Wüstwald'), "*in wuastinnu waldes*" ('in der Wüste des Waldes'), "*in waldes einôte*" ('in der Einöde des Waldes') bei Otfrid (I, 10, 28; 23, 9; 23, 19), "*in sinuueldi*" ('Wildnis'), in "*uualdes hleo*" ('Waldgebirge'), in des Waldes "*ênôdi*" ('Einöde') im *Heliand* (v. 1024 ff.; 1121 ff.). Dort wird Maria im Stile einer Frau aus dem Heldenliede geschildert, der für den Todesfall ihres Sohnes vorausgesagt wird: "Du wirst noch Schmerz leiden, Harm in deinem Herzen, wenn einst ihn Kriegsvolk mit Waffen tötet. Da musst du große Mühsal, Not musst Du dulden". Es ist bemerkenswert, dass die heroische Vorstellung vom 'Waffentod' so stark ist, dass sie sogar den Kreuzestod Christi zu überdecken vermag. Otfrid dagegen schildert Maria als adlige fromme Frau in ihrem Palast, ihrer "*palinza*" (I, 5, 9), mit dem Wirken edler Stoffe und der Lektüre des Psalters beschäftigt, "*divinis theoriis intendens*", wie es von einem entsprechend frommen Adligen der Karolingerzeit in seiner Vita heißt.

Man sollte erwarten, dass sich Sozial- und Kulturgeschichte die spezifische Welthaltigkeit der karolingischen volkssprachigen Bibelepen zu Nutze gemacht hätten. Das ist jedoch – nach durchaus beachtenswerten, vor allem auf die soziale und herrschaftliche Terminologie gerichteten Studien von Otto Plassmann,[7] Walter Schlesinger und Helmut Beumann[8] und trotz der bedeutsamen Studien von Ute Schwab zur Thematik von Herrschaft und Vasallität in der altsächsischen *Genesis*[9] – durchaus nicht der Fall gewesen. *Theodisca non leguntur.*

[7] J.O. PLASSMANN, "Reich und Gefolgschaft im 10. Jahrhundert", *Germanien* 15 (1943), S. 154-171.

[8] W. SCHLESINGER, *Die Entstehung der Landesherrschaft*, Bd. 1 (Dresden, 1941), S. 9 ff.; H. BEUMANN, *Widukind von Korvei. Untersuchungen zur Geschichtsschreibung und Ideengeschichte des 10. Jahrhunderts* (Weimar, 1950), S. 232 ff.

[9] U. SCHWAB, "Ansätze zu einer Interpretation der altsächsischen Genesisdichtung", *Annali Istituto Orientale di Napoli, Sez. Germ.* 17 (1974), S. 111-186; 18 (1975), S. 7-88; 19 (1976), S. 7-82; 20 (1977), S. 7-79; DIES., "Huld und Huldverlust in der altsächsisch-angelsächsischen Genesis", in: *Scritti in onore di Salvatore Pugliatti*, Bd. 5: *Scritti vari* (1978), S. 951-1003.

Die folgenden Überlegungen wollen an Hand von vier Beispielen zu zeigen versuchen, dass es sich lohnt, aus der Perspektive einer modernen Kulturgeschichte und einer historischen Semantik der Begriffe und des Verhaltens die beiden Bibelepen auf darin enthaltene Verhaltens- und Kulturmuster, auf Rituale, Bräuche und habituelle Sprechhandlungen hin zu analysieren.

1. Feste und Feiern als soziale Orte

Der Evangelist Markus (6,21) und mit ihm *Tatian* gibt den Geburtstag des Königs Herodes, an dem sich die Tötung Johannes des Täufers vollziehen soll, in einem einzigen nüchternen Vers: "*et cum dies oportunus accidisset Herodes natalis sui cenam fecit principibus et tribunis et primis Galilaeae*" ("Und als sein Geburtstag herankam, gab Herodes den Fürsten, Heerführern und Vornehmen Galiläas ein Festmahl").

Sehen wir zu, was der altsächsische Dichter, im Variationsstil des Stabreimepos arbeitend, daraus macht (*Heliand*, v. 2728-2742):

Thô uurðun an themu gêrtale Iudeo cuninges
tîdi cumana, so thar gitald habdun
frôde folcuueros, thô he gifôdid uuas,
an lioht cuman. Sô uuas thero liudio thau,
that that erlo gehuilic ôƀean scolde,
Iudeono mid gômun. Thô uuarð thar an thene gastseli
megincraft mikil manno gesamnod,
heritogono an that hûs, thar iro hêrro was
an is kuningstôle. Quâmun managa
Iudeon an thene gastseli; uuarð im thar gladmôd hugi,
blîði an iro breostun: gisâhun iro bâggeƀon
uuesen an uunneon. Drôg man uuîn an flet
skîri mid scâlun, skenkeon huurƀun,
gengun mit goldfatun: gaman was thar inne
hlûd an thero hallu, heliðos drunkun.

Da war im Jahreslauf des Judenkönigs die Zeit gekommen, die wussten weise Männer des Volkes, da er geboren war, da er gekommen war ans Licht. So war es des Stammes Sitte, dass diesen Tag jeder Vornehme aus dem Volke der Juden durch ein Gastmahl feiern sollte. Da sammelte sich in der Gasthalle eine mächtige Menge von Männern, im Haus des Herzogs, wo ihr Herrscher saß in seinem Königsstuhle. Es kamen viele vom Volk der Juden in diesen Gastsaal. Da ward ihnen der Sinn froh, heiter war ihnen ums Herz: Sie sahen ihren Ringspender in Wonne verweilen. Schieren Wein trug man in Schalen ins Haus, die Schenken drehten sich, eilten mit Goldkrügen: Lust ward da laut in der Halle, die Krieger tranken.

Aus diesem Stück lässt sich zunächst einmal ein beachtliches terminologisches Inventar rund um die Institution des Festes, des Festherrn, seiner Gäste, der Örtlichkeit und des präponderanten Ablaufs entnehmen:

Zwar wird der Brauch, das *anniversarium*, den Geburtstag, zu feiern, ausdrücklich als Brauch der betreffenden *gens* der Juden geschildert, doch war die rituelle Verpflichtung von Adligen und Großen zur Veranstaltung von Festen der frühmittelalterlichen Welt – wie chronikalische und andere Quellen zeigen – keineswegs unvertraut: *thau* m. < germ. **thawa* war das Wort für diese Verpflichtung neben *sidu* 'Sitte'. Die dazu verpflichteten Leute, die herausgehobenen Adligen, *edilinge* nach sächsischen Quellen, hießen *erlo(s)*, 'Earls, Vornehme', ein elitäres Wort, das einem Stamm des frühen Mittelalters, den *(H)Erulern* < germ. **Erulaz* (vgl. ae. *eorl*, an. *jarl*), seinen Namen gab. In diesem Fall ist der Herr, der Herrscher, ein *kuning*, der über das Herrschaftszeichen des *kuningstôl*, des 'Königsstuhles', verfügt, wobei offenbleiben muss, ob es sich um die durch Grabbeigaben, Abbildungen und sogar erhaltene Exemplare belegten prachtvollen Faltsessel (Klappstühle) handelt, welche selbst die nordfranzösisch-romanische Welt beeindruckten, so dass sie aus dem Wort *faltstuol* das Lehnwort *fauteuil* entwickelten, oder um ebenfalls (etwa im *Beowulf*, v. 1815) früh belegte Hochstühle in der Halle.[10]

Die Sachsen kannten keine Könige, doch seit merowingischer Zeit Herzöge, *heritogon*, wie zu Karls des Großen Zeiten Widukind einer war, und wie es zu Zeiten des *Heliand* die Brunonen (die späteren Ottonen) waren. Natürlich kannten sie aber die Institution des Königs, *rex*, von den Franken, dürften sie aber doch wohl supragentil interpretiert haben, als Herrschaft über mehrere Völker. So erscheint der Wechsel der Bezeichnung zwischen *cuning* und *heritogo* durchaus bemerkenswert, wobei *cuning* in einer noch nicht als Übersetzung von *rex* standardisierten Bedeutung von 'Oberhaupt eines Verwandtschaftsverbandes' bis zu 'Führer einer *gens*' schillern konnte. Es dürften wohl hinter diesem Wortgebrauch Verhältnisse stehen, wie wir sie bei den benachbarten Friesen, aber nicht nur dort, in der wechselnden Bezeichnung *dux* und *rex* für die Führer des Stammes oder eines Teilverbandes kennen.

Der Herrscher wird aber auch – mit einer ältestes Gut bewahrenden Formel – "*bâggeƀo*" ('Ringspender') genannt, mit einer Kenning also, der an anderer Stelle des *Heliand* der "*bôguuini*" ('Freund der Ringe', d. h. der durch die Gabe

[10] *Beowulf and the Fight at Finnsburg*, hg. v. F. KLAEBER (New York, ^{3}1950), hier S. 68. Diese Ausgabe wird den weiteren Zitaten zugrundegelegt.

von goldenen oder silbernen Armreifen, das meint nämlich *bôg, bâg* < germ. **bauga*, seinem Herrn verpflichtete Gefolgsmann). Man wird nicht zu Unrecht an die Schilderungen des *Hildebrandliedes* (v. 33 ff.)[11] über die aus römischem Gold geschmiedeten Ringe des "*chuning*", des "*huneo truhtin*", die der Protagonist dieses Liedes als Zeichen seiner Wertschätzung erwarb,[12] und an Stellen anderer Heldenlieder erinnert. Auch im *Beowulf* ist es vornehme Aufgabe des freigebigen Königs, Ringe an die Krieger zu verteilen (v. 81 f.; 1089 ff.; 1193 f.; 1967 ff.); genannt wird er deswegen "*beága bryttan*" ('Spender der Ringe', v. 35; 352; 1488) oder "*beág-gyfa*" ('Ringspender', v. 1102) oder "*sinces brytta*" ('Schatzspender', v. 607) und "*hringa fengel*" ('Herr der Ringe', v. 2345). König Gunnar/Gunther wird im altnordischen *Atlilied* (Str. 31),[13] das auf niederdeutsche Quellen des 9. Jahrhunderts zurückgeht, "Ringspender" genannt. Und bei Gregor von Tours (*Hist. Franc.* II, c. 42)[14] wird von den falschen Goldarmringen berichtet, mit denen sich König Chlodwig die Gefolgsleute seines Rivalen Ragnachar von Cambrai verpflichtete. Es ist eine archaische Welt, die hier heraufbeschworen wird um 840, die Welt des germanischen *heroic age*, und möglicherweise war *bâggeƀo* vorwiegend ein poetisches Synonym für 'Herrscher', doch war es zweifellos noch durchsichtig in seinen Bestandteilen. Auch wenn das Verhältnis zwischen Gefolgschaft und Herrn (längst) durch dingliche Substrate wie Lehen, Land und Leute abgelöst worden war, so müssen doch die archaischen Vorweltverhältnisse, die in dieser rezipierten Formel des Heldenliedes heraufbeschworen werden, dem Publikum noch verständlich gewesen sein.[15]

[11] *Die kleineren althochdeutschen Sprachdenkmäler*, hg. v. E. von STEINMEYER (Berlin, 1916), hier S. 5.

[12] N. WAGNER, "Cheisuringu gitan. Zu v. 33-35a des Hildebrandsliedes", *ZfdA* 104 (1975), S. 179-188. Vgl. zur frühmittelalterlichen Bedeutung des Fürstenschatzes und der Ringgaben jetzt grundlegend M. HARDT, *Gold und Herrschaft. Die Schätze europäischer Könige und Fürsten im ersten Jahrtausend* (Berlin, 2004).

[13] Hier zitiert nach der Übersetzung von A. HÄNY, *Die Edda. Götter- und Heldenlieder der Germanen. Aus dem Altnordischen übertragen, mit Anmerkungen und einem Nachwort versehen* (Zürich, 1987), hier S. 429.

[14] *Gregorii episcopi Turonensis Historiarum libri decem*, hg. und übersetzt v. R. BUCHNER (Darmstadt, 1977), Bd. 1, hier S. 138.

[15] Vgl. zur Formelwelt des altsächsischen Epos auch M.J. CAPEK, "A Note on Formula Development in Old Saxon", *Modern Philology* 67 (1969/70), S. 357-363; G. MANGANELLA, "Le formule dell' antica poesia sassone", *Annali Istituto Orientale di Napoli, Sez. Germ.* 5 (1962), S. 73-94; A.M. GUERRIERI, "Grammatica e Poesia del 'Heliand' nell'avvicendarsi di discorsi indiretti e diretti", *Annali Istituto Orientale di Napoli, Sez. Germ.* 28/29 (1985/86), S. 253-289; DIES., "Un segno della scrittura artistica di poeta del 'Heliand'", *Giornale Italiano di Filologia* 45 (1993), S. 67-90; H. HAFERLAND, "Mündliche Erzähltechnik im Heliand", *GRM* N.F. 52 (2002), S. 237-259.

Das Gastmahl selbst hieß "*gôma*" zu as. *gōmian*, ahd. *gouman* 'Acht geben, hüten, aufmerksam sein' schließlich auch 'bewirten'. Es ist also jenes Mahl anthropologisch als Teil der sozialen Aufmerksamkeit zu interpretieren, die der Herr seiner Gefolgschaft, dem 'Gesinde', der *familia*, zu erweisen hat.[16] Es findet statt im "*hûs*" des "*heritogo*", in der "*halla*" – wunderbar geschildert u. a. im altenglischen *Beowulf* (v. 67 ff.) – und dort in der "*gastseli*" (vgl. *Beowulf*, v. 994; dem "Saal", zu germ. **salja*), dem "*flet*" (der 'Trinkhalle'; vgl. *Beowulf*, v. 448: 'Methalle'; v. 482: 'Biersaal'; v. 655: 'Weinhalle'). Es fällt auf, wie der Wein, ein Luxusgut, und zwar reiner, unvermischter Wein, bevorzugt wird. Er wird in Schalen serviert, die Trinkkrüge ("*fatun*") sind aus Gold[17] – auch dies die Atmosphäre der Repräsentation akzentuierend.[18] Es fällt auch auf, dass das Trinkgelage im Geschehen privilegiert herausgestellt wird – Essen kommt nicht vor. Ziel ist der Rausch, die Herstellung von "*gaman*" ('Lust'), "*blîði*" ('Freude'), die sich laut äußern darf: das erzeugt "*gladmôd hugi*" ('frohen Sinn') bei allen, "*uunniu*" ('Wonne') auch beim Herrscher. Das Ziel der sozialen Einung durch trunkene Freude wird in diesem religiösen Text ganz unverblümt ausgesprochen – und das ist kein Einzelfall (vgl. auch die Gelageschilderungen im *Beowulf*, v. 117; 615 ff.).

Selbst wenn Christus und seine Mutter an einem solchen Gastmahl teilnehmen, an der "*gôma*" zu Kanaa, dort wo "*man êna brûd geƀan*" (v. 1996: 'eine Braut vergeben') sollte, eine "*munalîca magað*" (eine 'erinnerungswürdige Jungfrau') auch dann bleiben – ohne biblische Vorlage – die Elemente des Festritus gewahrt (v. 1999-2002, 2005-2013):

Managoro drohtin
geng imu thô mid is iungoron, godes êgan barn,
an that hôha hûs, thar thiu hêri dranc,

[16] Vgl. G. ALTHOFF, "Der friedens-, bündnis- und gemeinschaftsstiftende Charakter des Mahls im früheren Mittelalter", in: *Essen und Trinken im Mittelalter*, hg. v. I. BITSCH, T. EHLERT und X. VON ERTZDORFF (Sigmaringen, 1987), S. 13-25; ferner G. ALTHOFF, *Verwandte, Freunde und Getreue. Zum politischen Stellenwert der Gruppenbindungen im frühen Mittelalter* (Darmstadt, 1990).

[17] Vgl. die 'Goldschalen' im *Atlilied*, Str. 10: HÄNY, *Die Edda*, S. 434.

[18] Vgl. zur Rolle wertvollen Geschirrs in königlichen und fürstlichen Schätzen: M. HARDT, "Royal Treasures and Representation in the Early Middle Ages", in: *Strategies of Distinction. The Construction of Ethnic Continuity 300-800*, hg. v. W. POHL (Leiden, 1998: *The Transformation of the Roman World* 2), S. 255-280. DERS., "Silverware in Early Medieval Gift Exchange: Imitatio Imperii and Objects of Memory", in: *Franks and Alamanni in the Merovingian Period*, hg. v. I. WOOD (Woodbridge und San Marino, 1998), S. 317-342; zum Beispiel des gotischen Schatzes von Pietroassa vgl. nun R. HARHOIU, P. PIEPER und R. NEDOMA, "Pietroassa", *Reallexikon der Germanischen Altertumskunde*, Bd. 23 (Berlin, 2003), S. 147-155 mit Tafeln 6-12.

thea Iudeon an themu gastseli: he im ôc at them gômun was ...

... Uuerod blîðode,
uuârun thar an luston liudi atsamne,
gumon gladmôdie. Gengun ambahtman
skenkeon mit scâlun, drôgun skîrianne uuîn
mid orcun endi mit alofatun; uuas thar erlo drôm
fagar an flettea, thô thar folc undar im
an them benkeon sô bezt bliðsea afhôƀun
uuârun thar an uunneun. Thô im thes uuînes brast,
them liudiun thes lîðes ...

Der Herr der Vielen ging dorthin mit seinen *iuniores*, seinen Gefolgsleuten, Gottes eigenes Kind ging in das erhabene Haus, wo die Vornehmen [*maiores*] tranken, die Juden im Gastsaal: Er war auch bei dem Gastmahl ... Das Männervolk schwelgte in Freude, es waren da mit Lust die Leute zusammen, frohen Sinnes waren die Menschen. Es gingen die Diener, die Schenken trugen mit Schalen herbei schieren Wein in Kannen und [Bier]-Krügen; es jubelten die adligen Männer, wie es sich ziemt in der Trinkhalle, und das Volk unten auf den Bänken gab sich ausgelassener Fröhlichkeit hin, die Menschen weilten dort in Wonnen. – Da ging ihnen der Wein aus, der Saft den Leuten ...

Auch hier findet – ohne jede Vorgabe in den evangelischen Texten – die "*gôma*", die notwendige Bewirtung, während einer Hochzeit, in einem Adelshaus, einem "*hôhen hûs*" statt, in der "*gastseli*", dem Gastsaal, im "*flet*", der Trinkhalle, die mit Bänken gefüllt ist, wo es "*ambahtman*" ('Dienstleute') und Schenken gibt. Christus, gehüllt in die wohl alte Königsmetapher "*managoro drohtin*" (vgl. "*managoro mundburo*" 'Schutzherr der Vielen', v. 1274; "*thiodo drohtin*" 'Herr der Völker', v. 1284, 1386; "*landes hirdi*" 'Herr des Landes', v. 1286; "*cuningo rîkiost*" 'Mächtigster der Könige', v. 1334; "*landes uuard*" 'Schützer des Landes', v. 1382), erscheint mit seinen "*iungoron*", den Jüngern, einem Ausdruck, dem ebenfalls noch die Herkunft aus der sozialen Terminologie – *iuniores, pueri* – anhängt.[19] Das Fest atmet adlige Atmosphäre: es ist die "*hêri*" ('die Schar der Vornehmen'), es sind die "*erlos*", die trinken; daneben aber finden sich auch die "*liuti*", das "*folc*", die Schar der einfachen Krieger, bezeichnenderweise weiter unten an den Bänken, welche soziale Abstufung wir auch aus anderen Quellen des frühen Mittelalters kennen. Der schiere, unvermischte Wein dominiert das Gastmahl, privilegiert erscheint erneut das rituelle Trinken, das Gelage, bevor die Katastrophe "Der Wein ist aus" eintritt. Ziel ist

[19] Vgl. H. EGGERS, "Althochdeutsch *iungiro*, altsächsisch *iungro, iungaro*" (1964), in: DERS., *Kleine Schriften* (Tübingen, 1982), S. 36-53.

die Herstellung der sozialen Freude, die in zahlreichen terminologischen Varianten – "*blîðon*" ('sich freuen'), "*blîðsea*" ('Fröhlichkeit'), "*gladmôdi*" ('frohgemut'), "*drôm*" ('Jubel'), "*uunnea*" ('Wonne') – gefeiert wird.

Man kann hier die geradezu textgliedernd eingesetzten, repetierten Festmähler des *Beowulf* vergleichen, wo nach dem Einschenken des Bieres gesagt wird: "Da herrschte bei den Helden Frohsinn" (v. 494 ff.). Ein anderes Mal: "Wieder erhob sich frohes Treiben, brausender Bankjubel. Es brachten Mundschenken Wein in wundervollen Gefäßen" (v. 1160 ff.). Und wieder: "Da gab es ein prächtiges Gelage. Die Schar der Männer trank Wein" (v. 1232 f.).[20] Dem entspricht z. B. im nordischen Heldenlied das Weintrinken der burgundischen Krieger in der Halle im *Atlilied* (Str. 1 f.).[21]

Man wird sich der Einsicht nicht verschließen dürfen, dass in dieser farbigen Ausmalung der dürren biblischen Wirklichkeit, die Otfrid z. B. in beiden analogen Szenen nicht kennt, auch poetische Muster der mündlichen Dichtung nachwirken. Doch sind sie hier wie an vielen anderen Stellen der altsächsischen Bibeldichtung eingesetzt, um in einem Akt der sozialen Akkommodation und der kulturellen Amalgamierung das Heilsgeschehen welthaltig werden zu lassen. Es ist die Welt des frühen Mittelalters, die hier kreativ entsteht, gewiss in literarischer Brechung, doch stets im kulturellen Horizont des Publikums verbleibend. Es sind insbesondere die Elemente der Nobilitierung des Geschehens, die wir in anderen Szenen auch bei Otfrid finden, das Eindringen der frühmittelalterlichen Adelswelt, und dann die Intention der Herstellung des *gladmôd*, des 'frohen Sinnes', der *wunnea*, die nicht als Topoi hinwegerklärt werden können, sondern als kulturelle Muster ernst genommen werden müssen.[22]

2. Kampf und Tod als Fokus der Adelswelt

Krieg, Kampf und auch der Tod im Kampf waren Bedingungen adliger Herrschaft im frühen Mittelalter. Jeder Adlige der Karolingerzeit musste sich dieses dunklen Bodens seiner Existenz bewusst sein. Wir vergessen allzu leicht über den blendenden Schilderungen der Kunst- und Literaturerzeugnisse sogenannter 'karolingischer Renaissance', dass die Annalenwerke des fränkischen Reiches Jahr für Jahr von Kriegszügen gegen fremde Völker am Rande des

[20] Hier nach der Übersetzung von M. LEHNERT, *Beowulf. Ein altenglisches Heldenepos übertragen und herausgegeben* (Leipzig, 1986).

[21] HÄNY, *Die Edda*, S. 421.

[22] Vgl. die Beiträge in: *Feste und Feiern im Mittelalter*, hg. v. D. ALTENBURG, J. JARNUT und H.-H. STEINHOFF (Sigmaringen, 1991).

Imperium, von Aufständen im Innern und von Bürgerkriegen berichten. Die Welt des frühen Mittelalters war eine Welt des permanenten Krieges. Kampf und Krieg waren Existenzformen des adligen, zur Herrschaft berufenen und willigen Menschen der Zeit.[23]

Die evangelische Geschichte bot nur wenige Möglichkeiten, kriegerisches Geschehen darzustellen. Wo sie sich aber bot, hat der "*non ignobilis vates*", der Dichter des *Heliand*, sie intensiv genutzt – so in der berühmten Gefangennahme Christi durch die Kriegsknechte zu Gethsemane, da Petrus das Schwert ergreift und dem Malchus das Ohr abhaut. Die Evangelisten (Matth. 26: 47 ff.; Marc. 14: 43 ff.; Luk. 22: 47 ff.; Joh. 18: 2 ff.) hatten diese Szene nur kurz und teilweise dunkel angedeutet, am deutlichsten noch Johannes und mit ihm weitgehend *Tatian*: "*Simon ergo Petrus habens gladium eduxit eum et percussit pontificis servum et auriculam eius dextram; erat autem nomen servo Malchus*" ("Da hatte Simon Petrus ein Schwert und zog es aus und schlug nach des Hohepriesters Knecht und hieb ihm sein rechtes Ohr ab. Und der Knecht hieß Malchus").

Der *Heliand* gestaltet die Szene (v. 4854-4882) mit langem Atem im Stile heroischer Kampfschilderungen aus (übrigens auch in lateinischer Chronistik belegt; vgl. z. B. den Kampf des Bretonen Wurfand gegen eine Übermacht von Wikingern bei Regino von Prüm, Chronica ad a. 874):[24]

uuârun thoh sô strîdige man,
ahliopun eft up an themu holme, hugi fastnodun,
bundun briostgithâht, gibolgane gengun
nâhor mid nîðu, anttat sie thene neriendion Crist
uuerodo biuurpun. Stôdun uuîse man,
suîðo gornundie giungaron Kristes
biforan theru dereƀeon dâdi endi te iro drohtine sprâkun:
"uuâri it nu thîn uuillio", quâðun sie, "uualdand frô mîn,
that sie ûs hêr an speres ordun spildien môstin
uuâpnun uunde, than ni uuâri ûs uuiht sô gôd,
sô that uui hêr for ûsumu drohtine dôan môstin
beniðiun blêka". Thô gibolgan uuarð
snel suerdthegan, Sîmon Petrus,
uuell imu innan hugi, that he ni mahte ênig uuord sprekan:
sô harm uuarð imu an is hertan, that man is hêrron thar

[23] Vgl. HAUBRICHS, *Die Anfänge*, S. 127 ff.; ferner: *Kampf und Krieg*, hg. v. W. HAUBRICHS (Stuttgart, 1998: *LiLi* 109).

[24] *Quellen zur karolingischen Reichsgeschichte*, hg. v. R. RAU, 3. Teil (Darmstadt, 1966), S. 240 ff.

binden uuelde. Thô he gibolgan geng,
suîðo thrîstmôd thegan for is thiodan standen,
hard for is hêrron: ni uuas imu is hugi tuîfli,
blôð an is breostun, ac he is bil atôh,
suerd bi sîdu, slôg imu tegegnes
an thene furiston fiund folmo crafto,
that thô Malchus uuarð mâkeas eggiun,
an thea suîðaron half suerdu gimâlod:
thiu hlust uuarð imu farhauuan, he uuarð an that hôƀid uund,
that imu herudrôrag hlear endi ôre
beniuundun brast: blôd aftar sprang,
uuell fan uundun. Thô uuas an is uuangun scard
the furisto thero fiundo. Thô stôd that folc an rûm:
andrêdun im thes billes biti.

Doch waren sie außerordentlich streitbare Männer, stiegen wieder hinauf auf den Hügel, festigten ihren Sinn, schlossen ihre Gedanken ein in die Brust. Zornig geworden gingen sie näher heran, von Hass erfüllt, bis sie den Heiland Christus mit der Schar der Männer umringt hatten. Da standen die weisen Männer, die Gefolgsleute, die Jünger Christi, heftig klagend ob der grausamen Freveltat und sprachen zu ihrem Herrn (*frô*): "Wäre es nun auch dein Wille, waltender Herr mein, dass sie hier an Speeres Spitze uns spießen sollten, wund von Waffen, dann wäre uns nichts so lieb, als dass wir hier für unseren Gefolgsherrn (*drohtin*) sterben müssten, bleichen Leibes!" Da erzürnte sich der kühne Schwertmann, Simon Petrus, da schwoll ihm der Sinn, kein einziges Wort konnte er sprechen: so bitter ward ihm ums Herz, daß man seinen Herrn dort binden wollte. Zornvoll ging er da, der hochsinnige Held (*thrîstmôd thegan*), um vor seinen Herrscher (*thiodan*) sich zu stellen, kühn vor seinen Herrn: Kein Wanken kannte sein Sinn, keine Furcht sein Herz, die Klinge zog er, riss das Schwert von der Seite, schlug ein auf den vordersten der Feinde, mit der Kraft seiner Hände, so dass Malchus gezeichnet ward durch die Schärfe der Schneide, an der rechten Seite gezeichnet vom Schwert: das Ohr ward ihm zerhauen, er wurde am Haupte wund, dass ihm schwerblutig Wange und Ohr in Todeswunde barst: Blut sprang hervor, wallend aus der Wunde. Da wurde an seiner Wange schartig der vorderste der Feinde. Da wich das Kriegsvolk, sie scheuten den Biss des Schwertes.

Diese Szene des *Heliand* ist mit Recht berühmt. Sie könnte in jedem Heldenlied stehen, sie ist erfüllt nicht nur von Formeln und Stil der mündlichen Dichtung, sondern auch von der Mentalität des frühmittelalterlichen Kriegertums. Nur Weniges sei angeführt: So findet sich das Motiv vom Versagen der Sprache, vom wortlosen Zorn, mit dem die kriegerische Tat gegenüber dem Frevler angegangen wird, auch im Bericht eines spätmerowingischen Geschichtsschreibers, des *Liber Historiae Francorum* (c. 41), in seinem zweifellos auf eine heroische Sage zurückgehenden Bericht über den Sachsenkrieg Chlothars II., wo der König ebenfalls in schweigender, sprachloser Wut Rache an seinem Beleidiger, dem Sachsenherzog, übt. Die frühmittelalterliche Adelswelt wiederum spiegelt es – übrigens hier und anderswo – wenn der Gefolgsherr, für den der "*iungiro*",[25] der "*suerdthegan*" Petrus, kämpft, mit vielen zur Verfügung stehenden sozialen Termini der Herrschaft variierend umschrieben wird: "*uualdand frô*" ('waltender Herr'); "*hêrro*", d. i. *senior*, ein "*drohtin*" ('Gefolgsherr'), für den man zu sterben bereit ist; schließlich ein "*thiodan*" (ein 'Herrscher der *gens*, des Volkes'). Die Funktion dieser variierenden Terminologie ist eindeutig die, das soziale Geflecht des kriegerischen *comitatus*, die Mentalität der Gefolgschaft und der *familia* eines großen Herrn auf das Deutlichste für das Publikum zu evozieren.

Keinesfalls aber handelt es sich hier, wie man in früheren, keineswegs ruhmvollen Zeiten unserer Wissenschaftsgeschichte gemeint hat, um eine 'Germanisierung' (bzw. 'germanic transformation') oder auch nur eine 'Heroisierung' des Christentums – wie ja bereits Johannes Rathofer (1962) schlagend in seinem großen *Heliand*-Buch nachwies.[26] In der Szene selbst folgt der christliche Umschlag unmittelbar anschließend; die heroische Kampfkulisse ist vom Autor nur aufgebaut worden, um die Botschaft Christi, der auch kein 'Saxon Saviour' ist,[27] von der Gewaltlosigkeit um so eindrucksvoller hervortreten zu lassen: "*... ni sculun ûs belgan uuiht, uurêðean uuið iro geuuinne*" (v. 4895 f.: "... wir dürfen nicht zürnen, nicht widersetzen uns ihrem Streiten") und: "*... uui mid ûsun dâdiun ni sculun uuiht auuerdian*" (v. 4899 f.: "... wir mit unseren Taten könnten nichts wenden"). Erst der letzte Satz, die völlige Negierung des heroischen Tatensinns, lässt die Heldenpose des Petrus in ihrer ganzen Nichtigkeit aufscheinen.

[25] Vgl. Anm. 19.

[26] J. RATHOFER, *Der 'Heliand'. Theologischer Sinn als tektonische Form* (Köln, 1962), hier S. 51 ff.

[27] G.R. MURPHY, *The Saxon Savior. The Germanic Transformation of the Gospel in the Ninth-Century Heliand* (New York und Oxford, 1989); DERS., *The Heliand, the Saxon Gospel. A Translation and Commentary* (New York und Oxford, 1992). Leider wird der Begriff 'germanisch' auch recht unreflektiert – trotz interessanter Interpretationsansätze – gebraucht bei H. HAFERLAND, "Der Haß der Feinde. Germanische Heldendichtung und die Erzählkonzeption des 'Heliand'", *Euphorion* 95 (2001), S. 237-256. Auch die von ihm anderswo vorgetragene These, dass es sich bei dem *Heliand*-Dichter um einen laikalen mündlichen Dichter mit einem gelehrten Beraterstab gehandelt habe, ist mit einer gewissen Skepsis zu betrachten: H. HAFERLAND, "War der Dichter des 'Heliand' Illiterat?", *ZfdA* 131 (2002), S. 20-48, vor allem S. 43 ff.; ferner DERS., "Mündliche Erzähltechnik im 'Heliand'"; dazu HAUBRICHS, "Ludwig der Deutsche", S. 220 f. mit Anm. 50.

Noch an späterer Stelle, in der 60. Fitte (v. 5039-5049), nach der dreimaligen Leugnung des Petrus, wird die adlige, kriegerische *superbia* der Nichtigkeit geziehen:

Be thiu nis mannes bâg   mikilun bitherƀi,
hagustaldes hrôm: ef imu thiu helpe godes
gesuîkid thurh is sundeon,   than is imu sân after thiu.
breosthugi blôðora,   thoh he êr bihêt spreca,
hrômie fan is hildi   endi fan is handcrafti,
the man fan is megine.   That uuarð thar an themu mâreon skîn,
thegno bezton,   thô imu is thiodanes gisuêk
hêlag helpe.   Bethiu ni scoldi hrômien man
te suîðo fan imu selƀon,   huand imu thar suîkid oft
uuân endi uuilleo,   ef imu uualdand god,
hêr heƀenkuning   herte ni sterkit.

> Deswegen ist des Mannes Prahlen völlig unnütz, des jungen Helden (*hagustald*) hochmütiges Rühmen: wenn ihm die Hilfe Gottes versagt wird um seiner Sünden willen. Dann wird bald ihm furchtsam das Herz in der Brust, was immer er auch an Drohung aussprach, sich rühmend seiner Schwerttüchtigkeit und der Kraft seiner Hände, prahlend der Krieger mit seinem Vermögen. Das ward da offenbar an dem berühmten, dem besten der Krieger, als ihm seines Herrschers (*thiodan*) heilige Hilfe versagt wurde. Darum soll kein Krieger zu sehr seiner selbst sich rühmen; denn ihm entweicht gar schnell *uuân endi uuilleo*, Hoffnung und Zuversicht, wenn ihm der waltende Gott, der erhabene Himmelskönig das Herz nicht stärkt.

Auch in der berühmten Paraphrase von Johannes 11: 16, wo es um die Rückkehr Jesu in das feindliche Land der Juden geht, hat der Autor des *Heliand* das Ethos des heimischen Heldenliedes zwar benutzt, aber auch ebenso instrumental eingesetzt (v. 3986 ff.). Die vom Rückkehrplan abratenden Jünger reden Jesu als ihren Herrn an: "Warum strebst du nun danach, zu diesem kampflustigen Volk, wo der Feinde soviele sind, zu diesen übermütigen Edelleuten zu fahren?" Doch Thomas, der "*diurlîc drohtines thegan*" ('treffliche Gefolgsmann des Herrn'), antwortet: "'Wir wollen seine Tat nicht tadeln, noch wehren seinem Willen, sondern ihm getrost beistehen, leiden mit unserem Gebieter: das ist Pflicht des Gefolgsmannes, dass er mit seinem Herrn unbeugsam stehe, sterbe mit ihm in der Stunde des Ruhms. So lasst uns alle handeln, folgen seiner Fahrt: unser Leben soll fortan nichts gelten, bis wir im Kriegsvolk mit ihm, unserem Herrscher [*drohtin*] sterben. Dann lebt doch unser Nachruhm, gute Sage unter den Menschen!' So wurden des Mächtigen Jünger, die edelgeborenen Krieger, einmütigen Herzens, ihrem Herrn zu Willen".

Die Heroisierung dieser Szene verfolgt zwei Ziele: falsches heroisches Ethos wird denunziert im 'Übermut' der Juden – durchaus, wie der kampfwütende, ins Verderben führende *overmōd* des Königs Byrhtnoth gegenüber den Wikingern, denen er leichtfertig einen Kampfvorteil schenkt, in der *Battle of Maldon*, einem altenglischen heroischen Lied des zehnten Jahrhunderts, zeigt, eine heroische Eigenschaft.[28]

Die hier an das Johanneswort "*moriamur cum eo*" ("lasst uns mit ihm sterben") anknüpfende, aber im Stile des heroischen Kriegerethos gestaltete Todesbereitschaft der Jünger ist als Topos des heroischen Kampfes oft in der frühmittelalterlichen Chronistik belegt: So formulierte Nithard, selbst ein Adliger aus dem Stamme Karls des Großen, in analoger Situation als Geschichtsschreiber des westfränkischen Königs Karl des Kahlen a. 844:[29] "Die Großen zogen es vor, in edler Gesinnung (*nobiliter*) zu sterben als den verratenen König zu verlassen". Der schon erwähnte bretonische Herzog Wurfand stürzte sich – nach dem Bericht des um 908 schreibenden Chronisten Regino von Prüm[30] – im Kampf mit einem Konkurrenten um die Herrschaft auf eine dreißigfache Übermacht und weist jeden Gedanken an Rückzug von sich: "Fern sei es von mir, ihr mutigen Krieger, heute zu tun, was ich noch nie getan habe, nämlich meinen Feinden den Rücken zu zeigen und den Ruhm unseres Namens beschimpfen zu lassen. Besser ist es, rühmlich zu sterben als mit Schande das Leben zu retten ..." (vgl. auch *Beowulf*, v. 1383 ff.; 2890 f.). Ähnlich lässt der ottonische Historiograph Widukind um 967/68 Otto den Großen in schwieriger Lage der Lechfeldschlacht gegen die Ungarn 955 sagen: "Es ist besser, meine Krieger, wenn das Ende bevorsteht, ruhmvoll zu sterben, denn von den Feinden unterworfen ein knechtisches Leben zu führen".[31] Die Annalen des bayerischen Klosters Niederaltaich berichten zum Jahre 1042 von einem Ungarneinfall. Eine kleine Schar von "Adligen und Tapferen" entschließt sich, der feindlichen Übermacht entgegenzutreten – mit den Worten: "Ehrenvoller sei es, das Leben in Ehren (*cum honore*) zu verlieren, als es in Schande zu verlängern!"[32] Ähnlich reagiert die kleine Schar der schon verlorenen Krieger in der bereits erwähnten altenglischen *Battle of Maldon* im 10. Jahrhundert (v. 312 f.): "Unsere Gedanken müssen um so härter, unser Herz um so kühner, unser Geist um so großmütiger

[28] *The Battle of Maldon*, hg. v. E.V. GORDON. (London, 1966), S. 49 f., v. 89 ff.

[29] *Nithardi Historiae* II, 4, in: *Quellen zur karolingischen Reichsgeschichte*, hg. v. R. RAU, 1. Teil (Darmstadt, 1966), S. 408.

[30] Vgl. Anm. 24.

[31] *Widukindi Res gestae Saxonicae* III, 46, in: *Quellen zur Geschichte der Sächsischen Kaiserzeit*, hg. u. übertragen v. A. BAUER und R. RAU (Darmstadt, 1971), S. 150 f.

[32] *Annales Altahenses*, in: *MGH Scriptores rerum germanicarum in usum scholarum* 4 (1891), S. 30, Z. 7-15.

werden, je kleiner unsere Macht wird".[33] Es ist die gleiche *magnitudo animi* ('Größe des Herzens'), die Regino von Prüm an seinem bretonischen Helden lobte. Noch Wipo formulierte in seinen *Taten des Kaisers Konrad II.* (1024-1039), dass schlimmer als der Tod sei, "im Ruf der Feigheit" zu leben.[34]

Auf das Heilige bezogen finden wir schließlich diese heroische Mentalität in einer kleinen, aber bezeichnenden Mirakelgeschichte der Vita des hl. Fridolin von Säckingen (c. 32):[35] Dort erkennt ein Knecht namens *Wenilo*, dass bei einem Heideneinfall alle Mönche und Priester, obwohl aus dem Adel stammend, geflohen sind, der wunderträchtige Leib des Heiligen, seine Reliquien aber ungeschützt im Kloster verblieben sind. Er erkennt, "er selbst müsse sich auch auf die Gefahr hin, zu sterben, aus Liebe zu seinem Herrn schützend vor diesen stellen. Voll Gottvertrauen sprach er, nicht wie ein ungebildeter Mensch, sondern wie ein vornehmer Herr: 'Mir liegt nicht daran, länger zu leben, wenn ich sehe, wie mein Gebieter von den Heiden mit Feuer verbrannt wird' ". Die merkwürdige *militia* des Nichtkriegers, die heroische Tat, gelingt. Allein bringt er den ihm leicht werdenden schweren Steinsarkophag des Heiligen in die Sicherheit einer Burg.

Genug der Beispiele. Im *Heliand* dient die Evokation heroischer Todesbereitschaft dazu, dem in der heimischen Wertwelt lebenden Publikum der Bibeldichtung das heilsgeschichtlich notwendige, dennoch frei verantwortete, die Erlösung der Menschen vorbereitende Selbstopfer Christi verständlich zu machen. Auch dieses freilich scheint dem frühmittelalterlichen Menschen nur in der Gemeinschaft, im Verband von Herrn und Gefolgsleuten, die sich zu umfassender gegenseitiger Hilfe verpflichtet haben, denkbar. Dennoch wird sichtbar, wie sich im Wechsel der Perspektiven die dramatische Rede des Heldenliedes als kerygmatische, das Heil offenbarende Rede des Bibelepos enthüllt, die das tragische heimische mündliche Lied als Heilsdichtung, in dem der Tod des Helden einen neuen Sinn gewinnt, gleichsam erlöst. Es ist Christus – wie Gottschalk, auch Sachse und Schüler, freilich rebellischer, des Hrabanus Maurus, Abt von Fulda, sagte – "*custos*" und "*heros*" ('Wächter und Krieger').[36]

Umgekehrt lässt sich bei aller Instrumentalisierung adliger, kriegerischer Mentalität nicht übersehen, dass die evangelische Geschichte im *Heliand* durch

[33] *Battle of Maldon*, S. 61, v. 312 f.

[34] *Wiponis Gesta Chuonradi II. Imperatoris*, c. 2, in: *Quellen des 9. und 11. Jahrhunderts zur Geschichte der Hamburgischen Kirche und des Reiches*, hg. v. W. TRILLMICH und R. BUCHNER (Darmstadt, 1978), S. 542 f.

[35] M. PÖRNBACHER, *Vita Sancti Fridolini. Leben und Wunder des hl. Fridolin von Säckingen* (Sigmaringen, 1997), S. 258 ff.

[36] Gottschalk von Orbais, in: *MGH Poetae Latini* VI, 1, Nr. 1, Str. 1, S. 89.

diese Instrumentalisierung eine bemerkenswerte Nobilitierung erfährt. Uns verrät gerade diese Nobilitierung, dass kriegerische Mentalität, auch jene, welche die heroische Anstrengung des *experimentum virtutis*, im Angesicht des Todes die Ehre neu zu befestigen, verlangt, in der Adressatengesellschaft des altsächsischen Epos fest etabliert war.[37]

3. *Taufe und Namengebung*

Namengebung im frühen Mittelalter war ein bedeutsamer sozialer Akt, der normalerweise bei der Taufe vollzogen wurde.[38] Auch die Namen, die man vergab, konnten bedeutsam sein, ja waren in der Regel bedeutsam, bei den germanischen *gentes* wie auch bei den Romanen: Es gab sprechende christlich-romanische Namen, wie *Deodatus, Donatus, Desiderius, Desiderata, Christinus*; Nachbenennungen nach biblischen Gestalten wie *Jacob, Daniel, David, Salomo, Maria, Elisabeth* usw.[39] Auch in der germanischen Adelswelt wurden bedeutungsvolle Namen kreiert und in Akten der Nachbenennung spektakulär an Enkel und Söhne weitergegeben werden: *Chlodwig* oder *Ludwig*, 'berühmter Kämpfer'; *Chlothar* oder *Lothar*, 'berühmter Krieger'; *Chilpericus* oder *Hilperich*, d. h. *adiutor fortis* ('starker Helfer'). Namenelemente werden in einer Familie variiert: *Sigimund* und *Sigifrid*; *Karl* und *Karlmann, Chlodwig* und

[37] Vgl. zur heroischen Verknüpfung von Ehre und Tod: W. HAUBRICHS, "Ehre und Konflikt. Zur intersubjektiven Konstitution der adligen Persönlichkeit im früheren Mittelalter", in: *Spannungen und Konflikte menschlichen Zusammenlebens in der deutschen Literatur des Mittelalters*, hg. v. K. GÄRTNER, I. KASTEN und F. SHAW (Tübingen, 1996), S. 35-58; DERS., "Emotionen vor dem Tode und ihre Ritualisierung", in: *Codierungen von Emotionen in der Kultur und Literatur des Mittelalters und der frühen Neuzeit. Paradigmen und Perspektiven*, hg. v. S. JAEGER und I. KASTEN (Berlin, 2003), S. 70-97.

[38] Vgl. G. KRETSCHMAR, *Die Geschichte des Taufgottesdienstes in der alten Kirche* (Kassel, 1970: *Leiturgia. Handbuch des evangelischen Gottesdienstes* 5), S. 1-348.

[39] Aufkommen und mentaler Gehalt der neuen, in Spätantike und frühem Mittelalter erfolgreichen christlich-romanischen Namen sind noch unzureichend untersucht. Vgl. unterdessen H. SOLIN, "Zur Entwicklung des römischen Namensystems", in: *Person und Name. Methodische Probleme bei der Erstellung eines Personennamenbuches des Frühmittelalters*, hg. v. D. GEUENICH, W. HAUBRICHS und J. JARNUT (Berlin und New York, 2002: *Ergänzungsbände zum Reallexikon der Germanischen Altertumskunde* 32), S. 1-17 [mit. Lit.]; ferner: N. GAUTHIER, *Recueil des inscriptions chrétiennes de la Gaule antérieures à la Renaissance carolingienne*, Bd. I: *Première Belgique* (Paris, 1975), S. 82 ff. § 103 ff.; F. DESCOMBES, *Recueil des inscriptions chrétiennes de la Gaule,* Bd. XV: *Viennoise du Nord* (Paris 1985), S. 165 ff. § 229 ff.; W. HAUBRICHS, "Romanen an Rhein und Mosel. Onomastische Reflexionen", in: *Deutsche Sprache in Raum und Zeit. Festschrift für Peter Wiesinger* (Wien, 1998), S. 379-413, hier S. 385 ff.

Chlothar, Mero-wich und *Mero(w)-ing, Childebert* und *Childerich; Heribrand, Hildebrand* und *Hadubrand* – um nur berühmte Beispiele zu nennen.[40]

Die Namen lebten in den großen Familien und wurden in Übereinstimmung mit der Familientradition weitergegeben. Dies ist der Hintergrund für jene berühmte Szene, in der im *Hildebrandlied* (v. 9 ff.) der Protagonist seinen Gegner vor dem Kampf danach fragt, "*wer sin fater wari*" und "*welihhes cnuosles du sis; ibu du mi enan sages, ik mi de odre wet, chind, in chunincriche chud ist mir al irmindeot*". Er fragt also danach, "wer sein Vater wäre" und "welcher Abkunft du seist; wenn du mir einen [deiner Verwandten] nennst, weiß ich mir die andern, Jüngling, im Königreich ist mir alles Großvolk bekannt".[41]

Wenn in besonderen Fällen bedeutungsvoll von der Namentradition abgewichen wurde, so wurde das durchaus wahrgenommen. So erzählt die *Vita der hl. Genovefa von Paris* (c. 32), dass ein Kind in der Fastenzeit in einen Brunnen fiel, zunächst tot geborgen wurde, dann aber zu der Heiligen gebracht und von ihr wieder zum Leben erweckt wurde. Der Knabe habe dann bei der Taufe den Namen *Cellomeris* erhalten – "*eo quod in cellolam sepe dicte Genovefae vitam quam amiserat recipisset*" ("deswegen, weil er in der Zelle der bekannten Genovefa das Leben, das er verlor, wieder erhielt").[42] Und in der Vita des Friesenmissionars Wulfram von Sens erhält ein Knabe, der von ihm vor der Opferung an die Götter gerettet wurde, den (bitheriophoren) Namen *Wulf-hraban* des Missionars, einen Namen, der – wie ausdrücklich vermerkt wird – bis dahin beim Volke der Friesen unerhört war.[43]

[40] Vgl. zur Semantisierung germanischer Personennamen im frühen Mittelalter: W. HAUBRICHS, "Identität und Name. Akkulturationsvorgänge in Namen und die Traditionsgesellschaften des frühen Mittelalters", in: *Die Suche nach den Ursprüngen. Von der Bedeutung des frühen Mittelalters*, hg. v. W. POHL (Wien, 2004), S. 85-105; DERS., "Romano-germanische Hybridnamen des frühen Mittelalters nördlich der Alpen", in: *Akkulturation. Probleme der romanisch-germanischen Kultursynthese in Spätantike und frühem Mittelalter*, hg. v. D. HÄGERMANN, W. HAUBRICHS und J. JARNUT (Berlin und New York, 2004), S. 179-203.

[41] STEINMEYER, *Die althochdeutschen Sprachdenkmäler*, S. 2.

[42] Vgl. M. HEINZELMANN, "Vita sanctae Genovefae. Recherches sur les critères de datation d'un texte hagiographique", in: DERS. und J.-C. POULIN, *Les vies anciennes de sainte Geneviève de Paris. Etudes critiques* (Paris und Genf, 1986), S. 23-28. Es ist ein Name doppelter Interpretation, denn er kann – dies ist kein Einzelfall in den Interferenzräumen des frühen Mittelalters – auch fränkisch interpretiert werden: N. WAGNER, in: "Cillica, Cella, Cellomeris und Chillardus", *Beiträge zur Namenforschung* N.F. 31 (1996), S. 164-170.

[43] Vgl. W. HAUBRICHS, "Biographie und Onomastik", in: *Scripturus vitam. Lateinische Biographie von der Antike bis in die Gegenwart. Festgabe Walter Berschin*, hg. v. D. WALZ (Heidelberg, 2002), S. 1-23, hier S. 2 ff.; ferner HAUBRICHS, "Romano-germanische Hybridnamen", S. 192 f.

Welche Bedeutung Verwandtschaft im *Heliand* hat,[44] lässt sich an der Bearbeitung der dürftigen Angaben, welche die Evangelien und *Tatian* (c. 22)[45] anlässlich der Berufung der Apostel zu deren Herkunft machen, ablesen (v. 1225 ff.). Z. B. wird Jesu Verwandter mit folgenden Worten gewürdigt (v. 1263 ff.): Und er berief auch den anderen Jakob, "*is selƀes suuiri: sie uuârun fon gisustruonion tuuêm / cnôsles cumana, Krist endi Iacob / gôde gadulingos*" ("seinen eigenen Schwestersohn: sie stammten von zwei Schwestern, waren gekommen aus deren Geschlecht, Krist und Jakob, gute Sippenverwandte"). Das im *Hildebrandlied* und im *Heliand* aufscheinende Wort **knōt* ('*substantia*, Wesen, Art') dürfte ein Bedeutungsspektrum wie lat. *stirps* (z. B. in "*ex stirpe eorum*") besessen haben.[46]

In einer berühmten Passage der Evangelien, bei der Geburt des Täufers, des Sohnes der Elisabeth und des Zacharias, gibt es ein ähnliches Szenario (Luk. 1: 57 ff.):

> Als die Nachbarn und Verwandten [*cognati*] dies hörten ... freuten sie sich mit den Eltern. Am achten Tag, am Tag der Beschneidung, kamen sie und hießen den Knaben in einem Akt der Nachbenennung nach dem Vater Zacharias. Doch die Mutter protestiert und spricht: "Er soll Johannes heißen", wie es der Engel ihr verkündigt hatte. Die Verwandten aber widersprechen: "Es ist doch niemand in deiner Verwandtschaft [*cognatio*], der so heißt".

Erst die Bestätigung durch den Vater bringt die Entscheidung für den geoffenbarten, aber in der Sippe unerhörten Namen.

Wie haben die Bibelepen diese Szene, die die Ordnungen und Riten der Gesellschaften, für die sie geschrieben wurden, durchaus intensiv betraf, verarbeitet?

Bei Otfrid (I, 9) ist die Versammlung der Verwandten um den Neugeborenen bedeutend ausführlicher als bei Lukas erzählt. Es kommen die "*friunt*" (v. 3), die Angehörigen der *familia*, und die "*lántliut*", die *pagenses* aus der Nachbarschaft, sowie die "*mága*" (v. 5), die eigentlichen Verwandten. Es wird ausdrücklich als deren Aufgabe bezeichnet, das Kind zeremoniell zu begrüßen ("*quetten*") und ihm einen Namen zu schaffen (v. 8). Sie sind "*edilinge*" (v. 9:

[44] Vgl. dazu allgemein ALTHOFF, *Verwandte, Freunde und Getreue*; R. LE JAN, *Famille et pouvoir dans le monde franc* (Paris, 1995).

[45] *Die lateinisch-althochdeutsche Tatianbilingue Stiftsbibliothek St. Gallen Cod. 56*, hg. v. A. MASSER (Göttingen, 1994: *Studien zum Althochdeutschen* 25), hier S. 133.

[46] W. HAUBRICHS, "Die Erfindung der Enkel. Germanische und deutsche Terminologie der Verwandtschaft und Generationen", *LiLi* 30 (2000), S. 41-80, hier S. 65.

'Adlige') und einigen sich darüber, wie man das Kind zu nennen habe.[47] Sie sagen ausdrücklich, dass der schon alte Vater im Namen erneuert werden sollte; der Sohn solle seinen Namen um der *memoria* des Vaters willen tragen, damit man ihn in der "*námiti*" (v. 14), in der Benamung erinnere. So etwa wurde Ludwig das Kind, Sohn des Königs Arnulf (887-899), ausdrücklich in einem bewussten Akt der *memoria* von den bischöflichen Paten nach seinem Großvater Ludwig dem Deutschen benannt.[48] Dieses Verfahren wird bei Otfrid ausdrücklich als geziemend, als Brauch, bezeichnet, während der Vorschlag der Mutter nicht dem Brauch entspreche (v. 20 ff.). In typischem Wortspiel (*figura etymologica*) bemerkte Otfrid: "*Ni was in ther námo námi*" ("Der Name war ihnen nicht annehmbar"). "In deinem Geschlecht [*kunni*]", sagen sie der Mutter: "– Zähle es Mann für Mann durch – kann sich niemand erinnern, dass jemand diesen Namen führte".

Im *Heliand* (v. 198-239) wird die ganze Szene noch deutlicher individualisiert, wird nahezu ganz eingebettet in den einheimischen Brauch, in dem die Verwandten den Namen bestimmen, so dass das Scandalum des neuen, des unerhörten Namen (*Johannes*, d. h. 'Gott ist gnädig') noch schärfer hervortritt.

Iohannes quam
an liudeo lioht: lîk uuas im scôni,
uuas im fel fagar, fahs endi naglos,
uuangun uuârun im uulitige. Thô fôrun thar uuîse man,
snelle tesamne, thea suâsostun mêst,
uundrodun thes uuerkes, bihuî it gio mahti giuuerðan sô,
that undar sô aldun tuêm ôdan uurði
barn an giburdeon, ni uuâri that it gibod godes
selƀes uuâri: afsuoƀun sie garo,
that it elcor sô uuânlîc uuerðan ni mahti.
Thô sprak thar ên gifrôdot man, the sô filo consta
uuîsaro uuordo, habde giuuit mikil,
frâgode niudlîco, huuat is namo scoldi
uuesan an thesaro uueroldi: "mi thunkid an is uuîsu gilîc
iac an is gibârea, that he sî betara than uui,
sô ic uuâniu, that ina ûs gegnungo god fon himila

[47] Vgl. zum rituellen Akt der Namengebung in der Taufe B. JUSSEN, *Patenschaft und Adoption im frühen Mittelalter. Künstliche Verwandtschaft als soziale Praxis* (Göttingen, 1991), hier S. 238 ff.; DERS., *Spiritual Kinship as Social Practice. Godparentship and Adoption in the Early Middle Ages* (Newark und London, 2000), S. 181 ff.; J. JARNUT, "Avant l'an Mil", in: *L'anthroponymie. Document de l'histoire sociale des mondes méditerranéens médiévaux*, hg. v. M. BOURIN u. a. (Rom, 1996), S. 7-18, hier S. 11.

[48] Vgl. JUSSEN, *Patenschaft und Adoption*, S. 241.

selƀo sendi". Thô sprac sân aftar
thiu môdar thes kindes, thiu thana magu habda,
that barn an ire barme: "hêr quam gibod godes", quað siu,
"fernun gêre, furmon uuordu
gibôđ, that he Iohannes bi godes lêrun
hêtan scoldi. That ic an mînumu hugi ni gidar
uuendean mid uuihti, of ic is giuualdan môt".
Thô sprac ên gêlhert man, the ira gaduling uuas:
"ne hêt êr giouuiht sô", quað he, "aðalboranes
ûses cunnies eftho cnôsles. Uuita kiasan im ôðrana
niudsamna namon: he niate of he môti".
Thô sprac eft the frôdo man, the thar consta filo mahlian:
"ni giƀu ic that te râde", quað he, "rinco negênun,
that he uuord godes uuendean biginna;
ac uuita is thana fader frâgon, the thar sô gifrôdod sitit,
uuîs an is uuînseli: Thoh he ni mugi ênig uuord sprecan,
thoh mag he bi bôcstaƀon brêf geuuirkean,
namon giscrîƀan". Thô he nâhor geng,
legda im êna bôc an barm endi bad gerno
uurîtan uuîslîco uuordgimerkiun,
huat sie that hêlaga barn hêtan scoldin.
Thô nam he thia bôk an hand endi an is hugi thâhte
suîðo gerno te gode: Iohannes namon
uuîslîco giuurêt endi ôc aftar mid is uuordu gisprac
suîðo spâhlîco: habda im eft is sprâca giuuald,
giuuitteas endi uuîsun.

Johannes trat in den Sichtkreis der Menschen: Sein Leib war schön, hell waren seine Haut, sein Haar und seine Nägel, seine Wangen glänzten. Da kamen dort die weisen Männer rasch zusammen, es waren die meistvertrauten in der Verwandtschaft, wunderten sich über dieses Werk, wie solches überhaupt geschehen konnte, dass durch zwei so alte Leute ein Kind dem Geschlecht geschenkt wurde. Solches konnte nur durch das Gebot Gottes geschehen sein. Sie erkannten klar, dass es auf andere Weise nie so schön hätte werden können. Da sprach ein erfahrener Mann, der viele Worte der Weisheit in seinem Gedächtnis bewahrte, der reiches Wissen besaß; er fragte eifrig, welcher denn sein Name werden sollte in dieser Welt: "Mich dünkt, dass er nach seinem Wesen und nach seinem Verhalten besser sei als wir; so glaube ich, dass ihn uns in Wahrheit Gott selbst vom Himmel sandte". Da sprach gleich darauf die Mutter des Kindes, die diesen Sohn empfangen hatte, die getragen hatte den Sprössling in ihrem Schoße: "Zu uns kam das Gebot Gottes", sagte sie, "im vorigen Jahr, es gebot in bedeutungsvollem Worte, dass er nach der Weisung Gottes Johannes heißen sollte. Diesen Entschluss dürfen in meinem Sinn keine Wichte [Dämonen] wenden, ich muss ihn sorgsam befolgen". Da sprach ein vermessener Mann, der ihr Verwandter war: "So hieß bisher nicht einer von den Adligen unseres Geschlechts oder in der Verwandschaft, lasst uns einen anderen, einen angemessenen Namen wählen: davon kann er Nutzen ziehen". Da sprach aber der erfahrene Mann, der über so vieles klug zu sprechen wusste: "Nicht gebe ich solchen Rat", sprach er, "irgendeinem Mann, dass er das Wort Gottes zu verkehren beginne; es geziemt sich, den Vater zu fragen, der vor uns als ein Erfahrener sitzt, weise in seiner Weinstube: Zwar kann er kein einziges Wort sprechen, doch kann er mit Buchstaben ein Zeugnis ausstellen, den Namen schreiben". Da trat er an ihn heran, legte ihm ein Buch in den Schoß und bat ihn inständig, besonnen darein mit Schrift Zeichen zu schreiben, wie sie das heilige Kind nennen sollten. Da nahm dieser das Buch in die Hand und dachte in seinem Gemüte mit Inbrunst an Gott: Den Namen Johannes schrieb er mit Bedacht und sprach ihn danach auch mit eigenem Worte aus, klug und bedacht. Er hatte wieder die Gewalt über seine Sprache, über Ausdruck und Sinn.

Man darf zunächst einmal festhalten, in welcher Weise Auserwähltheit in dieser Gesellschaft (ohne jede biblische Vorlage) festgestellt wird: Schönheit, Glanz und Licht umgeben den *electus*, das "*hêlaga barn*". Die Szene enthält ferner geradezu ein Kompendium der Verwandtschaftsterminologie (v. 198 ff.) und die ganze Sippe nimmt an diesem Akt teil, auch wenn man von weiter her kommt (v. 201 f.): "*... thô fôrun thar uuîse man snelle tesamne, the suâsostun mêst ...*" ("Da kamen dort die weisen Männer rasch zusammen, es waren die meistvertrauten in der Verwandtschaft ...").

Nachdem die Mutter das Gebot Gottes, den Gottes Gnade verdankten Sohn Johannes zu heißen, verkündet hat, gibt es (erneut ohne biblische Vorlage) einen aus den Traditionen der Adelsgesellschaft heraus verständlichen Widerspruch aus dem Kreise der Verwandten (v. 221 ff.) "*thô sprac en gêlhert man, the ira gaduling was: 'ne hêt êr giouuiht sô', quađ he, 'ađalboranes ûses cunnies eftho cnôsles. Uuita kiasan im ôđrana niudsamna namon: he niate of he môti!'*" ("Da sprach ein vermessener Mann, der ihr Verwandter war: 'So hieß bisher nicht einer von den Adligen unseres Geschlechts oder in der Verwandtschaft, lasst uns einen anderen, einen angemessenen Namen wählen: davon kann er Nutzen ziehen!'")

Die Namen sind einer Sippe 'angemessen', also konventionalisiert, ihr speziell eigen und wohl auch erblich. Der Einzelne kann, indem er einem bedeutenden Namenträger nachbenannt wird, oder indem er sich in die Namentradition eines Verbandes einordnet, aus diesem bekannten Namen Nutzen ziehen. Er erhöht sein 'Renommée'. Der Name kann gar ein *prodigium* oder *veriloquium* enthalten.[49] So verweist nach Ermoldus Nigellus (*Carmen in hono-*

[49] Vgl. W. HAUBRICHS: "Namendeutung im europäischen Mittelalter", in: *Namenfor-*

rem Hludowici, I, v, 78 ff.) der Name Kaiser Ludwigs des Frommen durch seine Bestandteile *hludo-* ('berühmt') und *wicgch-* ('Kampf, Krieg') auf die kriegerischen Fähigkeiten des Herrschers, den schon in seiner Jugend sowohl Frömmigkeit als auch Mut auszeichneten.[50]

Weil der Akt der Namengebung den ganzen Verwandtenverband angeht, kommen – ganz analog dem biblischen Geschehen, aber durchaus noch narrativ ausgebaut – die wichtigsten Verwandten, die "*suâsostun*", die zum engeren Verband, der **swē* Gehörigen und daher Vertrauten, zu diesem Ereignis zusammen. Sie ergreifen das Wort, ein "*gaduling*" (zu germ. **gad-* 'zusammenkommen, passen'), ein Verwandter also, sucht die Interessen des Verwandtenverbandes zu wahren, indem er die Unerhörtheit (und die für den Neugeborenen drohende Schädlichkeit) des Tuns hervorhebt. Der Verband selbst wird durch zwei Wörter – nämlich "*cunni*"und "*cnōsal*" (zu ahd. *chnōt* 'Wesenheit, Natur') – umschrieben, deren genaue Differenzierung uns entgeht. Möglicherweise wird auch hier wie im *Hildebrandlied* zwischen dem allgemeinen Abstammungsverband und der, wie *aðalboran* 'edelgeboren' nahe legt, adligen Abkunft unterschieden.

In der vom Dichter des *Heliand* dramatisierten Szene kommt der Umschlag aus dem Kreise der Verwandten selbst. Es ist ein erfahrener, ein weiser Mann (v. 208), der den zu gebenden Namen von der Mutter erfragt hatte und deshalb wohl als Wortführer des *cunni*, des Verwandtenverbands gewertet werden darf. Er hatte schon aus der lichten Erscheinung des Kindes dessen besondere, 'bessere' Qualität abgeleitet, ja seine göttliche Sendung vermutet. Er ist es auch, der dem traditionsgebundenen *gaduling* widerspricht und den Vater um Entscheidung angeht, der den gottgesandten Namen bestätigt. Das Außerordentliche verlangt und erhält einen neuen Namen.

4. Sprechen und Verhalten

Zu den durchaus erstaunlichen Eigenheiten von Otfrids *Evangelienbuch* gehört es, daß der Autor die Personen der heiligen Handlung, besonders Christus, aber auch Engel, Maria, Augustus, Apostel usw. weit über die biblische Vorlage hinaus sprechen lässt, ja ihnen häufig genug auch Kommentar und

schung. Ein internationales Handbuch zur Onomastik, hg. v. E. EICHLER u. a., Teilbd. 1 (Berlin und New York, 1995), S. 351-360 [mit. Lit.].

[50] *Ermoldi Nigelli Carmen in honorem Hludouici Christianissimi Caesaris Augusti*, liber I, v. 78 ff., in: *MGH Poetae Latini*, Bd. II (Berlin, 1884), S. 6.

Deutung des Erzählten zugleich bereits in den Mund legt.[51] Dies ist schon inhaltlich eine erstaunliche Freiheit gegenüber einem verbalinspirierten heiligen Text, dem von der weitaus überwiegenden Mehrheit der zeitgenössischen Intellektuellen doch die Haltung verehrender Scheu, wortwörtlicher Bewahrung und skrupulöser Kommentierung entgegengebracht wird. Otfrid aber springt in diesem Falle – in größerem Maße als der *Heliand*[52] – mit Verve und Mut in die Lücken der evangelischen Handlung, um sie mit neuer Rede und neuem Dialog zu füllen.

Es fragt sich dabei, mit welchem kulturellen Gestus der gelehrte Teilhaber einer Buchkultur, der *litteratus* und *magister* Otfrid, Schreiber von Bibelkommentaren und Glossator grammatischer Traktate und doch gleichzeitig Teilhaber der von Mündlichkeit geprägten kommunikativen Mehrheitskultur seines Volkes,[53] wie er die gesprochene Sprache seiner Personen gestaltet hat.[54] Eine anderswo bereits versuchte breitere Analyse hätte sich nun genauer mit den vorkommenden Typen von Sprechakten,[55] mit den Sprechweisen und benutzten Redeformeln zu befassen. Hier soll es bei der Vorstellung eines entschieden kulturspezifisch (und das nicht nur in damaliger Zeit) konturierten Redetypus, der 'geziemenden Rede' gegenüber Frauen, sein Bewenden haben.

[51] Vgl. W. HAUBRICHS, "Otfrid von Weißenburg – Übersetzer, Erzähler, Interpret. Zur translativen Technik eines karolingischen Gelehrten", *Wolfram-Studien* 14 (1996), S. 13-45.

[52] Vgl. dazu B. SOWINSKI, *Darstellungsstil und Sprachstil im 'Heliand'* (Köln und Wien, 1985).

[53] Vgl. zur Stellung Otfrids zwischen Laienkultur und gelehrter Literatenkultur z. B. W. HAUBRICHS. "Eine prosopographische Skizze zu Otfrid von Weißenburg", in: *Otfrid von Weißenburg*, hg. v. W. KLEIBER (Darmstadt, 1978: *Wege der Forschung* 419), S. 397-413; DERS., *Die Anfänge*, S. 292 ff.; DERS., "Otfrid von Weißenburg", *Theologische Realenzyklopädie* 25 (1995), S. 541-544; E. HELLGARDT, *Die exegetischen Quellen von Otfrids Evangelienbuch* (Tübingen, 1981); W. KLEIBER, *Otfrid von Weissenburg. Untersuchungen zur handschriftlichen Überlieferung und Studien zum Aufbau des Evangelienbuches* (Bern und München, 1971: *Bibliotheca Germanica* 14); U. LUDWIG, "Otfrid in den Weißenburger Mönchslisten", *Zeitschrift für Geschichte des Oberrheins* 135 (1987), S. 65-82.

[54] Vgl. S. SONDEREGGER, "Reflexe gesprochener Sprache in der althochdeutschen Literatur", *Frühmittelalterliche Studien* 5 (1971), S. 176-192; DERS., "Althochdeutsch als Volkssprache", in: *Gedenkschrift für Ingerid Dal*, hg. v. J.O. ASKEDAL u. a. (Tübingen, 1988), S. 17-27; A. MASSER, "Wege zu gesprochenem Althochdeutsch", in: *Grammatica Ianua Artium. Festschrift Rolf Bergmann*, hg. v. E. GLASER und M. SCHLAEFER (Heidelberg, 1997), S. 49-70.

[55] W. HAUBRICHS, "Heilige Fiktion? Die Gestaltung gesprochener Sprache in Otfrids von Weißenburg *Liber Evangeliorum.* Vier Fallbeispiele zur inneren Sprachreflexion des karolingischen Dichtertheologen", in: *Vox-Sermo-Res. Beiträge zur Sprachreflexion, Literatur- und Sprachgeschichte vom Mittelalter bis zur Neuzeit. Festschrift Uwe Ruberg,* hg. v. W. HAUBRICHS, W. KLEIBER und R. VOSS (Stuttgart und Leipzig, 2001), S. 99-122.

Als der Erzengel Gabriel in der Annunziationsszene (Lk. 1: 26-38) Maria die frohe Botschaft verkündet (Otfrid I, 5), wird dies vom Weißenburger folgendermaßen gestaltet:[56]

Ward áfter thiu irscrítan sár, so moht es sin, ein halb jár,
mánodo after ríme thría stunta zuéne;
Tho quam bóto fona góte, éngil ir hímile,
bráht er therera wórolti diuri árunti.
Floug er súnnun pad, stérrono stráza,
wega wólkono zi theru ítis frono;
Zi édiles fróuun, sélbun sancta Máriun,
thie fórdoron bi bárne warun chúninga alle.
Gíang er in thia pálinza, fand sia drúrenta,
mit sálteru in hénti, then sáng si unz in énti;
Wáhero dúacho werk wírkento
díurero gárno, thaz déda siu io gérno.
Tho sprach er érlicho ubar ál, so man zi frówun scal,
so bóto scal io gúater, zi drúhtines muater:
"Heil mágad zieri, thíarna so scóni,
állero wíbo gote zéizosto!
Ni brútti thih múates, noh thines ánluzzes
fárawa ni wenti; fol bistu gótes ensti!
Fórosagon súngun fon thir sáligun,
wárun se allo wórolti zi thir zéigonti.
Gímma thiu wíza, magad scínenta,
múater thiu díura scált thu wesan éina.
Thú scalt beran éinan alawáltendan
érdun joh hímiles int alles líphaftes,
Scépheri wórolti (theist min árunti),
fátere gibóranan ebanéwigan.
Got gíbit imo wíha joh éra filu hóha
(drof ni zuívolo thu thés), Davídes sez thes kúninges.
Er ríchisot githíuto kúning therero líuto;
(thaz steit in gótes henti) ána theheinig énti.
Állera wórolti ist er líb gebenti,
tház er ouh inspérre hímilrichi mánne".
Thiu thíarna filu scóno sprah zi bóten frono,

[56] Vgl. hierzu W. HAUBRICHS, "Otfrids Verkündigungsszene", *ZfdA* 97 (1968), S. 176-189; DERS., "Heilige Fiktion?", S. 101 ff.; G. VOLLMANN-PROFE, *Kommentar zu Otfrids Evangelienbuch*, Teil I: *Widmungen, Buch I, 1-11* (Bonn, 1976), S. 191 ff.; M. SCHMIDT, "Otfrid I, 5, 56: Gidúat er imo frémidi thaz hoha hímilrichi. Zu Otfrids Verkündigungsszene", *PBB* (T) 94 (1972), S. 26-51.

gab si imo ántwurti mit súazera giwurti:
"Wánana ist iz, fró min, thaz ih es wírdig bin,
thaz ih drúhtine sinan sún souge?
Wio meg iz ío werdan wár, thaz ih werde suángar?
mih io gómman nihein in min múat ni biréin.
Háben ich giméinit, in múate bicléibit,
thaz ich éinluzzo mina wórolt nuzzo".

Danach mochte etwa ein halbes Jahr vergangen sein / – in Monaten gerechnet: dreimal zwei, / da kam ein Bote, ein Engel vom Himmel, / und brachte dieser Welt herrliche Botschaft. / Er flog auf dem Sonnenpfad, auf der Sternenstraße, / auf den Wolkenwegen zu der herrscherlichen Frau, / zu der Herrin von adliger Abkunft, zu Maria, der geheiligten. / Alle ihre Vorfahren waren Könige, von Generation zu Generation. / Der Engel betrat die Pfalz und fand sie im Nachdenken begriffen, / den Psalter in den Händen, den sie von Anfang bis Ende sang, / damit beschäftigt, schöne Stoffe herzustellen / aus kostbarem Garn, wie es ihre liebe Gewohnheit war. / Da sprach er voller Ehrerbietung, wie es sich einer Herrin gegenüber ziemt, / wie ein guter Bote stets zur Mutter des Herrn sprechen soll. / "Heil dir, liebliches, erlesenes Mädchen, du wunderschöne Jungfrau, / du unter allen Frauen die Gott liebste! / Erschrick nicht in deinem Herzen, und dein Antlitz / wechsle nicht die Farbe: erfüllt bist du von der Gnade Gottes. / Die Propheten haben von dir, du Gebenedeite, geweissagt / und haben alle Weltalter auf dich hingewiesen. / Leuchtender Edelstein, strahlende Jungfrau, / erhabene Mutter sollst du allein sein: / Du sollst gebären den einzigen Herrscher / über Himmel und Erde und alles Lebendige / den Schöpfer der Welt – dies ist meine Botschaft –, / den Sohn, gleich ewig dem Vater. / Gott wird ihm Heiligkeit und höchste Ehre verleihen / und den Thron König Davids – daran zweifle durchaus nicht. / Er wird glorreich als König herrschen über diese Menschen / für alle Zeit, das bewirkt Gottes Macht. / Der ganzen Welt wird er das Leben bringen / und damit auch das Himmelreich den Menschen öffnen". / Die überaus schöne Jungfrau sprach zum göttlichen Boten, / sie gab ihm Antwort mit artiger Freude: / "Mein Herr, wodurch bin ich würdig, / Gottes eigenen Sohn zu stillen? / Wie soll das geschehen, dass ich schwanger werde? / Noch nie hat ein Mann mein Herz berührt. / Ich hatte gedacht und war im Innersten entschlossen, / mein Leben allein zu verbringen".[57]

Otfrid hat die Szenenregie nicht unerheblich verändert, die Details beträchtlich aufgefüllt. Und das auch in der Kommentierung der sprachlichen Akte. Es heißt in des Weißenburgers Vorlage Lukas 1: 28 nur: "*angelus ad eam dixit*", bei Otfrid aber werden es zwei Langzeilen (v. 13 f.): "*Tho sprach er érlicho*

[57] Übersetzung auf der Grundlage derjenigen von G. VOLLMANN-PROFE, *Otfrid von Weißenburg: Evangelienbuch. Auswahl. Althochdeutsch/Neuhochdeutsch* (Stuttgart 1987: *RUB* 8384), S. 57 ff.

ubar ál, so man zi frówun scal, so bóto scal io gúater, zi drúhtines muater" ("Da sprach er voller Ehrerbietung, wie es sich einer Herrin gegenüber ziemt, wie ein guter Bote stets zur Mutter des/eines Herrn sprechen soll").

Es gehen sicherlich zunächst einmal auch literarische Traditionen in Eröffnung und Gestaltung dieser Szene ein: etwa die aus spätantiker Bibelepik erworbene Lizenz, biblische Erzählung gemäß eigener Erzählkonvention des Epos erweitern zu dürfen; auch die aus dem heimischen Stabreimepos ererbte Technik der Variation ("*so man ... scal*", "*so boto scal*" und "*zi frówun*", "*zi drúhtines muater*"). Dies ist aber noch nicht die eigentliche Funktion der Redeeinleitung. Es wird vielmehr in diesem Variationsgefüge von zwei Versen von Otfrid ein Sprechgestus aufgebaut – ohne biblisches Vorbild –, der dem Verhalten eines *missus* gegenüber einer vornehmen Frau, einer Königin etwa entsprechen soll. Maria ist im Erzählrahmen zuvor als "*ítis frono*" (v. 6: 'herrscherliche Frau'), variiert "*édiles frowa*" (v. 7: 'Herrin von adliger Abkunft'), bezeichnet worden; sie wurde als aus königlichem Geblüt stammend und in einer "*palinza*" (v. 9: 'Königspfalz') wohnend dargestellt. Wenn nun der 'englische Gruß', der Gruß des Engels, und die folgende Botschaft, die dann ja in weiterer Erzählung ergänzt und erläutert wird, "*Ave Maria gratia plena, dominus tecum, benedicta tu in mulieribus*" etc. von Otfrid mit (v. 15 ff.) "*Heil mágad zieri, thíarna so scóni, állero wíbo gote zéizosto! ... fol bistu gótes ensti!*" usw. ("Heil dir, liebliches, erlesenes Mädchen, du wunderschöne Jungfrau, du unter allen Frauen die Gott liebste ..., erfüllt bist du von der Gnade Gottes") wiedergegeben wird, so fragt sich, ob wir hierin, vor allem in den Abweichungen der Anrede, einen höfisch-adligen Sprechgestus wiederfinden, etwa im erlesenen Vokabular:

- "*zieri*" (v. 15) im Sinne von *cultus, decorus, ornatus* (vgl. *ziergarto* 'Paradies'); "*scóni*" (v. 15); "*zeizo*" ('*tener*') d. h. 'lieblich, schön, lieb' (v. 16).
- "*anst, ensti*" (v. 18), das gegenüber 'Gnade' seltene Wort für *gratia, eucharistia,* im Sinne von 'Gunst', evtl. 'Heil'.
- im Gebrauch von Hyperbolik und Elativ – "*so scóni, állero*" (v. 15 f.), "*zéizosto*" (v. 16).
- im Verschweigen des persönlichen Namen in der Anrede.

Auch das "*benedicta*" des Evangelisten wird andersartig wiedergegeben (v. 16), nämlich mit "*gote zéizosto*", wobei die hagiographische Idee der *cara dei* mitschwingt.

Wenn dann (v. 33 ff.) Maria dem Engel antwortet, wird ihr Sprechgestus folgendermaßen beschrieben: "*gab si imo ántwurti mit súazera giwurti*" ("Sie gab ihm Antwort mit artiger Freude"). In der folgenden wörtlichen Rede (v. 35 ff.) ferner gebraucht die als adlige *femina religiosa* gestaltete Maria gegenüber dem Engel die respektvolle Anrede "*fró min*" ('mein Herr'), d. h. romanisch *domne meo,* lateinisch *senior meus.*

Was bedeuten diese Sprechriten? Woher kommen die Vorbilder der Dialogführung und Sprechregie? Aus der lateinischen Bibelepik? Nein. Aus der einheimischen Epik? Kaum. Dann aus der mündlichen (in diesem Falle zeremoniellen) Kultur der Zeit? Wie wurden die Vorbilder, wenn man sie denn fassen könnte, umgesetzt?

In Kapitel II, 8 erzählt Otfrid das Wunder von Kana (Joh. 2: 1-11), die berühmte Geschichte von der Hochzeitsgesellschaft, der peinlicherweise der Wein ausging, aber seine Gestaltung ist eine ganz andere als die des *Heliand,* die oben behandelt wurde (v. 11-26):

Thó zigiang thes lídes joh brást in thar thes wínes;
María thaz bihúgita, joh Kríste si iz giságeta.
"Ich scal thir ságen, min kínd, then híon filu hébig thing,
theih míthon ouh nu wésta: thes wínes ist in brésta".
Spráh tho zi iru súazo ther ira sún zeizo
sconen wórton ubar ál, so sun zi múater scal:
"Wib, ich zéllu thir ein, waz drífit sulih zi úns zuein?
ni quam min zít noh so frám, theih óuge weih fon thír nam.
Sar so tház irscínit, waz mih fon thír rinit,
so ist thir állan then dag thaz hérza filu ríuag.
Thaz thu zi mír nu quáti inti eina klága es dati,
mit gótkundlichen ráchon scal man súlih machon".
Thiu muater hórta thaz tho thár; si wéssa thoh in álawar,
thaz íru thiu sin gúati nirzígi thes siu báti.
Gibót si then sar gáhun then thes lídes sahun,
so wás so er in giquáti, iz íagiliher dati.

Schließlich gingen ihre Getränke zu Ende und sie hatten keinen Wein mehr. / Maria bemerkte dies und sagte es Christus. / "Ich muss dir etwas sagen, lieber Sohn, was für die Brautleute sehr unangenehm ist / – ich habe es auch eben erst erfahren –: es fehlt ihnen an Wein". / Da sprach artig zu ihr ihr lieber Sohn / mit überaus schönen, passenden Worten, wie es sich für einen Sohn der Mutter gegenüber ziemt: / "Frau, ich darf doch fragen, was mag uns beide so etwas angehen? / Meine Zeit ist noch nicht so weit vorangeschritten, dass ich zeigen kann, was ich aus dir habe. / Aber wenn das offenbar wird, was mir von dir her zukam, / dann wird dir an diesem Tage dein Herz kummerschwer sein / Was du mir soeben erzählt und geklagt hast, / das wird jedoch durch göttliches Handeln behoben werden". / Dies bekam die Mutter damals darauf zur Antwort; dennoch wusste sie ganz sicher, /

dass seine Güte ihr nicht verweigern würde, worum sie gebeten hatte. / Sie ordnete sogleich an, dass alle, die sich um die Getränke zu kümmern hatten, / tun sollten, was er ihnen auftragen würde.[58]

Maria bemerkt also den Weinmangel und berichtet den Umstand ihrem Sohne, nicht ohne taktvoll – bei Otfrid (v. 13-14) – auf die Peinlichkeit dieser Lage für die Brautleute hinzuweisen. Beim Evangelisten Johannes folgt nun die reichlich schroffe Antwort Jesu: "*Quid mihi et tibi est, mulier?* [bei Otfrid als Marginalnotiz] *Nondum venit hora mea*". Was Luther zutreffend und kernig übersetzte: "Weib, was habe ich mit dir zu schaffen? Meine Stunde ist noch nicht gekommen". Die etwas rätselhafte Antwort wurde von den Kommentatoren als Hinweis auf Christi später zu leistende Offenbarung seiner Menschheit und seiner menschlichen Leidensfähigkeit in der Passion erklärt. Doch völlig inakzeptabel war für das frühe Mittelalter die ehrverletzende Form der Antwort Christi. Ausdrücklich hatte Alkuin in seinem Johanneskommentar bemerkt: "*Neque enim matrem suam inhonoraret qui nos iubet honorare patrem et matrem*".[59] Und Otfrid formuliert ausführlich die Ehrerbietigkeit der Antwort des Sohnes (v. 15-17):

Spráh tho zi iru súazo ther ira sún zeizo
sconen wórton uber al, so sun zi múater scal:
"Wib, ich zéllu thir ein, was drífit sulih zi úns zuein?"

Da sprach artig zu ihr ihr lieber Sohn mit überaus schönen, passenden Worten, wie es sich für einen Sohn gegenüber seiner Mutter ziemt: "Frau, ich darf doch fragen, was mag uns beide so etwas angehen?"

Die Schärfe der biblischen Antwort ist zusätzlich durch den neu eingeführten Bezug auf beide, Mutter und Sohn, gemildert. Und ebenfalls durch die Ausführlichkeit der Antwort. Mit "*scónen worton*" verweist Christus der Mutter die allzufrühe "*klága*" (v. 21): Für ihn ist die Angelegenheit am Ende seiner Rede nur Motiv "*gótkundlich*[*er*] *rách*[*a*]" ('göttlicher Handlung'), wobei das seltene Wort *gotkundlich* : *divinus* den hohen Akzent setzt. Ferner wird der adligen Herrenmutter aus Königsgeschlecht eine eigenständige Rolle zuerkannt: sie weiß, dass der Sohn ihren Wunsch erfüllen wird. Sie gibt den Dienern des Hauses als Erste Anweisung.

[58] Übersetzung auf der Grundlage derjenigen von VOLLMANN-PROFE, *Otfrid von Weißenburg*, S. 75 ff.

[59] Alkuin, *Commentaria in Sancti Ioannis Evangelium,* I, 3, in: MIGNE, *PL* 100 (1851), Sp. 766.

Schluss

Wir lernen also aus den beiden Dialogszenen mit 'Frauen', dass es offensichtlich in der volkssprachigen Kultur des frühen Mittelalters feste Vorstellungen über einen individueller Ehre entsprechenden Sprechstil und entsprechende Sprachformen und entsprechenden Wortschatz gab.

Aus den insgesamt sehr unterschiedlich dimensionierten, hier untersuchten Fällen scheint man jedoch vor allem lernen zu können, dass es möglich ist, die Spuren laikaler und oraler Kultur des frühen Mittelalters im *Heliand* und bei Otfrid aufzufinden, dass es möglich ist, die entwickelte, wenn auch je unterschiedliche, so doch welthaltige Narrativität der beiden großen volkssprachigen karolingerzeitlichen Bibelepen nach den in ihnen enthaltenen kulturellen Mustern und Riten abzusuchen.[60]

[60] Vgl. zum 'Trauerverhalten' in den Bibelepen auch B. JUSSEN, "*Dolor* und *Memoria*. Trauerriten, gemalte Trauer und soziale Ordnungen im späten Mittelalter", in: *Memoria als Kultur*, hg. v. O.G. OEXLE (Göttingen, 1995), S. 222.

Manuscripts for Reading: The Material Evidence for the Use of Manuscripts Containing Middle High German Narrative Verse

NIGEL F. PALMER

I

swer ez iemer hœre gesagen,
der scol in der wâren gotes minne
ain pater noster singe
ze helve mînem hêrren,
ze trôste allen geloubigen sêlen,
daz unsich got an rechtem gelouben mache veste,
daz uns an guoten werken niene gebreste,
unt mache uns sîn rîche gewis.
tu autem, domine, miserere nobis.[1]

Here, in the closing lines of the epilogue to his poem, Pfaffe Konrad calls on whoever may hear his work performed to sing a paternoster on behalf of his lord, Duke Henry (the Lion), and for all faithful souls, in order that God may maintain them in their righteous faith and good works, so that they may be sure of their place in the Kingdom of Heaven. Finally, tying the words of Latin into the body of his poem by the rhyme, he concludes with the liturgical formula adapted from Ps 40,11: *Tu autem, Domine, miserere*

[1] *Das Rolandslied des Pfaffen Konrad. Mittelhochdeutsch / Neuhochdeutsch*, ed. and trans. D. KARTSCHOKE (Stuttgart, 1993: *RUB* 2745), ll. 9086-9094. The end of the poem is preserved in only a single manuscript (P). Cf. *Das Rolandslied des Pfaffen Konrad. Faksimile des Codex Palatinus Germanicus 112 der Universitätsbibliothek Heidelberg*, ed. W. WERNER and H. ZIRNBAUER (Wiesbaden, 1970: *Facsimilia Heidelbergensia* 1), f. 123r.

nobis. These are the words sung by the deacon at the end of each of the twelve readings of matins, as prescribed for the divine office in a monastic community, to which the choir would respond *Deo gratias*.[2]

The main narrative of the *Rolandslied*, which concludes with the gruesome execution of Genelun, comes to an end somewhat earlier and is marked with a more standard, almost 'bookish' closure formula, announcing that 'this is the end of the poem':

durh dorne unt durh hagene,
an dem bûche unt an dem rücke
brâchen si in ze stücke.
sô wart diu untriuwe geschendet.
dâ mit sî daz liet verendet.[3]

This is followed by the section in which Konrad names and praises his patron as Duke Henry, comparing him to King David and closing with a prayer that Henry may be specially favoured when the Last Judgement comes:

an dem jungesten tage,
dâ got sîn gerichte habe,
daz er in ze gerichte niene vordere,
sunder er in ordene
zuo den êwigen gnâden,
dar umbe ruofe wir alle AMEN.[4]

The poet calls upon the audience to join him in the *Amen* at the end of his prayer, an *Amen* that forms part of the body of the text, but which also marks a stage in the process of closure for the whole work. This is particularly evident if we read the passage as it is set out in the unique complete manuscript of the *Rolandslied*, where the "*AMEN*" is written in majuscules and stands at the very end of the last line of the penultimate page.

A similar closure device, also with the liturgical formula *Amen*, is employed at the end of the Early Middle High German *Wiener Genesis*, where

[2] C. CALLEWAERT, "Tu autem Domine miserere nobis", *Collationes Brugenses* 28 (1928), pp. 471-475; repr. in: ID., *Sacris erudiri* (Steenbrugge, 1940), pp. 185-194. Cf. D.H. GREEN, *Medieval Listening and Reading. The Primary Reception of German Literature 800-1300* (Cambridge, 1994), pp. 78-79.

[3] *Rolandslied*, ll. 9012-9016.

[4] *Rolandslied*, ll. 9071-9076.

the poet moves swiftly from Joseph's death and burial to the commendation of his soul to eternal life:

Duo er zi fole redite, nieht langer er lebite.
man chlagit in sêre, bevalch in ziere.
Des nist zwîvil nieht, sîn sêle ist gote lieb.
daz muozze si sîn nû unt in êwin.
AMEN. deo gracias.[5]

Whereas here the two liturgical formulae, *Amen* and *Deo gratias*, stand outside the text and could be regarded as scribal (although *Amen* is preserved in all three manuscripts of the poem), in other works of this period the concluding *Amen* is tied into the rhyme scheme, for example at the end of Frau Ava's *Leben Jesu* in the Vorau Manuscript:

er warf den mennisken zware sehste halp tusent jare
von dem oberisten liehte, er brahte in ze niehte,
unze uns got getroste, von der vinstere er unsich loste
in voller siner gnaden, nu sprechen wir: amen.[6]

In the Görlitz manuscript of the same poem the concluding words have been modified by a redactor, so that the *Amen* stands outside the rhyme scheme, as in the *Wiener Genesis*:

Vntz vns got getrôste
do er vns von der vínste lôste. AM̄ [7]

[5] Cited from MS W. *Die frühmittelhochdeutsche Wiener Genesis. Kritische Ausgabe mit einem einleitenden Kommentar zur Überlieferung*, ed. K. SMITS (Berlin, 1972: *PhStQu* 59), ll. 3033-3037. In the Millstatt Manuscript (MS M) the *Genesis* concludes with: "*Amen. Got uns genade Amen.*"; cf. *Millstätter Genesis und Physiologus Handschrift. Vollständige Facsimileausgabe der Sammelhandschrift 6/19 des Geschichtsvereines für Kärnten im Kärntner Landesarchiv, Klagenfurt*, ed. A. KRACHER (Graz, 1967: *Codices selecti phototypice impressi* 10), f. 84v. In the *Vorauer Joseph* (MS V), which is taken over from the *Genesis*, the text ends with "*Amen*", but the words "*deo gracias*" are omitted; cf. *Die deutschen Gedichte der Vorauer Handschrift <Kodex 276 – II. Teil>. Faksimile-Ausgabe*, ed. K.K. POLHEIM (Graz, 1958), f. 87vb.

[6] *Die religiösen Dichtungen des 11. und 12. Jahrhunderts*, 3 vols, ed. F. MAURER (Tübingen, 1964-70), II, p. 491 (= 221,7-10). Facsimile: *Die deutschen Gedichte der Vorauer Handschrift*, ed. POLHEIM, f. 123ra.

[7] MAURER, *Religiöse Dichtungen*, II, p. 490.

Such use of *Amen* to mark the closure of a poem is not restricted to religious verse. But it must be noted that, for the most part, the process whereby the poet of a Middle High German narrative text directs the audience towards a religious perspective, or in which he establishes a common religious perspective to be shared by poet and audience, begins before the utterance of the liturgical formula itself. We have seen how this is done in the *Rolandslied.* It is also the case at the end of *Wigalois*, where the narration of the fact that Gwigalois and Larie lived happily to the end of their lives is followed by the statement that their virtue earned them a place in heaven, a comment which then serves to effect a transition to a prayer for the souls of the poet and his audience, followed by an *explicit* formula:

deheines herzen sin gemezzen mac
der vreude niht gelîche
diu ist in himelrîche;
dar uns noch got gesende
ûz disem ellende!
hie hât daz buoch ein ende.[8]

The words with which *Wigalois* concludes in manuscript A are the German rendering of a traditional Latin closure formula, in the manner of *Hic explicit liber* or *Hic est finis libri*, which, even though it is tied in by the threefold rhyme ("*gesende*"/"*ellende*"/"*ende*"), belongs to the book as a physical artefact and is not necessarily to be understood as spoken by the poet. Reference is to a *buoch* rather than a *liet* (as in *Rolandslied* l. 9016). Manuscripts B and M of *Wigalois* supply *Amen* after the last line, reverting to the perspective of the poet's prayer. The scribe of manuscript k was more radical and replaced the technical scribal formula *hie hât daz buoch ein ende* by a verse of his own in which he continues the prayer of the previous two lines: "*Got vns sine helffe sende. Amen.*" It is clear from this example, which is just one of many that could be cited, that the authors, redactors and scribes of Middle High German texts had different ideas about just how a text should end.

What are the implications when, in an Arthurian romance such as Wirnt von Grafenberg's *Wigalois*, the closure at the end of the poem is marked by a liturgical formula? Are we to imagine that the *Amen* is spoken by the poet or by his audience? How does the literary or codicological articulation of the end of

[8] *Wigalois der Ritter mit dem Rade von Wirnt von Gravenberc*, ed. J.M.N. KAPTEYN (Bonn, 1926: *Rheinische Beiträge und Hülfsbücher zur germanischen Philologie und Volkskunde* 9), ll. 11703-708. The manuscript variants cited here are from Kapteyn's critical apparatus.

the poem relate to what happened at the end of a performance, at the end of a reading? Where a double formula is employed, as in the example cited from the *Wiener Genesis*, are we to imagine that the *Amen* is spoken by the poet and the *Deo gratias* as a response by his audience? There is no straightforward answer to these questions. Whereas the move to a *wir*, embracing both poet and implied audience, is an extremely common feature of closure, we should resist the temptation to think of the *Amen* as a response from the audience. In a liturgical context *Amen*, although it can be used as a response, is commonly spoken by the celebrant, and in private prayer it is spoken by the voice that prays.[9] To argue, however, that the countless examples where *Amen* stands at the end of a literary work are simply to be explained through their local context as the conclusion of a prayer is to ignore the graphic or 'codicological' significance of the siglum, often written in majuscules, as the marker of an ending. In the Vorau Manuscript, our largest collection of Middle High German religious poems from the twelfth century, about one third of the texts end in *Amen*.[10]

Formulae such as *hie hât daz buoch ein ende* propagate a conception of the literary work as a written artefact, whereas conclusions like *Amen* and *Tu autem* are more reminiscent of the performance situation. Texts such as the *Rolandslied* and *Wigalois* were written in a period when attitudes towards literary texts and the status of texts in the oral and written culture were changing. This paper will be concerned to assess some of the material evidence for these changes in manuscripts of German verse from the period 1100-1230.

II

In 1973 Friedrich Ohly addressed some of these issues in an article devoted to the formula *Tu autem, Domine, miserere nobis*, in which he argued that the use of these words in the concluding line of the *Rolandslied* might be seen as a clue to the circumstances of performance envisaged by the authors of a number of vernacular works in the period from the ninth to the twelfth century ("vom

[9] For the history of the use of *Amen* in the medieval liturgy, see J. JEREMIAS and G. KRAUSE, "Amen", in: *Theologische Realenzyklopädie*, vol. 2 (Berlin/New York, 1978), pp. 386-402.

[10] For closure formulae combined with *Amen*, a prayer or an invocation see the numerous examples cited in: K. IWAND, *Die Schlüsse der mittelhochdeutschen Epen* (Berlin, 1922: *Germanische Studien* 16), pp. 18-32; M. HAMM, *Der deutsche 'Lucidarius'*, vol. 3: *Kommentar* (Tübingen, 2002: *Texte und Textgeschichte* 27), pp. 239-242. As a further example of the variability of closure formulae with *Amen* see J. STRIPPEL, *Schondochs 'Königin von Frankreich'. Untersuchungen zur handschriftlichen Überlieferung und kritischer Text* (Göppingen, 1987: *GAG* 252), pp. 342-343.

Ludwigslied bis zum Rolandslied").[11] He discusses how the *Tu autem* formula was used, not only for the lessons of the office, but also for readings in the refectory in monastic institutions, and suggests that wherever the *Tu autem* was integrated by rhyme into the conclusion of a vernacular verse text, this is a sure sign that the poem was composed with a view to being used in the divine office, for readings in the refectory, or at some similar occasion.[12] Performance of the text in this context, it is argued, must have had implications for the mode of performance, and we must imagine that it was rendered in a manner comparable to the readings of the liturgy.[13]

Ohly appears to have imagined the performance of German poetry as a kind of heightened recitation, such as would imply the use of a melody or the employment of particular melodic formulae for beginnings and ends, and possibly to mark the metrical structure, in accordance with his overall conception of the vernacular poetry of the period as being subject to the same implied rules of interpretation as the texts of public and private worship, and occupying a directly comparable 'Sitz im Leben'. It is easy to follow him when he argues that the use of the *Tu autem* formula implies an audience to whom its use at the end of a liturgical *lectio* was familiar,[14] but must it imply a similar performance situation? This problem demonstrates with exemplary clarity the beguiling force of analogy as a basis of historical interpretation – and the attendant dangers. At what point do the similarities between vernacular poetic texts and texts with a specific liturgical function become so overwhelming that we are entitled to imply that the same implicit rules of interpretation held for both, or the same mode of performance?

It should never be forgotten, in considering these questions, that the notion that very long texts were read out in a normal speaking voice is itself problematic, indeed hardly an acceptable fall-back position. The use of recitation tones for liturgical readings and of sung melodic formulae for the psalms is not simply a reflection of the dignity of the worship of God, it is also a device for protecting the voice during the performance of extremely long passages of text and a means of voice projection.

The analogy between the performance of vernacular poetry and the performance of the liturgy is the principal issue with which I shall be concerned in the

[11] F. OHLY, "Zum Dichtungsschluß *Tu autem, domine, miserere nobis*", *Deutsche Vierteljahrsschrift für Literaturwissenschaft und Geistesgeschichte* 47 (1973), pp. 26-69; repr. in: ID., *Ausgewählte und neue Schriften zur Literaturgeschichte und zur Bedeutungsforschung*, ed. U. RUBERG and D. PEIL (Stuttgart/Leipzig, 1995), pp. 1-33; quotation at p. 64/31.

[12] OHLY, "Dichtungsschluß", p. 62/29.

[13] OHLY, "Dichtungsschluß", pp. 62-68/29-33.

[14] OHLY, "Dichtungsschluß", p. 32/6.

following pages. To understand it is not tantamount to being able to provide a yes-or-no answer to the question whether German narrative poetry was 'sung'. My aim is to set out some of the material evidence for how Middle High German verse was understood in the period up to the early thirteenth century, namely that provided by punctuation in the manuscripts, and to do so for the first time on a systematic basis.

Three related issues need brief mention before I go further, each of which needs to be borne in mind, as a parallel, in assessing the evidence for how Middle High German couplet verse was intended to be read. First, we should remind ourselves that, for the ninth century, there is substantial evidence for the musical performance of long biblical poems, *Heliand* and Otfrid von Weissenburg's *Evangelienbuch*, in the form of neumes and other musical or accentual notation.[15]

Secondly, it is widely held, with good evidence, that Middle High German heroic epic in strophic verse was composed to a melody, so that the sung recital of long narrative texts which have come down to us in written form, such as the *Nibelungenlied*, *Kudrun* and the *Eckenlied*, may safely be assumed.[16] This is unlikely, of course, to have been the exclusive mode of performance.

Thirdly, there is evidence in a German gospel book of ca. 1200 (Vienna, Österreichische Nationalbibliothek, ser. nov. 249, ff. 7r-8v) for the liturgical intonation of a translation of the Gospel text. The evidence for the performance of the *Wien-Münchener Evangelienübersetzung*, which I have discussed elsewhere,[17] consists of 'passion letters' (c, t, and a) inscribed over the beginning of each sentence in a reading for Palm Sunday, indicating different modes of performance (in fact differences in pitch) for the voices of the Evangelist, the Saviour, and other speakers in the liturgical recitative. This differentiated mode

[15] GREEN, *Medieval Listening*, pp. 69 (with n. 80) and 182 (with nn. 100-106), to whom I refer for further literature on this subject. For a review of the isolated occurrence of neumes in the Heidelberg MS of Otfrid, the 'Romanus letters' in the Vienna MS, and the use of accents see also D.H. GREEN, "Zur primären Rezeption von Otfrids Evangelienbuch", in: *Althochdeutsch*, ed. R. BERGMANN *et al.*, 2 vols. (Heidelberg, 1987), I, pp. 737-771, here 762-764, and the literature quoted there. See in particular K. BERTAU, "Epenrezitation im deutschen Mittelalter", *Études Germaniques* 20 (1965), pp. 1-17, at pp. 3-6.

[16] For references, see GREEN, *Medieval Listening*, p. 68 (with n. 72). See in particular H. BRUNNER, "Epenmelodien", in: *Formen mittelalterlicher Literatur. Siegfried Beyschlag zu seinem 65. Geburtstag von Kollegen, Freunden und Schülern*, ed. O. WERNER and B. NAUMANN (Göppingen, 1970: *GAG* 25), pp. 149-178.

[17] N.F. PALMER, "Zur Vortragsweise der Wien-Münchener Evangelienübersetzung", *ZfdA* 114 (1985), pp. 95-118. For further analysis of passion-letter notation see: *Evangelistar Kaiser Heinrich III. Faksimile-Ausgabe des Codex Ms. b. 21 der Universitätsbibliothek Bremen. Kommentarband*, ed. G. KNOLL (Wiesbaden, 1993), pp. 40-42.

of performance was restricted to Eastertide. The argument that the German text was intended to be recited to the Gospel tone, in the manner of the Latin readings of the mass, is here entirely dependent on the principle of analogy, on the assumption that the identical marking of pitch in the German manuscript and in Latin liturgical manuscripts of the period can be taken as an indication that the same manner of performance was intended. The counter-argument, namely that the German translation contains performance cues which were followed when the passage was recited in Latin, but not when read out in German, seems implausible.

The example of the *Wien-Münchener Evangelienübersetzung* is important, because it is probably the most secure material evidence that we have for the intonation of a German text in the manner of the liturgy in the Middle High German period: a German gospel lectionary with layout and performance cues which are identical to what we would find in a Latin gospel lectionary. The most likely explanation is that it was used for reading at table in a community of monks or canons (or more likely: nuns or canonesses), where the reading which had been heard at mass earlier in the day was repeated in the German vernacular. It can usefully be compared, in its relationship to Latin, to two manuscripts in which a German hymn from the late twelfth century is marked up for sung performance with adiastematic neumes, exactly in the manner of a manuscript of the Latin sequence on which the German work is modelled; namely the *Mariensequenz aus Muri*, which is based on the text and melody of *Ave praeclara maris stella*.[18] But however unusual it may be, at this early date, for a German song to be accompanied by neumes, it cannot be surprising that a song was intended to be sung. The texts to which we must now turn are those Middle High German narrative poems for which the mode of performance is uncertain and which need to be reconsidered on the basis of a systematic examination of the material evidence.

III

In 1988 Ernst Hellgardt published a catalogue of 276 German vernacular manuscripts (codices and – mostly – fragments) for which an eleventh- or twelfth-

[18] Engelberg, Stiftsbibliothek, MS 1003, f. 115r (MS B); MAURER, *Religiöse Dichtungen*, I, pp. 453-61. Cf. K. KUNZE, in: ²*VL* 6 (1987), cols. 50-54. For a second manuscript and its melody see: B. GUTFLEISCH, "Eine ostoberdeutsche Handschrift der 'Mariensequenz aus Muri'", *ZfdA* 119 (1990), pp. 61-75; R. FLOTZINGER, "Zur Melodie der sog. 'Mariensequenz aus Muri' in Can. lit. 325 der Bodleian Library zu Oxford", *ibid.*, pp. 75-82.

century date had been proposed in the literature.[19] This list provided, for the first time, a basis for the systematic study of the German vernacular manuscript evidence, prose or verse, for the period during which Middle High German literature evolved, and the remarks about 'the material evidence for the use of manuscripts' that follow are based on as complete an examination as I could achieve of this corpus of material. I have augmented Hellgardt's list by one or two new discoveries and some further manuscripts from the first half of the thirteenth century, which I needed to complete the picture. I also take into account Karin Schneider's ground-breaking monograph on early gothic bookhands of 1987,[20] and the views expressed in the on-line digital archive 'Marburger Repertorium deutschsprachiger Handschriften des 13. Jahrhunderts'.[21]

I am only concerned with verse texts here, and in the first part of the appendix I provide information about 78 manuscripts of Middle High German verse which, in the current state of knowledge, can be dated to the period 1100-1200/20. This list is intended to be complete. The second part of the appendix lists, for the purposes of reference, a selection of manuscript sources from the thirteenth century which are relevant to the argument of this study. For every manuscript I provide a brief statement about the type of punctuation used, based on the literature, photographs, and where possible personal inspection.

Palaeographical evidence for performance, which would allow the analogy between the conventions of Latin liturgical manuscripts and the marking up of vernacular texts to be pressed into the service of a statement about the mode of oral delivery, has not yet been found for Middle High German verse texts. The first step, for which the appendix provides the basis, must be to analyse the evidential value of punctuation and layout for the earliest manuscripts of Middle High German verse. I concentrate here on the period up to about 1220/1230, on the grounds that this is the period before verse came to be written out in lines as a matter of course.

In examining the presentation of verse we will be particularly concerned with three variables: (1) the layout, whether copied continuously, and thus at

[19] E. HELLGARDT, "Die deutschsprachigen Handschriften im 11. und 12. Jahrhundert. Bestand und Charakteristik im chronologischen Aufriß", in: *Deutsche Handschriften 1100-1400. Oxforder Kolloquium 1985*, ed. V. HONEMANN and N.F. PALMER (Tübingen, 1988), pp. 35-81. I am grateful to Ernst Hellgardt for providing me with corrections to his list.

[20] K. SCHNEIDER, *Gotische Schriften in deutscher Sprache. I. Vom späten 12. Jahrhundert bis um 1300* (Wiesbaden, 1987). Cf. K. SCHNEIDER, *Paläographie und Handschriftenkunde für Germanisten. Eine Einführung* (Tübingen, 1999).

[21] http://www.marburger-repertorien.de. I wish to record my thanks to Christa Bertelsmeier-Kierst, who has worked on the Marburg Repertorium, for letting me have her notes on an earlier version of my own list.

first sight indistinguishable from prose, or set out with each new metrical unit (usually the verse, but occasionally the couplet) on a new line; (2) the type of punctuation marks employed to indicate the metrical units, if any, namely *punctus* or *punctus elevatus*; (3) the treatment of the beginning of the verse, which can be left unmarked with a small letter or given special prominence by a majuscule or otherwise accentuated letter form.

The repertory of punctuation marks employed by medieval scribes was of course different from that with which we are familiar today, but also different from that which had been used in the early Middle Ages. By the twelfth century the ancient system of *distinctiones* described by Donatus, according to which *punctus* ('points') were placed at different heights in an ascending order of importance (low point or *subdistinctio*, medial point or *media distinctio*, and the high point or *distinctio*) had been abandoned, and this principle was never to my knowledge employed in Middle High German manuscripts.[22] Most of the manuscripts use only a single punctuation mark, the *punctus* placed either on the line or in medial position, with no distinction of meaning, to mark a pause or the end of a line of verse. This simple punctuation was almost always combined with the use of majuscules, better described as *litterae notabiliores* to allow for the use of marking in red or offsetting to distinguish them from 'small letters', which in prose texts served to mark the beginning of the *sententia*, and with various features of layout, of which the most important is the move to a new line. Between the eighth and the tenth century a set of additional symbols known as *positurae* became available, which were used in manuscripts for liturgical recitation to mark different kinds of pause, each of which required a different inflection of the voice.[23] The most important *positurae* for the consideration of vernacular manuscripts are the *punctus versus* (often formed like a low semicolon) to indicate the end of a *sententia* containing a statement, the *punctus interrogativus* or question mark, and the *punctus elevatus* (⸵), to indicate a major medial pause within a *sententia* where the *sensus* is complete but the *sententia* is not.[24] The distinguishing mark of the *punctus elevatus* is the upwards sloping stroke placed over a point, indicating that the voice should be raised and that the sense is at this juncture not complete. The *positurae* were commonly employed in manuscripts of a non-liturgical character, where they

[22] On *distinctiones*, and more generally for what follows, see M.B. PARKES, *Pause and Effect. An Introduction to the History of Punctuation in the West* (Aldershot, 1992), pp. 13-14; for the twofold system developed in Carolingian times, pp. 31-32.

[23] PARKES, *Pause and Effect*, pp. 36-37. The term *positurae* is to be distinguished from Isidore's use of the term *positura* for a sign marking the end of a text (cf. PARKES, Pl. 7).

[24] These definitions verbatim from PARKES, *Pause and Effect*, p. 36.

serve as punctuation marks interpreting the syntax or metre, but not necessarily indicating specific melodic formulae.[25]

In the period from 1100 until ca. 1225 all German verse is written continuously. Forty-eight, that is to say two thirds of the twelfth-century manuscripts (section (a) in the appendix), follow a system whereby each line of verse begins with a small letter and finishes with a *punctus*, larger letter forms being reserved to mark the beginning of paragraphs. The opening of the *Rolandslied*, for example, is set out as follows in MS P (appendix no. 35):

> ***S**chephare allir dinge . cheiser allir chůnin*
> *ge . wol du oberister ewart . lere mich sel*
> *be diniu wort . dů sende mir zemunde .*[26]

This is by far the commonest way to punctuate verse in this period, and because the *punctus* is the only marker of the verse boundary it is virtually impossible in this system to use punctuation marks to clarify the sense. This punctuation is therefore metrical, not syntactic or rhetorical.

The standard presentation of Middle High German verse was not always the most convenient for readers, who needed to be able to interpret as they read, in order to communicate the sense to their audience. It seems likely that the recitation of a Middle High German text would need to be prepared carefully in advance, just as we know this was done by the monks whose turn it was to read the Latin lessons in the liturgy.[27] The material evidence for such preparation is largely lacking, but it is occasionally apparent that scribes anticipated the needs of readers and intervened in passages where special help was needed. A particular problem for those whose task it was to recite Middle High German verse was posed by direct speech and dialogue, and two examples can be cited here to show how scribes set out to help their readers.

[25] For a preliminary statement on these matters, as they apply to German, see my study "Von der Paläographie zur Literaturwissenschaft", *PBB* 113 (1991), pp. 212-250, at pp. 227-232. See also G. KARHOF, *Der Abschnitt als Vortragsform in Handschriften frühmittelhochdeutscher Dichtungen. Seine strukturbildende Funktion und Bedeutung für die Chronologie* (Diss. Münster, 1967), pp. 68-139.

[26] Facsimile: *Das Rolandslied des Pfaffen Konrad*, ed. WERNER/ZIRNBAUER, f. 1r (= ll. 1-5).

[27] The *Ecclesiastica officia* of the Cistercian order, for example, exempts those who are preparing readings from the general rule of silence during the *tempus lectionis* in the cloister; *Les 'Ecclesiastica officia' cisterciens du XIIème siècle. Texte latin selon les manuscrits édités de Trente 1711, Ljubljana 31 et Dijon 114*, ed. D. CHOISSELET and P. VERNET (Turnhout, 1993: *La Documentation cistercienne* 22), pp. 172-173 (cap. 71).

In the Millstatt text of the verse *Physiologus* (no. 48) Jacob is quoted as addressing Judah and asking "Oh warrior of Judah, you who are the lion's whelp, who will rouse up a man from your kin? No one but God!":

> ***D**o der gůte Jacob . sine sune*
> *gesegenot . unde sigewihte . uon der gotes bihte . do*
> *sprach er uil hewen welf des Lewen . bistu Juda*
> *réche . nu wer sol erwechen . uon dinem geslæhte*
> *einen man ⁄ ane got ⁄ nieman .*[28]

At the end of the rhetorical question "*nu wer sol erwechen / uon dinem geslæh-te einen man?*" the scribe places a *punctus elevatus* (apparently in lieu of the *punctus interrogativus*, which does not form part of this scribe's repertory).[29] The reply, which is a single four-beat line of verse, "*ane got nieman*", is punctuated with a *punctus elevatus* at the mid point, inviting the reader to raise his voice and pause for emphasis.

Another manuscript text which allows us to see how a scribe might anticipate the needs of a reader is the Wolfenbüttel fragment Wo of Veldeke's *Eneas* (no. 24) in which a passage of dialogue between Lavine and her mother is marked up for recitation, marking changes of speaker by a *littera notabilior* (in the manuscript marked with a red stroke, in the following transcription in bold):

> *[...] wand du doch*
> *minnen must plegen . ū minne* ***Turnum*** *den cu*
> *nen degen . den edelen fursten .* ***I****ch en mac noch en tor*
> *ste .* ***w****arumbe durch die arbeit .* ***I****o ist iz ein michel semph*
> *techeit .* ***w****ie mochte iz semphte gesin .* ***G****otweiz liebe*
> *tochter min . ich weiz wol daz du minnen must . swie*
> *ungerne du iz tust . [...]*[30]

[28] Facsimile: *Millstätter Genesis und Physiologus Handschrift*, ed. KRACHER, f. 85r (= ll. 15-24/3,1-5). Diplomatic transcription in MAURER, *Religiöse Dichtungen*, I, p. 174. The expression "*vil hewen*" (l. 19), which must be a filler, is unexplained (= "*vil eben*"?).

[29] The *punctus interrogativus* seems to be extremely rare in early manuscripts of German verse. SCHNEIDER, *Gotische Schriften*, Textband pp. 93 and 157, mentions occurrences in the Berlin/Cracow copy of Priester Wernher's *Maria* (no. 72) and in manuscript A of *Iwein* (no. 86). Further examples are the 'Stargard fragments' of Eilhart's *Tristrant* (no. 82) and the Koblenz fragment of Hartmann's *Erec* (no. 84).

[30] Wolfenbüttel, Herzog August Bibliothek, cod. 404.9 (4) Nov., recto (= ll. 9963-9972/265,31-40). The personal name "*Turnum*" is emphasized by being ruled through in red, a not uncommon device with personal names in manuscripts of this period.

In the fifth line (l. 9967), which must be read " *'warumbe?'* – *'durch die arbeit!'* ", the scribe has failed to observe that the speaker switches mid-line from mother to daughter.

A much less common variant of the standard system is that found in the latter part of the Heidelberg manuscript of *König Rother* (no. 96) and in the Erfurt fragment of the *Rolandslied* (no. 97)[31] In these manuscripts each line of verse begins with a majuscule, rather than with a small letter. In *König Rother* the scribe only goes over to this system in about l. 1000. In the first part of the poem he employs optional, but not infrequent majuscules at the beginning of the line, most commonly the letter D, and more often than not for the first line of a couplet rather than for the second.

The second largest group of manuscripts consists of those in which the rhyming couplet forms the basic unit of punctuation rather than the individual line of verse, and where the beginning of each couplet is marked by a majuscule, and thus distinguished from the second line, which has a small letter. Each line is concluded with a *punctus*. This can be seen in the following example from fragm. B of the *Mittelfränkische Reimbibel* (no. 51):

> *Á be them geslahte ther ivden . thie tho zelibe*
> *beliben . Scā heléna zů ierłm uant . thie*
> *turch thaz heilige cruce quam inthaz lant .*
> *Then sie gebote thaz sie ire sageten . war sie*
> *thaz heilige cruce uerborgen habeten .*[32]

Here, as with the first type, we have an essentially metrical principle of punctuation. It provides the reader with no help, for example, in understanding that ll. 529-530 ("those from the race of the Jews who had survived") constitute the object of the verb "*uant*" in l. 531, thus necessitating a different modulation for the pause after "*beliben*" (l. 530) from that at the end of the *sententia* after "*lant*" (l. 532). The scribe of this manuscript, like many of the period, follows the principle of drawing majuscules out into the margin, where as in l. 523 they

[31] For a discussion of the majuscules in the former poem see: *König Rother*, ed. T. FRINGS and J. KUHNT (Bonn/Leipzig, 1922: *Rheinische Beiträge und Hülfsbücher zur germanischen Philologie und Volkskunde* 3), pp. 30*-31*; for a plate showing the scribe's work in the latter part of the poem see: SCHNEIDER, *Gotische Schriften*, Tafelband Pl. 59. For *Rolandslied* E see the reproduction in: B. GUTFLEISCH-ZICHE, "Zur Überlieferung des deutschen 'Rolandsliedes'. Datierung und Lokalisierung der Handschriften nach ihren paläographischen und schreibsprachlichen Eigenschaften", *ZfdA* 125 (1996), pp. 142-186, at p. 179.

[32] Karlsruhe, Badische Landesbibliothek, cod. Donaueschingen A III 50, f. IIIr (= ll. 529-534). MAURER, *Religiöse Dichtungen*, I, p. 152.

occur at the beginning of a line in the page layout. At the beginning of a new paragraph, which this scribe sets out on a new line, both the first and the second lines of text are indented, to allow for a two-line initial. In l. 531, as also in l. 537, the name "*heléna*" has an acute accent on the second syllable, indicating that it should be recited with stress on the penultimate syllable (in contravention of the accent rules of Greek, Latin and German, but in line with later practice in Middle High German). We note the interplay between the system of punctuation, using the *punctus* and the majuscule, and features of page layout and accentuation.

In many early texts there is a tendency for the metrical couplet also to constitute the basic sense unit, forming what were once known as 'Langzeilen', and when this is the case the punctuation may appear to be metrical and syntactic at once. This gave out mixed messages to readers and scribes, and it is not surprising that there are a number of manuscripts in which the first two types are mixed. Irregular punctuation, due to an imperfect command of the system, is not infrequent (nos. 2, 4, 51, 52, 58, 65, 67, 74, 84, 91, 96), and this would no doubt be even more apparent if more complete manuscripts had survived, rather than just fragments.

A special feature of manuscripts of verse written out continuously, although not restricted to this group, is the use of the *punctus elevatus* as a punctuation mark.[33] We have already seen an example of its use sporadically, to provide help with the reading of a difficult passage. It occurs as a regular feature of the punctuation in 14 of the 104 manuscripts of Middle High German verse for which I have collected information. Its use here is to be explained by the fact that in Latin liturgical manuscripts the *punctus elevatus* was used to mark the conventional intonation of a medial pause where the sense might at first seem complete, but where the *sententia* in fact continued. Here is a Latin example from a thirteenth-century Bible manuscript:

> *(IN PRINCIPIO CREAUIT DEUS CELUM ET TERRAM terra autem erat inanis et uacua et tenebre super) faciem abyssi ⸵ et spiritus dei ferebatur super aquas. Dixitque deus. Fiat lux. Et facta est lux. Et uidit deus lucem quod esset bona ⸵ et diuisit lucem*

[33] For the *punctus elevatus* in Middle High German manuscripts, see: SCHNEIDER, *Gotische Schriften*, Textband (index under 'Interpunktion/Strichpunkt'); PALMER, "Von der Paläographie", pp. 237-238; C. BERTELSMEIER-KIERST, "Zur ältesten Überlieferung des 'Wigalois'. I. Die Handschrift E", *ZfdA* 121 (1992), pp. 275-290, at pp. 281-282. See also: KARHOF, *Der Abschnitt als Vortragsform*, pp. 68-113; H. BECKERS, "Paläographisch-kodikologische und sprachgeschichtliche Beobachtungen zu den alten Pergamentbruchstücken von 'Karl und Galie' und 'Morant und Galie'. Ein Beitrag zur Klärung ihrer überlieferungsgeschichtlichen Stellung", in: *Deutsche Handschriften 1100-1400*, ed. HONEMANN/PALMER, pp. 179-213, at pp. 190-191.

> *atenebris. Appellauitque lucem diem ⸮ et tenebras noctem. Factumque est uespere et mane dies unus.* (Gn 1:1-5)[34]

After the opening words of Genesis 1:1-2, which are set out in two different grades of display script (from "*In principio*" to "*super*"), the scribe employs standard syntactic/rhetorical punctuation to indicate how the text should be recited. The rhetorical structure of verse 2, which uses *tricolon* to report on the state of the earth, the darkness and the spirit of God, is conveyed by the *punctus elevatus* placed before the final *colon*, indicating that the reader should raise his voice before the final major pause, to show that the *sententia*, which requires the statement about the spirit of God to complete the *tricolon*, is not yet at an end. Verse 4 too uses the *punctus elevatus*. The statement that God saw that the light was good could stand on its own as a complete sense unit, but by placing a *punctus elevatus* after "*bona*" and before the statement "*et diuisit lucem atenebris*", the scribe requires of the reader that he should speak the whole of verse 4 as a single *sententia*, raising his voice before the medial pause to indicate that the division of light from darkness proceeds from the observation that the light was good. In the first part of verse 5 the *punctus elevatus* is employed to show that, although the *sensus* may be complete with the word "*diem*", the *sententia* is not.

Just as the intonation patterns indicated by the *positurae* served to clarify the sense for a listener in a liturgical context or in monastic readings at table, these same signs, when understood as punctuation marks, served to indicate the syntactic and rhetorical structure to a reader of any kind, and they were thus available as a means of clarifying the sense, irrespective of the mode of performance or reading anticipated. Nevertheless, the use of *positurae*, particularly of the *punctus elevatus*, in a German context clearly places the texts so punctuated within the clerical culture of those familiar with the conventions of the liturgy, and they are a strong indicator that the scribes knew that they were preparing the ground for the performative act of reading out loud. Their use in secular verse texts composed in the vernacular is also a clear marker of the close association of the copying and reading of vernacular poetry with that clerical culture.

[34] Freiburg, Universitätsbibliothek, Hs. 374. From Wasserburg, dated 1295. I quote from the reproduction of the first page of Genesis in: *Verborgene Pracht. Mittelalterliche Buchkunst aus acht Jahrhunderten in Freiburger Sammlungen*, ed. D. ZINKE (Lindenberg, 2002), p. 67.

Five of the 14 manuscripts[35] with *punctus elevatus* have it at the end of every verse, as in the following example from the work of the first scribe of manuscript A of Wirnt von Grafenberg's *Wigalois* (no. 76):

> *E in palas het div chvnegin : daz was marmelstei-*
> *nin : gezieret wol begarwe : von uierhande*
> *uarwe : rot . brun . weitín . vn̄ gel : daz hvs daz was*
> *sinvwel : beliewet vmbe vnde vmbe wol :*[36]

An advantage of this system was that it allowed a certain amount of syntactic/rhetorical pointing within the verse, as in the list of four colours in verse 226. The other examples are a group of texts in the Vorau Manuscript (no. 70) – namely the *Kaiserchronik*, the works of Frau Ava and the *Vorauer Sündenklage* (the latter two copied in sequence); the Klagenfurt fragment of the *Kaiserchronik* (no. 29); the short poem entitled *Meßgebet 'Got vater allir cristinheit'* (no. 46) preserved as an addition to a Latin psalter in a Fulda manuscript; and the Koblenz fragment of Hartmann's *Erec* (no. 84).[37] In the *Erec* fragment, which is one of the most eloquent witnesses to the early reception of Arthurian romance in Germany, the first letter of the line is frequently, but by no means always, a majuscule. This manuscript also uses the *punctus interrogativus* (f. 1v, l. 30; = *Erec*, l. 7991), and thus provides a rare example of the combination of *positurae* with metrical and syntactic/rhetorical function. A second sub-group is constituted by the five manuscripts in which a *punctus* is placed after the first rhyme word, in the middle of the couplet, while the end of the couplet is marked by a *punctus elevatus*, as in the Freiburg/Vienna/Beinecke fragments of Wirnt's *Wigalois* (fragm. E, no. 107):

> *Gwigaloys nv svmet evch niht : sp^{a}ch her Gawein der*
> *degen . vn̄ wil got des rehten phlegen : als er îe*

[35] In addition to the 14 manuscripts discussed here, I have noted sporadic use of the *punctus elevatus* in the manuscripts of the following texts: *Ältere Judith*, *Jüngere Judith*, *Ezzos Gesang* (MS V), Vorau *Physiologus*, *Arnsteiner Marienlied*, *Von der Siebenzahl* by Priester Arnold, Pfaffe Konrad's *Rolandslied* (fragm. S), 'Straßburg-Molsheimer Hs.', the poems of Der Wilde Mann.

[36] SCHNEIDER, *Gotische Schriften*, Tafelband Pl. 35 (= *Wigalois*, ll. 222-228).

[37] For the *Meßgebet* see SCHNEIDER, *Gotische Schriften*, Tafelband Pl. 47. For the Vorau texts see the facsimile editions, *Die Kaiserchronik des regul. Chorherrenstiftes Vorau in der Steiermark*, ed. P. FANK (Graz, 1953); *Die deutschen Gedichte der Vorauer Handschrift*, ed. POLHEIM, ff. 125ra-128rb. For *Erec* fragm. K see P. BROMMER, "Ein unbekanntes 'Erec'-Fragment in Koblenz", *ZfdA* 105 (1976), pp. 188-194, Pl. after p. 190. The *Kaiserchronik* fragment in Klagenfurt is unpublished.

hat getan . so wê vns niht geschaden chan ∴ ir ha
bet vil gut riterschaft . vñ wellent die ir trewen
chraft ∴ iv mit helfe erzeîgen hie .[38]

The other manuscripts with this system of punctuation are the *Baumgartenberger Johannes Baptista* (no. 6), *Vom Himmelreich* (no. 68), *Von der babylonischen Gefangenschaft* (no. 69), and the Vienna fragment of the *Kaiserchronik* (no. 27).[39] A third category in this group consists of four manuscripts in which a *punctus elevatus* is placed in the middle of the couplet, and a *punctus* at the end. One of these is represented by the second of the three scribes who copied manuscript A of *Wigalois*.[40] A second is the Berlin manuscript of Heinrich von Veldeke's *Eneas* (no. 91), which has an extensive passage predominantly punctuated in this way, with small letters at the beginning of each line, on ff. 1va/b and 3ra/b, before the scribe goes over, at the beginning of f. 3v, to setting out his verse in lines (and in three columns).[41] In the poem *Trost in Verzweiflung* (no. 65), the manuscript of which is now lost, and in the so-called 'Stargard fragments' of Eilhart von Oberge's *Tristrant* (no. 82) each couplet begins with a majuscule, the middle of the couplet is marked by a *punctus elevatus*, and its conclusion by a *punctus*, as in the following example from the scene where Tristrant sends Pilose as a messenger to Isalde:

P ylose wart do ∴ beide rvwích vñ vro . Vro daz er vorkos ∴ vñ dar vm
be vrŏweden los . Daz er si níet ne wolde sien ∴ e dar was vorgíen .
Als' gelobet hauete ∴ pilose do sagete . He' nv gebut mír ∴ ich wille
scheiden von dír .[42]

[38] This page is reproduced by BERTELSMEIER-KIERST, "Wigalois", p. 280 (= *Wigalois*, ll. 9910-9917).

[39] For the *Johannes Baptista* see MAURER, *Religiöse Dichtungen*, I, Pl. 15; for *Vom Himmelreich* see I, Pl. 17, and SCHNEIDER, *Gotische Schriften*, Tafelband Pl. 9. *Von der babylonischen Gefangenschaft* ('Maria Saaler Fragmente') is illustrated in SCHNEIDER, *Gotische Schriften*, Tafelband Pl. 16; *Katalog der Ausstellung. Handschriftenfragmente von 500-1500*, ed. H. GRÖCHENIG *et al.* (St. Paul im Lavanttal, 1977: *Armarium* 1), plate p. 154. The *Kaiserchronik* fragment is unpublished.

[40] BERTELSMEIER-KIERST, "Wigalois", p. 282 n. 32. I have not seen the manuscript. If this information is correct, then the account given by SCHNEIDER, *Gotische Schriften*, Textband pp. 84-85, allowing for only two scribes rather than Bertelsmeier-Kierst's three, needs to be corrected.

[41] *Heinrich von Veldeke: Eneas-Roman. Vollfaksimile des Ms.germ.fol.282 der Staatsbibliothek zu Berlin Preußischer Kulturbesitz*, ed. A. FINGERNAGEL and N. HENKEL (Wiesbaden, 1992).

[42] Eilhart von Oberg, *Tristrant. I. Die alten Bruchstücke*, ed. K. WAGNER (Bonn/Leipzig, 1924: *Rheinische Beiträge und Hülfsbücher zur germanischen Philologie und Volkskunde* 5),

Like the Koblenz *Erec* this manuscript also makes use of the *punctus interrogativus* to punctuate complex dialogue passages.

This last example exemplifies the application to Middle High German couplet verse of a system of punctuation which was commonly used for the pointing of the psalm verses in liturgical manuscripts, namely *punctus elevatus* in the middle and *punctus* at the end of the verse.[43] The following example of this practice is taken from the 'Psalter of St Elisabeth', a luxury psalter made for lay ownership (for Landgrave Hermann of Thuringia) in the early years of the thirteenth century (abbreviations resolved):

> ***Q****uare fremuerunt gentes* ⸮
> *et populi meditati sunt in á-*
> *nia.* ***A****stiterunt reges ter*
> *re et principes conuenerunt inunum* ⸮
> *aduersus dominum et aduersus christum eius.*
> ***D****isrumpamus uincula eorum et proiciamus*
> *anobis iugum ipsorum.* (Ps 2:1-3)[44]

In such manuscripts for private use, possibly under the influence of the breviary, the psalms were written out continuously, but marking the beginning of each psalm verse with a much bolder enlarged letter than was ever used for the couplet in poetry. The punctuation of the psalm verse can be quite simple, with just the *punctus* to mark the juncture(s) within the verse, or as here in verse 3 with only a point at the end. Frequently, however, the *punctus elevatus* is used to mark the medial pause, indicating that the *sententia* is not complete without what will follow.

That some kind of a link between the conventions of punctuation for German verse and the Latin psalter must exist is clear from the *Meßgebet 'Got vater allir cristinheit'* (no. 46) at Fulda, where the German poem is copied immediately after Psalm 100 by the same hand as the Latin text, carrying over a system of punctuation with *punctus elevatus* from the psalms on the upper part of the page to the *Meßgebet* below. The psalm text has *punctus elevatus* at the mid point of the verse, whereas the *Meßgebet* uses it to mark the end of every line of verse.

p. 42, St ll. 276-285.

[43] For a more positive discussion of this, with plates, see: N.F. PALMER, *German Literary Culture in the Twelfth and Thirteenth Centuries. An Inaugural Lecture delivered before the University of Oxford on 4 March 1993* (Oxford, 1993), especially p. 19.

[44] *Salterio di Santa Elisabetta. Facsimile del ms. CXXXVII del Museo Archeologico Nazionale di Cividale del Friuli*, ed. C. BARBERI (Udine, 2002), f. 15r/v.

The evidence collected here does not as yet permit a definitive statement about whether the common punctuation scheme is a coincidence, or whether the use of *punctus elevatus* is in fact directly modelled on the well-known system used for the psalms. If the latter were the case, then it would be necessary to find an explanation for the fact that the variant which mirrors the punctuation of the psalms most exactly (with *punctus elevatus* at the middle of the couplet) is the least frequently attested of the three types. Indeed the commoner types with *punctus elevatus* underscore the continuity of the flow of the verse from couplet to couplet, inviting the reader to think of each such rhymed unit as forming an incomplete link in a continuous chain of text, which is not at all how the psalms are constructed. There is also a case to be made against the view that the individual *positurae* indicate specific melodic formulae used in the recitation of German verse, like those used in the performance the psalms. We have noted the co-existence of three different types: (1) *punctus elevatus* at the middle and end of the couplet (five times); (2) at the end of the couplet with *punctus* in the middle (five times); (3) at the middle of the couplet with *punctus* at the end (four times). Should it be supposed that there were three quite different systems for articulating the couplet in the performance of German verse? This is unlikely.

The range of texts that employ the *punctus elevatus* might at first sight seem surprising, but if the chronology is examined a pattern emerges. The most important witnesses of this punctuation system from the twelfth century are the Vorau Manuscript, which could be as early as the 1180s, and *Vom Himmelreich*, which is datable to the year 1174. In the case of the Vorau Manuscript the scribes use different punctuation systems for different works, presumably responding to the exemplars from which they were working, and it is therefore likely that they had early copies of the poems of Frau Ava and of the *Kaiserchronik* in which the system with *punctus elevatus* was already used. These are all likely to have been monastic books, even if the Vorau Manuscript itself was not simply a creation of the monastic environment.[45] *Vom Himmelreich*, Frau Ava, and this copy of the *Kaiserchronik* document a firmly established, if sparsely attested tradition, which appears to have flourished in major monastic centres such as Windberg, Vorau, and perhaps Seckau, where the use

[45] For an important revision of received views on the origins of the Vorau Manuscript see K. GRUBMÜLLER, "Die Vorauer Handschrift und ihr *Alexander*. Die kodikologischen Befunde: Bestandsaufnahme und Kritik", in: *Alexanderdichtungen im Mittelalter*, ed. J. CÖLLN *et al.* (Göttingen, 2000: *Veröffentlichungen aus dem Göttinger SFB 529*, A 1), pp. 208-221. See the detailed study of lection marks in the Vorau Manuscript in KARHOF, "Der Abschnitt als Vortragsform", pp. 107-123.

of *positurae* deriving from liturgical use might well be an indicator of the mode of performance. The other manuscripts of early Middle High German religious poetry fit into this picture.

The challenge is to find an interpretation for the preponderance of manuscripts of secular poetry that use this system: three twelfth-century manuscripts of the *Kaiserchronik*, two of the earliest *Wigalois* manuscripts (datable ca. 1215-25 for MS A and ca. 1220-30 for fragm. E), the *Eneas* from the 1220s, and the manuscripts of Eilhart's *Tristrant* and Hartmann's *Erec*, which are likely to date from the 1230s. The use of the *punctus elevatus* in these manuscripts is not in itself an indication that the poems were to be intoned in the manner of liturgical recitative, but it is a strong indicator that the manuscripts offer texts that are to be performed. The group provides important evidence of a continuity in scribal presentation between twelfth-century religious poetry, vernacular historiography and works of courtly literature based on French models. But perhaps we can go further. The continuity is not just scribal, it extends to the conception of vernacular narrative poetry implicit in the material presentation. Just as there was a continuous tradition of linguistic formulae such as requests for attention, *Amen* and *Tu autem* that marked out the performative aspect of the literary text, so there was also a tradition of punctuation which not only served to help the reader with his specific task (however this may have been executed), but also said something about the nature of the text.

IV

Some time around 1220/30 a major change in the handling of layout took place. From now on, with increasing frequency, scribes started to set out Middle High German verse texts in lines, as if they were Latin hexameters (or pentameters).[46] In so doing they were following the precedent of French literary manuscripts of the later twelfth century. It was a return to a principle which had been relatively common in the copying of Old High German verse in the later ninth century, although at that time the basic unit for the purposes of page layout was the long line, with internal rhyme. Only a single surviving manuscript has carried the old layout forward into the twelfth century, that of the *Merigarto* (no. 45),

[46] See SCHNEIDER, *Gotische Schriften*, Textband p. 91. For the development of verse layout in France see G. HASENOHR, "Traductions et littérature en langue vulgaire", in: *Mise en page et mise en texte du livre manuscrit*, ed. J. MARTIN and J. VEZIN (Paris, 1990), pp. 231-349; B. FRANK, *Die Textgestalt als Zeichen. Lateinische Handschriftentradition und die Verschriftlichung der romanischen Sprachen* (Tübingen, 1994: *ScriptOralia* 67), pp. 168-179.

whose linguistic forms betray that this is an Old High German poem preserved in a later copy.[47] In the first part of the manuscript, which extends over two leaves, the long lines are copied continuously in the usual manner, but on the lower half of the second recto the scribe goes over to the earlier Latinate layout in which each long line of verse is set out on a new line.[48]

A precise chronology for the development of the new layout has not yet been established, and further work is needed on the principal manuscripts that document the transition. Given the impossibility of precise datings, on the basis of script alone, within a short period, it is best to regard the following ten manuscripts as forming a single group, and not to attach too much significance to the currently accepted relative datings (noted in the appendix), which stretch them out over the period ca. 1215-40: (1) Albrecht von Augsburg: *Ulrichslegende* (no. 80); (2) the Giessen manuscript of Hartmann's *Iwein,* MS B (no. 87); (3) the Linz fragment of Hartmann's *Iwein*, fragm. F (no. 88); (4) the Berlin manuscript of Veldeke's *Eneas*, MS B (no. 91); (5) the 'Meran fragments', in Munich, of Veldeke's *Eneas*, fragm. Me (no. 92); (6) the Basel fragments of the *Kaiserchronik*, version B (no. 32);[49] (7) the Frauenfeld fragments of Konrad Fleck: *Flore und Blanscheflur* (no. 100); (8) Der Stricker: *Karl der Große*, fragm. a (no. 60); (9) Der Stricker: *Karl der Große*, fragm. e (no. 61); (10) Cracow-Berlin fragments of Wirnt von Grafenberg: *Wigalois*, fragm. q (no. 108).

In the *Ulrichslegende*, a small-format manuscript, which has generally been held to be one of the earliest of the group, three different systems are employed for setting out the verses.[50] In the opening pages the couplet form is accentuated by a system of punctuation and page layout in which the first line of each couplet is introduced by a *littera notabilior* off-set to the left. For ff. 30v-33v the scribe reverts to a traditional system of continuously written verse. A third punctuation system, which is employed from f. 34r to the end, sets the verse out in lines and treats all lines equally, beginning each with a *littera notabilior*. The

[47] N.T.J. VOORWINDEN, *Merigarto. Eine philologisch-historische Monographie* (Leiden, 1973: *Germanistisch-Anglistische Reihe der Universität Leiden* 11), plates after p. 18.

[48] At f. 2r, ll. 16-30 (= str. 23-28)

[49] Not mentioned in the literature on the *Kaiserchronik*, and known to me from the discussion in J. WOLF, "Buch und Text. Literatur- und kulturhistorische Untersuchungen zur volkssprachlichen Schriftlichkeit im 12. und 13. Jh." (Habilitationsschrift Marburg, 2002), chapter I.1.4.1. I am grateful to Jürgen Wolf for allowing me to read his unpublished book.

[50] E. PETZET and O. GLAUNING, *Deutsche Schrifttafeln des IX. bis XVI. Jahrhunderts aus Handschriften der K. Hof- und Staatsbibliothek*, 5 vols. (Munich/Leipzig 1910-1930), II, Pl. 21; SCHNEIDER, *Gotische Schriften*, Tafelband Pl. 42. See in particular Schneider's detailed discussion of the layout, Textband p. 93.

Berlin manuscript of Veldeke's *Eneas* also makes use of more than one layout, which, as with the *Ulrichslegende*, it must be right to interpret as experimentation with an unfamiliar system of layout and punctuation. After rather uncertain application, on the first two pages (ff. 1v and 3r), of a traditional continuous layout in two columns, on f. 3v (at l. 273) the scribe goes over to a format with three columns, setting the verses out in lines. In the first column of f. 3v each couplet begins with a majuscule, the first line of the couplet is concluded with a *punctus elevatus*, whereas the second line begins with a small letter and is concluded with a simple point. In the second and third columns of f. 3v, and for the whole of the rest of the manuscript, the scribe adheres to the system of beginning each couplet with an off-set majuscule, leaving the second line indented and beginning with a small letter. It is evident that the scribe initially experienced difficulty in imposing a consistent layout of the new type on his text, whilst also responding to the need to accommodate a large quantity of text on the page. This was essential if the principle of alternating text pages and picture pages was not to make excessive demands on the artists. The inconsistencies in both these manuscripts would appear to result from inexperience in the 'codicological' implementation of the new verse layout, and are unlikely to be performance related.

A second group of manuscripts, represented by three as yet little studied fragments, documents the application of the new layout to long poems of historical content, Stricker's *Karl der Große* (two fragmentary half-leaves of remarkably similar appearance) and the *Kaiserchronik* (in the modernizing recension B). This is a category in which the Berlin *Eneas*, which is of similar date and appearance (but in three columns and with added illustrations), could also be included. These manuscripts employ a larger format (written area ca. 185 × 120/135 mm, ca. 30/37 lines on the page) and display the text in two columns. The individual line of verse is presented as the basic unit, marked by a majuscule (and off-set in the *Kaiserchronik* fragments). All three have been dated, on the basis of the script, towards the end of the first quarter of the thirteenth century.[51]

The third group comprises the earliest manuscripts of courtly romance to use the new layout. They are generally dated to the beginning of the second

[51] For the *Kaiserchronik* see the Marburg Repertorium. For the fragments of Stricker's *Karl der Große* see SCHNEIDER, *Gotische Schriften*, Textband pp. 99-100; EAD., *Die Fragmente mittelalterlicher deutscher Versdichtung der Bayerischen Staatsbibliothek München (Cgm 5249/1-79)* (Stuttgart, 1996: *ZfdA Beiheft* 1), pp. 24-25 (Cgm 5249/5a). Schneider's (cautious) dating of Cgm 5249/51 to the first quarter is questioned by C. BERTELSMEIER-KIERST, review of SCHNEIDER, *Fragmente*, in: *PBB* 121 (1999), pp. 299-302, at pp. 299-300, but she gives no evidence to support her later dating.

quarter of the century, but that they 'look' later than the historical epics could be a function of their more elegant appearance. Two manuscripts of *Iwein* (B and L) document the adaptation of the new layout to a small format (126 x 82/85 mm and 164 x 97 mm), displaying the verses in a single column with off-set minuscule letters at the beginning of every line. The *Wigalois* fragments follow the same punctuation system (but with off-set majuscules), also in a small format, but this manuscript has unusual elongated pages (196 x 75 mm, written area 186 x 43 mm, 47-52 lines), as can sometimes be found with manuscripts of Latin poetry. The fragments of *Flore und Blanscheflur*, which are less elegant in appearance (unusually, with a simple minuscule at the beginning of each line and rhyme points set out aligned in the right-hand margin of each column), show how layout in lines could be adapted to a small-format manuscript in two columns (170 x 114 mm, written area ca. 140 x 95 mm, 30/31 lines). The small-format manuscripts of courtly romance, comparable in size to books that in the monastic world were used for private devotions (such as the diurnal), may have been intended as an invitation to private reading, setting out visually through the layout of the verses the metrical structure which at a traditional reading would for the most part have only been heard.

For the rest of the thirteenth and for the fourteenth century the two basic forms of layout that we encountered in the *Ulrichslegende*, stressing either the couplet or the individual line of verse as the basic unit, continue to be employed. Whereas in the transitional period the Berlin *Eneas* is the only manuscript which consistently displays the couplet as the basic unit, this presentation became commoner in the second half of the thirteenth and in the first half of the fourteenth century, especially in the south-east.[52] For a long time the older layout, with verses written out continuously, continued to be retained as an alternative form, most commonly for strophic poems such as the *Nibelungenlied* and the *Titurel*, where the continuously written pattern is the norm, but also for religious verse.[53]

In part the new layout of German verse was a matter of fashion. In this respect it must be noted that French and Anglo-Norman scribes had already

[52] See the discussion by SCHNEIDER, *Gotische Schriften*, Textband pp. 91-92.

[53] On the use of the continuously written form for strophic epic see, most recently, H. HAFERLAND, "Der auswendige Vortrag. Überlegungen zur Mündlichkeit des 'Nibelungenliedes' ", in: *Situationen des Erzählens. Aspekte narrativer Praxis im Mittelalter*, ed. L. LIEB and S. MÜLLER (Berlin/New York, 2002: *Quellen und Forschungen zur Literatur- und Kulturgeschichte* 20 [254]), pp. 245-282. Haferland must surely be wrong when he argues that verses set out in lines were much easier to read out (pp. 269-270). To judge from liturgical manuscripts, which regularly use continuously written layout for hymns and psalms, the opposite seems rather to have been the case.

gone over to setting verse out in lines by at least the middle of the twelfth century, the first example being the Oxford manuscript of the *Chanson de Roland.* Nonetheless, many of the earliest manuscripts of the Middle High German courtly romances based on French models are written out continuously. This holds for Veldeke's *Eneas*, Eilhart's *Tristrant*, Hartmann's *Erec*, Wolfram's *Parzival*, Wirnt's *Wigalois*, *Reinhart Fuchs*, but not for Gottfried's *Tristan.*[54]

An alternative suggestion might be that the change in layout has more to do with changes in the way the cultural practice of reading texts written down in books was understood, – not simply with the process whereby texts that had been read out or declaimed from manuscripts to an audience now came to be read privately, perhaps silently, but rather with changes in the way that the linguistic structure of narrative verse texts was conceived. Verses written out in lines provide a strong visual marker of the literary form of the verse. Among the manuscripts written out continuously those that provide the strongest visual markers are those that mark the couplet, either by punctuation with the *punctus elevatus* or by majuscules. The manuscripts that give prominence to the individual line of verse as the minimal repeated unit accentuate the continuous flow of the language, presenting this as something that overrides the metrical structure of the rhyming couplets. Those that give prominence to the rhyming couplets as the minimal repeated unit accentuate the metrical form, which for the poets of the later twelfth and early thirteenth century generally stood in counterpoint to the syntax.

Seen in this context the history of the graphic representation of couplet verse in the twelfth and thirteenth centuries could be set out as follows. First we observe a process whereby new forms of punctuation were developed for the traditional, continuously written verse which gave special stress to the metrical form. This took place in a period which saw increasing sophistication in the way Middle High German poets handled the interplay of syntax and metre. This awareness of the potential of the visual design of the page to symbolize the linguistic structure of the poetic discourse was given new impetus when the layout of verse set out in lines, as in French (and many Latin) manuscripts, was introduced, in the period 1215-40, as an alternative to the previous practice. The new layout meant a sharp break with tradition and some adjustment was necessary, on the part of scribes – and readers too no doubt, as they came to terms with the new visually conceived text, which needed to be seen as well as

[54] For early manuscripts of *Parzival* written continuously see the fragments nos. 77 and 109; also the codices Munich, Bayerische Staatsbibliothek, Cgm 19 and 61 (MSS. G and G^{m}), which both date from the first half of the century. I am grateful to Michael Stolz for discussion of the *Parzival* manuscripts.

heard. Initially the new layout presented the verse as a continuum of short lines, but in the course of the thirteenth century an alternative layout gained ground which gave visual embodiment to the interplay of the rhyming couplet and the syntax. This process whereby increasingly the visual appearance of the manuscript came to symbolize and embody the poetic form depended on the adaptation of traditional graphic features for the representation of texts to the needs of readers whose office it was to perform, or to engage in private reading.

Appendix: Middle High German Verse Texts in Manuscripts from the Period 1100-1250

Conventions

[aa] means that the lines of verse rhyming a a b b c c (etc.) are written out continuously, with neither capitalization nor punctuation. **[A̲:a.]** means that each couplet begins with a *littera notabilior* (A), touched in red (A̲), with a *punctus elevatus* (:) in the middle of the couplet, that the second line begins with a small letter (a), and has a *punctus* (.) at the end. Where each verse is set out on a new line, as in the layout of verse today, this is indicated by a vertical stroke, so **[|A.|a.]** means couplets introduced by a *littera notabilior* and with each verse on a new line. Where the first letter at the beginning of a verse is off-set, this is marked by a hyphen, so **[|A̲-.|a.]** means that the verses are copied out in lines, each couplet beginning with an off-set *littera notabilior* splashed in red, whereas the second verse begins with a non off-set small letter. All texts listed are composed in rhyming couplets, unless there is a statement to the contrary.

Literature

References are minimal, for reasons of space. The titles of texts are as far as possible those used in the *Verfasserlexikon*. I use four main points of reference: H (= HELLGARDT, "Die deutschsprachigen Handschriften im 11. und 12. Jahrhundert", as in n. 19); M (= MAURER, *Die religiösen Dichtungen des 11. und 12. Jahrhunderts,* as in n. 6); S (= SCHNEIDER, *Gotische Schriften*, as in n. 20); MR (= Marburger Repertorium deutschsprachiger Handschriften des 13. Jahrhunderts, http://www.marburger-repertorien.de [accessed 9 August 2003]). Facsimiles and reproductions of individual pages are cited wherever possible, including those in: P/G (= PETZET/GLAUNING, *Deutsche Schrifttafeln des IX. bis XVI. Jahrhunderts*, as in n. 50) and ^{36}MF II (= *Des Minnesangs Frühling. II: Editionsprinzipien, Melodien, Handschriften, Erläuterungen*, ed. H. MOSER and H. TERVOOREN [Stuttgart, ^{36}1977]).

Dating

Section (a) lists all manuscripts plausibly dated to before about 1200/1220. All dates are to be understood as plus or minus 15/20 years. To suppose that objective distinctions can be made between '12th C, last quarter', 'ca. 1200' and '12th C, 1st quarter' is illusory. These gradations refer to the type of script employed, and do not give an absolute chronology. The most important point of reference is Schneider, *Gotische Schriften*. For the Munich fragments I follow SCHNEIDER, *Fragmente* (as in n. 51). Datings from the Marburg Repertorium are also given and attributed, wherever there is a difference of opinion.

Section (b) lists a selection of manuscripts from the transitional period between the first and second quarters of the thirteenth century. For a proper study of these manuscripts a more refined approach to the dating of manuscripts assigned to '13th century, 1st quarter', 'ca. 1220-30' and '13th century, 2nd quarter' is needed than I have felt it appropriate to aim at here.

(a) Manuscripts dating from before ca. 1220

1 Priester Adelbrecht: *Johannes Baptista* + *St. Veit* (fragm.). St. Paul im Lavanttal, Stiftsbibl., Fragm. 25/8. Ca. 1200/13th C, inc. (SCHNEIDER). H 151 (1). M, nos. 37 and 63; III, Pl. 6. MR. GRÖCHENIG, *Handschriftenfragmente* (as n. 39), plate p. 154. **[a.a.] for both poems, midline red initials.**

2 *Ägidius* (fragm.). Berlin, SBB-PK, Nachlaß Grimm 132,11. 12th C, end. H 161. **[a.a.], occasional majuscules.**

3 *Andreas* (fragm.). Petrohrad (Petersburg, NW Bohemia), s.n. 12th C, 2nd half. H 134. *Germania* 12 (1867), pp. 76-80. **[A.a.].**

4 *Arnsteiner Marienlied* + *De spiritu sancto* (fragm.). Wiesbaden, Hauptstaatsarchiv, Abt. 3004 C 8, ff. 129v-135v. 12th C, 2nd half, not before 1170 (SCHNEIDER). H 137. M, no. 19; I, Pl. 18. S, Pl. 29. **Strophes. [a.a.], [aa], [a.aː], [a.aː], also [aːa.] and [aːaː], – irregular.**

5 *Ave Maria* (4 verses). Graz, UB, cod. 1287 (formerly 42/69 4°), front pastedown. 12th C, end. H 167. *ZfdA* 18 (1875), p. 160. **[a.a.].**

6 *Baumgartenberger Johannes Bapista* (fragm.). Linz, Studienbibl., cod. 317, f. 119v. 12th C, 2nd half. H 129. M, no. 27; I, Pl. 15. **[a.aː], sections marked with Roman numerals.**

7 *Benediktbeurer Gebet zum Meßopfer*. Munich, BSB, Clm 4616, f. 54r/v. 13th C, inc. (SCHNEIDER). H 179. M, no. 35. MR. P/G II, Pl. 23. **[a.a.].**

8 *Christ ist erstanden*. Salzburg, UB, cod. M II 6, f. 67r. 12th C (ca. 1160). H 143. ^{2}*VL* I, col. 1197. **Only the incipit of strophe 1, with neumes.**

9 *Crescentia* + *Scoph von dem lone* + *Cantilena de conversione S. Pauli*. Colmar, Archives départ. du Haut-Rhin, Fragments de Ms nos 559-560. 12th C, last quarter (SCHNEIDER). H 164. M, no. 32 and 6; I, Pl. 13-14. S, Pl. 24. *ZfdA* 40 (1896), pp. 305-331. **[a.a] ('Cantilena') and [A.a.], with some additional pointing; the 'Cantilena' is in 8-line strophes.**

10 *Denkspruch* ('Namenloser IV'). Vienna, ÖNB, cod. 160, f. 100v. 12th C, end (MOSER/TERVOOREN) (listed as 13th C in MR). H 188. ^{36}MF II, Pl. 16. **Strophe. [a.a.].**

11 *Denksprüche* ('Namenlose I-III'). Zurich, Zentralbibl., cod. C 58, f. 73v (MS of the *Arzenibuoch Ipocratis* and *Züricher Predigtsammlung*). 12th C, end (SCHNEIDER) (listed as 13th C in MR). H 194. [36]MF II, Pl. 15. **Strophe. [a.a.].**

12 *Deutung der Meßgebräuche*. Munich, BSB, Cgm 39, ff. 132v-142r (MS of the *Speculum ecclesiae*). 12th C, 2nd half, ca. 1170-1200 (SCHNEIDER). H 146. **[a.a.], new sections begin on a new line.**

13 *Deutung der Meßgebräuche* (fragm.). Wolfenbüttel, HAB, cod. 404.9(12) Novi. Ca. 1200. H 238. M, no. 34. *ZfdA* 32 (1888), pp. 117-118. **[a.a.].**

14 *Du bist mîn, ich bin dîn* (lyric). Munich, BSB, Clm 19411 (*Tegernseer Briefsammlung*), f. 114v. 12th C, last quarter (datable 1178-86). H 181. S, Pl. 2. P/G II, Pl. 16B. **Strophe. [a.a.].**

15 Eilhart von Oberge: *Tristrant* (fragm. M). Cracow, Bibl. Jagiellońska, Berol. Ms. germ. 4° 661. Ca. 1200 ('1. Dr. 13.Jh.' MR). H 158. MR. Ed. H. BUSSMANN (Tübingen, 1969: *ATB* 70), Pl. 2. **[a.a.], new paragraph on a new line (initial not executed).**

16 Eilhart von Oberge: *Tristrant* (fragm. R). Karlsruhe, LB, cod. Donaueschingen 69 + Munich, BSB, Cgm 5249/31 + Regensburg, Bischöfl. Zentralbibl./Proske-Musikbibl., s.n. (lost). 13th C, inc. (SCHNEIDER). H 155. MR. Ed. BUSSMANN, Pl. 1. **[a.a.], 2-line red initials on a new line.**

17 *Ezzos Gesang* + *Memento mori*. Strasbourg, BNU, cod. 1-2 (All. 278), ff. 74v, 154v-155r. 12th C, shortly after 1130. H 103. M, nos. 7 and 5; I, Pl. 12. **[a.a.], the first poem with 4-line strophes introduced by majuscules.**

18 *Friedberger Christ und Antichrist* (fragm.). Giessen, UB, cod. 660a. Ca. 1200/13th C, inc. (SCHNEIDER). H 68. M, no. 25; I, Pl. 11-11a. S, Pl. 58. MR. **[a.a.], sections beginnings with 2-line initials on a new line.**

19 *Graf Rudolf* (fragm.). Braunschweig, StB, cod. 5 + Göttingen, SUB, cod. philol. 184 VII. 13th C, inc. (SCHNEIDER). H 163. S, Pl. 61-62. **[a.a.], mid-line red initials.**

20 Heinrich: *Reinhart Fuchs* (fragm. S). Kassel, Murhardsche u. LB, cod. 8° Ms. poet. et roman. 1. 13th C, inc. (SCHNEIDER). H 251. S, Pl. 53. MR. O. EHRISMANN, *Der mittelhochdeutsche Reinhart Fuchs: Abbildungen und Materialien zur handschriftlichen Überlieferung* (Göppingen, 1980: *Litterae* 72). **[a.a.], mid-line red initials.**

21 *Heinrichs Litanei*. Graz, UB, cod. 1501 (formerly 39/59 8°), ff. 70r-105r. 12th C, 2nd half (listed as 13th C in MR). H 127. M, no. 51; III, Pl. 1 and 3. **[a.a.].**

22 Heinrich von Rugge: *Leich*. Munich, BSB, Clm 4570, ff. 239v-240v. Late 12th C, shortly after 1190 (listed as 13th C in MR). H 157. S, Pl. 25. MR.

P/G II, Pl. 24. [36]MF II, Pl. 6a-c. **Strophes. [a.a.].**

23 Heinrich von Veldeke: *Eneas* (fragm. R). Munich, BSB, Cgm 5249/19. 12th C, end/ca. 1200 (SCHNEIDER). H 177. S, Pl. 18. MR. P/G III, Pl. 31A. **[a.a.], 2-line red initials.**

24 Heinrich von Veldeke: *Eneas* (fragm. Wo). Wolfenbüttel, HAB, cod. 404.9(4) Novi. Ca.1200 (listed as 13th C in MR). H 237. **[a.a.], dialogue marked up with majuscules splashed in red.**

25 *Herzog Ernst* (version A, fragm. M). Cracow, Bibl. Jagiellońska, Berol. Ms. germ. 4° 1303, Nr. 5. 12th C, end ('1.V.13.Jh.' MR). H 159. MR. **[a.a.].**

26 *Kaiserchronik* (version A, fragm. no. 8a/b). Freiburg, UB, Hs. 447 + private ownership G. Fischer, Mainz, in 1803 (lost). 12th C, 2nd half. H 123. MR. **[a.a.], mid-line red initials.**

27 *Kaiserchronik* (version A, fragm. 9). Vienna, ÖNB, cod. 13006. 12th C, end (dated to the early 13th C by BERTELSMEIER-KIERST, "Wigalois" [as n. 33], p. 282 n. 31). H 192. MR. **[a.a:], mid-line red initials.**

28 *Kaiserchronik* (version A, fragm. no. 10). Graz, UB, cod. 1703 Nr. 133 + Innsbruck, Ferdinandeum cod. FB 1519/V. 12th C, 2nd half ('1.V.13.Jh.' MR). H 112. MR. *ZfdA* 19 (1876), pp. 208-210. **[a.a.], mid-line red initials.**

29 *Kaiserchronik* (version A, fragm. no. 11). Klagenfurt, Kärntner Landesarchiv, cod. GV 6/26. 12th C, 2nd half. H 113. MR. *WSB* 6 (1851), pp. 328-342. **[a:a:], mid-line red initials.**

30 *Kaiserchronik* (version A, fragm. no. 13). Nuremberg, GNM, Hs. 22067. 13th C, inc. ('1.H.13.Jh.' MR). H 264. MR. **[a.a.], mid-line red initials (2 cols), majuscules for sub-sections.**

31 *Kaiserchronik* (version A, fragm. F). St. Florian, Stiftsbibl., Fragm. 29 + (?) Schwaz (Tyrol), Franziskanerkloster, s.n. (lost). 13th C, inc. ('1. Dr. 13. Jh.' MR). H 267 and 182. MR. *ZfdPh* 83 (1964), pp. 34-41. **[a.a.], paragraphs beginning on a new line (2 cols).**

32 *Kaiserchronik* (version B, fragm.). Basel, UB, Cod. N I 3 Nr. 89. 13th C, 1st third, probably ca. 1220-30 ('1.V.13.Jh.' MR). MR. WOLF, "Buch und Text" (as n. 49), chapter I.1.4.1, ill. 22. **[|A-|A-].**

33 *König Rother* (fragm. M). Munich, BSB, Cgm 5249/1. Ca. 1200 (SCHNEIDER). H 176. S, Pl. 19. MR. **[a.a.], mid-line red initials.**

34 Pfaffe Konrad: *Rolandslied* (fragm. A). Strasbourg, Bibl. de la ville, destroyed in 1870. 12th C, last third. Printed by SCHERZ in 1729. H 147. GUTFLEISCH, "Rolandslied" (as n. 31), pp. 147-148. No information.

35 Pfaffe Konrad: *Rolandslied* (MS P). Heidelberg, UB, Cpg 112. Ca. 1200 (SCHNEIDER/GUTFLEISCH) (listed as 13th C in MR). H 169. GUTFLEISCH, "Rolandslied" (as n. 31), pp. 148-159. Facsimile ed. WERNER/ZIRNBAUER (as n. 1). S, Pl. 33. **[a.a.], 2-line red initials on a new line.**

36 Pfaffe Konrad: *Rolandslied* (fragm. S). Schwerin, LB Mecklenburg-Vorpommern, s.n. 12th C, end/ca. 1200 (GUTFLEISCH) ('1. Dr. 13.Jh.' MR). H 183. MR. GUTFLEISCH, "Rolandslied" (as n. 31), pp. 159-167, plate p. 163. **[a.a.], mid-line red initials.**

37 *Linzer Antichrist*. Linz, Studienbibl., cod. 33, ff. 171r-180r. Ca. 1200/ 13th C, inc. H 215. M, no. 54; III, Pl. 5. **[a.a.].**

38 *Makkabäer* (fragm.). M.V. Lomonossov Moscow State University, Fond 40, opis 1, ed. khr. 39, formerly Halberstadt, Bibl. des Domgymnasiums, Fragm. 6. 13th C, inc. M, no. 61. H 250. **[a.a].**

39 *Mariengebet* (6 verses). Munich, BSB, Clm 19463, f. 35r. Probably ca. 1200/13th C, inc. H 79. *Germania* 24 (1879), p. 297. No information on layout or punctuation.

40 *Mariensequenz aus Muri* (MS A). Sarnen, Bibl. des Benediktiner-Kollegiums, cod. 69 ('Gebetbuch aus Muri'), ff. 33v-36r. Ca. 1200. H 229. M, no. 20. **Irregular strophes. [aa], [a.a.].**

41 *Mariensequenz aus Muri*. (MS B). Engelberg, Stiftsbibl., cod. 1003, f. 115r/v. 12th C, end (listed as 13th C in MR). H 122. M, no. 20. A. Bruckner, *Scriptoria medii aevi Helvetica*, vol. 10 (Geneva, 1964), Pl. XIV. **Irregular strophes. [a.a.], with neumes.**

42 *Mariensequenz aus Muri* (MS O). Oxford, Bodleian Library, MS Can. misc. 325, f. 12v. Ca. 1200. MR. **Irregular strophes. [a.a.], mid-line red initials, with neumes.**

43 *Mariensequenz aus Seckau.* Graz, UB, cod. 287 (formerly 39/17 f°). 13th C, inc. (SCHNEIDER). H 210. M, no. 21; I, Pl. 19. S, Pl. 41. **Irregular strophes. [a.a.], mid-line red initials.**

44 *Melker Marienlied.* Melk, Stiftsbibl., cod. 391 ('Melker Annalen'), f. 1r (pag. 3). 12th C (datable 1123-1142). H 102. M, no. 13; I, Pl. 16. **6-line strophes with refrain, a new line and off-set majuscule for each strophe. [a.a.].**

45 *Merigarto*. Karlsruhe, LB, cod. Donaueschingen A III 57. 12th C, 1st half. H 101. M, no. 1. VOORWINDEN, *Merigarto* (as n. 47), with Pl. **[a.a.], tending towards [|a.a.].**

46 *Meßgebet 'Got vater allir cristinheit'* (13 verses). Fulda, LB, Hs. Aa 46, f. 81v. 13th C, inc. (SCHNEIDER). H 124. S, Pl. 47. MR. *ZfdA* 18 (1875), pp. 455-456. **[a:a:].**

47 *Meßgebet 'Vater herre, vater got'.* Salzburg, Stiftsbibl. St. Peter, cod. A V 31, f. 58r. Ca. 1200. H 228. *ZfdA* 17 (1874), pp. 425-427. No information.

48 'Millstätter Handschrift' (collection of eight 11th/12th C poems). Klagenfurt, Kärntner Landesarchiv, cod. GV 6/19. Ca. 1200/13th C, inc. (SCHNEIDER). H 213. S, Pl. 37. Facsimile ed. KRACHER (as n. 5). **[a.a.], mid-line red initials.**

49 *Millstätter Sündenklage* (fragm.). Munich, BSB, Cgm 5249/60a. 12th C, end. *ZfdA* 124 (1995), pp. 298-302, reproductions pp. 301-302. **[a.a.].**

50 *Mittelfränkische Reimbibel* (fragm. A, A*). M.V. Lomonossov Moscow State University, Fond 40, opis 1, ed. khr. 37, formerly Halberstadt, Bibl. des Domgymnasiums, Fragm. 3 + Halle, UB, cod. Yg 34. 4°. 12th C, 1st half. H 91. *ZfdPh* 10 (1879), pp. 129, 131. **[A.a.].**

51 *Mittelfränkische Reimbibel* (fragm. B, B*). Karlsruhe, LB, cod. Donaueschingen A III 50 + Hall (Tyrol), Franziskanerkloster, s.n. (lost). 12th C, mid. H 111. M, no. 3. *Germania* 12 (1867), pp. 90-96. *ZfdA* 59 (1922), pp. 17-18. **[A.a.], but small letters where the rhyme has not been recognized.**

52 *Mittelfränkische Reimbibel* (fragm. C). M.V. Lomonossov Moscow State University, Fond 40, opis 1, ed. khr. 38, formerly Halberstadt, Bibl. des Domgymnasiums, Fragm. 4. 12th C, 1st half. H 88. M, no. 3. **[A.a.], [a.a.].**

53 *Monatsregeln für die Wahl eines Freundes.* Vienna, ÖNB, cod. 2245, ff. 54v-58v. 12th C, end. H 190. *ZfdA* 8 (1851), pp. 542-544. No information.

54 *Oberdeutscher Servatius* (fragm. n). Nuremberg, GNM, Hs 29774. 12th C, last quarter (ca. 1200 KURRAS, '1.V.13.Jh.' MR). H 225. MR. **[a.a.].**

55 *Paternostergedicht + Von der Siebenzahl.* Innsbruck, UB, cod. 652, ff. 72r-79v (MS of the *Innsbrucker Arzneibuch*). 12th C, 3rd quarter (HELLGARDT). H 70. M, nos. 10-11. **Regular 12-line strophes. [a.a.], with some syntactic pointing.**

56 *Psalter, gereimter + Johannes Baptista* (fragm.). Klagenfurt, Archiv der Diözese Gurk, Bestand der Mensalbibl. der Bischöfe von Gurk, ad cod. XXIX e 27. H 252. 13th C, inc. *ZfdA* 67 (1930), pp. 258-260. **[A.a.], 2-line initials on new line.**

57 *Rheinauer Paulus* (fragm.). Zurich, Zentralbibl., cod. Rh 77, ff. 1r and 53v. 12th C, 1st third. H 84. M, no. 23. **[aa], majuscules only at beginning of section, paragraph signs.**

58 *Rittersitte.* Vienna, ÖNB, cod. 2871, f. V verso (fragm.). 12th C, last quarter. H 106. *ZfdA* 68 (1931), pp. 153-163. **[a.a.], with occasional majuscules [A.a.].**

59 ‘Straßburg-Molsheimer Hs.’ Der arme Hartmann: *Credo + Heinrichs Litanei + Straßburger Alexander + Pilatus*. Strasbourg, Bibl. de la ville, cod. C. V. 16. b. 4°. Destroyed in 1870. 13th C, inc. (C. MACKERT). H 156. *ZfdA* 130 (2001), pp. 143-165, with Pl. after p. 146. **[a.a.].**

60 Der Stricker: *Karl der Große* (fragm. a). Munich, BSB, Cgm 5153e. 13th C, end of 1st quarter (SCHNEIDER). S, Pl. 46. MR. **[|A-.|A-.].**

61 Der Stricker: *Karl der Große* (fragm. e). Munich, BSB, Cgm 5249/5a. 13th C, end of 1st quarter (SCHNEIDER) (‘zwischen 1220-1240’ C. BERTELSMEIER-KIERST, in: *PBB* 121 [1999], pp. 299-302). S, Pl.45. MR. **[|A-.|A-].**

62 *Summa theologiae* (fragm., 6 verses). Wolfenbüttel, HAB, cod. 268 Gud. lat. 4°, ff. 172v-173r. Ca. 1100. Probably somewhat later, if the use of Honorius Augustodunensis, *Elucidarium*, as a source can be regarded as secure. H 62. M, no. 8. *PBB* 26 (1901), p. 312. **Irregular strophes. [aa].**

63 *Summa theologiae* (strophe 28 only). Nuremberg, GNM, Hs 1966, f. 122v. 12th C, 2nd half. H 119. **Sporadic pointing.**

64 *Trierer Ägidius + Trierer Silvester + Trierer Floyris*. Trier, StB, Mappe X, Nr. 13-14. Ca. 1200/13th C, inc. (SCHNEIDER). H 185. S, Pl. 63. H. KIENHORST, *De handschriften van de Middelnederlandse ridderepiek. Een codicologische beschrijving*, 2 vols. (Deventer, 1988: *Deventer Studiën*), II, Pl. 39. **[a.a.], mid-line red initials.**

65 *Trost in Verzweiflung* (fragm.). Privately owned in Memmingen in 1813 (lost). Ca. 1200. H 239. M, no. 38. **[A⹎a.], with variations.**

66 *Übermuot diu alte*. Munich, BSB, Cgm 5249/42a. Ca. 1200/13th C, inc. (SCHNEIDER). H 259. [36]MF II, Pl. 17. *Codex Manesse. Katalog der Ausstellung*, ed. E. MITTLER and W. WERNER (Heidelberg, [2]1988), plate p. 550. **One strophe. [a.a.], with neumes.**

67 *Uppsalaer Sündenklage*. Uppsala, Universitetsbibliotek, cod. C 226, ff. 157v-158v. 12th C, end (listed as 13th C in MR). H 186. *Germania* 31 (1886), pp. 99-104. **[a.a.], sometimes [A.a.].**

68 *Vom Himmelreich*. Munich, BSB, Clm 9513, f. 1r-7r. 12th C (datable ca. 1174). H 153. M, no. 14; I, Pl. 17. S, Pl. 9. **Long lines with endrhyme: [a.a⹎]. Marginal addition (v. 12,1-12) set out in lines: [|a.|a⹎]. Gamma as an end-marker.**

69 *Von der babylonischen Gefangenschaft* (fragm.). St. Paul im Lavanttal, Stiftsbibl., Fragm. 26/8. 12th C, last quarter/ca. 1200 (SCHNEIDER). H 151 (2). MR. *PBB* (T) 82 (1960), pp. 89, 92. S, Pl. 16. GRÖCHENIG, *Handschriftenfragmente* (as n. 39), plate p. 158. **[a.a⹎].**

70 'Vorauer Handschrift'. *Kaiserchronik* and a large collection of 11th/12th C poems. Vorau, Stiftsbibl., cod. 176, ff. 1r-135v. 12th C, last quarter (SCHNEIDER). H 187. S, Pl. 10. Facsimile in two parts: *Kaiserchronik*, ed. FANK (as n. 37); *Die deutschen Gedichte*, ed. POLHEIM (as n. 5). **[a.a.] and [a:a:], punctus versus as end-mark, mid-line red initials.**

71 *Vorauer Sündenklage*. Zwettl, Stiftsbibl., cod. Zwetl. 73, ff. 116r-117r. Ca. 1200/13th C, inc. H 85. M, no. 50. MR. O. PAUSCH, in: *Jahrbuch für Landeskunde von Niederösterreich* N.F. 46/47 (1981), ill. 3. **[a.a.].**

72 Priester Wernher: *Marienleben* (MS D). Cracow, Bibl. Jagiellońska, Berol. Ms. germ. 8° 109. 13th C, 1st quarter (SCHNEIDER). H 204. N. HENKEL, in: *Scrinium Berolinense. Festschrift Tilo Brandis*, 2 vols. (Berlin, 2000), I, pp. 271-275. **[a.a.], 2-line pen-work initials on a new line, occasional majuscules for minor divisions.**

73 Priester Wernher: *Marienleben* (fragm. E^1 and E^2). Innsbruck, Landesmuseum Ferdinandeum, Cod. FB 1519/IX + Nuremberg, GNM, Hs 18065. Ca. 1200 ('Anfang 13. Jh.' WESLE/MR). H 212. MR. *ZfdA* 101 (1972), p. 210. **[a.a.], mid-line red initials.**

74 Wernher von Elmendorf: *Moralium dogma philosophorum*. Berlin, SBB-PK, Ms. germ. 8° 226. 12th C, end (BUMKE). H 160. MR. J. BUMKE, in: *Festschrift U. Pretzel* (Berlin, 1963), plate after p. 34. Ed. J. BUMKE *et al.* (Tübingen, 1974: *ATB* 77), ill. 1. **[a.a.], [A.a.], [A.a] – mixed, roman numerals for sections.**

75 *Wiener Genesis + Physiologus + Exodus*. Vienna, ÖNB, cod. 2721. 12th C, last quarter (SCHNEIDER). H 150. S, Pl. 11. Facsimile: *Codex Vindobonensis 2721*, ed. E. PAPP (Göppingen, 1980: *Litterae* 71). **[a.a].**

76 Wirnt von Grafenberg: *Wigalois* (MS A). Cologne, Historisches Archiv der Stadt, cod. W* 6. 13th C, 1st quarter (probably ca. 1215-25) (SCHNEIDER). S, Pl. 35-36. MR. **Hand 1 [a:a:], hand 2 [a:a.], hand 3 [a.a.], initials on new line.**

77 Wolfram von Eschenbach: *Parzival* (fragm. G^h). Munich, BSB, Cgm 5249/3c. 13th C, 1st quarter (SCHNEIDER, MR) ('1. Hälfte 13. Jh.' BONATH/LOMNITZER). MR. G. BONATH and H. LOMNITZER, "Verzeichnis der Fragment-Überlieferung von Wolframs 'Parzival'", in: *Studien zu Wolfram von Eschenbach. Festschrift W. Schröder* (Tübingen, 1989), pp. 114-115 (no. 26). **[a.a.], mid-line red initials.**

78 Wolfram von Eschenbach: *Willehalm* (fragm. F 13). Munich, BSB, Cgm 193/I. 13th C, 1st quarter, ca. 1220 ('um oder bald nach 1220' SCHNEIDER). S, Pl. 38-40. MR. **[a.a.].**

(b) *13th-century manuscripts (selection)*

79 *Albanus* (fragm.). Cracow, Bibl. Jagiellońska, Berol. Ms. germ. 4° 665. 13th C, 1st half. ('2.V.13.Jh.' MR). H 271. M, no. 62. MR. **[A.a.].**

80 Albrecht von Augsburg: *Ulrichslegende*. Munich, BSB, Cgm 94, ff. 25r-81v. 13th C, 1st quarter (SCHNEIDER). H 255. S, Pl. 42. P/G II, Pl. 21. **[|A-.|a.], [A.A.], [|A.|A.].**

81 *Ave Maria* (4 verses). Graz, UB, cod. 737 (formerly 39/21 f°), f. 121v. 13th C, 1st half. H 272. No information.

82 Eilhart von Oberge: *Tristrant* (fragm. St) + *Tagzeitengedicht* + Pfaffe Lamprecht: *Tobias* ('Stargard fragments'). Cracow, Bibl. Jagiellońska, Berol. Ms. germ. 4° 1418. 13th C, 2nd quarter, ca. 1230 (13th C, inc. MR). H 203. MR. **Eilhart and Lamprecht: [A⸵a.], 2-line red initials on a new line, punctus interrogativus; 'Tagzeitengedicht': [|A.|A.] (set out in lines).**

83 Hartmann von Aue: *Der arme Heinrich* (fragm. C). Berlin, SBB-PK, Ms. germ. 2° 923,7a. 13th C, 1st half. MR. *Aderlass und Seelentrost. Die Überlieferung deutscher Texte im Spiegel Berliner Handschriften und Inkunabeln*, ed. P.J. BECKER and E. OVERGAAUW (Berlin, 2003), pp. 69-70 with colour Pl. **[a.a.].**

84 Hartmann von Aue: *Erec* (fragm. K). Koblenz, Landeshauptarchiv, Best. 701 Nr. 749, Bl. 14b. 13th C, 2nd quarter. MR. BROMMER, "Erec" (as n. 37), with plate. **[a⸵a⸵], [A⸵a⸵], punctus interrogativus.**

85 Hartmann von Aue: *Gregorius* (fragm. N). Berlin, SBB-PK, Fragm. 275. 13th C, 1st half. MR. *Aderlass und Seelentrost* (as no. 83), pp. 217-219 with colour Pl. **[a.a.].**

86 Hartmann von Aue: *Iwein* (MS A). Heidelberg, UB, Cpg 397. 13th C, second quarter. S, Pl. 87. MR. L. OKKEN, *Hartmann von Aue, "Iwein". Ausgewählte Abbildungen und Materialien zur handschriftlichen Überlieferung* (Göppingen, 1974: *Litterae* 24), plates pp. 1-7, 12-16, 37. **[a.a.], punctus interrogativus.**

87 Hartmann von Aue: *Iwein* (MS B). Giessen, UB, cod. 97. 13th C, 2nd quarter. H 249. Facsimile: H.M. HEINRICHS, *Hartmann von Aue. Iwein. Handschrift B* (Cologne and Graz, 1964: *Deutsche Texte in Handschriften* 2). S, Pl. 79. **[|a-.|a-.].**

88 Hartmann von Aue: *Iwein* (fragm. F). Linz, Studienbibl., cod. 599. 13th C, 2nd quarter. MR. OKKEN, *Hartmann von Aue*, plates pp. 17-18. WOLF, "Buch und Text" (as n. 49), chapter II.2.3. **[|a-.|a-.].**

89 Hartmann von Aue: *Iwein* (fragm. V). Kremsmünster, Stiftsbibl., Fragm. VI/275. 13th C, 1st quarter. H 253. MR. *ZfdA* 107 (1978), plate after p. 194. **[a.a.], mid-line red initials.**

90 *Der heimliche Bote*. Munich, BSB, Clm 7792, f. 59r. 13th C, 1st quarter (SCHNEIDER). H 262. S, Pl. 54. MR.

[a.a.], majuscules for new paragraph (mid-line).

91 Heinrich von Veldeke: *Eneas* (MS B). Berlin, SBB-PK, Ms. germ. 2° 282. Ca. 1220-30 (SCHNEIDER). H 270. S, Pl. 43. Facsimile ed. FINGERNAGEL/HENKEL (as n. 41). **First pages irregular: [|A-.|a.], [|A-⸮.|a⸮.], [a⸮.a.], [a.a.]; thereafter [|A.|a.], and from f. 5vb [|A-.|a.].**

92 Heinrich von Veldeke: *Eneas* (fragm. Me). Munich, BSB, Cgm 5199. Ca. 1220-30 (SCHNEIDER). H 217. S, Pl. 44. MR. **[|A-|A-], 2-line red initials on a new line.**

93 Heinrich von Veldeke: *Servatius* (fragm.). Karlsruhe, Bibl. des Bundesgerichtshofs, Ph 1767 (formerly: Berlin, Bibl. des Obersten Gerichts der DDR) + Munich, BSB, Cgm 5249/18, 1a-c. 13th C, 1st half (SCHNEIDER). H 205. *ZfdA* 120 (1991), plates pp. 16-20. **[A.a.], midline red initials.**

94 *Herzog Ernst* (version A, fragm. n and P). Berlin, SBB-PK, Ms. germ. 8° 225 + Prague, Národní knihovna ČR, Fragm. germ. 19 and 37 (= cod. XXIV C 2). 13th C, 2nd quarter (inc.) (SCHNEIDER). H 248. MR. H.-J. BEHR, *Herzog Ernst: Eine Übersicht über die verschiedenen Textfassungen und deren Überlieferung* (Göppingen, 1979: *Litterae* 62), plates pp. 1-5; *Aderlass und Seelentrost* (as no. 83), p. 58 with colour plate. **[A.a.], two-line red initials.**

95 *Idsteiner Sprüche der Väter* (fragm.). Wiesbaden, Hauptstaatsarchiv, Abt. 3004 C 26a.b. 13th C, 2nd quarter (HELLGARDT) ('Mitte 13. Jh.' MR). H 274. M, no. 2. MR. **[A.a.], [a.a.], [Aa.], punctuation generally following the syntax and rhetorical structure.**

96 *König Rother* (MS H). Heidelberg, UB, Cpg 390. 13th C, 1st quarter. H 170. S, Pl. 59. **[a.a.], [A.A.], midline red initials.**

97 Pfaffe Konrad: *Rolandslied* (fragm. E). Erfurt, UB, cod. Ampl. 4° 65. 13th C, 1st half (not before 1220) (GUTFLEISCH). H 207. MR. GUTFLEISCH, "Rolandslied" (as n. 31), pp. 175-181, plate p. 179. **[A.A.], mid-line red initials.**

98 Pfaffe Konrad: *Rolandslied* (fragm. T). Sondershausen, Stadt- und Kreisbibl., Hs.-Br. 2. 13th C, 1st quarter (GUTFLEISCH). H 184. MR. GUTFLEISCH, "Rolandslied" (as n. 31), pp. 167-172, plate p. 169. **[a.a.].**

99 Pfaffe Konrad: *Rolandslied* ('Kauslersches Fragm.', W). Formerly in private ownership in Stuttgart, von Kausler (1838). 13th C, 1st quarter. H 196. GUTFLEISCH, "Rolandslied" (as n. 31), pp. 172-175. Script sample published in: *Ruolandes liet*, ed. W. GRIMM (Göttingen, 1838), appendix. **[a.a.].**

100 Konrad Fleck: *Flore und Blanscheflur* (fragm. F). Frauenfeld, Archiv der katholischen Kirchgemeinde, Cod. III Bg. 13th C, 2nd quarter.

MR. **[|a.|a.], the *punctus* offset to the right of the column.**

101 *Mariengebet* (rhymed) + *Mariensequez aus Muri* (MS C). Munich, BSB, Clm 935 ('Gebetbuch der Hl. Hildegard von Bingen'). 13th C, 2nd quarter. H 178. M, no. 20. Facsimile: *Hildegard-Gebetbuch*, ed. H. HAUCKE *et al.* (Wiesbaden, 1982). **Irregular strophes. [a.a.].**

102 *Marienlegenden* (fragm.). Munich, BSB, Cgm 5249/11. 13th C, 1st half (ca. 1220-40) (SCHNEIDER). H 257. MR. *Germania* 25 (1880), pp. 82-88; H. HILG, in: ²*VL* 6 (1987), col. 31. **[a.a.], mid-line red initials.**

103 *Niederrheinischer Tundalus* (fragm.). Cracow, Bibl. Jagiellońska, Berol. Ms. germ. 4° 642. 13th C, 1st quarter. H 202. *ZfdPh* 108 (1989) Sonderheft, plate after p. 128. **[A.A.].**

104 *Patriciuslegende* (fragm.). Munich, BSB, Cgm 5249/38. 13th C, 2nd quarter (SCHNEIDER). H 258. MR. **[a.a.], mid-line red initials.**

105 *Von Christi Geburt* (fragm.). Innsbruck, UB, Hs.-Frg. 69. 13th C, 1st half. H 92. M, no. 26. MR. **[A.a.].**

106 *Vorauer Moses* (fragm.). Linz, Oberösterr. Landesarchiv, Buchdeckelfunde Sch. 3 Nr. II/4a. 13th C, 1st quarter ('1.H.13.Jh.' MR). H 243. MR. *Germania* 7 (1862), p. 231. **[a.a.], mid-line red initials.**

107 Wirnt von Grafenberg: *Wigalois* (fragm. E). Freiburg, UB, Hs 445 + Vienna, ÖNB, cod. 14612 + New Haven, Beinecke Library, MS 481, no. 113. Ca. 1220-30 (BERTELSMEIER-KIERST). MR. BERTELSMEIER-KIERST, "Wigalois" (as n. 33), ill. p. 280. **[a.a:], mid-line red initials.**

108 Wirnt von Grafenberg: *Wigalois* (fragm. q). Cracow, Bibl. Jagiellońska, Berol. Ms. germ. 4° 1689. 13th C, 2nd quarter ('2.Dr.13.Jh.' SCHIEWER). MR. **[|a-.|a-.].**

109 Wolfram von Eschenbach: *Parzival* (fragm. r). Erlangen, UB, Ms. B 1. 13th C, 1st half. BONATH/LOMNITZER, "Verzeichnis" (as no. 77), p. 103 (no. 14). MR. **[a.a.], mid-line red initials.**

Some Aspects of Orality in the Anglo-Norman *St Modwenna*

TONY HUNT

The Anglo-Norman *Life of Saint Modwenna*[1] runs to 8692 octosyllabic lines arranged in monorhyme quatrains and seems to date from ca.1230, though Legge has suggested an earlier date of composition.[2] It is longer than any other Anglo-Norman saint's life except that of St Francis[3] (8727 lines, not quite complete) and the unpublished Life of St Clement, Pope, in Cambridge, Trinity College MS R.3.46 (14988 lines, unfinished). It survives in two manuscripts, Oxford, Bodleian Library, Digby 34 (s. XIII^{med}), and the celebrated 'Campsey manuscript' (London, BL Add. 70513, formerly Welbeck Abbey I C 1.2, s. XIV^{in}), so called because in the fourteenth century it belonged ("*cest livre est a covent de Campisse*") to the convent of Augustinian canonesses at Campsey, near Woodbridge in Suffolk.[4] In this MS it is described as "*le romanz de la vie seinte Modwenne noneyne*", where *romanz*, of course, merely draws

[1] *St. Modwenna*, ed. A.T. BAKER and A. BELL (Oxford, 1947: *ANTS* 7). For the source see now *Geoffrey of Burton: Life and Miracles of St. Modwenna*, ed. R. BARTLETT (Oxford, 2002: *Oxford Medieval Texts*).

[2] M.D. LEGGE, *Anglo-Norman Literature and its Background* (Oxford, 1963), p. 261: "This has been dated 1230, but is either earlier or is modernized from a late twelfth-century text".

[3] See *La Vye de seynt Fraunceys d'Assise*, ed. D.W. RUSSELL (London, 2002: *ANTS* 59-60).

[4] See J. WOGAN-BROWNE, *Saints' Lives and Women's Literary Culture c.1150-1300: Virginity and its Authorizations* (Oxford, 2001), pp. 6-12, 170-176. We owe the most thorough study of the MS to D. RUSSELL, "The Campsey Collection of the Old French Saints' Lives: A Re-examination of its Structure and Provenance", *Scriptorium* 57 (2003), pp. 51-83. I am very indebted to the kindness of Professor Russell in allowing me to read his article before publication.

attention to the fact that it is written in the French vernacular, as indeed are all the thirteen rhymed saints' lives, which are largely concerned with insular, female saints, contained in the Campsey MS. The Anglo-Norman *Life* has attracted little critical attention: Jocelyn Price (now Wogan-Browne)[5] has sought to clarify its position as a witness to a literary culture of women in medieval England, and it has been carefully examined, from selected points of view, in a recent survey of insular French hagiography by Françoise Laurent.[6]

Against this rather meagre critical background the *Life* has not been investigated for one of its most striking features, a high density of 'oral' elements which are suggestive of a special relationship between its style, mode of performance, and intended audience. The many features of orality in the work point to the need to situate it on the scale which extends from Manfred Scholz's emphasis on reception through individual reading[7] (according to which aural elements tend to be interpreted as constituting a 'Hörerfiktion') to the traditional, and sometimes simplistic, acceptance of oral recitation,[8] via Dennis Green's intermediate mode which allows for both.[9] Price speculates on the intended audience of the *Life*, suggesting that "*Modwenne* may have been written for a monastic or for a secular audience, composed perhaps, as Legge suggests, of guests and patrons at Burton [the Benedictine abbey of Burton-on-Trent, Staffs.], but it is at all events written for a courtly audience". What is meant by "a courtly audience" is not at all clear, but "it does not exclude a lay audience as well as, or as part of, a courtly ecclesiastic audience".[10] Thus the

5 "*La Vie de Sainte Modwenne*: a neglected Anglo-Norman hagiographic text, and some implications for English secular literature", *Medium Aevum* 57 (1988), pp. 172-189.

6 F. LAURENT, *Plaire et édifier: les récits hagiographiques composés en Angleterre aux XIIe et XIIIe siècles* (Paris, 1998). M. THIRY-STASSIN in her brief survey of Anglo-Norman hagiography in: *Hagiographies*, ed. G. PHILIPPART, 2 vols. (Turnhout, 1994, 1996: *Corpus Christianorum*), I, pp. 407-428, describes *Modwenne* simply as "pouvant être lue par sections par un appel aux auditeurs" (p. 420).

7 M.G. SCHOLZ, *Hören und Lesen. Studien zur primären Rezeption der Literatur im 12. und 13. Jahrhundert* (Wiesbaden, 1980). See the review by D.H. GREEN in: *MLR* 77 (1982), pp. 479-485.

8 See, for example, P. GALLAIS, "Recherches sur la mentalité des romanciers français du moyen âge", *CCM* 7 (1964), pp. 479-493 and 13 (1970), pp. 333-347. The most ardent, though perhaps somewhat uncritical, proponent of oral performance from memory is E.B. VITZ, *Orality and Performance in Early French Romance* (Woodbridge, 1999), who summarizes her position on p. 267: "The central argument of this book has been that early French romance had strong roots in oral culture and that it was frequently performed from memory in a way that drew significantly on the resources of both the voice and the body of the performer".

9 D.H. GREEN, *Medieval Listening and Reading. The Primary Reception of German Literature 800-1300* (Cambridge, 1994).

10 PRICE, "*La Vie de Sainte Modwenne*", pp. 175, 176.

Life is said to be "superbly designed to engage courtly audiences, lay, ecclesiastical and mixed".[11] We shall return to the question of adaptability. Suffice to say for the present that the word *courtois* and its derivatives make no appearance in the text,[12] the heroine is, in Legge's submission, "a rather colourless person",[13] and the work is soberly written, if not plain in style, making only very sparing use of literary effects,[14] almost none of them involving *figurae verborum*. In the absence of external evidence, indicators of intended reception have to be collated with many other details of the text. The *Life of Modwenna* is a long text, as hagiographical compositions go (it is certainly the longest in the Campsey MS), and its form of monorhyme quatrains unusual, so that neither feature seems to relate to conventional audience expectations. But the sheer density of oral techniques, including the high incidence of phatic elements, seems to presuppose a listening audience.[15]

The first line of the text, "*Oez, seignurs, pur Deu vus pri*", immediately presents three characteristic and frequently occurring features of the author's style: s/he exhorts the audience to listen, the audience is identified as male, and the narrator employs the first person. Throughout frequent use is made of the first person,[16] not least the first person plural[17] which Laurent associates with hagiography rather than the romances. The audience seems to become one of the *dramatis personae*, so frequently are the narrator's remarks directed to it.[18] Narrative terminology is a significant factor when investigating the intended reception of a work, as both Scholz and Green emphasize. The word *oïr* in the

[11] PRICE, "*La Vie de Sainte Modwenne*", p. 185. On the links between monastic, clerical and lay literary publics see GREEN, *Medieval Listening*, pp. 217-219 and 284-288.

[12] Cf. W. MACBAIN, "Some religious and secular uses of the vocabulary of *fin' amor* in the early decades of the northern French narrative poem", *French Forum* 13 (1988), pp. 261-276 and J.D. BURNLEY, "*Fine amor*: its meaning and context", *Review of English Studies* N.S. 31 (1980), pp. 129-148.

[13] *Anglo-Norman Literature*, p. 262.

[14] For example similes at ll. 160-162, 697-700, 787-788, 1829-1892, 3141-3142, 8311-8312, 8315-8316.

[15] Note the important distinctions and cautions of C. SEGRE, "Dalla memoria al codice", in: *La Filologia romanza e i codici: Atti del convegno Messina-Università degli studi-Facoltà di lettere e filosofia 19-22 Dicembre 1991*, ed. S. GUIDA and F. LATELLA (Messina, 1993), pp. 5-13.

[16] Narratorial addresses to the audience in the first person singular number over 50, whilst narratorial observations also with frequent reference to the audience total just over twice that number.

[17] The instances number just over forty.

[18] Apart from the above examples which exhibit the narrator's use of the first person pronoun, singular and plural, there are a further 70 or so references to the audience without the personal pronoun. The total of all references to the audience exceeds 225.

context of narrative performance or reception occurs some 70 times[19] (*entendre*/*attendre* at ll. 7418, 7588, 7730, 8370) and in the imperative it appears 11 times with "*seignurs*", which identifies the audience and is a form of address which occurs on a further 11 occasions without the injunction to listen.[20] This is not the only feature which recalls, for example, the narrator's interventions in Beroul's *Tristran.*[21] The figure of the reciting narrator is ever-present:

> *Par telz vertuz, cum vos oez*
> *E cum avant oïr purrez,*
> *Ke vus dirai, si vus volez,*
> *Si jo sui ci bien escutez.* (ll. 6181-6184)

> *Ore dirrai un conte ici,*
> *Cum jo l'ai suvent oï:*
> *Pur ceo, seignur, pur Deu vus pri,*
> *S'il vus pleist, entendez!* (ll. 7585-7588)

> *Qui ore voldra bon cunte oïr,*
> *La noise face un poi queissir,*
> *Kar del cunter l'en voil servir*
> *A mun poer tuit a pleisir.* (ll. 8073-8076)

The use of the word *geste* recalls its function in Old French epic:

> *Modewenne, la Deu amie,*
> *La qui mort e la qui vie*
> *En cest escrit avez oïe,*
> *Dunt la geste n'est pas finie.* (ll. 8177-8180)

[19] *oez* ll. 1, 25, 49, 270, 296, 651, 810, 1139, 1383, 1386, 4057, 4446, 1599, 2353, 2392, 3959, 5460, 6039, 6181-6182, 6193, 6268, 6313, 6856, 6861 ("*Tanette l'ai oï numer*") (note *entendre* at ll. 7418, 7588, 7730), 7586, 7737, 8026, 8073, 8179; repeated expressions include *cum vus oez* ll. 1408, 1842, 5626, 6181; *dunt vus oiez* ll. 454, 1564, 1773, 2870, 3875, 6193; *que avez oï(e)* ll. 1110, 2298, 2718, 2744, 3547; *cum poez oïr* ll. 1952, 3852, 3862; *cum vus orrez* ll. 2354, 4112, 8345; *cum nus l'avum oÿ cunter* ll. 4333 (*legi audire*), 8030,8096; *oïr numer* ll. 5633, 6674, 6861. Note also *dunt m'oez cunter* l. 4640, *cum avant oïr purrez* l. 6182, *cum vus purrez aprés oïr* l. 7737, *oïr purrez* l. 8369.

[20] See ll. 1*, 25*, 296*, 341, 350, 574*, 1561, 2053, 2298*, 3062, 3630*, 4057*, 4109, 4561, 5589, 6026*, 6108*, 6274*, 6850, 7587, 7905*, 8370 (the asterisk denotes the presence of *oez*).

[21] See E. BIK, "Les interventions d'auteur dans le *Tristan* de Béroul", *Neophilologus* 56 (1972), 31-42. For 'epic style' in the *Life of St Modwenna* see LAURENT, *Plaire et édifier*, pp. 74-76.

The verb of narration par excellence is *cunter* which makes more than 70 appearances. But *chanter* is used in l. 5286 ("*par les paroles, que vus chant*")[22] and as part of a proverbial saying on the avoidance of tedium:[23]

L'em [le] dit en reprovier:
Suvent ennue beau chanter.
Pur ceo mun cunte *voil terminer,*
Que nuls ne nust mun lung parler.

Nel di *pur ceo que seit fini*
Cest miracle, que avez oï,
Ainz l'ai pur ceo en dous parti
Pur le[s] enuis, dunt jo vus di. (ll. 1105-1112)[24]

Regular use is also made of *faire memorie*,[25] *tucher* ('relate, treat of, speak of'),[26] *faire menciun* (l. 2787), *mustrer*,[27] *dire*,[28] *parler*,[29] *deviser*,[30] *descrire*,[31] and *retraire*,[32] which help to foreground the notion of telling, which is also reflected in the widely employed direct speech (dialogue) in the work.

The *Life* is made up of a series of miracles, which are almost invariably termed *miracles* when understood as stories and *merveilles* when treated as divine works causing wonderment.[33] The miracle stories function like exempla, clearly presented as lessons, sometimes explained for the audience's benefit,[34] and offered at the audience's convenience and pleasure. It is a particularly striking feature of the *Life* that the miracle stories are marked by transitional passages, 31 in all, which represent a clear structuring device employed by the

[22] See S. CERRITO, "*Dire* e *chanter* nel lessico poetico dell'antico francese", *Annali (sezione romanza) dell'Istituto Universitario Orientale* 29 (1987), pp. 325-335.

[23] See J.W. HASSELL, Jr., *Middle French Proverbs, Sentences, and Proverbial Phrases* (Toronto, 1982: *Subsidia Mediaevalia*), p. 64, C57.

[24] Cf. ll. 1874-1876, 2053-2054, 5195.

[25] ll. 1129, 1714, 2301, 2443, 5750, 5818.

[26] ll. 893, 4139, 5595, 5742.

[27] ll. 5192, 5366, 5590, 5627, 5707, 5724, 6122, 7020, 7040, 7384, 7569, 7652, 8364, 8619.

[28] ll. 6872, 7280, 7413, 8413, 8456.

[29] ll. 2033, 5190, 5637, 5674, 5797, 6112, 6133, 6268, 6359, 6426, 6870, 7584, 7597, 8314, plus the *vois parlant* formula: ll. 4337, 4383, 4337, 4383, 6133, 6185, 7745, 7809, 8034.

[30] ll. 5956, 7026, 7100, 7298.

[31] ll. 3959, 5608.

[32] ll. 7712, 7944.

[33] The same distinction is made in the *Miracles de Notre Dame* of Gautier de Coinci; see B. CERQUIGLINI, "Les énonciateurs Gautier", *Médiévales* 2 (1982), pp. 68-75.

[34] See LAURENT, *Plaire et édifier*, pp. 208-214.

narrator. Of these passages 18 are constructed according to a consistent formula, a fixed set of motifs which may be summarized as follows:[35]

a. the descriptive term *miracle*[36]
b. the notion of completion (*finer*, *terminer*)[37] and the intention not to say more[38]
c. the notion of rest (*repos*[*er*])[39]
d. the will to narrate another, even greater wonder[40]
e. deference to the will or pleasure of the audience[41]
f. having another miracle ready (*prest*)[42]
g. the idea of the narrator serving the audience.[43]

Characteristically, it is the motif concerning the pleasure and concurrence of the audience (e) which is the most frequently represented, another indication, perhaps, of adaptability to the requirements of different audiences. The passages which indicate performance breaks incorporate on average three motifs, but the following displays almost all:

Ici, seignurs, si vus agree,
Voldrum faire reposee;
Ne mie pur ço que finee
Seit la reisun ne terminee

De cest miracle mes pur tolir
Le ennui de vus, que dei servir.
Quant vus vendra a pleisir,
Le remanant purrez oïr. (ll. 2053-2060)

[35] In the footnotes those line references for each motif which are printed in italics belong to the passages which indicate a performance break (iii).

[36] *St. Modwenna*, ll. 445, 625, 837, *1107*, *1465*, *1589*, *2057*, 2309, *2434*, 2916, *3393*, *3677*, *4109* (*merveille*), 4135, 4585, 5191, *5739*, 6325, *7409*, 7569, 7729, 8655-8656 (*vertu*).

[37] ll. 837, *1107*, *1465*, *1589*, *2055-2056*, 3393, 3677, 3953, 4585, *5739*, 6325, *6849*, 7591, 8655-8656, *8677*.

[38] ll. 827, 2309, *2433*, 4135, 6325.

[39] ll. *1465*, *1589*, *2053*, *2434*, *5739*, *6171*, *6489*, *7407*, *8677*.

[40] ll. 628, 839, *1592*, 2311, 3062, 3393.

[41] ll. 840, *1465*, *1589*, *2436*, *2920*, 3064, 3393, 3684, 3956, 4110, 4587, 5194, *6165*, 6183, *6849*, *6856*, *7409*, *7413*, 7729, 8076.

[42] ll. *1592*, *2053*, *2058*, 2919, 3393, *7420*,7572.

[43] ll. 2058, 3955, 7739, 8075.

A single quatrain may contain four motifs:

Cest miracle voil finer,
Ne voil plus dire ne cunter.
Un autre grant voil cumencer,
Si vus pleist a escuter. (ll. 837-840)

Such motifs are found in two ([ii] and [iii]) of the following three categories of narratorial address which are found in the *Life*:

(i) General addresses or exhortations to the audience at appropriate moments but with no clear structuring function. These characteristically include the *audite/attendite* formula as in the following:

Seignurs, issi cum vus oez (l. 25)

Oez merveille de beste mue (l. 270)

Oez, seignurs, quel aventure! (ll. 296, 574, 6108)

Seignurs, aiez en remembrance (l. 341)

Ore oez par quel vesdie (ll. 651, 1139)

Oez merveille e verité (ll. 810, 1386)

Ne vus devez esmerviller (l. 1036)

Or oiez en quel manere (l. 1383)

Seignurs, pur Deu ore esgardez
En [voz] curages ... (ll. 1561-1562)

Veez merveille dé dous chaitifs
Dont avant memorie fis (ll. 1713-1714)

Qui oï mes tel aventure? (ll. 2392, 5956)

Oiez, seignurs, merveille grant (ll. 2704, 6274)

Veez, seignurs, quel aventure (l. 2841; *Oiez*, l. 3630)

Unc tel [merveille] ne fud oï
Cum vus purrez oïr ici (ll. 2851-2852)

Oiez, seignurs, ne quidez mie
Ke iceste prophecie
Ne seit tuit bien acumplie (ll. 4057-4059)

Ore oez cum grant dolur (l. 4446)

Si out, seigneurs [= *grant aventure*] (l. 4561)

Oez, seignurs, qu'est avenu (l. 6026)

Oïr poez merveille grant,
Si estre volez entendant (ll. 6039-6040)

Or oez, nus la vus dirrum (l. 6872)

Issi, seignurs, cum vus oez (l. 7905)

Merveille grant oïr purrez,
Si vus, seignurs, i attendez (ll. 8369-8370)

(ii) Addresses which function as miracle markers, demarcating the conclusion of the *miracle* that has been narrated and the start of a new one. There are 21 such addresses.[44]

De cest miracle ne voil plus dire,
Ne mie pur ceo que la matire
Se defaille, ainz voil descrire[45]
Un autre grant, u mis queor tire.[46] (ll. 625-628)

The motif of avoiding tedium sometimes appears:

Pur ço vus voil issi cunter
Iceste estoire, que lung parler

[44] ll. 341-352, 445 ff., 625-628, 837-844, 1973-1976, 2309-2312, 2916-2920, 3061-3064, 3081, 3393-3396, 3677-3684,3953-3960, 4109-4112, 4135-4136, 4585-4588, 5189-5196, 5625-5630, 6149-6152, 6325-6328, 7569-7573/7585-7588, 7729-7732, 8029-8032, 8072-8076.

[45] Cf. ll. 61, 95.

[46] Cf. ll. 96, 3958.

Ne vus peuse ennuer[47]
Ne la brefté de rien grever. (ll. 1873-1876)

The notion of a rest break (*reposee*) may be the only element missing:

Cest miracle est terminez
Mes tant tost cum vus voldrez
Un autre grant oïr purrez,
Qui vus est ja aprestez. (ll. 3393-3396)

The word *miracle* may be replaced by *aventure* or *cunte*:

Icest cunte m'estot finir
E mun chemin avant tenir,
Quant ai enpris de vus servir
A mun poer tuit a pleisir.

Un autre vus voil cunter e dire,
U mun curage e trait e tire,
Cum oï l'avum descrire,
A cels qui sorent la matire. (ll. 3953-3960)

The absence of a break may be explicitly signalled:

Seignurs, merveille cunté ai,
Mais, s'il vus pleist, tut sanz delay
Asez greignur vus cunterai.
E vus l'orrez, tres bien le sai. (ll. 4109-4112)

The narrator marks his offer of a new miracle story with courteous deference ("*A un autre a vos cungez /Mettrum la main*", ll. 4587-4588) and sometimes with the promise of brevity ("*Brevement le voil cunter*", l. 5196).

(iii) Addresses, 10 in number,[48] which, unlike the miracle markers, suggest a performance break. These are the only structuring devices recognized by Laurent, who is guided by the use of the terms *terminer* and *reposer*,[49] despite the fact that the latter term does not occur in the first such narratorial address at

[47] Cf. ll.1108,2058,5195.
[48] ll. 1105-1112, 1465-1468, 1589-1592, 2053-2060, 2433-2436, 5739-5740, 6165-6172, 6849-6856, 7105-7120, 8677-8678.
[49] LAURENT, *Plaire et édifier*, p. 293 n. 39.

ll. 1105-1112 and that there are 8 other addresses in (ii) above which share a set of motifs forming similar interventions, but without the word *reposer*:

> *Ore me voil ici* reposer
> *E cest* miracle terminer.
> *Bien i purrez* recovrer,
> *Quant il vus* plarra *de l'esculter.* (ll. 1465-1468)
>
> *Ne voil plus dire ne cunter*
> *De cest* miracle *sanz* reposer.
> *Quant vus* plarra *de l'escuter,*
> *Plus vus dirrai sanz danger.* (ll. 2433-2436)

The break may be given more extensive treatment:

> *Icest* miracle *finé avum,*
> *Un petitet nus* reposum;
> *Quant vus* plerra, *vus redirum*
> *Un autre* grant, *kar prest l'avum.*
>
> *L'en le dit en reprover,*
> *Ke promettre e rien doner*
> *Fait le fol recunforter,*
> *Mais jo de ceo n'ai mester.*
>
> *Ma promesse vus voil tenir,*
> *Ne vus puis a ceo faillir;*
> *Ore n'i ad fors de l'oïr,*
> *S'il* vus veint a plaisir. (ll. 1589-1600)
>
> *Ici, seignurs, si* vus agree,
> *Voldrum faire* reposee;
> *Ne mie pur ço que* finee
> *Seit la reisun ne* terminee
>
> *De cest* miracle *mes pur tolir*
> *Le ennui de vus,* que dei servir.
> *Quant vus* vendra a pleisir,
> *Le remanant purrez oïr.* (ll. 2053-2060)

The narrator sometimes provides a proleptic allusion to the next narrative after the break:

Cum nus aprés vus cunterum,
Quant a iço venu serrum. (ll. 6169-6170)

The same two lines introduce another transitional passage (ll. 7405-7420) which announces the forthcoming matter as two miracles which took place in Scotland and the founding of the abbey at Burton.

The 'interval' is at the audience's discretion:

Iceste vie est termine[e]
Pur ço, seignurs, s'il vus agree,
Ici seit bien la reposee.
Nus la ferum sanz tresturnee

Kar la matire vient siwant,
Que est pur veir plener[e] e grant;
Pur ço larrum ici a tant
Desqu'il vus pleise oïr avant. (ll. 6849-6856)

In the one passage in this category where the word *reposer* is not used, the narrator explains the nature of the break:

Nel di pur ceo que seit fini
Cest miracle, que avez oï,
Ainz l'ai pur ceo en dous parti
Pur le[s] enuis, dunt jo vus di. (ll. 1109-1112)

As we can now see, the *Life* is notable for the density of oral references and the systematic function of transitional passages marking the end of a miracle story or the insertion of a performance break. The emphasis on presentation of the material and its emotive aspect (there are over 40 occurrences of the words *merveille*, *esmerveillier* etc.) far outweighs in this work any rhetorical, decorative aspect, which is unremarkable. There are few texts which foreground phatic elements quite as clearly as does this text. But how are we to interpret them?

It is tempting to answer the question by straightaway citing the evidence of the Campsey MS, where on f. 265v a fourteenth-century hand has written "*Ce livre deviseie a la priorie de Kanpseie de lire a mangier*".[50] It is clear, though,

[50] RUSSELL, "The Campsey Collection", pp. 63-64, reviews some of the interpretations that have been offered of *deviser*, including the sense of 'bequeath'. There is no conclusive indication and the most plausible explanation is that the Campsey MS represents the adaptation of an earlier manuscript for use at Campsey. It is possible, but unproven, that such an adaptation was made at the instigation of Isabel de Warenne, Countess of Arundel.

that the *Life of St Modwenna* was not actually composed at Campsey (the only link is really only supplied by an interpolation in the *Life of St Osyth*, which does have East Anglian connections). The conclusion of the *Life* refers to the work or composition as a whole as "*liveret*":

> *Pur ceo voil ci terminer*
> *Icest liveret e reposer.* (ll. 8677-8678)

If we study the size of the passages demarcated by miracle markers or performance breaks, the results are so variable as to suggest little practical applicability to performance. The sequence of miracle stories, marked by the narrator, produces a series of sections of the following lengths: 446-182-216-1032-436-608-144-332-288-276-152-24-452-608-434-522-176-1245-159-300-44. The division of the text into performance sessions yields even more disparate results, as can be seen from the following figures: 1112-356-124-468-376-3304-432-684-264-1558. The evidence might suggest that what we have here is textual *imitation* of oral recitation techniques, rather than their *implementation*. Michèle Perret remarks concerning narratorial interventions in the epic:

> *On peut néanmoins se demander s'il s'agit là d'une véritable situation de communication directe, ou de sa représentation mimétique, une vocalisation d'un texte déjà très élaboré ... on peut donc supposer que ces signes de la communication du locuteur avec son public, inutiles tant que la récitation du texte se produisait dans un espace commun, deviennent de plus en plus importants à mesure que l'on s'éloigne d'une situation de pure oralité.*[51]

She concludes,

> *L'oralité dont il est question n'est, bien entendu, que celle de la récitation du texte, un texte 'vocalisé' par son scripteur, qui a distribué, pour souligner les points forts de son récit, des marques d'oralité à l'intention d'un locuteur conçu comme un simple exécutant. ... de fréquentes interventions ... montrent bien, en effet, qu'il y a ici mimésis d'une situation de pure oralité, où locuteur et public seraient en présence, et où l'énonciation du texte correspondrait à sa production.*[52]

After these elements, or perhaps we should say simulacra, of oral recitation attributed to the narrator, it is worth considering the implications of the text's

[51] M. PERRET, "De l'espace romanesque à la matérialité du livre. L'espace énonciatif des premiers romans en prose", *Poétique* 13 (1982), pp. 173-182, at p. 176.

[52] "De l'espace romanesque", pp. 176 n. 7, 177.

formal composition in monorhyme quatrains. These have been held by Robson to represent "an archaic stanza form, a pattern of Romance versification peculiar to this country", to derive from a medieval Latin hymn form, and hence to suggest that they were sung.[53] There are several caveats that need to be entered in this respect. First, the octosyllables (sometimes heptasyllables) are rather clearly divided into hemistichs. Second, the author makes considerable use of enjambement. Third, this enjambement extends over multiple stanzas, in such a way as to suggest that stanza divisions are of little significance.[54] The whole work comprises 2173 quatrains. Of these approximately 25% (588) form pairs through enjambement; 198 form triads; 80 compose quartets; 30 are arranged in pentads; 18 represent three groups of hexads; 7 form a heptad, and nine a group of 9. These figures mean that 900 quatrains, approximately 41.4% of the total, do not represent autonomous units.[55] Another consideration is the relatively high percentage, 32.6% (2840 lines), of speech/dialogue in this hagiographical narrative. Despite Legge's assertion that "the question whether *St. Brendan* and *St. Modwenna* were ever sung must remain an open one, but at any rate it can be stated that they are written in a form which is singable",[56] it seems very unlikely, given the highly variable internal structures of the poem (length of narrative episodes, grouping of quatrains) that the *Life* was intended for singing.

The Campsey MS provides special indications of its own concerning the use to which the *Life of St Modwenna* may have been put. First, each stanza begins with a decorated initial, alternating red and blue (the same is true of the other stanzaic text in the MS, the *Life of Becket* by Guernes de Pont-Sainte-Maxence), with even larger initials marking major sections of text. Second, physical marking of places in the texts is indicated by holes and threads which suggest that *scedulae* were attached with the function of bookmarks. In the case of the *Life of St Modwenna* such a *scedula* is found three times: opposite the opening historiated initial, opposite one of the textual divisions of the poem at l. 1600, and at another division at l. 3961, thus dividing the text into three unequal sections of roughly 12, 22 and 35 folios, evidence perhaps of a one-time reading, but not necessarily a public one. Third, in place of a concluding rubric the text is equipped with an epilogue of nine stanzas, forming ll. 8657-8692, not

53 C.A. ROBSON, review of *St. Modwenna*, ed. BAKER and BELL, *Medium Aevum* 18 (1949), pp. 49-60 , at p. 50.

54 LEGGE, *Anglo-Norman Literature*, p. 262: "In *St. Modwenna* there is often enjambement between the stanzas, but this is not an incontrovertible argument that it was read".

55 Cf. ROBSON, p. 51: "It seems possible that performer and hearers regarded the four-line monorhymed stanza as a single rhythmic unit".

56 LEGGE, *Anglo-Norman Literature*, p. 262.

found in the Digby MS,[57] but printed by Baker and Bell, ending "*La paternoster dium a tant*". This is followed by text in Latin consisting of an antiphon, versicle and prayer, written as if forming two six-line stanzas, a purely visual effect, since the line-breaks do not correspond with the rhymes and the final prayer is in any case in prose:

> *Prudens et vigilans virgo qualis es cum sponso illo que te elegit de mundo, quam pulcra quam mirabilis, quanta luce spectabilis inter Syon juvenculas et Jherusalem filias thalamo guades regio conjuncta dei filio. V~. Diffusa est.* **oro~** *Omnipotens sempiterne deus, auctor virtutis et amator virginitatis, da nobis quis sancte Moduenne virginis placitis tibi meritis commendari, cuius vita merito castitatis tibi conplacuit, per [Christum dominum nostrum].*[58]

Russell remarks that "the intercessional power of the virgin Modwenna is given special emphasis by the antiphonal liturgical coda in Latin" and comments thus on the conclusion:

> It would seem this ending in fact was meant to be performed communally, and what might be seen as simply a rhetorical stance adopted by the narrator in other epilogues, here is instead a literal transition to audience participation and response. The emphasis on communal response to, and sharing in, the life of Modwenna may account for the absence of a reference to the narrator as author or translator in an epilogue.[59]

Meal-time reading, of course, was a well established monastic and conventual custom and much is known from monastic reading lists about texts destined for reading in the refectory or at collations which sometimes continued readings which had been begun in liturgical offices. Saints' lives were a staple diet, though usually considerably shorter and less ambitious than those included in the Campsey MS, but evidence persists that readings from extensive works did also take place. The consistent addressing of the audience as "*seigneurs*" suggests that the works were originally written for a male monastic audience[60] and that no alteration was felt necessary (on account of their frequency and metrical position) in presenting the collection of lives to an audience of nuns.

[57] The Campsey MS has a further 139 stanzas (ll. 4333-4884) which are absent from the Digby MS.

[58] Quoted from RUSSELL, "The Campsey Collection", p. 81.

[59] RUSSELL, "The Campsey Collection", pp. 63, 61.

[60] See I. SHORT, "The Patronage of Beneit's *Vie de Thomas Becket*", *Medium Aevum* 56 (1987), pp. 239-256, at p. 250 n. 43 and GALLAIS, "Recherches", pp. 333-334.

What conclusions may be drawn from this survey of a much neglected text? The Anglo-Norman *Life of St Modwenna* turns out to be rich in material concerning performance and audience. The choice of verse form, monorhyme quatrains, is unusual. Robson's view was that the author deliberately mixed eight- and seven-syllable lines to produce stanzas which regularly show 30 syllables. Since the *Life* is a long poem, it is apparently divided by the translator into "a series of fits convenient for chanting or reciting at a sitting, each with an epilogue announcing the subject of the next".[61] Clearly, saints' lives rely on techniques of both oral and written traditions.[62] The question of orally composed poetry in Old French is particularly delicate. One reason is the prompt textualization of poetry after it is thought to have been composed, so that evidence of improvisation is elusive. There is a real difficulty in distinguishing textual mobility (*mouvance*) that comes from improvisation and adaptation, and the variation, or incidence of variants, produced by creative and quite independent scribes (*variance*). This last factor has led some text-critics to challenge even the idea of an archetype. Certainly nothing was fixed for long! But perhaps these factors lead us to the crux of the matter: the essential flexibility, adaptability and versatility of the medieval text. In the interests of taxonomy texts have been over-rigidly identified and allocated to generic types and classes. But the evidence of their manuscript context and the possible modes of reception and transmission may present, as Keith Busby has shown,[63] a quite different picture. The evidence of 'oral' elements in the *Life of St Modwenna* is unusually rich and yet all we can confidently state is that the text lends itself to episodic recital and is written in a style which creates the impression (illusion?) of intimacy with a carefully targeted audience. It may be, of course, that both manuscript copies have modified the original along these lines. But the genesis of the text is irrecoverable and we should compensate by an alert awareness of the adaptability of medieval literature, which, however rich or poor its transmission, must have circulated on circuitous paths and been used to respond to varied requirements of patrons and audiences alike.[64] This is the position provided for by Dennis Green's recognition that oral recitation and private reading might coexist as optional realizations of the presentation of texts.

[61] LEGGE, *Anglo-Norman Literature*, p. 263.

[62] See E.B. VITZ, "Vie, légende, littérature: traditions orales et écrites dans les histoires des saints", *Poétique* 18 (1987), pp. 387-402.

[63] K. BUSBY, *Codex and Context: Reading Old French Verse Narrative in Manuscript*, 2 vols. (Amsterdam and New York, 2002).

[64] For an excellent illustration of these points see A. VÀRVARO, "Elaboration des textes et modalités du récit dans la littérature française médiévale", *Romania* 119 (2001), pp. 1-75.

Fictions of Orality in Troubadour Poetry

SIMON GAUNT

La brisure marque l'impossibilité pour un signe, pour l'unité d'un signifiant et d'un signifié, de se produire dans la plénitude d'un présent et d'une présence absolue. C'est pourquoi il n'y a pas de parole pleine. (Jacques Derrida)[1]

Nos textes ne nous livrent qu'une forme vide et sans doute profondément altérée de ce qui fut, dans un autre contexte sensori-moteur, parole pleine. (Paul Zumthor)[2]

Received wisdom on troubadour poetry tends to stress the orality of its rhetoric, its phatic and dramatic nature, the need to envisage performance in order to understand its humour, social reference, and power to move. Thus, even while cautioning against a reading of early troubadour poetry that relies on "overemphasis on the oral performative mode" precisely so he can begin to examine how early troubadours are "performed" more than a century later in the different (written) medium of the *chansonniers*, that is to say in the books through which we know them, Stephen G. Nichols insists on "the importance of oral performance and transmission for representing and preserving the songs".[3] Unlike some scholars, Nichols does not assume that the apparent immediacy of performance precludes the displacements and artifice of

[1] J. DERRIDA, *De la Grammatologie* (Paris, 1967), p. 102.

[2] P. ZUMTHOR, *La Poésie et la voix dans la littérature médiévale* (Paris, 1987), p. 68.

[3] S.J. NICHOLS, "The Early Troubadours: Guilhem IX to Bernart de Ventadorn", in: *The Troubadours: an Introduction*, ed. S. GAUNT and S. KAY (Cambridge, 1999), pp. 66-82, at p. 68.

representation,[4] but he does nonetheless assume a primary orality for early troubadour poetry, grounded in what he calls a "performative presence", which he then contrasts to a "performative absence" that characterizes a subsequent written tradition.[5]

In this chapter, my intention is to argue for the importance of writing in the transmission and reception of troubadour poetry not only in the period that led up to the production of the great *chansonniers* from which we edit these texts, but also in the twelfth-century heyday of the tradition. Let me be clear: I am not suggesting that troubadour lyrics were never performed orally. Nor am I seeking to deny their dramatic quality. My point rather is to call into question – from a perspective that is informed by Jacques Derrida's early writing – the category of the 'oral' that inflects so much writing about the troubadours (and indeed about much early medieval literature) with a view to putting forward a rather different view of troubadour poetry as generated by a culture in which the importance and pre-eminence of writing was increasingly recognized. I should stress, however, that by writing I mean not simply the physical act of writing and its material product, but rather what Derrida means by the term *écriture*, that is a conception of language grounded in a view of the sign itself as deriving from the written word as opposed to speech. My purpose is therefore to counter the nostalgia for the presence and immediacy of oral performance that in my view underscores some scholarship on troubadour poetry (and indeed on many medieval texts). I wish to suggest that precisely because this nostalgia is to some extent at least encouraged by the texts themselves, the representation of orality in the troubadour tradition should to be seen as an *effect*, even as a fiction, of a textual culture: to take what is said about orality in these written sources at face value is therefore perhaps to read uncritically. Indeed, the actual oral and performative dimensions of medieval texts cannot be recuperated by reading in this way. Furthermore, we should not assume that oral communication *necessarily* guarantees immediacy or presence in any case.

There will be three sections in what follows: I shall begin with some theoretical reflections; the second section will give a brief outline of the representation of orality in troubadour songbooks; finally, I will offer a case study of the centrality of writing to the lyrics and poetics of one early troubadour, namely Marcabru, before drawing some conclusions.

[4] On this point Rhoda Sutherland's classic article remains indispensable: D.R. SUTHERLAND, "L'élément théâtral dans la *canso* chez les troubadours de l'époque classique", *Revue de Langue et de Littérature d'Oc* 12-13 (1962-63), pp. 95-101.

[5] NICHOLS, "Early Troubadours", p. 70.

The Nature of Writing

Medieval literary scholarship has long considered orality to be crucial to any authentic understanding of medieval texts (and I use the word 'authentic' advisedly). The quotation from Zumthor given as an epigraph illustrates neatly the widespread hostility towards writing that paradoxically seems to underscore the work of people who devote their life to reading old books, which gives in turn the belief that what medievalists find on the page is but an empty, much diluted record of a *parole pleine* that preceded it, an oral *parole* that would have been characterized by immediacy, presence, authenticity. This tendency to value the spoken word over the written work is altogether characteristic generally of scholars who work on orality. Thus Walter Ong, author of several influential books on orality, writes: "By contrast with natural, oral speech, writing is completely artificial. There is no way to write 'naturally'. Oral speech is fully natural to human beings in the sense that every human being in every culture who is not physiologically or psychologically impaired learns to talk".[6] 'Oral' speech here is deemed to be natural (thereby implicitly marked as good), whereas writing by contrast (and also by inference) is cultural (thereby implicitly marked as bad). Tellingly the idea that speech is 'natural' is not questioned here, nor elsewhere in Ong's work.[7]

For French medievalists, the drive to establish literary genres such as the lyric, the *chansons de geste* or the *lai* as 'oral' reflects a desire to claim for these texts an unmediated immediacy in their original context that would contrast them to the arch artificiality and ironic distance of other (written) genres, most notably of course courtly romance, though it has been argued recently (implausibly in my view), that even courtly romance, was originally an oral, performed genre.[8] To turn specifically to troubadour lyric, this is apparently the

[6] W.J. ONG, *Orality and Literacy: the Technologizing of the Word* (London and New York, 1982), p. 82. Although Ong remarks defensively that "to say writing is artificial is not to condemn or praise it", he speaks of writing as "contrived" and involving "alienation", words which in my view have implicitly negative connotations.

[7] A cogent critique of Ong, informed by Derrida, is, however, offered by J. DAGENAIS, "That Bothersome Residue: Toward a Theory of the Physical Text", in: *Vox Intexta: Orality and Textuality in the Middle Ages*, ed. A.N. DOANE and C. BRAUN (Madison and London, 1991), pp. 246-259.

[8] Apart from Zumthor, proponents of orality among French medievalists include notably J. RYCHNER, *La Chanson de geste: Essai sur l'art épique des jongleurs* (Geneva, 1955) and E.B. VITZ, *Orality and Performance in Early French Romance* (Woodbridge, 1999). For the argument against proponents of orality in Old French literature, see S. GAUNT, *Retelling the Tale: An Introduction to Medieval French Literature* (London, 2001), particularly the Introduction and Chapters 1-3.

oral genre *par excellence* since the poems are sung rather than simply voiced, and therefore necessarily performed. By and large Zumthor's account of orality in the 1970s and 80s has been strongly endorsed by a number of important books. For example Amelia Van Vleck argues that the form of troubadour lyrics often anticipates and encourages oral transmission and adaptation in and through performance; she even goes so far as to suggest that some troubadours evince hostility to writing.[9] Similarly, although she disagrees with Zumthor on some fundamental points, Sarah Kay broadly accepts his account of the orality of troubadour lyric and in a chapter entitled "Performance", she writes "the attitudes adopted by the Occitan lyric towards different media privilege oral over written communication precisely because of the subjective value invested in orality as presence".[10] Now unlike Van Vleck, Kay is also fully aware that "the categories of orality and writing are neither stable nor discrete",[11] and this is a point I wish to pursue. But I see the implications of the interpenetration of orality and writing as more far-reaching than Kay since, if one follows Derrida's argument about writing and orality, the very notion of orality is and can only be the product of a written culture, while the primacy of the written sign to the culture of the troubadours that I shall be advocating calls into question the very idea of presence.[12]

The single most influential piece of scholarship today on orality and literacy in medieval Western Europe today is undoubtedly Michael Clanchy's *From Memory to Written Record.*[13] It remains a constant source of surprise to me, however, that advocates of the orality of medieval vernacular texts cite Clanchy's work as evidence for the persistent orality of medieval culture when this is a book about the astonishing rise, if not of literacy in the Middle Ages, then certainly of the dependence on the written word. What Clanchy shows is a dramatic – and initially purely pragmatic – increase in the use of writing for record keeping in the twelfth century – particularly in England and France during the reigns of Henry II and Philip Augustus. To be sure most individuals in all classes could not read or write, but to infer from this that we are dealing with what Zumthor calls *une oralité mixte* is perhaps to oversimplify.[14] In any case, the literacy of the laity – including that of the chivalric classes – has

[9] A. VAN VLECK, *Memory and Re-Creation in Troubadour Lyric* (Berkeley, 1991).

[10] S. KAY, *Subjectivity in Troubadour Poetry* (Cambridge, 1990), pp. 132-133.

[11] KAY, *Subjectivity*, p. 133.

[12] Kay in fact suggests that troubadour lyric "only rarely" supports the idea of *écriture* proposed by Derrida; see *Subjectivity*, p. 134.

[13] M.T. CLANCHY, *From Memory to Written Record: England 1066-1307* (London, 1979).

[14] By *oralité mixte*, Zumthor seems to mean an oral culture in which the influence of writing is felt, but remains secondary, see *Poésie*, p. 49.

probably been underestimated.[15] We might also usefully turn to the work of Brian Stock, which deserves attention at least as much as Clanchy's, though it is cited less frequently, perhaps because of its theoretical difficulty.[16] Stock, like Clanchy sees the twelfth century as the key period in the rise of literacy. Whereas both scholars are interested in considering the impact of the increased use of documents on all people – the illiterate as well as the literate – Stock, in a move explicitly informed by Derrida's *De la Grammatologie*, seeks to trouble the opposition between orality and writing, and he therefore sees the implications of the rise of literacy as more far-reaching than Clanchy.

For Stock, in a society for which writing was becoming a prime means of record keeping or intellectual debate, *all* discourse, whether spoken or written, becomes subject to what he calls "a new style of reflection", which includes of course reflection on language itself. Thus: "the written did not simply supersede the oral, though that happened in large measure: a new type of interdependence also arose between the two. In other words, oral discourse effectively began to function within a universe of communications governed by texts".[17] The fundamental changes in *mentalité* of which Stock speaks here are, of course, happening in precisely the same period that sees the rise of vernacular literature in France and Occitania.

Stock further argues that the notion of orality itself needs calling into question: "The present range of meaning of the pair [orality and writing] does not exist much before the nineteenth century ... The intellectual origins of both ideas are Western, and to non-Westerners they smack of ethnocentrism ... it may be asked whether as literates, we understand orality as anything but the opposite of literacy ... studies of orality are sometimes nostalgic pleas on behalf of traditions that have disappeared or are threatened. Such works imply a rejection of the literate norms of today in favour of an earlier, 'purer' state of mind".[18] Quite apart from the scepticism I share with Stock about the folksy and nostalgic view of a Middle Ages in which people sang to each other a lot, the anachronistic nature of 'orality' as an intellectual tool for examining

[15] See M.B. PARKES, "The Literacy of the Laity", in: *Literature and Western Civilisation*, ed. D. DAICHES and A. THORLBY, vol. 2: *The Medieval World* (London, 1973), pp. 555-577; and R.V. TURNER, "The *Miles Literatus* in Twelfth- and Thirteenth-Century England: How Rare a Phenomenon?", *American Historical Review* 83 (1978), pp. 928-945.

[16] B. STOCK, *The Implications of Literacy: Written Language and Models of Interpretation in the Eleventh and Twelfth Centuries* (Princeton, 1983); see also his *Listening for the Text: On the Uses of the Past* (Philadelphia, 1996).

[17] STOCK, *Implications*, p. 3.

[18] STOCK, *Listening*, p. 9.

medieval literature, particularly when 'oral' textuality is contrasted with 'written' textuality, needs, in my view, to be taken seriously.

Any straightforward opposition between orality and writing is hard to sustain. There is, for instance, overwhelming evidence that the majority of vernacular manuscripts were not read silently, but read aloud.[19] Indeed for Laura Kendrick, the troubadour lyric is from the outset grounded in an "audio-visual aesthetic", playing on ambiguities and uncertainties generated by "the unreliability of the 'technology of writing'" and by the movement of the lyrics between their written form and performance.[20] Written texts were "voiced" and a written text will often assume an *audience* of *listeners* while nonetheless invoking a written text or even specifically signalling the mediation or presence of a book. Consider these examples from Marie de France:

Les contes que jo sai verais,
dunt li Breton unt fait les lais,
vos conterai assez briefment.
El chief de cest comencement
sulunc la letre e l'escriture
vos mosterrai une aventure,
ki en Bretaigne la menur
avint al tens anciënur.[21]

I will briefly tell you the tales that I know to be true, about which the Bretons composed *lais*. As this work opens, according to what is recorded in writing, I will relate for you an adventure from olden times that came about in Brittany.

De lur amur e de lur bien
firent un lai li ancïen;
e jeo ki l'ai mis en escrit

[19] This argument is made strongly in relation to later medieval texts by J. COLEMAN, *Public Reading and the Reading Public in Late Medieval England and France* (Cambridge, 1996: *Cambridge Studies in Medieval Literature* 26); see also D.H. GREEN, *Medieval Listening and Reading: The Primary Reception of German Literature 800-1300* (Cambridge, 1994).

[20] See L. KENDRICK, *The Game of Love: Troubadour Wordplay* (Berkeley, Los Angeles and London, 1989), pp. 30-31 and p. 48; but see also the whole chapter "Reading Troubadour Verse: the Adventure of the Signifier" *passim* (pp. 24-52). Kendrick's suggestive and provocative book nonetheless clings to a binary opposition between writing and orality which I find unsatisfactory, see for example p. 31: "For the medieval reader, the written text of a lyric was only a *semblance* or visible sign of the oral text".

[21] Marie de France, *Lais*, ed. K. WARNKE and trans. L. HARF-LANCNER (Paris, 1990), *Guigemar*, ll. 19-26.

el recunter mult me delit.[22]

The people from olden times composed a *lai* about their love and happiness; and I, who transposed it to writing, take great pleasure in relating it.

Asez me plest e bien le vueil
del lai qu'um nume Chievrefueil
que la verité vus en cunt
coment fu fez, de quei e dunt.
Plusur le m'unt cunté e dit
e jeo l'ai trové en escrit
de Tristram e de la reïne.[23]

It pleases me and gives me pleasure to tell you the truth about the *lai* that is known as *Chievrefeuil*, how it was composed, about what and why. Quite a few people have told and related it to me and I found it written down, about Tristan and the queen.

A direct address to an audience, the use of verbs like *oïr*, *dire*, *cunter*, *recunter*, *escouter* do not necessarily indicate that a text is simply a reflection of an originally textless performance. Indeed, markers of oral presentation often sit alongside clear indications that texts were composed and transmitted using the medium of writing, as we see here. Thus Chrétien de Troyes refers to his *Chevalier de la Charrete* as his *livre* while directly addressing his audience 'orally' as *vos* throughout, and *La Mort le roi Artu* concludes with Walter Map "falling silent", but as he "finishes his book".[24] Furthermore, the very notion of 'orality' derives from an intellectual perspective that is imbued with writing. A truly oral culture, one which had never encountered writing, could not, by

[22] *Lais*: *Milun*, ll. 531-534.

[23] *Lais*: *Chievrefueil*, ll. 1-7.

[24] See *Les Romans de Chrétien de Troyes III: Le Chevalier de la Charrete*, ed. M. ROQUES (Paris, 1963), l. 25 and, for a famous instance of his addressing his audience as *vos* but in a manner which interestingly supposes familiarity with the mechanisms of writing, see ll. 4550-4551, "*Bien poez antendre et gloser / vos qui avez fet autretel*" ("You who have done the same can indeed understand and gloss this"); see also *La Mort le roi Artu*, ed. J. FRAPPIER, 3rd edition (Geneva, 1964), § 204, 8-13: "*Si se test ore atant mestre Gautiers Map de l'Estoire de Lancelot, car bien a tout mené a fin selonc les choses qui en avindrent, et fenist ci son livre si outreement que aprés ce n'en porroit nus riens conter qui n'en mentist de toutes choses*" ("Now Master Walter Map falls silent about the story of *Lancelot*, since he has brought everything to a conclusion, following events as they happened, and he finishes his book here to the bitter end so that nothing more can be said afterwards which would not be downright lies").

definition have any sense of the 'oral', as the category itself only makes sense in relation to the 'written'.

The assumption that the oral can somehow be self-sufficient, independent of writing is of course precisely the position that Derrida attacks throughout *De la Grammatologie.* As I have already noted, for scholars of orality, such as Zumthor, Ong, and in Derrida's view Saussure, speech is primary, natural and a marker of presence, whereas writing is secondary and derivative because it *represents* speech, and thereby marks an absence: "il y a donc une bonne et une mauvaise écriture: la bonne et naturelle, l'inscription dans le cœur et l'âme: la perverse et l'artificieuse, la technique, exilée dans l'extériorité du corps".[25] For Derrida, however, all language marks absence and deferral. As Christina Howells puts it (with useful clarity): "Language is 'originally' figurative, 'direct' painting is already allegorical ... The supposed supplementarity of writing is precisely what constitutes human society. Alienation from presence is thus paradoxically originary ... it is supplementarity itself which is originary ... The articulation of writing is not a pale substitute of the living presence of the accents of speech: it is the origin of language itself".[26] An oral, primary and originary, language in which the speaker is totally present ("*une parole pleine*" as Derrida puts it in the quotation used here as an epigraph) is a myth constituted by the supplementarity of all language: "la prétendue dérivation de l'écriture ... n'a été possible qu'à une condition: que le langage 'originel', 'naturel', etc. n'ait jamais existé, qu'il n'ait jamais été intact, qu'il ait toujours été lui-même une écriture".[27] This gives rise to the notion of *archi-écriture*, which designates the supplementarity and *différance* of all language.

Writing, then, becomes less important in Derrida's argument than the fact that writing illustrates how all language functions (rather than speech, which was Saussure's starting point). He does, however, continue to insist throughout *De la Grammatologie* on the role writing plays in shaping our conception of language. Most importantly, without writing, we can have no theory of the sign: "il n'y a pas de signe linguistique avant l'écriture"; or at more length, he says:

> *Le système de l'écriture en général n'est pas extérieur au système de la langue en général ... l'écriture en général n'est pas 'image' ou 'figuration' ... c'est qu'un certain modèle d'écriture s'est nécessairement mais provisoirement imposé ...*

[25] DERRIDA, *Grammatologie*, p. 30.

[26] C. HOWELLS, *Derrida: Deconstruction from Phenomenology to Ethics* (Cambridge, 1999), p. 60.

[27] DERRIDA, *Grammatologie*, p. 83.

> *comme instrument et technique de représentation d'un système de langue. Et que ce mouvement, unique dans son style, a même été si profond qu'il a permis de penser,* dans la langue, *des concepts comme ceux de signe, de technique, de représentation, de langue.*[28]

Representations of Orality in Troubadour Songbooks

My contention in the final section of this chapter will be that Marcabru's poetry represents language and evinces a notion of the sign that resonates strongly with Derrida's theory of *écriture* rather than with any sense of primary or unmediated orality. Before turning to Marcabru, however, I should like to offer a few brief observations on the troubadour *chansonniers*, since these make an interesting case study of the relation between orality and literacy in medieval vernacular culture, being as they are written repositories for texts that are supposedly initially oral. Indeed the *chansonniers* will often represent the texts they transmit as oral performances. In my conclusion, I will endeavour to reconcile this representation of troubadour song as primarily oral with my more esoteric findings in relation on Marcabru.

Some *chansonniers* include *vidas* and *razos* that seek either to give a brief outline of a troubadour's life, often suggesting a biographical explanation of his songs, or alternatively to explain the circumstances that lay behind the composition of an individual lyric. *Vidas* and *razos* will often portray texts as orally performed, and also by implication as orally composed and transmitted. One of the more interesting examples of this is this *razo* to a song by Arnaut Daniel:

> *E fon aventura qu'el fon en la cort del rey Richart d'Englaterra, et estant en la cort, us autres joglars escomes lo com el trobava en pus caras rimas que el. Ar-*naut[z] *tenc so ad esquern e feron messios, cascu[s] de son palafre, que no fera, en poder del rey. E.l rey[s] enclaus cascu en una cambra. E.N A*rnaut[z], *de fasti que n'ac, non ac poder qe lasses un mot ab autre. Lo joglar[s] fes son cantar leu e tost; e[t] els non avian mas detz jorns d'espazi, e devia.s jutgar per lo rey a cap de cinc jorns. Lo joglar[s] demandet a.N A*rnaut *si avia fag, e.N A*rnaut[z] *respos que oc, passat a tres jorns; e no.n avia pessat. E.l joglar[s] cantava tota nueg sa canso, per so que be la saubes. E.N A*rnautz *pesset co.l traysses isquern; tan que venc una nueg, e.l joglar[s] la cantava, e.N A*rnaut[z] *la va tota arretener, e.l so. E can foro denan lo rey, N'Arnaut[z] dis que volia retraire sa chanso, e comenset mot be la chanso que.l joglar[s] avia facha. E.l joglar[s], can l'auzic, gardet lo en*

[28] DERRIDA, *Grammatologie*, pp. 26 and 63.

> *la cara, e dis qu'el l'avia facha. E.l reys dis co.s podia far; e.l joglar[s] preguet al rey qu'el ne saubes lo ver; e.l rey[s] demandec a.N* Arnaut *com era estat. E.N* Arnaut[z] *comtet li tot com era estat, e.l rey[s] ac ne gran gaug e tenc so tot a gran esquern; e foro* aquitiat li gatge, *et a cascu fes donar bels dos. E fo donatz lo cantar a.N* Arnaut Daniel, *que di: "Anc yeu non l'ac, mas ela m'a".*[29]

> And it so happened that he was at king Richard of England's court, and there was another minstrel at court who challenged him, claiming he could compose in richer rhymes. Arnaut thought this was hilarious and each bet his palfrey that the other could not do this, with the king as arbiter. And the king shut each one up in a room. And Arnaut, because he was bored, could not string two words together. The minstrel composed his song swiftly and promptly: the court was staying put for no more than ten days and the king was to deliver his judgement after just five days. The minstrel asked Sir Arnaut if he had composed his song and Arnaut replied that he had, three days earlier; but he had not actually thought of anything. And the minstrel was singing his song all night so that he might know it well. And Sir Arnaut thought of a good joke to play on him: when night came and the minstrel was singing his song, Sir Arnaut sets about retaining the whole thing, including the tune. And when they were before the king, Sir Arnaut said that he wished to sing his song, and began heartily to sing the song the minstrel had composed. When the minstrel heard it, he looked him in the face and said that he had composed it. And the king asked how this could be; and the minstrel asked the king to get to the bottom of this; and so the king asked Sir Arnaut what was going on. And Sir Arnaut told him everything that had happened; and the king thought this was very funny and a jolly good joke; and the bets were acquitted and he gave each one fine gifts. And the song, which says "*Anc yeu non l'ac, mas ela m'a*" was given to Sir Arnaut Daniel.

No mention is made of writing when the two minstrels are locked in their separate rooms here. It seems implicit in this text that the two poets are expected to compose without the aid of writing. Indeed, it is also implicit in this story that a song could be transmitted orally with relative ease. Arnaut learns to perform his rival's song simply by hearing it rehearsed throughout the night and this *razo* apparently, therefore, offers an intriguing representation of a particularly bizarre instance of oral transmission, which nonetheless apparently goes to show that oral transmission was unproblematic and unsurprising.

[29] Cited from *Biographies des troubadours: textes provençaux des XIIIe et XIVe siècles*, ed. J. BOUTIÈRE and A.H. SCHUTZ, 2nd edition (Paris, 1973), IX, B.

Fig. 1 Paris, Bibliothèque Nationale, fr. 12474, f. 1r. Photo: Bibliothèque Nationale de France.

In a number of other *razos*, songs are represented as impacting upon people's lives because they are performed orally, because people hear them. For example, in the celebrated 'eaten heart' story that is retold as a *razo* to Guillem de Cabestaing's "*Li dous cossire*",[30] the jealous husband is provoked into action by hearing the song performed: "*E quant R[aimons] de Castel Rossillon auzi la canson q'En G[uillems] avia faita, el entendet e creset qe de sua moillier l'agues faita*" ("And when Raimon de Castel Roussillon heard the song that Sir William had composed, he understood and believed that he had composed it about his wife").[31] Similarly, in the *razo* to "*Mout eron doutz miei cossier*", Alfonso II of Aragon is said to become jealous when he hears the songs that Arnaut de Maruelh composes about the Countess of Bézier, with whom they are both smitten.[32]

This representation in the *chansonniers* of songs circulating orally and impacting through oral performance on the lives of those that hear them as well as on the lives of the people whose feelings they ostensibly record resonates

[30] See *Les Chansons de Guilhem de Cabestanh*, ed. A. LÅNGFORS (Paris, 1924), V.

[31] *Biographies des troubadours*, XCIV, C, *H*, § 10.

[32] *Biographies des troubadours*, VII, B, § 3.

strongly with the famous and much-cited stanza in which Jaufre Rudel sends his song off into the world "*senes breu de pargamina*" ("without parchment sheet"), a statement which is often taken as firm proof of the grounding of early troubadour lyric in oral rather than written culture.[33] We might also consider, as Giuseppe Noto has remarked, that representations of troubadours' writing in *chansonniers* – whether this be in the lyrics themselves or in *vidas* and *razos* – are extremely rare,[34] and that troubadours are usually illustrated in poses that suggest singing, or some activity with which they are associated (such as riding a horse), but not reading or writing. An obvious and illustrious exception here is Giraut de Borneil, who in *chansonnier M*, is famously illustrated in somewhat resplendent scholarly garb sitting at a lectern reading (see fig. 1, Paris, Bibliothèque Nationale fonds français 12474, f. 1r; the rubric reads "*Chansos qe fes Girars de borneilh*", that is "the songs that Giraut de Borneil composed"). But this could be taken to be the exception that proves the rule, in that Giraut is of course celebrated as the "*maestre dels trobadors*" ("master of the troubadours") because "*savis hom fo de letras*" ("he was a wise and lettered man").[35] The *chansonniers* seem therefore to record an oral court culture, in which songs were composed and transmitted orally and in which writing was the exception rather than the rule. Why then am I reluctant to accept this picture at face value?

The Nature of the Sign in Marcabru

In this section I shall take Marcabru as an exemplary early troubadour to examine the importance of writing (real writing) in the composition and transmission of his texts. Secondly, but more importantly, I will argue that Marcabru's theory of the sign marks his poetry as what Derrida calls *écriture*.

What evidence is there then for written composition and transmission in the Marcabru corpus? On one occasion at least Marcabru represents his song implicitly as a written text:

[33] See *Il canzoniere di Jaufre Rudel*, ed. G. CHIARINI (Rome, 1985), III, 29. For an influential example of scholarship that takes this stanza as evidence of orality, see R. PICKENS, "Jaufré Rudel et la poétique de la mouvance", *CCM* 20 (1977), pp. 32-37. But on the equivocal nature of this stanza as evidence of oral transmission, see S. GAUNT, "Orality and Writing: the Text of the Troubadour Poem", in: *The Troubadours: an Introduction*, pp. 228-245, at pp. 232-233.

[34] G. NOTO, *Il giullare e il trovatore nelle liriche e nelle "Biografie" provenzali* (Turin, 1998), pp. 181-182.

[35] *Biographies des troubadours*, VIII, §§ 2-3.

Messatgier cortes, ben parlans,
vai t'en en Urgelh ses falhir,
e sias del vers despleyans
a.n Cabreira, que lo remir,
e potz li dir senes guabar,
qu'en tal loc ai tornat ma sort
on elh poiria pro muzar.[36]

Courtly, eloquent messenger, go to Urgel without fail and unfold my poem to Lord Cabreira, so that he may contemplate it, and you can say this to him, without boasting, that I have placed my destiny in the hands of someone new before whom he could wait in vain for a long time.

"*Despleyans*" in line 45 may be ambiguous; *despleyar* means 'to unfold', but also 'to explain' and there are numerous examples of troubadours using the verb in connection with a poem. As Laura Kendrick points out, Marcabru combines the verb here with another (*remir*) which suggests *visual* interaction with the text;[37] so the sense of *despleyar* may literally be 'to unfold' as in to unfold a piece of parchment with writing on it, which is how it is often used elsewhere.[38] The messenger who is enjoined to transmit the text to its addressee is therefore implicitly represented as doing so in writing here, which suggests that writing was playing a role from the outset in the life of these lyrics.

If we move beyond the circulation of these texts in the lifetime of the poets, writing is still demonstrably central to their transmission. In the Marcabru corpus, there is little evidence indeed for oral transmission and such evidence as there is tends to be in manuscripts that are marginal to the main tradition of *chansonniers*.[39] The evidence for written transmission is overwhelming in the face of the impressionistic assertions of oral transmission. I will content myself with one illustration, the first stanza of the exchange between Marcabru and Audric:

[A]d un estrun
vei, Marcabrun,
qe.l comjat voletz demandar:
de mal partir

[36] *Marcabru: A Critical Edition*, ed. S. GAUNT, R. HARVEY and L. PATERSON (Cambridge, 2000), XXXIV, ll. 43-49.

[37] KENDRICK, *Game*, pp. 38-39.

[38] Compare *The Romance of Tristran by Beroul*, ed. A. EWERT (Oxford, 1971), l. 686: "*Cel brief li faites desploier*".

[39] For details see *Marcabru*, p. 12.

non ai cossir,
tant sabetz mesura esgardar.[40]

Marcabru, I can see that you want to ask leave to depart in a hurry: I do not worry that your departure might be unpleasant, because you know so well how to restrain yourself.

No manuscript gives a satisfactory version of the first line:

ACIKR Dun estrun (*CIK* estru), *D* Tot aestrum, *a*[1] Tot aist rim

The reading in *ACIKR* is hypometric although it makes acceptable sense. *Da*[1] both transmit the line with what are presumably copying errors, but both are united in rendering the first two syllables of the line "*tot a*" which suggests that the line should read "*Tot a estrun*", a well-attested expression and the reading adopted by previous editors. However, since *Da*[1] do not otherwise converge to produce a correct reading against all the other MSS and since neither produces an acceptable version of the line (both have a faulty rhyme), it is possible that their readings here result from independent attempts to restore the metre of faulty sources, particularly when it is considered that *a*[1] transmits a later thirteenth-century *remaniement* of the poem that alters the form, and *D* a version in which the versification has been botched.[41] The uniformity of *ACIKR*'s "*Dun estru*(*n*)" suggests all these MSS derive from a common source and an obvious explanation of this hypometric first line could then be that this source had a missing initial, either because it had been removed, or because it had yet to be filled in. If "*Dun estru*(*n*)" is the result of a missing initial then the obvious missing letter is "A", the expression *a un estrun* being well attested in Occitan.[42]

If this analysis is correct, the agreement of *ACIKR* in this instance is significant. *AIK* are closely related thirteenth-century Italian *chansonniers* thought to derive from a written source taken to Italy in the late twelfth or early thirteenth century. *CR* are fourteenth-century Occitan *chansonniers* representing a tradition thought to be inflected by a longer continued tradition of performance.[43] The two traditions are therefore believed to have diverged in the late

[40] *Marcabru*, XX, ll. 1-6.

[41] On *D*, see *Marcabru*, p. 277; for the text in *a*[1] and an analysis of the process of *remaniement*, see pp. 289-294.

[42] For a more detailed account of the textual problems here, see *Marcabru*, p. 284; and for the relation of the manuscripts in the transmission of this poem, see *Marcabru*, p. 277.

[43] On the relationship between the *chansonniers*, see D'A.S. AVALLE, *I manoscritti della*

twelfth century with the Italian tradition becoming more fixed by writing; frequently they transmit substantially different versions of the same lyric. Disagreements at a local level are ubiquitous. In the Marcabru corpus, for example, *CR* transmit so-called vulgate versions of some famous lyrics (the *pastorela*, the *lavador*) that look like thirteenth-century *remaniements*.[44] However, the example of Marcabru's "[*A*]*d un estrun*" suggests that before these traditions diverged they nonetheless derived from a common *written* source.

Written transmission, however, does not in itself suggest a notion of *écriture* as Derrida uses the term. Indeed from a Derridean perspective whether or not troubadours used writing to compose and transmit their lyrics is perhaps less interesting than whether they evince a view of language that resonates with Derrida's notion of *écriture*, or indeed whether they theorize language at all. Does Marcabru overtly theorize the sign and if so how? Consider the following lyric:

Per savi teing ses doptanza
celui qu'e mon chan devina
cho que chascus moz declina,
si com la razos despleia,
qu'eu meteis sui en erranza
d'esclarzir paraula escura.

Trobador a sen d'enfanza
movon als pros ataïna
e torno a desceplina
çho que veritaz autreia,
e fan los moz per esmanza
entrebescaz de fraitura.[45]

I unhesitatingly consider wise the man who can divine in my song what each word means, as the theme unfolds, for I myself have difficulty in clarifying obscure speech.

Childish troubadours make trouble for the worthy and turn into strife what truth grants, and they deliberately interweave words with fragmentation.

letteratura in lingua d'Oc, second edition by L. LEONARDI (Turin, 1993). Avalle and indeed most Italian editors of troubadour poetry presume written transmission.

[44] See *Marcabru*, p. 12; the *pastorela* and the *lavador* are Poems XXX and XXXV respectively.

[45] *Marcabru*, XXXVII, ll. 1-12.

In his fascinating *Space Between Words*, Paul Saenger writes "languages that exist only in oral form do not have a word for 'word' because they do not have a conception of the linguistic unit that constitutes a word".[46] As Saenger shows, there is no such thing as a phonetic script; indeed the most important thing in writing is in fact the gaps between words. If words are conceived as divisible from each other, then they are necessarily also being conceived as written on the page and they will then be represented *spatially*, rather than *temporally*. One might usefully recall here Susanne Fleischman's work on the important distinction between spatial and temporal deictic markers in Old French narratives (*Ci dist* 'it says here', contrasting with *Or dist* 'it says now'), with the former having as its reference a written text ('here' meaning 'at this point in this book') and the latter a spoken delivery of that story ('now' meaning 'now, as I tell you this').[47] In Marcabru's poem we see most obviously that the poet indeed has an idea of the word. But perhaps more importantly that words are conceived as concrete objects existing in a *spatial* medium in that they can be broken or shattered. Such a representation of the word makes little sense in relation to sound or speech, or more accurately it only makes sense if the word is conceived in relation to writing.

For Derrida words are always alienated from themselves, there is no such thing as a *parole pleine* (a self-sufficient spoken word that is always true to itself), there is always only *brisure*. And *brisure* is precisely the metaphor that Marcabru uses here, as well as in other poems such as "*Doas cuidas*", where he announces "*En dos cuiars ai consirier / a triar lo fraich del entier*" ("In these two ways of thinking, I am concerned to distinguish the whole from the broken").[48] The opening stanzas of "*Per savi teing*" have been considered in relation to ethics, hermeneutics, aesthetics and form.[49] But perhaps they may also have a theoretical dimension in that they appear to evince a nostalgia for a 'whole' way of writing, what Derrida (and indeed Zumthor) would call *une*

[46] P. SAENGER, *Space Between Words: The Origins of Silent Reading* (Stanford, 1997), p. 253.

[47] S. FLEISCHMAN, "Philology, Linguistics and the Discourse of the Medieval Text", *Speculum* 65 (1990), pp. 19-37.

[48] *Marcabru*, XIX, ll. 10-11.

[49] See for example KENDRICK, *Game*, pp. 17-18; U. MÖLK, *Trobar clus: trobar leu* (Munich, 1968), pp. 70-75; L.M. PATERSON, *Troubadours and Eloquence* (Oxford, 1975), pp. 15-18; A. RONCAGLIA, "Riflessi di posizioni cistercensi nella poesia del XII secolo: discussione sui fondamenti religiosi del 'trobar naturau' di Marcabuno", in: *I cistercensi e il Lazio* (Rome, 1978), pp. 11-22, at pp. 16-17; M. SHAPIRO, "*Entrebescar los motz*: Word-weaving and Divine Rhetoric in Medieval Romance Lyrics", *Zeitschift für romanische Philologie* 100 (1984), pp. 355-383, at pp. 361-362.

parole pleine, in which there is no possibility of deferral/ambiguity/fracture. But since Marcabru himself says that he too is incapable of "clarifying obscure speech", his nostalgia in fact confirms what it seeks to deny, revealing the idea of 'whole speech'/*parole pleine* is an impossible ideal, produced by and yet excluded from the trickier *écriture* in which he is obliged to engage.

The spatial dimension of the theory of the sign is evident elsewhere in Marcabru. In the earliest lyric in the troubadour corpus to use derived rhyme, he represents his poem either as a kind of patterned round dance, or as a form of weaving or braiding, depending on what one takes the terms *tresc* and *tresca* to mean:[50]

> *Selh qui fes lo vers e.l tresc*
> *no sap don si mou la tresca.*
>
> *Marcabrus a fag lo tresc*
> *e no sap don mou la tresca.*[51]
>
> He who composed the poem and the dance-tune does not know where the round-dance begins.
>
> Marcabru composed the dance-tune and yet does not know where the round-dance begins.

But whether one takes *tresc* to suggest dancing or braiding, the image conceives of the rhymes patterned spatially rather than temporally (as they might be in a song conceived in purely oral terms). And elsewhere in Marcabru's corpus, the poem is a space on the page from which he wishes nothing to be erased:

> *Auias de chan com enans' e meillura,*
> *e Marcabru, segon s'entensa pura,*
> *sap la razo del vers lasar e faire*
> *si que autre no l'en pot un mot raire.*[52]
>
> Hear how the song progresses and improves, and Marcabru, according to his pure intention, knows how to make and bind up the theme of the *vers* so that no one can erase a word from it.

[50] On the meaning of *tresc* see *Marcabru*, p. 199. "Derived rhyme" is not strictly speaking rhyme, but rather the technique entails placing words from the same root at the rhyme.

[51] *Marcabru*, XIV, ll. 55-58.

[52] *Marcabru*, IX, ll. 1-4.

Here the audience may be asked to listen, but the poem is nonetheless represented as an entity that is independent of performance and there is therefore a split between its articulation and its 'text'. Consider also the characteristic way in which Marcabru names himself here in the third person, which, I would argue, is a mark of absence or *brisure* rather than presence, indeed the marker of a *nostalgia* for a presence that never existed.

For many commentators, Marcabru's poetics are encapsulated by his idea of *trobar naturau*, which one might translate as the 'natural art of composing':

Esegon trobar naturau
port la peira e l'esca e.l fozill,
mas menut trobador bergau
entrebesquill
me torno mo chant en badau
e.n fan gratill.[53]

According to the natural art of composition, I carry the flint and tinder and steel, but petty, silly, muddled troubadours make my song pointless and an object of mockery.

Again these lines have been considered in relation to ethics, hermeneutics, aesthetics and form. The purity of Marcabru's 'natural' art is contrasted to the muddled, or more literally 'interwoven' art of other troubadours who bowdlerize Marcabru's work.[54] But perhaps the real problem for Marcabru is that his texts are always already, of necessity if not 'interwoven with fragmentation', certainly 'bound together', or 'braided', that is crafted. After all, the markers he carries here of *trobar naturau* are tools, indicative of the fact that far from being 'natural' his *trobar* is in fact the result of artifice, a product of culture rather than nature. There is thus in fact nothing 'natural' about the nature of the sign in Marcabru and one might read his laments on the 'broken' language of other troubadours as analogous to the nostalgia for a pure and 'natural' form of language that underscores the work of scholars of orality such as Walter Ong, though unlike Ong Marcabru seems to acknowledge its impossibility.

Marcabru's comments on how he sees language working do not leave any clear cut distinctions between good and bad uses of language, that is between 'natural' and 'broken' language intact. Furthermore, his view of language is by

[53] *Marcabru*, XXXIII, ll. 7-12.

[54] On the meaning and formation of *entrebesquill*, see *Marcabru*, p. 422.

no means unusual in the troubadour tradition and poets: poets as various as Guilhem IX, Peire d'Alvernhe, Giraut de Borneil and Arnaut Daniel evince a sophisticated and complex sense of how language works.[55] Indeed the very term used to denote composition in troubadour lyric – *trobar* – marks poetic language as always already secondary, as derivative, as the product of a displacement. The troubadour's task is less to compose his song, than to 'find' it, as if the lyric is an object that pre-exists any act of creativity, waiting to be found or rediscovered.[56] The metaphors that are often used to vaunt the quality of a poem enhance this sense of the artificial or secondary nature of poetic language: the poem is polished and planed; it is an exquisite jewel, fashioned and carved like a statue.[57]

The picture that the *chansonniers* paint of a culture of oral immediacy that is innocent of the artifices of writing should thus not necessarily be taken at face value. Arnaut Daniel's *vida* tells us that "*abandonet las letras e fetz se joglars*" ("he abandoned letters and became a minstrel")[58], as if 'letters' and being a minstrel were somehow incompatible. But we need to remember that the *vidas* and *razos*, like the *chansonniers* themselves are seeking to preserve a culture that by the time these books come to be written is long gone.[59] They are steeped in nostalgia for a lost world of courtly purity. It is therefore unsurprising, but also perhaps instructive to consider that like modern scholars of orality they offer an idealized view of the 'oral' nature of the texts that interest them. They offer less a record of an earlier oral culture than fictions of orality, and as several eminent scholars have demonstrated the practice of fiction is in itself a product of writing.[60]

Much recent scholarship stresses the relation between troubadour lyric and clerical culture, suggesting that even the lyrics of aristocratic troubadours such as Guilhem IX, or those of hypercourtly figures like Bernart de Ventadorn, bear the marks of their clerical education (understood in the broadest possible

[55] See particularly PATERSON, *Troubadours*.

[56] For an interesting analysis of this point see J. LACAN, *L'Ethique de la psychanalyse: le séminaire VII* (Paris: Seuil, 1986), p. 143.

[57] On this point see also GAUNT, "Orality and Writing", p. 234.

[58] *Biographies des troubadours*, IX, A, §3.

[59] See W.E. BURGWINKLE, "The *chansonniers* as books", in: *The Troubadours: an Introduction*, pp. 246-262; NOTO, *Giullare*; and also W.E. BURGWINKLE, *Love for Sale: Materialist Readings of the Troubadour Razo Corpus* (New York and London, 1997).

[60] I have used the idea of 'fictions of orality' elsewhere in relation to Marie de France, see *Retelling the Tale*, pp. 49-70. On fiction and literacy see, for instance, GREEN, *Medieval Listening*, pp. 268-269 and F.H. BÄUML, "Varieties and Consequences of Medieval Literacy and Illiteracy", *Speculum* 55 (1980), pp. 237-265.

terms).[61] The supposed 'orality' of the troubadour tradition consequently needs to be examined critically. Indeed, occasionally we may catch a glimpse behind the fictional façade of orality that the texts – and the manuscripts that transmit them – construct:

Bos es lo vers e chantador,
En volgra bon, entendedor,
Per Deu. Bel clerc, tu me l'escriu![62]

The *vers* is good and by God it would want a good singer and one who understands well. Fair clerk, write it down for me!

[61] See, for instance, L. LAZZERINI, *Letteratura medievale in lingua d'Oc* (Modena, 2001), p. 79.

[62] Arnaut Tintinhac, cited by NOTO, *Giullare*, p. 181.

Psalter und Gebetbuch am Hof: Bindeglieder zwischen klerikal-literater und laikal-mündlicher Welt

JÜRGEN WOLF

Bis ins 13. Jh. hinein spielen Schrift und Schriftlichkeit im kulturellen Leben des weltlichen Hofs eine zweitrangige Rolle. Das höfische Leben fußt auf mündlich-visueller Kommunikation: dem (Fest-)Vortrag, dem Gesang, dem Sprechen, dem Zuhören und dem Schauen. Bücher spielen in einem solchen illiteraten Milieu kaum eine Rolle und sind nur über die mündliche Vermittlung der wenigen Schriftkundigen zugänglich – so jedenfalls eine alte, in ihrer Eindimensionalität nicht zuletzt durch die Arbeiten von D.H. Green mittlerweile überholte Vorstellung. "It is now generally accepted that the question of the primary reception of medieval literature cannot be answered in terms of a simple antithesis (either listeners or readers), but that many works were meant for both kinds of reception".[1] Curschmann erklärt dieses Phänomen mit der "Symbiose aus mündlichen und schriftlichen Lebensformen" in einer "Zwischenkultur der höfischen Elite".[2] Joachim Bumke spricht vom "*vir quasi litteratus*" bzw. vom "*miles quasi litteratus*".[3]

[1] Grundlegend D.H. GREEN, *Medieval Listening and Reading. The primary reception of German literature 800-1300* (Cambridge, 1994) und DERS., "Vrume rîtr und guote vrouwen / und wise phaffen. Court Literature and its Audience", in: *German narrative literature of the twelfth and thirteenth century. Studies presented to Roy Wisbey*, hg. v. V. HONEMANN u.a. (Tübingen, 1994), S. 7-23, hier S. 7.

[2] M. CURSCHMANN, "Hören – Lesen – Sehen. Buch und Schriftlichkeit im Selbstverständnis der volkssprachlichen literarischen Kultur Deutschlands um 1200", *PBB* (T) 106 (1984), S. 218-257, hier S. 221-222.

[3] J. BUMKE, *Wolfram von Eschenbach* (Stuttgart und Weimar, ^{7}1997), S. 7. BUMKE entwickelt ein solches Bild mit Blick auf den von Lambert von Ardes in seiner *Geschichte der*

Vielleicht mehr als jede andere Textsorte läßt eine in der Literaturgeschichtsschreibung bisher wenig beachtete Textspezies die weitreichenden Konsequenzen dieser Thesen sichtbar werden. Es handelt sich um die an (allen?) größeren Höfen in *Buchform* präsenten Texte der Glaubenspraxis. Unter Sammelbegriffen wie 'Psalter', 'Brevier', 'Gebetbuch', 'Stundenbuch', 'Erbauungsbuch', 'Liber Precum' oder 'Privatgebetbuch' begegnen höchst unterschiedliche Textsammlungen zur Glaubenspraxis, die alle gemein haben, daß sie auf der Bibel fußen und auch außerhalb der Klostermauern eine zentrale Rolle bei der Ausübung des christlichen Kultus spielen.[4] Ich unterscheide im vorliegenden Untersuchungszusammenhang deshalb nicht zwischen den klassischen lat. Psaltertypen als Teil der Überlieferung des Bibeltextes (u.a. *Psalterium Romanum* und *Gallicanum*[5]) oder den sog. 'Privatgebetbüchern liturgischer Provenienz' (Psalter, z.T. Stundenbuch) und 'nichtliturgischer Provenienz' (Erbauungsbuch, Gebetbuch, z.T. Stundenbuch). Auch kann sich mein Blick trotz der Fokussierung auf den weltlichen Hof nicht auf volkssprachige Psalterien/Gebetbücher beschränken. Die folgenden Ausführungen werden vielmehr zeigen, daß selbst in der vermeintlich illiteraten Sphäre des weltlichen Hofs bis weit über das 13. Jh. hinaus das Latein auch die Psalterrezeption der *laici* dominierte.[6] Außerdem changieren viele Psalter/Gebetbuchhandschriften

Grafen von Guînes stilisierten halbgebildeten Ritter und die psalterlesenden adligen Frauen.

[4] Vgl. etwa E.J. THIEL, "Die liturgischen Bücher des Mittelalters. Ein kleines Lexikon zur Handschriftenkunde", *Börsenblatt für den Deutschen Buchhandel. Frankfurter Ausgabe* 23 (1967), S. 2379-2395; P. OCHSENBEIN, "Deutschsprachige Privatgebetbücher vor 1400", in: *Deutsche Handschriften 1100-1400. Oxforder Kolloquium 1985*, hg. v. V. HONEMANN und N.F. PALMER (Tübingen, 1988), S. 379-398; *Mittelalterliche Andachtsbücher. Psalterien. Stundenbücher. Gebetbücher. Zeugnisse europäischer Frömmigkeit. Eine Ausstellung der Badischen und der Württembergischen Landesbibliothek 1992*, hg. v. H.-P. GEH und G. RÖMER, bearb. v. F. HEINZER und G. STAMM mit einer Einführung v. F.O. BÜTTNER (Karlsruhe, 1992), S. 11-54; K. SCHREINER, "Psalmen in Liturgie, Frömmigkeit und Alltag des Mittelalters", in: *Der Landgrafenpsalter. Vollständige Faksimile-Ausgabe im Originalformat der Handschrift HB II 24 der Württembergischen Landesbibliothek Stuttgart, Kommentarband* (Graz und Bielefeld, 1992: *Codices Selecti* 113), hg. v. F. HEINZER, S. 141-183, sowie allg. zum Psalter die von E. ZENGER herausgegebene Festschrift *Der Psalter in Judentum und Christentum* (Freiburg, Basel und Wien, 1998), darin vor allem der Überblick von E. ZENGER, "Der Psalter als Buch", S. 1-57, und speziell zum Psalter im Mittelalter T. LENTES, "Text des Kanons und Heiliger Text", S. 323-354. Im hier besonders interessierenden paraliturgischen und privaten Bereich fehlt nach wie vor ein zuverlässiges Begriffsinventar.

[5] Zur Textgeschichte des lat. Psalters vgl. den Überblick bei K. KIRCHERT, *Der Windberger Psalter. Band 1: Untersuchung* (München, 1979: *MTU* 59), S. 111-115.

[6] Zur Komplexität des Laienbegriffs, der schon im 12. Jh. längst nicht mehr automatisch mit Analphabet gleichzusetzen ist, vgl. zusammenfassend GREEN, "Court Literature and its Audience", S. 10-19.

mit ihren Auftraggeber(inne)n, Besitzer(inne)n, Stifter(inne)n und Nutzer(inne)n zwischen Hof und Kloster.

I. Der Psalter als (privates) Gebetbuch am weltlichen Hof

Literarische Inszenierung

In der Aachener *Institutio sanctimonalium* aus dem Jahr 817 wird die Bedeutung des Psalters für die religiöse Unterweisung der jungen Frauen herausgehoben. Man stützte sich auf die Ausführungen des Kirchenvaters Hieronymus, der den Psalter ausdrücklich als Lehrbuch empfohlen hatte.[7] Auf dieser Folie war die Lektüre des Psalters bald im kulturellen Kanon der gesellschaftlichen Eliten verankert. So überrascht es nicht, wenn beispielsweise Otfrid von Weißenburg in seinem *Evangelienbuch* die heilige Maria während der Verkündigung in einer typischen Hofsituation ("*in thia pálinza*") als gedankenversunkene, nachdenkliche Rezipientin des Psalters stilisiert: "*mit sálteru in hénti, then sáng si unz in énti*" (Otfrid I, 5,10). Seine literarische Inszenierung dürfte schon im 9. Jh. kein Staunen mehr erregt haben.[8] Psalterrezipierende *vrouwen* begegnen jetzt vieler Orten: Ich erinnere an Bischof Prudentius von Troyes (843-861), der *Flores Psalmorum* für eine Aristokratin verfaßte; an Königin Mathilde († 968), die im Kloster Herford am Psalter die *disciplina literalis* lernte und an Dhuoda, die Gattin des Grafen von Septimanien, die selbst ein *Manuale*[9] zur Unterweisung zusammengestellt hatte. "Sie besaß auch ein ein-

[7] Zur Frühgeschichte des Psalters auf dem Weg zum Heiligen Text (ab dem 3./4. Jh.) vgl. den mit reichen Literaturangaben versehenen Überblick bei LENTES, "Text des Kanons und Heiliger Text" sowie grundlegend J. BLACK, "Psalm Uses in Carolingian Prayer Books", *Medieval Studies* 64 (2002), S. 1-60 und F. HEINZER, *Wörtliche Bilder. Zur Funktion der Literal-Illustration im Stuttgarter Psalter (um 830)* (Berlin *et al.*, 2005, im Druck).

[8] Ob Otfrid damit "maßgeblich dazu bei[trug], Maria zum Prototyp der lesenden Frau zu machen", wie SCHREINER, "Psalmen in Liturgie", S. 166, andeutet, wäre bei der relativ geringen Breitenwirkung des *Evangelienbuchs* kritisch zu hinterfragen. Wir haben es hier wohl eher mit einem direkt auf der lateinischen Glaubenspraxis bzw. entsprechenden apokryphen Bibelstellen (insb. das *Evangelium Ps.-Matthaei*) fußenden Phänomen zu tun, das im Gefolge der hoch- und spätmittelalterlichen Marienbegeisterung (volkssprachliche Belege u.a. im *Passional* und in Bruder Philipps *Marienleben*) zu einem 'Massenphänomen' in Text, Bild und Plastik avancierte; vgl. grundlegend zur Stelle G. VOLLMANN-PROFE, *Kommentar zu Otfrids Evangelienbuch. Teil 1* (Bonn 1976), S. 199-200, und zur spätmittelalterlichen Tradition vgl. S. LÜKEN, *Die Verkündigung an Maria im 15. und frühen 16. Jahrhundert* (Göttingen, 2000: *Rekonstruktion der Künste* 2).

[9] *Liber Manualis Dhuodane*, hg. v. P. RICHÉ (Paris, 1975: *Sources Chrétiennes* 225).

schlägiges Handbuch, das Alkuin zugeschriebene *De psalmorum usu*[10] ('Vom Gebrauch der Psalmen'). Sie sagt ausdrücklich, daß sie den Stoff ihres *Manuale* aus vielen Werken, die sie selbst gelesen habe, zusammengestellt habe, und zwar zum Zwecke der Unterrichtung ihres Sohnes".[11] Auch Kaiserin Gisela († 1043), die Gemahlin Konrads II., ließ sich bei ihrem Besuch im Kloster St. Gallen im Jahr 1027 von Notker (s. u.) eine Abschrift seiner Psalter-Übersetzung anfertigen "for her personal use (*Kisila imperatrix operum eius avidissima Psalterium ipsum et Job sibi exemplari sollicite fecit*)".[12]

Im ausgehenden 12. Jh. scheint die aktive Psalterrezeption im Kloster, aber auch am Hof mehr denn je alltägliche Praxis.[13] Die volkssprachlichen Belege häufen sich: In der *Nibelungenklage* ist es "*Uote diu vrowe hêre / ze Lôrse in ir hûse ... , dâ si venjete unde las / an ir salter alle ir tagezît, in einem münster (daz ist wît) / des si von êrste dâ began*" (*Klage* B, v. 3682-3686). Auch Chrétien de Troyes berichtet im *Yvain* von einer Dame, die die Psalmen "*an un sautier ses paumes / Anluminé a letres d'or*" (*Yvain*, v.1414 f.) liest.[14]

Chrétiens Hinweis auf die Verzierungen mit Goldlettern ("*letres d'or*") erweist sich übrigens als exakte Beschreibung vieler kostbarer zeitgenössischer Psalterhandschriften, wie sie an den Höfen des Hochadels präsent waren und als 'heilige Bücher' verehrt wurden.[15] Woher Chrétien seine Detailkenntnisse

[10] MIGNE, *PL* 101 (1851), Sp. 466-508.

[11] Diese und weitere Beispiele bei W. HAUBRICHS, *Die Anfänge. Versuche volkssprachiger Schriftlichkeit im frühen Mittelalter (ca. 700-1050/60)*, (Tübingen, ^{2}1995), S. 50-60, hier S. 59; vgl. K. SCHMID, *Gebetsgedenken und adliges Selbstverständnis im Mittelalter. Ausgewählte Beiträge* (Sigmaringen, 1983), S. 631-634 und SCHREINER, "Psalmen in Liturgie", S. 155, mit einer kurzen Paraphrase der neun Verwendungsregeln im Buch *De psalmorum uso* und ebd. S. 158 ff. mit weiteren Beispielen für königliche Psalternutzer(innen).

[12] Eintrag in einem Exemplar von Ekkeharts IV. *Liber benedictionum*; vgl. D.H. GREEN, "The primary reception of the works of Notker the German", *Parergon* 2 (1984), S. 57-78, hier S. 58, und HAUBRICHS, *Die Anfänge*, S. 205.

[13] Man wird sich vor pauschalen Urteilen hüten müssen, denn zwischen Wunsch (bzw. literarischer Inszenierung) und Wirklichkeit gab es erhebliche Diskrepanzen. Der dramatische Bericht Wipos zur darniederliegenden literarischen Ausbildung (im *Tetralogus* von 1041) oder der nicht minder berühmte Bericht zur Erziehung des späteren Abts Dietrich von St. Hubert am väterlichen Hof zeichnen ein konträres Bild der Hofkultur; vgl. mit weiteren 'bildungsfeindlichen' Beispielen J. BUMKE, *Höfische Kultur,* 2 Bde. (München, 1986), S. 601-606.

[14] In Hartmanns *Yvain*-Adaption fehlt dieser explizite Hinweis auf den Psalter (*Iwein*, v. 1597 ff.). Überhaupt erwähnt Hartmann anders als Chrétien und Wolfram nirgendwo den Psalter.

[15] Zu den bebilderten Psalter-Handschriften nach wie vor grundlegend A. HASELOFF, *Studien zur deutschen Kunstgeschichte. Eine thüringisch-sächsische Malerschule des 13. Jahrhunderts* (Straßburg, 1897); vgl. auch G. HASELOFF, *Die Psalterillustration im 13. Jahrhundert. Studien zur Geschichte der Buchmalerei in England, Frankreich und den Niederlanden* (Diss.

bezog, liegt auf der Hand: An seinen Wirkungsstätten am Hof der Marie de Champagne und am Hof Philipps von Flandern sind entsprechend gestaltete Psalterexemplare nachgewiesen. Die Allgegenwärtigkeit gerade solcher besonders kostbarer Psalterhandschriften ist zur gleichen Zeit auch in einem dt. Spielmannsepos Gegenstand der Inszenierung von Hofkultur. In *Salman und Morolf* ist es die Königin, von der wir erfahren, daß "*man gap ir einen salter in ir sne wisse hant. / mit guldenen buchstaben / was er geschriben allersant*" (13,3-5).

Die Psalter-Handschriften, die sich Wolfram von Eschenbach bei Sigune – sie "*truoc ein salter in der hant*" (*Parzival*, 438,1) – und Ginover, die am frühen Morgen in der Kapelle des Artushofs "*den salter*" (644,24) liest, vorstellte, könnten ähnlich kostbar gewesen sein. Trevrizent besitzt ebenfalls ein Exemplar – jetzt wohl ein einfaches, schmuckloses Gebrauchsmanuskript –, das er, ohne dem weltlichen Ritter Parzival nur mit einem Wort die Funktionsweise erklären zu müssen, zur Berechnung der Zeit benutzen kann: "*ame salter las er im über al / diu jâr und gar der wochen zal, / die dâ zwischen wâren hin*". Parzivals Antwort vermittelt einen Eindruck von der Selbstverständlichkeit eines solchen Berechnungsvorgangs: "'*alrêrst ich innen worden bin / wie lange ich var wîselôs ...*'" (*Parzival*, 460,25-27 und 28 f.). Selbst der ungeschlachte Ritter Parzival war demnach mit dem Psalter in seiner technisch-kalendarischen Funktion vertraut, und zwar schon vor der aufwendigen Unterweisung durch den Einsiedler.[16] Auch in der *Kaiserchronik* (v. 9058), in *Salman und Morolf* (v. 4,3f., 13,3, 591,5), in *Flore und Blanscheflur* (v. 6222 ff.), in *Barlaam und Josaphat* (v. 13586), im *Titurel* (87,1-4), in *Tandareis und Flordibel* (v. 12892 ff.), in der *Virginal* (130,9 f.) und in Ulrichs von Etzenbach *Alexander* (v. 14808 ff.) singen, lesen und hören die Laien – meist sind es die *frou-*

[Kiel],1938), V. LEROQUAIS, *Les Psautiers. Manuscrits latins des bibliothèques publiques de France 1* (Mâcon, 1940/41) und *Mise en page et mise en texte du livre manuscrit,* hg. v. H.-J. MARTIN und J. VEZIN (Paris, 1990), *passim*, sowie die zahlreichen Monographien, Ausstellungskataloge und Faksimiles zu einzelnen Psalterhandschriften.

[16] Zu den Psalterstellen vgl. *Wolfram von Eschenbach: Parzival*, nach der Ausgabe v. K. LACHMANN revidiert und kommentiert v. E. NELLMANN, übertragen v. D. KÜHN (Frankfurt a.M., 1994: *Bibliothek des Mittelalters* 8), Bd. 2, S. 659, 672 und 739, sowie speziell zum Gebrauch des Psalters bei Wolfram J. BUMKE, *Höfische Kultur*, S. 474-475; H. HAFERLAND, "Parzivals Pfingsten. Heilsgeschichte im Parzival Wolframs von Eschenbach", *Euphorion* 88 (1994), S. 263-301, hier S. 263, *passim*, und zur Zeitrechnung mittels des Psalters A. BÜCHLER, "Psalter und Zeitrechnung in Wolframs 'Parzival'", *ABäG* 50 (1998), S. 95-109.

wen – selbstverständlich aus dem *salter*.[17] Bei Berthold von Regensburg (I 515,11) erscheint der Vorgang alltäglich:

> *Daz dir der munt gar ze kurz wirt, swenne dû das pater noster sprechen soll unde daz ave Marîâ unde den gelouben, oder swenne ir den salter lesen sult, ir frouwen, und iuwer tagezît. Ir sît gelêret oder ungêleret, so soltet ir iuwer tagezît sprechen.*[18]

Die Psalterliebe scheint letztlich so weit gegangen zu sein, daß Steinmars sarkastisch-ironische Klage über die "*saltervrouwen*"[19] (Steinmar 11,36), die nichts anderes mehr im Sinn haben als den Psalter, bei seinem höfischen Publikum auf fruchtbaren Boden fallen konnte. Warum man bei Hofe so sehr auf den Psalter fixiert war, formuliert der Dominikanerlesemeister Eggebrecht eindrücklich: "*Dez salters gesanch machet die sel schon, er ladet die engel ze helfe, er vertribet die vntvgent, er machet heilich, er spiset di sel, er tiliget die svnde*" usw.[20] Die letzte Konsequenz einer solchen Vorstellung wird an der Figur der Hl. Elisabeth in den Protokollen zur Kanonisation und in den späteren Viten faßbar, wenn berichtet wird, daß Elisabeth – gerade fünfjährig – "sich vor dem Altar auf der Wartburg niedergeworfen und dabei vor sich einen Psalter auf-

[17] Weitere Belege z.B. im LEXER II,586 und bei BUMKE, *Höfische Kultur*, S. 474. Die bei GREEN, *Medieval Listening and Reading*, S. 316-323 (bes. S. 320-321) gesammelten *lese*-Belege in der mhd. Literatur untermauern eine solche Vorstellung.

[18] GREEN, *Medieval Listening*, S. 320, faßt den Nachsatz ("*Ir sît gelêret oder ungêleret, so soltet ir iuwer tagezît sprechen*") so auf, daß nur diejenigen, die *gelêret* sind, zum *lesen* angehalten seien. Für *alle* gelte nur, daß sie die *tagezît* *s p r e c h e n* sollten. Angesichts der hier zusammengetragenen Belege wird man jedoch den Kreis der zumindest rudimentär *gêlereten frouwen*, die lesen, als sehr groß einschätzen müssen.

[19] BUMKE übersetzt hier durchaus gewollt despektierlich mit "Betschwestern" (Höfische Kultur, S. 474).

[20] Zitiert nach SCHREINER, "Psalmen in Liturgie", S. 148. Eggebrechts Ausführungen setzen das Verständnis des Psalters als 'Heiliges Buch', als *totius scripturae diuinae thesaurus* (Cassiodor, *Expositio Psalmorum*) voraus und erinnern an zahllose ebenso grundlegende wie omnipräsente theologische Schriften zur Bedeutung des Psalters (etwa von Hieronymus, Alkuin, Einhard, Petrus Lombardus, Gilbert von Poitiers u.v.a.). Zum Psalter als "Heilsmaterie" vgl. LENTES, "Text des Kanons und Heiliger Text", S. 335 und ebd. S. 338 zur Bedeutung der "viel zu wenig untersuchten Prologe". Als Ein- bzw. Anleitung begleiten die alten Psalterprologe selbst deutsche Psalterien des Spätmittelalters, vgl. etwa die rein volkssprachliche Münchner Psalterhandschrift Cgm 440 (Schwaben, 1390) mit am Schluß (!) angefügter Psalter-Vorrede und Hieronymus-Prolog und den rein volkssprachlichen Baseler Psalterkodex Basel, UB, A. IV. 44 (Dominikanerinnenkloster in Schlettstadt, um 1360) mit Pseudo-Augustinus *De virtute Psalmorum* am Schluß.

geschlagen habe, wie um zu beten”.[21] Gott, personifiziert im heiligen Buch, und die Auserwählte verschmelzen in einer von Marienanalogien durchdrungenen Erweckungsbotschaft.

Plastische Inszenierung

Zahlreiche Plastiken visualisieren genau dieses in der Literatur entworfene Bild der psalterlesenden *vrouwen*. Ein aufgeschlagenes Buch – offensichtlich den Psalter – halten z.B. die Gräfin Berchta (Abb. 1) im Westchor des Naumburger Doms und Eleonore von Aquitanien († 1204) im Grabmal in Fontévraud in der Hand.

Wohl dasselbe, nun geschlossene Buch finden wir in der Hand der Gräfin Gerburg im Naumburger Dom (Schubert, *Naumburger Dom*, Nr. 88), in der Hand der Landgräfin Elisabeth von Thüringen in der Elisabeth-Kapelle des selben Bauwerks (Abb. 2) und in der Hand einer

Abb. 1 Gräfin Berchta (?), Stifterfiguren im Naumburger Dom. Abbildungsnachweis: E. SCHUBERT, *Der Naumburger Dom. Fotos von Fritz Hege* (Berlin, 1968), Nr. 116; mit freundlicher Genehmigung des Domarchivs Naumburg – Bildarchiv.

[21] SCHREINER, “Psalmen in Liturgie”, S. 161.

der beiden Frauen des Grafen von Gleichen im Erfurter Mariendom (Abb. 3). Die Reihe der Beispiele ließe sich beinahe beliebig fortführen.

Abb. 2: Heilige Elisabeth, kurz nach 1235, Elisabeth-Kapelle des Naumburger Doms. Abbildungsnachweis: SCHUBERT, *Der Naumburger Dom*, Nr. 54; mit freundlicher Genehmigung des Domarchivs Naumburg – Bildarchiv.

Die *vrouwe* mit dem Psalter/Gebetbuch in der Hand erweist sich als eines der ikonographischen und literarischen Grundmuster des gesamten Mittelalters. Gespeist wird die Popularität eines solchen Bildes wohl nicht zuletzt durch den im *Evangelium Ps.-Matthaei* und in seiner Nachfolge bei Otfrid beschriebenen Verkündigungsvorgang: Er zeigt Maria bei der Arbeit – bei Otfrid und Ps.- Mattheus die Psalmen singend (s.o.). Bei der überragenden Bedeutung der Marienfigur für die Glaubenswelt der *Laici* – unter anderem dokumentiert in den überwältigenden Überlieferungserfolgen des *Passionals*[22] und Bruder Philipps *Marienleben* – dürften sie bzw. dieses Bild es sein (neben einigen anderen hier nicht zur Debatte stehenden ikonographischen Grundmustern), über die der geradezu selbstverständliche Konnex von Buch und Frau im laikal-höfischen Diskurs verankert war. In hoch- und spätmittelalterlichen Gebetbüchern wie dem Lichtenthaler Psalter (Abb. 4) aus dem 13. Jh. Oder dem *Buves-Studenbuch* aus dem 15. Jh. finden wir die Verkündigungsszene entsprechend ausgestaltet.

II. Die tatsächliche Präsenz von Psalter und Gebetbuch in der Lebenswirklichkeit

Doch es bleiben Zweifel. Gehörte dieses *Buch* und seine *aktive* Nutzung tatsächlich zur Lebenswirklichkeit der weltlichen Höfe oder sind wir hier nur

[22] Das Bild der (psalter-)lesenden Maria ist im Passional integraler Bestandteil der Verkündigungsszene (*Passional* 14,5-17).

Abb. 3: Grabplatte des Grafen von Gleichen, um 1250, Mariendom Erfurt. Abbildungsnachweis: Foto, Kunstverlag Peda 1996; mit freundlicher Genehmigung des Domstifts Erfurt.

Abb. 4 Lichtenthaler Psalter, Verkündigungsszene (Maria mit dem Psalter im Arm), Karlsruhe, Badische Landesbibliothek, Cod. Lichtenthal 26, f. 1r; mit freundlicher Genehmigung der Badischen Landesbibliothek.

einer didaktisch-missionarisch motivierten Wunschinszenierung der vorwiegend klerikal gebildeten Autoren dieser Texte aufgesessen? Haftet allen literarischen und plastischen Sekundärzeugnissen nicht der Geruch der klerikalen Einflußnahme, der Inszenierung an?

Ob die psalterlesenden *vrouwen* mehr als eine Fiktion und der allgegenwärtige Psalter-Kodex mehr als ein christlich-höfischer Bildungstopos sind, wird letztlich nur auf positivistischem Terrain zu klären sein. Werfen wir deshalb einen Blick auf die Bücher selbst, "*die zu gotis dienste gehoren*". Und wir haben Glück: Im Gegensatz zu den meist verlorenen literarischen Handschriften können wir ungewöhnlich früh auf eine Fülle erhaltener Kodizes zurückgreifen. Besonders interessieren dabei solche Manuskripte, die volkssprachliche Ein- und Nachträge, Rubriken, Bildbeischriften und Übersetzungen (s. Anhang) überliefern. Sie weisen am deutlichsten auf eine Nutzung außerhalb der engeren monastischen Sphäre.

Wenn im folgenden primär die Psalterien/Gebetbücher des deutschen Sprachraums Berücksichtigung finden, ist dies allein arbeitsökonomischen Gesichtspunkten geschuldet. Die Entwicklungen in Frankreich/England verliefen analog,[23] in der Chronologie allerdings nicht ganz deckungsgleich. Wie bei anderen geistesgeschichtlichen Entwicklungen geht der Westen bisweilen einige Jahre, was die quantitative Präsenz der Volkssprache betrifft, mitunter einige Jahrzehnte voraus. Dies mag mit einer entwickelteren Literarizität der dortigen weltlichen Höfe zusammenhängen, dürfte aber auch mit innovativen, vom Westen ausgehenden religiösen Reformbewegungen hin zu einer allumfassenden Laienfrömmigkeit zusammenhängen. Die engen Verflechtungen innerhalb der europäischen Hocharistokratie sorgten jedoch dafür, daß letztlich jederzeit an fast jedem Ort beinahe jede innovative Neuentwicklung, sei sie nun schreib- und buchtechnischer Art oder einem veränderten Ritual geschuldet, zugänglich sein konnte, freilich nicht sein mußte.

Das in den Medien inszenierte Bild von der aktiven Präsenz des Psalters/Gebetbuchs wird durch die Überlieferungsrealität mit einer gewaltigen Zahl von erhaltenen Psalterien eindrucksvoll bestätigt. Im schier unermeßlichen Strom der Psalter-/Gebetbuchhandschriften gelingt es freilich eher selten, konkrete Entstehungs- und Nutzungsszenarien nachzuweisen. Meist bleiben wir auf Vermutungen angewiesen: Besonders kostbare Exemplare erscheinen durch Widmungsgedichte, Dedikationsbilder, Besitz- und Nekrologeinträge überproportional häufig mit der Sphäre der großen Fürstenhöfe verwoben. Aus dem engsten monastischen Zirkel hinaus weisen zudem die Psalterien/ Gebetbücher, die nachträglich mit volkssprachlichen Textpartikeln oder Einträgen versehen

[23] In England gilt dies erst für die Zeit nach der normannischen Eroberung.

wurden. Hier lassen sich neben weiblichen Religiosen immer wieder *vrouwen* des Hofs als Nutzerinnen/Besitzerinnen identifizieren. Die von vorneherein mit volkssprachlichen Gliederungselementen (dt. Rubriken) und Nutzungshilfen (Anweisungen zur Nutzung) versehenen Manuskripte sind dagegen vornehmlich in den seit dem späten 12. Jh. in großer Zahl entstehenden Frauenklöster zu lokalisieren, wobei in beiden Fällen häufig die Grenzen zwischen monastischer und höfischer Sphäre verschwimmen.

Der Psalter zwischen klerikaler Innenwelt und höfischer Außenwelt

Für die gottesdienstliche Praxis außerhalb der klerikalen Sphäre und die private Andacht nutzen *clerici*, aber auch primär weibliche Laien seit frühester Zeit den Psalter (s.o.). Zu den anfangs rein lateinischen Manuskripten treten bald mit volkssprachlichen Elementen durchsetzte, kommentierte und interlinear- bzw. parallelübersetzte Kodizes hinzu.[24]

Eine Sonderrolle kommt Notkers *Psalter* zu: Notker III. von St. Gallen überträgt im frühen 11. Jh. den Psalter ins Deutsche. Seine Psalterübersetzung ist wie einige ältere Interlinearübersetzungen unmittelbar für den Gebrauch im Kloster konzipiert. Notkers zugleich kommentierende Psalterübersetzung erfreute sich im St. Galler Lehrbetrieb großer Beliebtheit. Außerhalb der monastischen Welt erregte sein volkssprachlicher *Psalter* ebenfalls Aufmerksamkeit. Kaiserin Gisela bestellte sich eine Abschrift für die private Nutzung. Das Beispiel der Kaiserin machte allerdings gerade keine Schule. Nur im St. Galler Umfeld des berühmten Lehrers entstanden weitere, meist sparsam ausgestattete, klar gegliederte und z.T. mit Akzenten versehene Abschriften. Sie waren allesamt für den klösterlichen Schulbetrieb bestimmt und wirkten nicht über die Klostermauern hinaus. Für die private Andacht und den Gottesdienst blieb Notkers Übersetzung ohne Bedeutung.

[24] Altirische, altenglische und althochdeutsche Psalterbearbeitungen belegen ein frühes Interesse an diesem Buch. Auf den Inseln begegnen seit etwa 850 neben volkssprachlich-interlinear glossierten, übersetzten und ggf. kommentierten Versionen auch schon poetische Vollübersetzungen. Vergleichbare Entwicklungen sind im Karolingerreich zu beobachten. Mit der normannischen Eroberung nivellieren sich etwaige Unterschiede zum Kontinent. Einen knappen Überblick bietet A. GIER, "Psalmen, Psalter", *LMA* 7 (1999), Sp. 299-300. Vgl. auch R. CONSTANTINESCU, "Alcuin et les 'Libelli precum' de l'époque carolingienne", *Recherches de théologie ancienne et médiévale* 50 (1974), S. 17-56 und die Nachweise entsprechender frz. Kodizes im *INVENTAIRE systématique des premiers documents des langues romanes*, ed. par B. FRANK und J. HARTMANN, avec la collab. de H. KÜRSCHNER (Tübingen, 1997: *ScriptOralia* 100, I-V), hier Bd. 2.

Im Zuge der religiösen Aufbruchsbewegungen in der zweiten Hälfte des 12. Jh.s rückten Psalter und Gebetbuch als zentrale Glaubenselemente dennoch mehr denn je in den Focus auch der Laienfrömmigkeit. Man griff dazu auf die an vielen Höfen vorhandenen 'alten' Prachtexemplare zurück. Sich verändernden Anforderungen trug man in diesen 'Erbstücken' mit marginal ergänzten volkssprachlichen Gebrauchsanweisungen und nachgetragenen volkssprachlichen Gebeten, Liedern, Sprüchen etc. Rechnung. Es ist dieser letztlich konventionelle, allenfalls mit wenigen volkssprachlichen Elementen und Zusatztexten aufbereitete lateinische Psaltertyp, der sich im Kloster und an fast jedem größeren weltlichen Hof als geistliches Grundlagenwerk wiederfindet. Für Schwestern wie Laien genügte es, die lateinischen Psalterexemplare – wo nötig – mit begleitenden volkssprachlichen Rubriken (vgl. Anhang Nr. 4, 22, 26, 28-30, 32-41, 64, 67, 93), Bildbeischriften (vgl. Anhang Nr. 13, 19, 58, 62, 67, 77), Gebeten oder Gebetsanweisungen (vgl. Anhang Nr. 1-3, 6-11, 13, 14, 17-20, 22, 24, 25, 45, 47, 49, 51, 52, 56, 57, 59-62, 64, 70, 71, 75, 76, 78, 81-83, 90-92) versehen zu haben.[25]

Mit den so aufbereiteten 'alten' Psalterhandschriften konnte der anscheinend explosionsartig steigende Buchbedarf schon bald nicht mehr gedeckt werden. Am Beispiel der Psalterproduktion in Frankreich und England läßt sich bereits mit dem Ausgang des 12. Jahrhunderts,[26] am Beispiel der thüringisch-sächsischen Malerschule und eines fränkischen Schreib- und Malzentrums im Reich seit dem frühen 13. Jh. die werkstattmäßige Produktion von Psalterien in großer Zahl belegen.[27] In großer Zahl entstanden nun auch von vornherein mit volkssprachlichen Elementen durchsetzte Psalterien. Zunächst waren meist nur Überschriften (Rubriken), Bildbeischriften, kurze Paraphrasen und einzelne Gebetsanweisungen in der Volkssprache abgefaßt. Dabei wurden in Frankreich

[25] Einige lat. Psalterien liefern mit dem Alkuin zugeschriebenen *liber de psalmorum usu* die Gebrauchsanweisung gleichsam als Praefatio mit; vgl. exemplarisch den aus dem 12. Jh. stammenden Seckauer Codex Graz, UB, Cod. 698. Inwieweit die volkssprachlichen Gebetsanweisungen auf solchen lateinischen Mustern fußen, wäre zu überprüfen.

[26] Vgl. R.H. ROUSE und M.A. ROUSE, "Statim invenire: Schools, Preachers and New Attitudes toward the Page", in: *Renaissance and Renewal in the Twelfth Century*, hg. v. R.L. BENSON und G. CONSTABLE (Oxford, 1982), S. 201-225.

[27] *Die Gotischen Handschriften der Württembergischen Landesbibliothek Stuttgart. Teil 1: Vom späten 12. bis zum frühen 14. Jahrhundert*, bearb. v. C. SAUER, mit Beiträgen v. U. KUDER (Stuttgart, 1996), S. 20-25; zur Verbreitung und Nutzung des Psalters im 13. Jh. vgl. G. ACHTEN, *Das christliche Gebetbuch im Mittelalter. Andachts- und Stundenbücher in Handschrift und Frühdruck* (Berlin, ^{2}1987: *Ausstellungskatalog SBPK* 13), SCHREINER, "Psalmen in Liturgie", und H.-W. STORK, "Psalter/Hymnar", in: *Bibliotheca Apostolica Vaticana. Liturgie und Andacht im Mittelalter, Katalog der Ausstellung vom 9. Oktober 1992 bis 10. Januar 1993*, hg. v. Erzbischöflichen Diözesanmuseum (Köln und Stuttgart, 1992), S. 52-54.

und England Psalterien für das höfische Publikum sowohl früher als im Reich als auch deutlich zahlreicher mit volkssprachlichen Elementen aufbereitet oder mit Bibelteilübersetzungen, volkssprachlichen Legenden, Heiligenleben, Liedern, Versen und glaubenspraktischen Basistexten ergänzt.[28] Als herausragendes Beispiel für diese neue Art der volkssprachlich aufbereiteten Psalter kann der lateinische *Eadwine Psalter* gelten. Er erhielt als Anhang (Bl. 275 ff.) eine ganze Reihe französisch übersetzter Texte der Glaubenspraxis: *Te Deum, Gloria, Pater Noster, Credo, Symbole d'Athanase*. Das Buch erlaubte damit seinem Besitzer, den christlichen Ritus zu vollziehen.[29]

Ochsenbein sieht die volkssprachlichen 'Einsprengsel' als Hilfen, "damit die Schwester weiß, wann und wofür der einzelne Psalm zu rezitieren sei".[30] "Bestimmte Psalmen konnten z.B. gegen Krankheiten, Herzweh, schwierige Geburten, Rechtsstreitigkeiten und in der Todesstunde helfen".[31] Im *Arenberg-Psalter* (Anhang Nr. 10)[32] heißt es zu Psalm 1: "*Dissen salmen saltu wizzen daz david dichte unde goddes denest da mite richte*", und zu Psalm 26: "*dissen sprich so dich boser dinch geluste daz dich der tůvel dinem engele nich beneme*".[33] Im *Comburger Psalter* (Anhang Nr. 9) liest man zu Psalm 51 den Hinweis: "*Den sprich daz dir got uerlihe dines sinnes daz du im mit trwen wider antwurtest sine cunst di er dir gab do er dir die sel beualch*".[34] Auch im *Augs-*

[28] Vgl. *Inventaire*, Nr. 2054-2074 und 2093 f., 2098 sowie mit kleineren volkssprachlichen Ergänzungen Nr. 2075-2091.

[29] Einige Handschriften mit einer ähnlichen Konstellation von lateinischem Haupttext (Psalter) und begleitenden glaubenspraktischen Texten in französischer oder occitanischer Übersetzung sind für die Zeit bis 1250 im *Inventaire* nachgewiesen; vgl. ebd. Nr. 2044 (*Eadwine Psalter*) und Nr. 2046-2049. Ergänzungen wie die alttestamentarischen Cantica für die Matutin gehören seit karolingischer Zeit zum selbstverständlichen Inhalt des Psalters im Sinne eines Andachtsbuchs – so schon im *Utrecht Psalter* von 830 (vgl. grundlegend HEINZER, *Wörtliche Bilder*). Neu ist die volkssprachliche Übertragung.

[30] P. OCHSENBEIN, "Latein und Deutsch im Alltag oberrheinischer Dominikanerinnenklöster des Spätmittelalters", in: *Latein und Volkssprache im deutschen Mittelalter 1100-1500. Regensburger Colloquium 1988*, hg. v. N. HENKEL und N.F. PALMER (Tübingen, 1992), S. 42-51, hier S. 49.

[31] G. SUCKALE-REDLEFSEN, "Buchkunst zur Zeit der Andechs-Meranier in Bamberg", in: *Die Andechs-Meranier in Franken. Europäisches Fürstentum im Hochmittelalter. Katalog zur Ausstellung in Bamberg vom 19.6. bis 30.9.1998* (Mainz, 1998), S. 239.

[32] Vgl. J.-C. KLAMT, "Zum *Arenberg-Psalter*", in: *Munuscula Discipulorum. Festschrift Kauffmann*, hg. v. T. BUDDENSIEG und M. WINNER (Berlin, 1968), S. 147-155 und Abb. 103-111 mit Abdruck, Übersetzung und Abbildung der Einträge (ebd. S. 147, 149 und Abb. 105). Im Psalter finden sich weitere deutsche Gebetsanweisungen zu den Psalmen 7, 27, 99, 100.

[33] Nahezu wörtlich auch im *Münchner Psalter* Clm 23111 (Anhang Nr. 61) zu Psalm 26: *Den sprich so dich boͤser dinge geluste vnd dich der tiuvel dem engel benem vnde den naehsten danach* (Bl. 21r).

[34] Im Psalter finden sich weitere, z.T. gereimte deutsche Gebetsanweisungen zu den

burger Psalter (Anhang Nr. 7) wird zu fast jedem Psalm vermerkt, in welcher Lebenssituation er hilfreich sein kann: Die Psalmen 6 und 40 "*sprih den siechen*".[35] "*So du groze angest habest so lis diesen salmen*" (Psalm 39) und "*sprih so du for den altare stest unde in die kirchen gest*" den Psalm 25. Einige der Anweisungen sind gereimt:

Lis den salmen morgenes frů
So get dir heil zů (zu Psalm 62).

Für eine Frau – "*pro me peccatrice*" ("für mich arme Sünderin") (Bl. 47) – war der *Donaueschinger Psalter* bestimmt (Anhang Nr. 78). Und wieder soll das Gebet vor allem vor der Angst schützen. Einer aufwendigen Kreuzigungsminiatur auf Bl. 45 ist die Anweisung beigefügt: "*Swen angest ane get, der spreche disse vuonf salme in di ere der funf wunden vnses heren godes so wiert er schiere irlediget vnde irloset*". Entgegen des pauschalen Verweises von Ochsenbein auf die "Schwestern" macht die Provenienzanalyse zumindest bei diesen Gebetbüchern mit marginalen bzw. marginal nachgetragenen Gebrauchsanweisungen auffallend häufig einen Gebrauch außerhalb der monastischen Sphäre, am Hof, wahrscheinlich.[36]

Dezidiert in monastische Zusammenhänge verweisen dagegen die schon in der Grundkonzeption zweisprachig angelegten Kodizes mit deutschen Rubriken und genauen volkssprachlichen Instruktionen zur Glaubenspraxis. Als Gliederungs- und Orientierungshilfen, aber auch als Handlungs- und Gebrauchsanweisungen für die Seckauer Chorfrauen dienten beispielsweise die auffällig gestalteten deutschen Rubriken in zahlreichen Gebetbüchern (Anhang Nr. 4, 22, 26, 28-30, 32-41, 64, 67, 93). "Für all diese Handschriften läßt sich zeigen, daß sie zum Gebrauch des Frauenkonvents bestimmt waren, der den Seckauer Chorherren schon früh, mindestens seit 1149 beigeordnet war. Im einfachsten Fall, so bei den Handschriften 832 [Anhang Nr. 33], 1257 [Anhang Nr. 37] und 1549 [Anhang Nr. 38], bezeugt das der Eintrag '*Breviarium monalium*' oder gar '*liber abatissae*' in den Handschriften selbst, so in 1257".[37]

Psalmen 1, 9, 17, 26, 27, 37, 39, 43, 47, 51, 56, 68, 87, 92.

[35] Ebenfalls nahezu wörtlich auch im *Münchner Psalter* Clm 23111 (Anhang Nr. 61) zu Psalm 6: *Den sprich den siechen* (Bl. 4v). Psalm 40 ist mit einer anderen Anweisung versehen: *Daz dich got ze rehtem leben sterke* (Bl. 34v); Übereinstimmungen zeigen sich auch zum *Wilheringer Psalter* (Anhang Nr. 83).

[36] Vgl. SCHREINER, "Psalmen in Liturgie", S. 157 Anm. 65, mit Belegen dafür, "daß im späteren Mittelalter Gebetsanweisungen für Laien und Gebetsanweisungen für geistlich lebende Personen weitestgehend identisch sind".

[37] E. HELLGARDT, "Seckauer Handschriften als Träger frühmittelhochdeutscher Texte. Hugo Kuhn in memoriam", in: *Die mittelalterliche Literatur in der Steiermark. Akten des*

Vergleichbare Nutzungskontexte sind beim *Züricher Psalter* (Anhang Nr. 91) auszumachen. In der *Züricher Gebetsanweisung* finden wir die Instruktion: "*Sinc den saltare unde tů dine uenie zu ieglichemo salmen unt sprih 'Gloria patri' unt 'Requiem eternam'* ". Es folgen detaillierte Anweisungen zur Almosenpraxis:

> *Gip zu ieglicher uenie ein almůsen unt ein cherzen gemezzen nah demo mitteristemo uingere diner zesewen unt tů daz nahtes. unt bit die brieste daz si die sele dines friuntes dem almahtigen gote beuelhen mit uollemo ambahte alsame da men den lichnamen der erde beualch. Daz tu an dem sibenten unt zu iegelichemo drizegisten so chumit dir diu sele zegesihte alnah diu so ir dinc stet.*

Die Anweisung hat wohl eine "Klosterfrau (aus einem Walburgis-Kloster)" des späten 12. Jh.s auf einer leeren Seite (106v) nach fünf Psalmen in das sonst rein lateinische Gebetbuch eingetragen.[38] Anweisungen zur Glaubenspraxis hält auch der in Allerheiligen (Schaffhausen) angefertigte *Fuldaer Psalter* (Anhang Nr. 25) bereit: "*In der stillvn messe sol ... sprechin. so man vnsirs herrin lichnami vf hebit*". Das angesprochene, dem Freidank-Korpus zugerechnete Meßgebet (Freidank, *Bescheidenheit* 181,10-21)[39] *Got uater allir cristinheit* folgt als einziger deutscher Text direkt im Anschluß. Charakteristisch für ein monastisches Interessengeflecht ist wieder, daß das Meßgebet integraler Bestandteil des Psalters (Layout, Einrichtung, Schrift) ist und in der für diese Handschrift üblichen Gestaltung mit einleitender Lombarde nach Psalm 100 folgt.[40] Jakobi-Mirwald favorisiert das dem Abt von Allerheiligen unterstellte Frauenkloster St. Agnes in Schaffhausen als Entstehungsort.[41] "Die Funktion der deutschen Rubriken in den liturgischen Büchern der Seckauer Chorfrauen [und vieler anderer Frauenkonvente, J.W.] wird man am besten im Hinblick auf Frauen

Internationalen Symposions Schloß Seggau bei Leibnitz 1984, hg. v. A. EBENBAUER, F.P. KNAPP und A. SCHWOB (Bern *et al.*, 1988: *Jahrbuch für internationale Germanistik, Reihe A: Kongreßberichte* 23), S. 103-130, hier S. 104.

[38] Abdruck der Gebetsanweisung in *Denkmäler deutscher Prosa des 11. und 12. Jahrhunderts*, hg. und mit Kommentar und Einleitung versehen v. F. WILHELM, Abt. A: Text, Abt. B: Kommentar (München, 1914/16: *Münchener Texte* 8), [A] S. 107.

[39] Es ist fragwürdig, ob man dieses weit verbreitete Meßgebet zum engeren Freidank-Komplex hinzurechnen kann, denn es findet sich auch in anderen Überlieferungskontexten ohne Freidank-Bezug.

[40] Vgl. *Die illuminierten Handschriften der hessischen Landesbibliothek Fulda. Teil 1: Handschriften des 6. bis 13. Jahrhunderts. Textband*, bearb. v. C. JAKOBI-MIRWALD auf Grund der Vorarbeiten v. H. KÖLLNER (Stuttgart, 1993), S. 147, mit der irrigen Annahme, bei dem Meßgebet handele es sich um einen Nachtrag. Nachgetragen wurden im 14. Jh. andere Freidank-Stellen.

[41] JAKOBI-MIRWALD, *Fulda*, S. 146.

eines mittleren Bildungsstandes verstehen, als Orientierungshilfe und Belehrung beim Gebrauch von Büchern, deren Verständnis im Prinzip fundiert, im einzelnen aber noch oder überhaupt nicht gefestigt war".[42]

Von Bedeutung mag sein, daß sich bei vielen dieser am Kloster und am Hof genutzten Gebetbücher auffällige Normierungserscheinungen zeigen. Selbst manche der marginal ein- und nachgetragenen volkssprachlichen Gebrauchsanweisungen gleichen sich in den verschiedenen Handschriften bis hin zu wörtlichen Übereinstimmungen. Man wird hier, wie bei den Büchern selbst, sowohl von grundsätzlichen, weit verbreiteten identischen Muster ausgehen dürfen als auch von verschränkten Nutzungskontexten. Möglicherweise lassen sich derartige Übereinstimmungen als Indizien für eine hohe sowohl horizontale (zwischen einzelnen Höfen) als auch vertikale (zwischen Hof und Kloster) Mobilität der sie nutzenden Personen deuten.[43]

Nutzungshorizonte

Die große Spannbreite unterschiedlicher Ausstattungsmuster von der kostbar, ganzseitig illuminierten Prachthandschrift bis hin zu einfachen, fast schmucklosen Alltagsexemplaren verdeutlicht, wie die Psalterien/Gebetbücher völlig unterschiedliche Funktionen im Rahmen des christlichen Kultus ausfüllen konnten und wie unterschiedlich die mit dem Buch verwobenen Interessenlagen waren. Die Kodizes wurden zur privaten Andacht, dem öffentlichen Gottesdienst, aber auch als Reliquie, zur Repräsentation und zur Stiftung genutzt. Daß dabei rein volkssprachliche Gebet- bzw. Stundenbücher und Psalterien noch lange eine untergeordnete Rolle spielten,[44] überrascht insofern nicht,

[42] HELLGARDT, "Seckauer Handschriften", S. 108.

[43] Vgl. SCHREINER, "Psalmen in Liturgie", S. 157 Anm. 65.

[44] Vgl. etwa die bei K.E. SCHÖNDORF, *Die Tradition der deutschen Psalmenübersetzung. Untersuchungen zur Verwandtschaft und Übersetzungstradition der Psalmenverdeutschung zwischen Notker und Luther* (Köln und Graz, 1967: *Mitteldeutsche Forschungen* 46) aufgelisteten Psalmenübersetzungen. Eine gereimte deutsche Psalter-Paraphrase überliefern die Klagenfurter Fragmente aus dem 1. Viertel des 13. Jh.s. Vollständige Übersetzungen bzw. Interlinearversionen bieten neben Notker die *Windberger Gruppe*, die *Trierer Interlinearversion zum Psalter* (um 1200), die *Leipziger Psalmen-Fragmente* (um 1200), das *Koeppelsche Psalter-Fragment* (um 1200), die *Schlierbacher Psalmen-Fragmente* (um 1200), die *Sonnenburger Psalmen-Fragmente* mit dt. Interlinearversion (um 1220/30), die etwa gleich alte *Linzer Psalmenübersetzung* (lat. mit dt. Parallelübersetzung) und das *Berliner Psalter-Fragment* (2. Viertel 13. Jh.). Volkssprachliche, anfangs noch oft bilinguale Psalter/Gebetbücher halten erst im ausgehenden 13. Jh. massiv Einzug in die Glaubenspraxis. Vorboten einer solchen Entwicklung sind z.B. der zweisprachige *Psalter der Anna von Bolanden* (Anhang Nr. 46) und ein um 1320

als die Ausübung des christlichen Kultus am Hof nicht anders als im Kloster an vorgeformte Normen und an die heilige Sprache gebunden blieb, wozu am Hof eine literarische Grundausbildung befähigte:

Das ich ûch sage das ist wâr:
er dette sie teuffen und lerte sie
den salter ein gantz jar. (*Salman und Morolf*, 4,1-3)

Grundsätzlich sind zwei Tradierungstypen zu unterscheiden. Auf der einen Seite entstehen im Umfeld der gesellschaftlichen Eliten eine ganze Reihe kostbarster Prachthandschriften. Diese oft mit historisierten Initialen und Miniaturen ausgestatteten Psalterien/Gebetbücher bleiben dem Latein verpflichtet.[45] Wie viele rein lateinische Prachtpsalterien etwa aus dem Besitz der

- Landgrafen von Thüringen: *Elisabethpsalter* (mit wenigen dt. Elementen; vgl. Anhang Nr. 13) und *Landgrafenpsalter* Hermanns I. und seiner Frau Sophie[46];
- der Welfen: Psalterien Heinrichs des Löwen, Kaiser Ottos IV. und Mechthilds von Anhalt;[47]

entstandener, durchgehend zweisprachig angelegter *Wiener Psalter* (ÖNB, Cod. 2767; vgl. A. FINGERNAGEL und M. ROLAND, *Mitteleuropäische Schulen I [ca. 1250-1350], Textband. Mit 78 Abbildungen* [Wien 1997: *WSB Denkschriften*, Bd. 245; *Veröffentlichungen der Kommission für Schrift- und Buchwesen des Mittelalters* I,10], Nr. 96). Endgültig vollzogen erscheint ein solcher Entwicklungsschritt hin zur Volkssprache in einem weiteren, etwa gleichzeitigen rein volkssprachlichen Wiener Psalter (ÖNB, Cod. 2756; vgl. ebd. Nr. 67). Für das fortschreitende 14. und das 15. Jh. ist die Zahl der rein dt. Psalterien/Gebetbücher dann kaum noch zu quantifizieren.

[45] Zur nicht allein textillustrierenden Funktion von historisierten Initialen und Illustrationen als 'Mittel der Andacht' und/oder als 'Gegenstand der andächtigen Betrachtung' vgl. *Mittelalterliche Andachtsbücher*, S. 11-12, *passim*, ACHTEN, *Das christliche Gebetbuch im Mittelalter*, S. 10 ff., J.F. HAMBURGER, "A Liber Precum in Sélestat and the Development of the Illustrated Prayer Book in Germany", *The Art Bulletin* 73 (1991), S. 209-236 und N. LARGIER, "Der Körper der Schrift. Bild und Text am Beispiel einer Seuse-Handschrift des 15. Jahrhunderts", in: *Mittelalter. Neue Wege durch einen alten Kontinent*, hg. v. J.-D. MÜLLER und H. WENZEL (Stuttgart und Leipzig, 1999), S. 241-271, bes. S. 262 ff.

[46] Vgl. *Hessen und Thüringen. Von den Anfängen bis zur Reformation. Eine Ausstellung des Landes Hessen* (Marburg, 1992), Nr. 234-235 (mit Abbildung eines Blattes aus dem Landgrafenpsalter) und U. PETERS, *Fürstenhof und höfische Dichtung. Der Hof Hermanns von Thüringen als literarisches Zentrum* (Konstanz, 1981: *Konstanzer Universitätsreden* 113), S.18-19.

[47] Vgl. B. KLÖSSEL, "Buchmalerei in Braunschweig", in: *Heinrich der Löwe und seine Zeit. Herrschaft und Repräsentation der Welfen 1125-1235. Katalog der Ausstellung*, hg. v. J. LUCKHARDT und F. NIEHOFF (Bd. 3 zusammen mit G. BIEGEL), 3 Bde. (München, 1995), S. 452-477, und dazu die Abbildungen des *Löwen-Psalters* (London, BL, Lansdowne MS 381) ebd. Nr. D 93,

- der Andechs-Meranier: *Psalterium Nocturnum* und *Gebetbuch der heiligen Hedwig*;[48]
- oder der Plantagenets: *Kopenhagen-Psalter* Mathildes bzw. Geoffroy Plantagenets;[49]

belegen, verstand man in höchsten Adelskreisen geradezu selbstverständlich mit diesen rein lat. Büchern umzugehen. Volkssprachliche Bildbeischriften, Gebets- und Gebrauchsanweisungen oder Gebete kommentierten oder erklärten zwar durchaus häufiger die lateinischen Texte und halfen bei ihrer adäquaten Verwendung, übersetzten sie aber nicht: Wir finden Hinweise darauf, wie und wann man einen Psalm singen sollte, welcher Psalm sich als Beschwörungsformel bei Krankheiten, Gebrechen, Not und Plagen eignete, welches Gebet ggf. ergänzend zum Psalm gesprochen werden mußte und einiges mehr. Diese oft unglaublich kostbaren Handschriften – Lentes spricht treffend von der "Auratisierung des Kodex"[50] – "waren wahrscheinlich zum größten Teil für Frauen bestimmt".[51] Ich greife exemplarisch das *Gebetbuch der heiligen Hedwig von Schlesien* heraus (Anhang Nr. 62). Der aufwendig bebilderte, mit dt. Gebetsüberschriften und -anweisungen, dt. Bildbeischriften und einem dt. Gebet versehene Codex wird dem familiären Umkreis der Hl. Hedwig von Schlesien († 1243) aus dem Geschlecht der Andechs-Meranier zugeschrieben und entstand wahrscheinlich im unmittelbaren Zusammenhang der Gründung des Klosters Trebnitz in Schlesien (1202/03). Mit der später heilig gesprochenen Hedwig – der Klostergründerin – kam der Kodex vermutlich als Teil der fundierenden Grundausstattung nach Trebnitz.[52] Die deutschen Elemente dürf-

des *Mechthild-Psalters* (Berlin, SBBPK, Ms. Theol. Lat. qu. 31) ebd. Nr. E 29 und des *Otto-Psalters* (Privatbesitz) ebd. S. 462.

[48] Vgl. G. SUCKALE-REDLEFSEN, "Buchkunst zur Zeit der Andechs-Meranier in Bamberg", in: *Die Andechs-Meranier in Franken. Europäisches Fürstentum im Hochmittelalter. Katalog zur Ausstellung in Bamberg vom 19.6. bis 30.9.1998* (Mainz, 1998), S. 239-261, hier S. 248-250 und Abb. 155 (Breslau, UB, Cod. membr. I F 440). Daneben besaß die heilige Hedwig ein prachtvoll illuminiertes lateinisches Gebetbuch mit einigen deutschen Gebeten, Gebetsanweisungen, Bildbeischriften (Anhang Nr. 62).

[49] Abbildung und Beschreibung in *Heinrich der Löwe*, Nr. D 95: "Die luxuriöse Ausstattung einerseits, die Zufügung des Alphabets zwischen den Texten des *Gloria* und des *Pater noster* andererseits weisen darauf hin, daß der Psalter für einen hochgestellten jugendlichen Besitzer hergestellt wurde, der aus diesem Gebetbuch auch elementares Wissen, Lesen und Latein lernen sollte".

[50] LENTES, "Text des Kanons und Heiliger Text", S. 335.

[51] BUMKE, *Höfische Kultur*, S. 474.

[52] Nach E.P. GOLDSCHMIDT: *The Hours of St. Hedwig, Duchess of Silesia. A Twelfth Century Manuscript containing a Picture Bible* (London, 1928) entstand der Codex zwischen 1189 und 1202 in Ostbayern (Regensburg oder Salzburg?) im Auftrag Ottos (VIII.) von

ten den neuen Konventualinnen die glaubenspraktische Anwendung der Buchinhalte erleichtert haben.

Ein zweiter, zunächst primär im monastischen Umfeld zu verortender Buchtyp scheint vorrangig pragmatischen Gesichtspunkten verpflichtet. Auf ein repräsentatives Äußeres wird nur begrenzt Wert gelegt. Charakteristisch für diese Variante des 'Alltagsgebetbuchs' ist ein mitunter größerer Anteil volkssprachlicher Passagen, die teilweise organisch mit den lateinischen Abschnitten verbunden bzw. sogar im selben Text miteinander verschränkt sind. Im Laufe des 13. Jh.s nehmen die volkssprachlichen Anteile in diesem Gebetbuchtyp mehr oder weniger kontinuierlich zu: In den Grazer Gebetbüchern des ausgehenden 12. und frühen 13. Jh.s sind es noch ausschließlich Rubriken und kleinste Einsprengsel (Anhang Nr. 26 ff.), in den um/nach 1300 entstandenen Gebetbüchern der Wöltingeroder Zisterzienserinnen (Anhang Nr. 84 ff.) überwiegen sie bereits. Charakteristika dieses Gebetbuchtyps sind die z.T. extreme Varianz der Inhalte und die enge Verzahnung von Latein und Volkssprache. Die Kodizes werden nach individuellen Bedürfnissen zusammengestellt und verlangen in der heterogenen Mischung auch aufwendigerer lateinischer und volkssprachlicher Passagen eine elaborierte Lesekompetenz. Die Provenienzbestimmung ergibt denn auch kaum zufällig eine signifikant enge Verflechtung mit dem monastischen Bereich (Frauenklöster). Dennoch wirkte dieser Gebetbuchtyp über personale (Verwandtschaft, Stiftung) und seelsorgerische Verbindungen aus dem Kloster auch direkt in die Hofkultur hinein. Letztlich scheint mit diesem Buchtyp der Weg zum rein volkssprachlichen, bald überall präsenten Gebet- und Stundenbuch des Spätmittelalters beschritten.

Wittelsbach für die Hl. Hedwig und ihre Gründung Trebnitz. W. SEMKOWICZ, "Der Kalender von Trzebnica aus der ersten Hälfte des XIII. Jhdts.", *Bulletin International de l'Académie Polonaise des Sciences et des Lettres* 35 (1930), S. 198-204, sieht im Benediktinerinnenkloster Kitzingen bei Würzburg den Entstehungsort des Stundenbuchs, wo die Hl. Hedwig erzogen und ihre Schwester Mechthild Äbtissin wurde. Auch Bischof Eckbert von Bamberg, ein Bruder der Hl. Hedwig, und die Schreibstube des Benediktinerklosters Michelsberg wurden in die Überlegungen einbezogen. Die Sprache der Bildbeischriften weist in den bair.-md. Grenzbereich, was sowohl böhm. als auch ostfrk. Herkunft möglich erscheinen läßt; vgl. *The Pierpont Morgan Library. A Review of the Growth, Development and Activities of the Library during the Period between its Establishment as an Educational Institution in February 1924 and the Close of the Year 1929* (New York, 1930), S. 53-55 und SUCKALE-REDLEFSEN, *Buchkunst zur Zeit der Andechs-Meranier*, S. 248, 373 f. und Abb. 148, 154, 162, 365.

Den Psalter lesen

Könnte man bei den Psalmen selbst noch eine relativ hohe Quote passiver, d.h. auswendig gelernter Textpräsenz annehmen, eine aktive Lesefähigkeit der potentiellen Rezipienten so vielleicht sogar negieren, machen volkssprachliche Ein- und Nachträge als Gebrauchsanweisungen nur Sinn, wenn die Rezipient(inn)en dieser Bücher sie auch selbst *lesen* konnten. Da die volkssprachlichen Gebrauchsanweisungen und die dazugehörigen lateinischen Psalmen in der Regel kommunikativ verflochten waren, d.h. dem deutschen Paratext ohne den lateinischen Basistext, der sich durch die volkssprachlichen Anweisungen eben nicht automatisch erschließt, die Sinnebene fehlte, ist weiter zu folgern, daß auch der lat. Psalm aktiv präsent sein mußte.[53]

Die hoch normierten und sicher in weiten Teilen – auch – schriftfrei memorierten Psalmen setzten allerdings keine größeren Schrift- und Lateinkenntnisse oder gar ein aktives Lateinwissen voraus. Es reichten elementare Grundkenntnisse. "This level of Latinity would still exclude them from an appreciation of Latin literature and its techniques".[54] Auf genau diese bescheidenen Grundkenntnisse spielt Albert von Stade bei der Charakterisierung Hildegards von Bingen despektierlich an.[55] Von ihr heißt es in Alberts *Cronica* – geringschätzig – "*nichil umquam didicerit, nisi solum psalterium more nobilium puellarum*" (*MGH SS* 16, S. 330) – "sie hatte nichts weiter gelernt als den Psalter, wie es bei adligen Mädchen Brauch ist". Aber sie hatte ihn gelernt, und es war bei adligen Mädchen eben *Brauch*, ihn zu lernen! Albert berichtet hier offensichtlich von einer um 1250 – oder gar schon zu Lebzeiten Hildegards? – gängigen Praxis bei Hofe. Diese durchaus verbreiteten rudimentären Kenntnisse sind es aber, die der laikalen Hofgesellschaft einen Zugang zur Schriftkultur sichern. Bis ins 11./12. Jh. gilt dies freilich nur für die dünne Schicht der hoch-

[53] LENTES, "Text des Kanons und Heiliger Text", S. 340 f., geht hier viel zu pauschal davon aus, daß "der lateinische Text kaum verstanden wurde" und reduziert seine Wirkung deshalb zum "Apotropaion" (vgl. dazu grundlegend D.C. SKEMER, "Amulet Rolls and Female Devotion in the Middle Ages", *Scriptorium* 55 (2001), S. 197-227). Ich denke, daß man hier genau zwischen dem sehr wohl verstandenen Text (vgl. dazu die *lese*-Belege) auf der einen und der apotropäischen Nutzanwendung – also der Magie des Wort(laut)es und des Buchkörpers – unterscheiden muß. Selbst im laikalen Umfeld wird man beide Rezeptionsebenen als 'Normalität des Alltags' annehmen dürfen.

[54] GREEN, "Court Literature and its Audience", S. 19.

[55] Albert von Stade bezieht sich hier offensichtlich auf die Hildegard-Vita des Theodoricus Epternacensis, wo die gesamte Szenerie freilich die unmittelbare, eben nicht auf eine genaue Schriftkenntnis bauende Verbindung der heiligen Nonne zu Gott dokumentieren will. Über den Bildungsstand ist bei Theodoricus also nichts gesagt, aber Albert will diese Szene wohl in seinem Sinne, d.h. falsch, verstehen.

adligen Elite. Angesichts der danach schnell ansteigenden Überlieferungszahlen auch weit weniger kostbarer Alltagsexemplare und der zunehmend größeren Zahl volkssprachlich aufbereiteter älterer lat. Exemplare (s. Anhang), darf man jedoch spätestens im ausgehenden 12. Jh. mit einer erheblichen Durchdringungstiefe im adligen sowie im späteren 13. Jh. auch im städtischen Milieu rechnen. Für die Zeit um/ab 1200 wird Alberts Aussage von literarischen Zeugnissen etwa in der *Klage*, im *Parzival* (s.o.) oder in *Flore und Blanscheflur* eindrucksvoll bestätigt:

alle naht unz ez taget
liset sî an ir salter,
daz iuch got an iuwer alter
mit genâden bringe;
und ist daz ir gedinge (*Flore und Blanscheflur*, v. 6222-6226)

An dieser Stelle sei nachdrücklich auf Eike von Repgow verwiesen, denn er dokumentiert eine solche Allgegenwärtigkeit des *seltere* und verwandter Bücher juristisch unanfechtbar im Erbrechtsartikel I, 24 §3 des *Sachsenspiegel*-Landrechts (um 1220/30; Abb. 5). Unter der Rubrik: "*Waz zu morgengabe, musteile, gerade, erbe gehort*" heißt es: "*Si nimt ouch alliz, daz zu der gerade gehort, daz sint alle schaf, unde gense, ... vingerlin unde armgolt, sappile, seltere unde alle buchere, die zu gotis dienste gehoren, die vrowen phlegene zu lesene*". Psalter und "*alle buchere, die zu gotis dienste gehoren*", sind also Teil der Grundausstattung einer (adligen) Dame,[56] und, was entscheidend ist, die "*vrowen*" pflegten diese Bücher "*zu lesene*"!

Die Aufnahme in das populärste volkssprachlichen Rechtsbuch des Spätmittelalters erklärt sich wohl nur, wenn eine von alters her bekannte, gängige Besitz- und damit auch Bildungspraxis gespiegelt wird. Einige Jahrzehnte später (um 1270) teilen übrigens die süddeutschen Verfasser des *Schwabenspiegels* kommentarlos Eikes Einschätzung. Im *Schwabenspiegel* nennt die entsprechende Stelle vom "*varnden gute*" der "*vrowen*" wie gehabt "*selter vnd alle puch die zv dem gotes dienste gehörent*" (Langform M Landrecht 25/26, S. 154).[57] Zu

[56] Ganz anders die typische Habe der Männer: In dem der *gerade* entsprechenden *hergewäte* (*Sachsenspiegel* I, 22) taucht kein einziger Hinweis auf ein Buch auf.

[57] Wo immer Eikes Ausführungen nicht (mehr) mit der Situation einige Jahrzehnte später im Süden übereinstimmen, griffen die *Schwabenspiegel*-Autoren massiv in den Text ihrer Vorlage ein. Sie kommentierten, ergänzten, strichen oder überarbeiteten die Vorgaben Eikes. Im Fall der glaubenspraktischen Bücher gab es an Eike nichts auszusetzen. Der Passus wird wörtlich übernommen; vgl. zu den Überarbeitungstendenzen exemplarisch J. WOLF, "Zwischen Mündlichkeit und Schriftlichkeit: Die frühen deutschen Judeneide im 13. Jahrhundert", in: *Magister et amicus. Festschrift Gärtner*, hg. v. V. BOK und F. SHAW (Wien, 2003), S. 839-874.

Abb. 5: Oldenburger Bilderhandschrift des *Sachsenspiegel*, f. 19r: gerade. Abbildungsnachweis: W. PETERS, “Der Rechtswortschatz in Land und Stadt Oldenburg”, in: *Beiträge und Katalog zu den Ausstellungen Bilderhandschriften des Sachsenspiegels – Niederdeutsche Sachsenspiegel und Nun vernehmet in Land und Stadt – Oldenburg – Sachsenspiegel – Stadtrecht*, hg. V. E. KOOLMAN, E. GÄSSLER und F. SCHEELE, 2., verbesserte Aufl. (Oldenburg, 1995: *Veröffentlichungen des Stadtmuseums Oldenburg* 21 = *Schriften der Landesbibliothek Oldenburg* 29), S. 361-372, hier S. 367 Abb.76.; mit freundlicher Genehmigung der Sparkasse Oldenburg.

denken gibt nur der fehlende Hinweis, daß die Frauen die Bücher auch zu lesen pflegten: Hatte drei, vier Jahrzehnte nach Eikes Aufzeichnung die Lesefähigkeit nachgelassen? War im Süden (in Augsburg?) die Lesefähigkeit geringer als im Norden (in Magdeburg?)? Oder brauchte es um 1270 eines solchen Hinweises gar nicht mehr, da das Lesen – erst jetzt – völlig selbstverständlich geworden war? Die große Zahl der nun überall aus dem Boden schießenden städtischen Schulen läßt Letzteres am plausibelsten erscheinen, wobei man sich allerdings gerade im Süden auffallend lange Zeit mit der Gründung ließ.[58]

[58] Vgl. K. SCHNEIDER, *Gotische Schriften in deutscher Sprache, I. Vom späten 12. Jahrhundert bis um 1300, Text- und Tafelband* (Wiesbaden, 1987), S. 206-207 und 260-261,

Aber diese Bücher, die zum Gottesdienst gehörten, boten weit mehr als das Grundinventar zum Vollzug des christlichen Ritus. Der Psalter (mit Kalendar, Gebeten, Vaterunser etc.) war ständiger Begleiter, Ratgeber, Dialogpartner bei der alltäglichen Ausübung der Glaubenspraxis (Dialog mit Gott), Helfer in verschiedensten Lebenslagen, Kalender und Schatztruhe für die Memoria des eigenen Geschlechts. Ein meist vorangehendes Kalendar konnte zu diesem Zweck fortlaufend mit aktuellen Einträgen – in der Regel Sterbedaten von Familienmitgliedern und Heiligenfesten – gefüllt und damit zu einem Nekrolog ausgebaut werden. Von Generation zu Generation weitergereicht, verschmolzen so private Andacht, überindividueller Gottesdienst und personale Erinnerung zeitlos miteinander. Und auch dies machte nur Sinn, wenn die Verfasser wie die Adressaten über eine gewisse Schreib-/Lesekompetenz verfügten. Typische Beispiele für solche bi- (Andacht – Memoria) oder sogar trifunktionale (Andacht – Memoria – Fundation) Kodizes können wir mit dem als fundierenden Stiftungsexemplar verwendeten *Gebetbuch der Heiligen Hedwig von Schlesien* (Anhang Nr. 62), dem *codex rotundus* einer Gutha (Anhang Nr. 69) und dem *Psalter der Anna von Bolanden* (Anhang Nr. 46) fassen, wobei in allen drei Fällen die spezifischen volkssprachlichen Anteile auf einen zwischen Hof und Kloster changierenden Nutzungskontext verweisen. Solche Gebetbücher waren lebendiger Bestandteil einer Glaubenspraxis, wie sie der liturgische Rahmen vorgab. Innerhalb eines solchen Rahmens hatte die Volkssprache auch am weltlichen Hof noch lange nur eine dienende Funktion. Sie half bei der Anwendung der *lateinischen* Psalmen und diente zur Ausführung der Glaubenspraxis (Gebete, Beichte, Vaterunser, Glaubensbekenntnis). Umfangreichere, als gleichzeitige Einheit mit dem lateinischen Psalter konzipierte volkssprachliche Passagen blieben nicht zuletzt deshalb bis ins ausgehende 13. Jahrhundert ausgesprochen selten und sind dann speziellen Interessenkonstellationen geschuldet (zur grundsätzlich anderen Funktion von dt. Rubriken s.o.). Zwei Beispiele von ganz unterschiedlicher Funktionalität seien herausgegriffen: Einen größeren, von vornherein in den lateinischen Textverbund integrierten deutschen Text enthält z.B. der 1276 vollendete *Magdeburger Psalter* (Anhang Nr. 54).[59] Die kostbaren Illustrationen lassen an ein bedeutendes Adelsgeschlecht als

sowie zusammenfassend und mit weiterführender Literatur A. WENDEHORST, "Wer konnte im Mittelalter lesen und schreiben?", in: *Schulen und Studium im sozialen Wandel des hohen und späten Mittelalters*, hg. v. J. FRIED (Sigmaringen, 1986: *Vorträge und Forschungen* 30), S. 9-33, hier S. 28-33, und M. KINTZINGER, "Schule und Schüler in der gegenwärtigen interdisziplinären Mittelalterforschung", in: *Schule und Schüler im Mittelalter. Beiträge zur europäischen Bildungsgeschichte des 9. bis 15. Jahrhunderts*, hg. v. M. KINTZINGER, S. LORENZ und M. WALTER (Köln, Weimar und Wien, 1996: *Beihefte zum Archiv für Kulturgeschichte* 42), S. 1-10.

[59] Der Kodex ist seit dem 2. Weltkrieg verschollen.

Auftraggeber denken, das aufgrund gewichtiger Indizien im Raum um Magdeburg verortet werden kann.[60] Der ungewöhnliche, dem Psalter vorgeschaltete volkssprachliche *Zweifler* (Bl. 8v-9v) rückt den Kodex zudem in die Nähe zisterziensischer Laienfrömmigkeit. Der dt. Verstext enthält eine frühe Fassung der Legende vom Mönch Felix, der bekanntlich Zisterzienser war.[61] Ansonsten fällt auf, daß der Autor über den Nibelungenstoff unterrichtet ist. Zur Relativität von weltlichem Besitz vermerkt er:

> *Waz half den nibelungen ir hort*
> *do si erslagen vorden dort*
> *in vremedem lande.* (Hardenberg[62] 35-38)

Der Verfasser mahnt weiter, "*gůt vnde werltliche ere*" (Z. 43) nicht zu überschätzen, denn "*Ez ist allez toub vnde blint / vnde ein trovm da mit die werlt vert*" (Z. 46 f.). Insgesamt erweckt der *Zweifler* den Eindruck einer prologartigen Anleitung zur rechten christlichen Lebensführung. Mit den auf die Relativität weltlicher Güter anspielenden Lehrsätzen versucht der Autor wohl die aus höchsten Adelskreisen stammende Auftraggeberin auf den rechten Pfad der Tugend zu führen. Man könnte sich ein solches Buch gut am (anhaltinischen?) Hof zur Unterweisung des fürstlichen Nachwuchses oder als Dedikationsexemplar für die Neugründung eines dem adligen Stifter besonders nahestehenden (Zisterzienser-)Klosters vorstellen.[63] Etwa zur gleichen Zeit entstand

[60] In der Bildgestaltung bestehen engste Verbindungen zu einem aus dem Magdeburger Raum (um 1265) stammenden Psalter mit Totenoffizium (München, BSB, Clm 23094; vgl. E. KLEMM, *Die illuminierten Handschriften des 13. Jahrhunderts deutscher Herkunft in der Bayerischen Staatsbibliothek. Text- und Tafelband* [Wiesbaden, 1998: *Katalog der illuminierten Handschriften der Bayerischen Staatsbibliothek in München* 4], S. 262-266, Abb. XVI, 663-670, und zur Gruppe verwandter sächsischer Psalterien ebd. S. 263, 265). Weitere Indizien für Magdeburg: Die Handschrift wurde im Jahr *Dusent zweihundert vnd sechse und sůbenzec* (1276) von *heinrich de vnisborch* (Bl. 190v) angefertigt. Unseburg a.d. Bode liegt bei Magdeburg. Auch das Kalendar weist wie der Schreibdialekt des volkssprachlichen Teils (Mitteldeutsch mit nd. Einschlag bzw. Elbostfälisch) nach Magdeburg; vgl. grundlegend LEROQUAIS, *Les Psautiers*, S. 268-270, mit Teilabdruck des Kalendariums und Abbildungen der Bildseiten ebd. Pl. XCV-CII) und R. KROOS, "Die Miniaturen", in: *Das Buch der Welt. Kommentar und Edition zur Sächsischen Weltchronik; Ms. Memb. I 90, Forschungs- und Landesbibliothek Gotha*, hg. v. H. HERKOMMER (Luzern, 2000), S. 47-117, hier S. 47-48, 58-59 und Abb. 3, 23.

[61] In einigen Fassungen wird direkt auf ein Zisterzienserkloster angespielt. Die Magdeburger Version enthält diese eindeutigen Hinweise nicht.

[62] C. VON HARDENBERG, "Geistliches Gedicht des XIII. Jahrhunderts", *Germania* 25 (1880), S. 339-344.

[63] Dem *Zweifler* ist auf Bl. 10r zum Abschluß eine ganzseitige Miniatur beigefügt (LEROQUAIS, *Les Psautiers*, Abb. XCVIII). Sie zeigt einen Mönch (den Mönch Felix?) vor einem Kloster (einem Zisterzienserkloster?), wie er dem Gesang der Vögel lauscht; vgl. grundlegend

für einen "privaten Benutzer (im Grenzbereich zwischen Regensburg und Franken?)"[64] der mit zahlreichen dt. Gebetsanweisungen aufbereitete Münchner Psalter Clm 2641 (Anhang Nr. 60). Das Buch wurde in den folgenden Jahrzehnten – an einem Hof? – intensiv genutzt. Kurz nach 1300 ergänzte man die Handschrift auf der letzten, ursprünglich leeren Seite (Bl. 151v) um ein *Marienlied.* Anders als beim *Zweifler*, der seine Einleitung wohl dem didaktischen Anspruch des herstellenden Psalter-Skriptoriums oder dem Wunsch der Auftraggeberin verdankt, wird in diesem einzigen umfangreicheren deutschen Text der Münchner Psalterhandschrift die persönliche Marienbegeisterung des aktuellen Besitzers bzw. der Besitzerin sichtbar.[65] Der *Münchner Psalter* erweist sich damit auch viele Jahrzehnte nach seiner Fertigstellung als 'lebendiger' Teil der Glaubenspraxis.

III. Psalter und Gebetbuch als Schlüssel zur Literarizität der Hofkultur

Ziehen wir Bilanz. An der aktiven Präsenz des Psalters bzw. des Gebetbuchs in der laikalen Hofkultur des 12. und dann vor allem des 13. Jh.s lassen die im Anhang zusammengestellten Nachweise von beinahe 100 lateinischen Psalterien/Gebetbücher mit dt. Ein- und Nachträgen keinen Zweifel. Mehr noch als der unmittelbar an ein höfisches Publikum gerichtete volkssprachliche Einleitungstext des *Magdeburger Psalters* und das aus der aktuellen Nutzung resultierende volkssprachliche *Marienlied* des Münchner Psalters erlauben die volkssprachlichen Marginalien und Einträge faszinierende Einblicke in die Lebenswirklichkeit dieser Textsorte. Sie verweisen immer wieder auf einen – auch – laikalen Nutzungshorizont und zeigen die Interferenzen zwischen klerikal-lateinischer und laikal-volkssprachlicher Welt. Die beinahe an jedem Hof als Standardinventar präsenten "*seltere unde buchere, die zu gotis dienste gehoren*", geben zudem Zeugnis von der frühen literarischen Durchdringung der sich scheinbar erst langsam an die Schriftlichkeit herantastenden laikalen Hofgesellschaft. Und was entscheidend ist, die Fähigkeit, die Bücher *lesen* zu können, war Bestandteil der Grundausbildung wenigstens der "literate noblewo-

N.F. PALMER, "Der Zweifler", ^{2}*VL* 10 (1999), Sp. 1621-1622. PALMER denkt vor allem an eine Verwendung als Dedikationsexemplar.

[64] KLEMM, *Die illuminierten Handschriften,* S. 63-65 Nr. 4 und Taf. XII, Abb. 124-129 (hier S. 65).

[65] Vgl. G. KORNRUMPF, "Ein deutsches Marienlied des 13. Jahrhunderts, eine Cantio – und eine Minnelied-Melodie?", in: *Fata Libellorum. Festschrift Fj. Pensel* (Göppingen, 1999: *GAG* 648), S. 101-112, mit Abdruck und Abbildung.

man".[66] Dazu gehörte die Fähigkeit, einzelne Passagen in allen Lebenslagen betend, beschwörend, heilend, singend, klagend richtig einzusetzen. Wohl kaum zufällig bieten viele besonders kostbar illuminierte Psalterien, wie man sie an den großen Fürstenhöfen vermuten darf, genau an dieser Stelle markante volkssprachliche 'Gebrauchsanweisungen'.[67]

Nimmt man Eikes von Repgow Erbrechtsartikel, die literarischen Zeugnisse, die Skulpturen und vor allem die gewaltige Zahl der Buchexemplare ernst, dürften die Beobachtungen grundsätzliche Folgen für die Bewertung des höfischen Lebens im 12./13. Jh. haben. Die weltlichen Höfe erscheinen damit schon früh – lange bevor in der 2. Hälfte des 13. Jahrhunderts eine nennenswerte volkssprachliche Schriftproduktion faßbar wird[68] – mittelbar (rezipierend) in der Schriftlichkeit verankert. Vor allem die ein- oder nachgetragenen Gebrauchsanweisungen, Gebete, Nekrologeinträge und viele andere unmittelbare Nutzungszeugnisse sind es, die in einzigartiger Weise die alltägliche Glaubenspraxis am Hof spiegeln. Psalter und Gebetbuch sind damit authentische Zeugnisse der von einer tiefen Religiosität durchdrungenen höfischen Lebenswirklichkeit, die sich, und dies sei einmal mehr nachdrücklich betont, auch am weltlichen Hof nicht zuletzt aus Büchern speist. Und diese Bücher bieten weit mehr als die schriftlich fixierten Glaubensinhalte. Sie sind als Transportbehälter, Andachtsobjekte und Reliquien zugleich Muster für andere, sich z.T. erst auf dieser Folie entwickelnde literarische Emanzipationsversuche. Die "*buchere, die zu gotis dienste gehoren*", öffnen damit die vermeintlich illiterate Welt des laikalen Hofs der hoch entwickelten klerikalen Schriftlichkeit.

Daß eben diese allgegenwärtigen Bücher des Glaubens, die man an vielen (allen?) Höfen *schouwen* konnte, in Gestaltung, Ausstattung und Einrichtung wichtige Vorbilder für die Tradierung der höfischen Literatur wurden, erscheint da nur als logische Konsequenz: Einige der Artusepen Chrétiens de Troyes, verschiedene Handschriften des französischen Prosa-Artuszyklus, die Berliner Bilder-Handschrift von Heinrichs von Veldeke *Eneas*, der Gießner *Iwein*, manche Textzeugen der Werke Wolframs von Eschenbach, mehrere bebilderte Reimchroniken und einige der berühmtesten französischen und deutschen Lyrikhandschriften werden in psalterähnlichen Kodizes tradiert. In einzelnen Fällen sind sogar explizit Skriptoriumszusammenhänge zwischen Psalter- und

[66] GREEN, "Court Literature and its Audience", S. 14-19.

[67] Damit werden pauschale (Fehl-)Urteile relativiert, wenn nicht falsifiziert, wie man sie z.B. in dem Ausstellungskatalog von ACHTEN, *Das christliche Gebetbuch im Mittelalter*, S. 15, nachlesen kann: "Der private Psalter diente in dieser Zeit wohl mehr als frommes Bilderbuch und Statussymbol, denn als biblisches Gebetbuch".

[68] Vgl. J. WOLF, "Buch und Text. Literatur- und kulturhistorische Untersuchungen zur volkssprachlichen Schriftlichkeit im 12. und 13. Jh." (Marburg, 2002: Habil. masch.).

Epenwerkstätten auszumachen.[69] Für den deutschen Sprachraum am markantesten dürfte dabei die Gruppe der Kodizes rund um die umfangreich bebilderte Vadiana-Sammlung mit Strickers *Karl* und Rudolfs von Ems *Weltchronik* sein (St. Gallen, StB Vadiana, Ms. 302 Vad.): Aus der selben Malwerkstatt stammen unter anderem mehrere kostbar illustrierte lateinische Psalterien (Graz, UB, Cod. 1029, Wien, ÖNB, Cod. 1982), eine lateinische Bibel (Graz, UB, Cod. 130) und ein vermutlich für Gregor von Falkenstein und seine Gemahlin entstandenes Zisterzienserbrevier (Luzern, Zentralbibliothek, P.4.4°).[70] Enge Verwandtschaft besteht ferner zum *Lilienfelder Missale* und weiteren Kodizes aus dem Umfeld des Lilienfelder Meisters. Dazu zählen u.a. das volkssprachliche Münchner Nonnengebetbuch (München, BSB, Cgm 101) und ein um 1310 angefertigtes deutsches Stundenbuch ('s-Heerenberg, Huis Bergh, Hs. 52).[71]

Pauschale (Vor-)Urteile zur Illiterarizität der laikalen Hofgesellschaft wird man vor dem Hintergrund dieser überall präsenten Bücher endgültig zu den Akten legen können, auch wenn der Psalter an so manchem Hof und in so manchem Patrizierhaus vielleicht überhaupt das einzige Buch war. Geradezu selbstverständlich wird das Bild einer besonders engen Verflechtung von weltlichem Hof und Glaube bestätigt. Letztlich erscheint über den Psalter ein von christlichen Idealen durchdrungenes klerikales Bildungsprogramm überhaupt als das zentrale Fundament des höfischen Lebens wirkmächtig präsent. Die von Otfrid von Weißenburg, Chrétien de Troyes, Wolfram von Eschenbach, Rudolf von Ems, Berthold von Regensburg und vielen anderen vermittelte Selbstverständlichkeit des Konnexes von Psalter und Hof bestätigt scheinbar vorbehaltlos eine solche Vorstellung. Doch wie passen die despektierlichen Äußerungen Alberts von Stade über Hildegard von Bingen und vor allem Steinmars Klage über die

[69] Vgl. mit Beispielen aus der Chrétienüberlieferung A. STONES, "The Illustrated Chrétien Manuscripts and their Artistic Context", in: *Les Manuscrits de Chrétien de Troyes,* 2. Bde., hg. v. K. BUSBY, T. NIXON, A. STONES und L. WALTERS (Amsterdam und Atlanta, 1993: *Faux Titre* 71), S. 227-322 (bes. S. 251-253 und Abb. 65-76 zur Princetoner Chrétien-Handschrift und dem 'Psalter des Guy du Boisrouvray') sowie mit Beispielen aus dem dt. Sprachraum N.F. PALMER, "Von der Paläographie zur Literaturwissenschaft. Anläßlich von Karin Schneider, Gotische Schriften in deutscher Sprache, Bd. I", *PBB* 113 (1991), S. 213-250, hier S. 247-248, zu dem wohl aus einer "auf die Herstellung liturgischer Bücher spezialisierten Werkstatt" stammenden 'Gießner *Iwein*' und WOLF, "Buch und Text", *passim.*

[70] Vgl. grundlegend J. RAEBER und A. BRÄM, "Das Zisterzienserbrevier P4.4° in der Zentralbibliothek Luzern. Eine Bilderhandschrift aus der Freiburger Werkstatt der *Weltchronik* des Rudolf von Ems, Vad. 302", *Zeitschrift für Schweizerische Archäologie und Kunstgeschichte* 54 (1997), S. 59-68. Die Falkenstein-These stützt sich freilich nur auf Indizien (Beweisführung ebd. S. 64).

[71] Vgl. grundlegend die Beträge von E.J. BEER und K. SCHNEIDER in: *Rudolf von Ems, Weltchronik. Der Stricker, Karl der Große. Kommentar zu Ms 302 Vad. der Kantonsbibliothek (Vadiana) St. Gallen*, hg. v. E. J. BEER u.a. (Luzern, 1987).

psalterverliebten 'Betschwestern' in einen solchen Rahmen? Bekommt das gerade erst entworfene Bild einer wenigstens leidlich gebildeten, von einer tiefen Religiosität durchdrungenen Hofkultur schon wieder Risse? Sind die Psalterien, so wie wir sie in den Epen kennenlernen, eventuell nur Accessoires der Hofkultur (zur apotropäischen Funktion s. o. Anm. 53) – nicht anders als Schwerter, Rüstungen und Pferde? Hatte das über den Psalter transportierte Glaubensprofil vielleicht eine viel geringere Akzeptanz am weltlichen Hof, als es uns die Texte (und damit die *clerici*!) glauben machen wollen? Lassen sich einige der höfischen Epen – ich denke vor allem an die im französischen Sprachraum sehr populären Gralepen und den Prosa-Artuszyklus – nicht sogar als Gegenentwurf zum Psalter, als separates 'Evangelium für den Ritter' lesen und ist die über den Psalter faßbare Brücke zwischen Kirche und *clerici* auf der einen sowie Hofkultur und *laici* auf der anderen Seite vielleicht brüchiger als es die Omnipräsenz der Bücher glauben macht?

Anhang. Lateinische Psalterien/Gebetbücher des 12. und 13. Jh.s mit dt. Gebetsanweisungen, Rubriken, Ein- und Nachträgen[72]

Grundlegende Literatur

SCHÖNDORF, *Die Tradition der deutschen Psalmenübersetzung* (wie Anm. 44); H. ENGELHART, "Gebetsanweisungen in lat. Psalterhandschriften", ^{2}*VL* 1 (1980) Sp. 1129-1130; M. WALLACH-FALLER, *Ein Alemannischer Psalter aus dem 14. Jahrhundert* (Freiburg i.d. Schweiz, 1981: *Spicilegium Friburgense* 27), S. 144-146; E. HELLGARDT, "Die deutschsprachigen Handschriften im 11. und 12. Jahrhundert. Bestand und Charakteristik im chronologischen Aufriß", in: *Deutsche Handschriften 1100-1400* (wie Anm. 4), S. 34-79; E. HELLGARDT, "Deutsche Gebetsanweisungen zum Psalter in lateinischen und deutschen Handschriften und Drucken des 12.-16. Jahrhunderts", in: *Deutsche Bibelübersetzungen des Mittelalters. Beiträge eines Kolloquiums im Deutschen Bibel-Archiv*, unter Mitarbeit v. N. HENKEL hg. v. H. REINITZER (Bern *et al.*, 1991: *Vestigia Bibliae* 9/10), S. 400-413; E. HELLGARDT, "Lateinisch-deutsche Textensembles in Handschriften des 12. Jahrhunderts", in: *Latein und Volkssprache* (wie Anm. 30), S. 19-31; P. OCHSENBEIN, "Deutschsprachige Privatgebetbücher vor 1400" (wie Anm. 4; ergänzend mit 19 deutschsprachigen Privatgebetbüchern des folgenden Jahrhunderts) sowie die Internet-Datenbanken MR13 (http://www.uni-marburg.de/hosting/mr13/welcome.html) und MANUSCRIPTA MEDIAEVALIA (http://www.manuscripta-mediaevalia.de/hs/kataloge-online.htm).

1 **Admont, SfB, Cod. 567**
lat. Martyrologium – Mitte 12. Jh.
– dt. Profeßformel (Nachtrag)
– dt. Gebetsanweisung zum Psalter
H.U. SCHMID, "Mittelhochdeutsches aus dem Frauenkloster Admont", in: *Deutsche Literatur und Sprache von 1050-1200. Festschrift für Ursula Hennig*, hg. v. A. FIEBIG und H.-J. SCHIEWER (Berlin, 1995), S. 217-220, hier S. 218-219.

2 **Admont, SfB, Cod. 575**
lat. Psalter – 12. Jh.
– dt. Gebetsanweisungen, marginal wohl von einer Nonne des Admonter Nonnenklosters um 1200 nachgetragen
SCHMID, "Admont", S. 219-220.

3 **Aschaffenburg, Hofbibl., Ms. 5**
lat. Psalter – 2. Hälfte 13. Jh.
– dt. Gebetsanweisungen

[72] Die folgenden Beschreibungen sollen und können nicht mehr als einen ersten Zugriff zu den Handschriften bieten: Kurz charakterisiert werden die lat. Primärtexte und die dt. Anteile; die Datierungen stützen sich auf die Forschungsliteratur (meist die genannten Handschriftenkataloge) und sind meist nach Autopsie oder Mikrofilm geprüft. An dieser Stelle sei N. Palmer ganz besonders gedankt. Er hat nicht nur mit zahlreichen Hinweisen zum gewaltigen Umfang des Anhangs beigetragen, sondern in vielen fruchtbaren Diskussionen meinen Blick für die Probleme der Materie geschärft. Daß nicht alle seine Anregungen umgesetzt werden konnten, hat seine Ursachen ebenso in der Heterogenität der Materie wie im begrenzten Raum.

J. HOFMANN und H. THURN, *Die Handschriften der Hofbibliothek Aschaffenburg* (Aschaffenburg, 1978: *Veröffentlichungen des Geschichts- und Kunstvereins Aschaffenburg e. V.* 15), S. 12-16.

4 **Aschaffenburg, SfB, Ms. Perg. 35**
lat. Liber precum – 2. Hälfte 12. Jh.
– dt. Rubriken
J. HOFMANN und U.H. HAUKE, *Die Handschriften der Stiftsbibliothek und der Stiftskirche zu Aschaffenburg* (Aschaffenburg, 1978: *Veröffentlichungen des Geschichts- und Kunstvereins Aschaffenburg e. V.* 16), S. 74-76.

5 **Augsburg, SStB, 2° Cod. 5**
lat. Psalter – Anfang 13. Jh.
– einzelne marginal nachgetragene dt. Angaben zu Gebetszeiten
H. SPILLING, *Die Handschriften der Staats- und Stadtbibliothek Augsburg 2° Cod 1-100* (Wiesbaden, 1978: *Handschriftenkataloge der Staats- und Stadtbibliothek Augsburg* 2), S. 9-11.

6 **Augsburg, SStb, 2° Cod. 6**
lat. Psalter – Anfang 13. Jh. (vor 1212?)
– dt. marginal eingetragene Gebetsanweisungen
SPILLING, *Augsburg*, S. 11-13; HELLGARDT, "Deutsche Gebetsanweisungen", S. 403; DERS., "Handschriften im 11. und 12. Jahrhundert", S. 73 Nr. 247.

7 **Augsburg, UB, Cod. I.2.4° 19**
lat. Augsburger Psalter – um 1220
– dt. marginal eingetragene Gebetsanweisungen
HELLGARDT, "Handschriften im 11. und 12. Jahrhundert", S. 63 Nr. 120.

8 **Bamberg, SB, Ms. bibl. 49**
lat. Psalter – nach 1300
– dt. Gebetsanweisungen
F. LEITSCHUH und H. FISCHER, *Katalog der Handschriften der königlichen Bibliothek zu Bamberg* (Bamberg, 1887-1912), S.43-44; HELLGARDT, "Deutsche Gebetsanweisungen", S. 403.

9 **Bamberg, SB, Cod. I Q a 2 + Stuttgart, LB, Cod. bibl. 2° 46**
lat. *Comburger Psalter* – um 1220/30
– dt. Gebetsanweisungen
W. IRTENKAUF, *Stuttgarter Zimelien. Württembergische Landesbibliothek. Aus den Schätzen ihrer Handschriftensammlung* (Stuttgart, 1985), S. 94; HELLGARDT, "Deutsche Gebetsanweisungen", S. 403.

10 **Berlin, Kunstbibl. , 4000-99,332 (verschollen) + Chicago, Art Institute, Coll. Joel Spitz acc. No. 24671 + New York, Coll. B.H. Breslauer + Paris, BN, Nouv. acq. lat. 3102 + Washington, National Gallery of Art, Rosenwald Coll.**
lat. *Arenberg-Psalter* – um 1230/40
– dt. Gebetsanweisungen marginal nachgetragen im gesamten Codex (dt. Teile um 1300)
KLAMT, "Zum Arenberg-Psalter" (wie Anm. 32), S. 147-155 und Abb. 103-111; F. AVRIL und C. RABEL, *Manuscrits enluminés d'origine germanique, Tome 1: X^e-XIVe siècle* (Paris, 1995), S. 141-144 und Abb. L, CXVI-CXIX (mit Nachweis der älteren Literatur); HELLGARDT, "Deutsche Gebetsanweisungen", S. 403; http://www.maryvillecollege.edu/cartlidge/apoc1400/APOC1420.htm

11 **Beuron, SfB, Frgm. 110**
lat. Psalter – 2. Hälfte 12. Jh.
– dt. Gebetsanweisungen
HELLGARDT, "Handschriften im 11. und 12. Jahrhundert", S. 63 Nr. 121; DERS., "Deutsche Gebetsanweisungen", S. 403.

12 **Cambridge, University Library, Ms. Add. 4080**
lat. *Medinger Gebetbuch* (Osterteil) – vor 1291
– nd. Interpolationen
Deutsche Handschriften in England, beschr. v. R. PRIEBSCH, Bd. 1: *Ashburnham-Place, Cambridge, Cheltenham, Oxford, Wigan. Mit einem Anhang ungedruckter Stücke* (Erlangen, 1896), S. 31-34 (mit Abdruck der dt. Teile).

13 **Cividale, Museo Archeologico Nazionale, Ms. CXXXVII**
lat. *Elisabethpsalter* – vor 1208
– dt. Gebetsanweisung zum *agnus dei* (nachgetragen)
– vereinzelte, nachgetragene dt. Bildbeischriften
H. WOLTER-VON DEM KNESEBECK, *Der Elisabethpsalter in Cividale del Friuli. Buchmalerei für den Thüringer Landgrafenhof zu Beginn des 13. Jahrhunderts* (Berlin, 2001), *passim* (bes. S. 91 u. 352).

14 **Cologny-Genf, Bibl. Bodmeriana, Cod. Bod. 30 (Teil 1)**
lat. Psalter, Hymnen etc. – um 1200
– dt. nachgetragene z.T. gereimte Fasten- und Gebetsanweisungen (14. Jh.) sowie vier Spruchstrophen in einem sonst nicht bekannten Ton mit der Subscriptio: *Gedenke eins cůnrat. Amen* (Ende 13. Jh.)
E. PELLEGRIN, *Manuscrits latins de la Bodmeriana* (Cologny-Genf, 1982), S. 66-79; RSM 1 (1994), S. 160; *Deutsche Handschriften des Mittelalters in der Bodmeriana*. Katalog bearb. v. R. WETZEL. Mit einem Beitrag von K. SCHNEIDER zum ehemaligen Kalocsa-Codex (Cologny-Genève, 1994: *Bibliotheca Bodmeriana Kataloge* VII), S. 213-215.

15 **Darmstadt, Hess. LB, Inc. IV/124 (Makulatur)**
lat. Brevierfragment – um 1200 s. Nr. 67 (Codex Discissus)
N. KOUBEK, "Ein illuminiertes Brevierfragment um 1200 in einem Straßburger Einband des 15. Jahrhunderts", *Bibliothek und Wissenschaft* 26 (1992/93), S. 1-7.

16 **Dillingen, Studienbibliothek, Cod. XV Frgm. 7**
lat. Psalter – 13. Jh.
– dt. Stoßgebet in einer Initiale
A. SCHRÖDER, "Mitteilungen. Bruchstücke von lateinischen und deutschen Handschriften im Besitz der Kreis- und Studienbibliothek Dillingen", *Archiv für die Geschichte des Hochstifts Augsburg* 5 (1916-1919), S. 620-629, hier S. 624.

17 **Erlangen, UB, Ms. 116**
lat. Psalter – 13. Jh.
– dt. Gebetsanweisungen
H. FISCHER, *Katalog der Handschriften der Universitätsbibliothek Erlangen*. Bd. 1: *Die Lateinischen PergamentHandschriften* (Erlangen, 1928), S. 123-124; HELLGARDT, "Deutsche Gebetsanweisungen", S. 403.

18 **Erlangen, UB, Ms. 117 (olim Irm. 412)**
lat. Psalter – um 1220/30
– dt. Gebetsanweisungen
FISCHER, *Katalog Erlangen*, S. 124; E. LUTZE, *Die BilderHandschriften der Universitätsbibliothek Erlangen* (Erlangen, 1936: *Katalog der Handschriften der Universitätsbibliothek Erlangen* 6; Nachdr. Wiesbaden 1971), S. 42 und 44.

19 **Erlangen, UB, Ms. 143 (olim Irm. 590)**
lat. Psalter – Mitte 13. Jh.
– dt. Gebetsanweisungen
– dt. Bildbeischriften
– dt. Prosagebete an Christus und Maria [Bl. 159v-162r]; dt. Reimgebet an Maria

[Bl. 162r-168r]; dt. Beichtspiegel [Bl. 168r-174r]; dt. Prosagebet an Johannes Baptista [Bl. 174r-176r]
– dt. [Gebete; Nachtrag 14. Jh.]
FISCHER, *Katalog Erlangen*, S. 147-148; LUTZE, *Bilderhandschriften*, S. 177-180 und Abb. 90-92.

20 **Erlangen, UB, Ms. 151**
lat. Gebetbuch – 13. Jh.
– dt. Gebetsanweisungen
FISCHER, *Katalog Erlangen*, S. 157; HELLGARDT, "Deutsche Gebetsanweisungen", S. 403.

21 **Frankfurt am Main, StUB, Ms. germ. oct. 51**
lat. Psalter einer *uestra Anna* – um 1250/70
– dt. Gebete (Mariengebete; Gebet beim Empfang der Eucharistie, Bl. 204v-208r)
B. WEIMANN, *Die mittelalterlichen Handschriften der Gruppe Manuscripta Germanica* (Frankfurt a. M., 1980: *Kataloge der Stadt- und Universitätsbibliothek Frankfurt a. M.* 5,4), S. 150-152.

22 **Frankfurt am Main, StUB, Ms. lat. oct. 274**
lat. Brevierfragment (Temporale und Sanctorale) – 2. Hälfte 13. Jh.
– dt. Rubriken
– dt. Gebetsanweisungen
K. BREDEHORN und G. POWITZ, *Die mittelalterlichen Handschriften der Gruppe Manuscripta Latina* (Frankfurt a. M., 1979: *Kataloge der Stadt- und Universitätsbibliothek Frankfurt a. M.* 3), S. 172.

23 **Freiburg i. Br., UB, Hs. 24**
lat. Psalter – 1. Hälfte 13. Jh.
– dt. Gebet an den Gekreuzigten [Bl. 1r/v]
W. HAGENMAIER, *Die lateinischen mittelalterlichen Handschriften der Universitätsbibliothek Freiburg im Breisgau* (Wiesbaden, 1974: *Kataloge der Universitätsbibliothek Freiburg im Breisgau* I.1), S. 23-26.

24 **Freiburg i. Br., UB, Hs. 355**
lat. Psalter – 2. Hälfte 12. Jh.
– dt. marginal nachgetragene Gebetsanweisungen (13. Jh.)
W. HAGENMAIER, *Die lateinischen mittelalterlichen Handschriften der Universitätsbibliothek Freiburg im Breisgau* (Wiesbaden, 1980: *Kataloge der Universitätsbibliothek Freiburg im Breisgau* I.3), S. 93f.; HELLGARDT, "Deutsche Gebetsanweisungen", S. 403.

25 **Fulda, LB, Cod. Aa 46**
lat. Psalter – 1. Viertel 13. Jh.[1]
– dt. Freidank
– dt. Meßgebet *Got vater allir cristinheit*
– dt. Gebetsanweisung
– dt. Messegesang
– dt. Nachträge (Freidank-Korpus)
SCHNEIDER, *Gotische Schriften*, S. 101 und Abb. 47; JAKOBI-MIRWALD, *Fulda* (wie Anm. 40), S. 147-148.

[1] Die Datierung der Handschrift ist umstritten. JAKOBI-MIRWALD, *Fulda*, S. 147, nimmt im Vergleich mit zwei ganz ähnlichen, ebenfalls in Allerheiligen entstanden Handschriften (davon Zürich, ZB, Rheinau 85 auf 1253 datiert) die Mitte des 13. Jh.s an. SCHNEIDER, *Gotische Schriften*, S. 101, plädiert mit paläographischen Argumenten für das 1. Viertel des 13. Jh.s und verweist auf einen weiteren, vermutlich aus dem selben Skriptorium stammenden "bald nach 1200" entstandenen Psalter (Stuttgart, WLB, Cod. Donaueschingen 180). Für Informationen zur Handschrift und zum besonderen Status des Meßgebets danke ich ganz herzlich Barbara Leupold, Marburg.

26 **Graz, UB, Cod. 204 (Teil 1)**
lat. Psalter und Hymnar – 13. Jh.
– dt. Rubriken

A. KERN und M. MAIROLD: *Die Handschriften der Universitätsbibliothek Graz*, 3 Bde. (Wien und Leipzig, 1942-1967), hier Bd. I, S. 101-102; HELLGARDT, "Seckauer Handschriften" (wie Anm. 37), *passim*.

27 **Graz, UB, Cod. 287, Bl. 1-12**
lat. Brevier – nicht vor 1200
– dt. 'Grazer Monatsregeln' als Teil eines lat. Kalendarium [Bl. 1v-7r]
– dt. Zeittafeln und Osterberechnung, lat. [Bl. 7v-8r]
– dt. 'Mariensequenz aus Seckau' [Bl. 8v]
KERN und MAIROLD I, S. 156-157; HELLGARDT, "Seckauer Handschriften", *passim*.

28 **Graz, UB, Cod. 763**
lat. Brevier – 2.Hälfte 12.Jh; Interlinearversionen: Ende 12. Jh./um 1200
– dt. Rubriken
– dt. 'Christ ist erstanden' [Bl. 187v]
– dt. Interlinearversionen [Bl. 269r-272r und 275r-276v]
KERN und MAIROLD II, S. 32; HELLGARDT, "Seckauer Handschriften", *passim*.

29 **Graz, UB, Cod. 770**
lat. Brevier – 2. Hälfte 12. Jh.
– dt. Rubriken
KERN und MAIROLD II, S. 35-36; HELLGARDT, "Seckauer Handschriften", *passim*.

30 **Graz, UB, Cod. 778**
lat. Brevier – 2. Hälfte 12. Jh.
– dt. Rubriken
KERN und MAIROLD II, S. 39; HELLGARDT, "Seckauer Handschriften", *passim*.

31 **Graz, UB, Cod. 784**
lat. Rituale – 12. Jh.
– dt. Hagelsegen als Nachtrag (Anfang 13. Jh.) auf der letzten Seite
A. SCHÖNBACH, "Segen aus Grazer Hss.", *ZfdA* 18 (1875), S. 78-81, hier S. 78-79 (mit Abdruck des Segens); KERN und MAIROLD II, S. 42.

32 **Graz, UB, Cod. 789**
lat. Brevier – 13. Jh.
– dt. Rubriken
KERN und MAIROLD II, S. 44; HELLGARDT, "Seckauer Handschriften", *passim*.

33 **Graz, UB, Cod. 832**
lat. Brevier – 2. Hälfte 12. Jh.
– dt. Rubriken
KERN und MAIROLD II, S. 65; HELLGARDT, "Seckauer Handschriften", *passim*.

34 **Graz, UB, Cod. 864**
lat. Brevier – Ende 12./ um 1200
– dt. Rubriken
KERN und MAIROLD II, S. 86; HELLGARDT, "Seckauer Handschriften", *passim*.

35 **Graz, UB, Cod. 1119**
lat. Brevier – Ende 12. Jh.
– dt. Rubriken
KERN und MAIROLD II, S. 232; HELLGARDT, "Seckauer Handschriften", *passim*.

36 **Graz, UB, Cod. 1244**
lat. Brevier – Ende 12. Jh.
– dt. Rubriken
KERN und MAIROLD II, S. 267; HELLGARDT, "Seckauer Handschriften", *passim*.

37 **Graz, UB, Cod. 1257**
lat. Brevier – Ende 12. Jh.
– dt. Rubriken
– dt. Nachträge 13./14. Jh.
Sprüche, u.a. 6 Verspaare Freidank(-Corpus) [Bl. 231v = Randnachtrag]

– dt. Interlinearversion zu Psalm 88 [Bl. 237r-239v]
KERN und MAIROLD II, S. 272-273; HELLGARDT, "Lateinisch-deutsche Textensembles", S. 24; DERS., "Seckauer Handschriften", *passim.*

38 **Graz, UB, Cod. 1549 + Graz, UB, Cod. 1202, Bl. 278-281**
lat. Brevier – Anfang 13. Jh.
– dt. Rubriken
KERN und MAIROLD II, S. 255, 352-353; HELLGARDT, "Seckauer Handschriften", *passim.*

39 **Graz, UB, Cod. 1550**
lat. Brevier – 2. Viertel 13. Jh.
– dt. Rubriken
– dt. 'St. Lambrechter Gebete' (B) [Bl. 67r-73r]
HELLGARDT, "Seckauer Handschriften", S.104, 115, *passim.*

40 **Graz, UB, Cod. 1645**
lat. Gebetbuch – 1. Hälfte 13. Jh.
– dt. Rubriken
– dt. Schreibervers [2 Verse, Bl. 85v]
KERN und MAIROLD II, S. 386; HELLGARDT, "Seckauer Handschriften", *passim.*

41 **Graz, UB, Cod. 1646**
lat. Brevier – 1. Hälfte 13. Jh.
– dt. Rubriken
KERN und MAIROLD II, S. 386; HELLGARDT, "Seckauer Handschriften", *passim.*

42 **Hamburg, SUB, Cod. 84 in scrin.**
lat. Psalter – um 1200
– dt. Überschriften
– dt. Nachträge (Anfang und 3. Viertel 13. Jh.): Gebet; Moralisierendes Alphabet; Ordinarium [Bl. 1r, 7r-v]
T. BRANDIS, *Die Codices in scrinio der Staats- und Universitätsbibliothek Hamburg 1-110* (Hamburg, 1972: *Katalog der Handschriften der Staats- und Universitätsbibliothek Hamburg* VII), S. 135-137.

43 **Hamburg, SUB, Cod. 85 in scrin.**
lat. Psalter – um 1220
– dt.: 'Hamburger Beichte' [Bl. 10v-11r] (Nachtrag 1. Hälfte 13. Jh.)
A. HASELOFF, *Studien zur deutschen Kunstgeschichte* (wie Anm. 15), Nr. IV; BRANDIS, *Katalog Hamburg*, S. 138-140; DERS., "Zu den altdeutschen Beichtformeln. Eine bisher unbekannte mittelfränkische Beichtformel des 13. Jahrhunderts", in: *Deutsche Handschriften* (wie Anm. 4), S. 171-176 (mit Abdruck).

44 **Hohenfurt (Vyšší Brod) in Böhmen, SfB, Cod. XLIX**
lat. Psalter – 13. Jh.
– dt. Marginalglossen
R. PAVEL, *Beschreibung der im Stifte Hohenfurt befindlichen Handschriften* (Wien, 1891: *Xenia Bernhardina* II,2), S. 183.

45 **Karlsruhe, LB, Cod. Lichtenthal 25**
Lat. Psalter – 2. Hälfte 13. Jh.
– dt. Gebetsanweisungen (nachgetragen) und interlineare Wortübersetzungen; vorgebunden bzw. z.T. auch nachgetragen sind dt. Gebete und ein dt. Magnifikat (14./15. Jh.)
Die Handschriften von Lichtenthal, beschr. v. F. HEINZER und G. STAMM (Wiesbaden, 1987: *Die Handschriften der Badischen Landesbibliothek in Karlsruhe* 11), S. 108-110 (mit Nachweis der älteren Literatur).

46 **Karlsruhe, LB, Cod. Lichtenthal 37**
Psalter der Anna von Bolanden – um/nach 1300
– abschnittsweise dt. Übersetzung
HEINZER und STAMM, *Lichtenthal*, S.128-130.

47 **Karlsruhe, LB, Cod. St. Peter perg. 58**
lat. Psalter/Brevierauszüge – um 1260 mit Nachträgen (aus einem Zisterzienserinnenkloster).
– dt. Gebetsanweisungen im Psalterteil
– dt. Gebet zu der Marginalminiatur Christus an der Geißelsäule [Bl. 128v] (Nachtrag Ende 13. Jh.)
HEINZER und STAMM, *Die Handschriften von St. Peter im Schwarzwald: Teil 2. Die Pergamenthandschriften* (Wiesbaden, 1984: *Die Handschriften der Badischen Landesbibliothek in Karlsruhe* 10,2), S. 135-137; HELLGARDT, "Deutsche Gebetsanweisungen", S. 403.

48 **Karlsruhe, LB, Cod. E.M. 5**
lat. Psalter – 13. Jh.
– dt. Nachtrag (Ende 13. Jh.): Ps.-Beda 'De meditatione passionis Christi' [Bl. 112v]
K. PREISENDANZ, *Die Handschriften des Klosters Ettenheim-Münster, Neudruck der Ausgabe Karlsruhe 1932 mit bibliographischen Nachträgen* (Wiesbaden, 1973: *Die Handschriften der Badischen Landesbibliothek in Karlsruhe* 9), S. 8-9 und 93; V. HONEMANN: "Beda", ^{2}*VL* 1 (1978) Sp. 662.

49 **Korneuburg, StA, ohne Sign.**
lat. Psalter – 2. Hälfte 13. Jh.
– dt. Gebetsanweisungen
HELLGARDT, "Deutsche Gebetsanweisungen", S. 403.

50 **Liverpool, University Library (Sydney Jones Libr.), Ms. M 8951 (Dauerleihgabe des Liverpool Museums, früher Mayer Museum, Ms. 895/M)**
lat. Psalter (illuminiert) – 2. Viertel 13. Jh.
– dt. Traumsequenz mit Geburtsprognosen nach Wochentagen (nachgetragen)
N.R. KER, *Medieval Manuscripts in British Libraries*, Bd. 3 (Oxford, 1983), S. 216-218; N.F. PALMER und K. SPECKENBACH, *Träume und Kräuter. Studien zur Petroneller 'Circa instans'-Handschrift und zu den deutschen Traumbüchern des Mittelalters* (Köln und Wien, 1990: *Pictura et Poësis* 4), S. 130-131 (mit Abdruck).

51 **London, BL, Ms. Add. 11846**
lat. Psalter – um 1200
– Gebetsanweisungen
HELLGARDT, "Handschriften im 11. und 12. Jahrhundert", S. 67 Nr. 173; DERS., "Deutsche Gebetsanweisungen", S. 403.

52 **London, BL, Ms. Add. 11847**
lat. Psalter – Ende 12. Jh.
– dt. Gebetsanweisungen
– dt. Reisesegen und lat. Gebet mit dt. Nachschrift von Haupthand auf Bl. 186r eingetragen.
– dt. Nachträge des 15.Jhs.
Deutsche Handschriften in England, beschr. v. R. PRIEBSCH. Bd. 2: *Das British Museum. Mit einem Anhang über die Guildhall-Bibliothek* (Erlangen, 1901), S. 119; HELLGARDT, "Handschriften im 11. und 12. Jahrhundert", S. 67 Nr. 174.

53 **Manchester, John Rylands Library (Bibliotheca Lindesiana), Lat. 105**
lat. Psalter – 13. Jh.
– dt. gynäkologische Einträge (Nachträge 14. Jh.)
Hinweis N.F. Palmer; *Deutsche Handschriften in England*, beschr. v. R. PRIEBSCH. Bd. 1 (wie Nr. 12), S. 189-190 (mit Abdruck der dt. Teile).

54 **Metz, Bibliothèque Médiathèque du Pontiffroy, Ms. 1200**
lat. *Magdeburger Psalter* – um 1260

– dt. Vorrede: 'Der Zweifler'
VON HARDENBERG, "Geistliches Gedicht des XIII. Jahrhunderts" (wie Anm. 62; mit Abdruck des 'Zweiflers'); LEROQUAIS, *Les Psautiers* (wie Anm. 15), S. 268-270 und Pl. XCV-CII (mit Teilabdruck des Kalendariums und allen Bildseiten).

55 **München, BSB, Cgm 73**
Münchner Gebetbuch – nach 1300
– dt. Memento-Gebet
Vgl. E. PETZET, *Die deutschen Pergament-Handschriften Nr.1-200 der Staatsbibliothek in München* (München, 1920: *Catalogus codicum manu scriptorum bibliothecae Monacensis* 5,1), S. 117-123; SCHNEIDER, *Gotische Schriften*, S. 274 Anm. 286; OCHSENBEIN, "Deutschsprachige Privatgebetbücher", S. 383-384.

56 **München, BSB, Cgm 5250 Nr. 5a, b-e**
lat. Psalter – um 1200
– dt. Gebetsanweisungen (Randbeschriftung)
HELLGARDT, "Handschriften im 11. und 12. Jahrhundert", S. 71 Nr. 219-220; DERS., "Deutsche Gebetsanweisungen", S. 403.

57 **München, BSB, Cgm 5250 Nr. 5g**
lat. Psalter – 2. Hälfte 13. Jh.
– in den Text integrierte dt. Gebetsanweisungen und liturg. Texte zur Kollekte

58 **München, BSB, Clm 935**
lat. *Gebetbuch der Hildegard von Bingen* – 1. Hälfte 13. Jh. (Bildbeischriften nicht vor dem 2.Viertel des 13. Jh.s)
– dt. Bildbeischriften [Bl. 2r-72r]
– dt. Mariengebete [Bl. 23r, 24r]
– dt. 'Mariensequenz aus Muri' (C) [Bl. 70r]
K. SCHNEIDER, "Die deutschen Texte in Clm 935", in: *Hildegard-Gebetbuch. Faksimile-Ausgabe des Codex-Latinus Monacensis 935 der Bayerischen Staatsbibliothek München, Kommentarband* (Wiesbaden, 1987), S. 51-69.

59 **München, BSB, Clm 2640**
lat. Psalter – um 1260, Augsburg
– dt. Gebetsanweisungen
E. KLEMM, *Die illuminierten Handschriften des 13. Jahrhunderts* (wie Anm. 60), S. 135-138 Nr. 118 + Taf. XIV, Abb. 330-332, 335-344; KORNRUMPF, "Marienlied" (wie Anm. 65), S. 101.

60 **München, BSB, Clm 2641**
lat. Psalter – um 1270
– dt. Gebetsanweisungen
– dt. Marienlied als Nachtrag
A. BIRLINGER, "Eine alemannische und eine bairische Gebrauchsanweisung zu den Psalmen aus dem XII XIII Jarhundert (!)", *Alemannia* 12 (1884), S. 82-98 (mit Abdruck der dt. Gebrauchsanweisung); HELLGARDT, "Deutsche Gebetsanweisungen", S. 403; KLEMM, *Illuminierte Handschriften*, S. 63-65 Nr. 4 + Abb. XII, 124-129; KORNRUMPF, "Marienlied", S. 101-112.

61 **München, BSB, Clm 23111**
lat. Psalter – um 1200
– dt. Gebetsanweisungen (marginal nachgetragen, 13. Jh.)
C.M. BLAAS und K. BARTSCH, "Psalterien mit deutschen Randbemerkungen", *Germania* 27 (1882), S. 339-350 (Abdruck der dt. Einträge); HELLGARDT, "Deutsche Gebetsanweisungen", S. 403.

62 **New York, Pierpont Morgan Library, Cod. M. 739**
Gebetbuch der heiligen Hedwig – 1. Viertel 13. Jh.
– dt. Gebetsüberschriften und Gebetsanweisungen

– dt. Bildbeischriften im Miniaturenteil [Bl. 9r-24v]
– dt. Gebet [Bl. 53v-54r]
SUCKALE-REDLEFSEN, "Buchkunst zur Zeit der Andechs-Meranier" (wie Anm. 48), S. 248, 373-374 + Abb. 148, 154, 162, 365.

63 **New York, Theological Seminary, The Burke Library, Ms 57**
s. Nr. 67 (Codex Discissus)

64 **Nürnberg, StB., Cod. Cent. VIII 17**
lat. Brevier – um 1300
– dt. Rubriken
– dt. Gebetsanweisungen
– dt. Gedicht (Nachtrag des 15. Jh.s)
K. SCHNEIDER, *Die deutschen mittelalterlichen Handschriften* (Wiesbaden, 1965: *Die Handschriften der Stadtbibliothek Nürnberg* 1), S. 414.

65 **Nürnberg, GNM, Graph. Slg., Mm 173 kl. F**
s. Nr. 67 (Codex Discissus)
E.W. BREDT, *Katalog der mittelalterlichen Miniaturen des GNM* (Nürnberg, 1903), S. 16/17 Nr. 11.

66 **Paris, BN, lat. 1081**
lat. Psalter – 1. Viertel 13. Jh.
– dt. Namen
AVRIL und RABEL, *Manuscrits enluminés* (wie Nr. 10), S. 155-156 Nr. 137.

67 **Paris, BN, lat. 9377 (ff. 29-32) + Darmstadt, Hess. LB, Inc. IV/124 (Makulatur) + Hamburg, Privatbesitz + New York, Union Theological Seminary, The Burke Library, Ms. 57 + Nürnberg, GNM, Graph. Sammlung, Mm. 173 kl. F**
lat. Brevier – Anfang 13. Jh.
– dt. Rubriken und Bildbeischriften
AVRIL und RABEL, *Manuscrits enluminés*, S. 152-153, Nr. 134.

68 **Paris, BN, lat. 9486**
lat. Rituale (aus Neuweiler) – 1. Drittel 13. Jh. (Bl. 108v: *Anno M°CC°XVII°*).
– dt. Gebet als (gleichzeitiger?) Eintrag auf dem ehemals leeren vorletzten Blatt [Bl. 108v]
AVRIL und RABEL, *Manuscrits enluminés*, S. 128-129 Nr. 115.

69 **Paris, BN, lat. 10526**
lat. Gebetbuch (*Codex rotundus*) – um 1200[1]
– dt. Gebet [Bl. 236 ff.]
AVRIL und RABEL, *Manuscrits enluminés*, S. 159-160 Nr. 140.

[1] Bl. 182 nennt sich die Besitzerin: *Gůtha, der waz dise bůche, unde gedenchent ir ze Gooth mith owerme Gebethe.* Im Kalender wird besagte Gutha als am 28. November verstorben aufgeführt: *obiit Guota.*

70 **Prag, SUB, Cod. XIII.E.14.b**
lat. Psalter – 13. Jh.
– gereimte dt. Überschriften zu den Psalmen
– dt. Gebetsanweisungen
W. DOLCH, *Katalog der deutschen Handschriften der k. k. öff. und Universitätsbibliothek zu Prag. I. Teil. Die Handschriften bis etwa z. J. 1550* (Prag, 1909), S. 43 Nr. 101; HELLGARDT, "Deutsche Gebetsanweisungen", S. 403.

71 **Rom, BAV, Cod. Pal. lat. 36**
lat. Psalter – um 1300
– dt. Gebetsanweisungen
HELLGARDT, "Deutsche Gebetsanweisungen", S. 403.

72 **Rom, BAV, Cod. Vat. lat. 4763**
lat.-dt. (Nonnen-)Gebetbuch – 2. Viertel 13. Jh.
– dt. 'Vatikanische Gebete' [Bl. 107r-128v]
SCHNEIDER, *Gotische Schriften*, S. 112-113, 161.

73 **Sarnen, Kollegiumsarchiv der Abtei Muri-Gries, Ms. Membr. 69**
lat. *Gebetbuch von Muri* – um 1200
– dt. 'Sarnener Ausfahrtsegen' [Bl. 8v-9r]
– dt 'Mariensequenz aus Muri' (A) [Bl. 33v-36r]
– dt. 'Sarnener Morgensegen' [Bl. 41v-44v]
P. OCHSENBEIN, "Das Gebetbuch von Muri als frühes Zeugnis privater Frömmigkeit einer Frau um 1200", in: *Gotes und der werlde hulde. Literatur in Mittelalter und Neuzeit. Festschrift für Heinz Rupp*, hg. v. R. SCHNELL (Bern und Stuttgart, 1989), S. 175-199.

74 **Sávár, Kathedralbibliothek, Cod. Lat. 1**
lat. Brevier – 2. Hälfte 13. Jh.
– dt. Osterlied als Nachtrag des 14./15. Jh.s
P. RADÓ, *Libri Liturgici Manuscripti Bibliothecarum Hungariae et Limitropharum Regionum* (Budapest 1973), S. 278-283.

75 **St. Gallen, SfB, Ms. 25**
lat. Psalter aus dem Katharinenkloster – 12. Jh.
– dt. Gebetsanweisungen (Ende 13. Jh. für Dominikannerinnen nachgetragen)
WALLACH-FALLER, *Alemannischer Psalter*, S. 145.

76 **St. Gallen, SfB, Ms. 492**
lat. Psalter aus dem Katharinenkloster – Ende 13. Jh.
– dt. Gebetsanweisungen (um 1300)
WALLACH-FALLER, *Alemannischer Psalter*, S. 145.

77 **Stuttgart, LB, Cod. bibl. 4° 10 + Cod. HB II 25**
lat. Psalter – 2. Hälfte 13. Jh.
– dt. Bildunterschrift(en)
– 'Weingartner Reisesegen' [Bl. 123v]
GEH und RÖMER, *Mittelalterliche Andachtsbücher* (wie Anm. 4); HELLGARDT, "Handschriften im 11. und 12. Jahrhundert", S. 75 Nr. 273.

78 **Stuttgart, LB, Cod. Donaueschingen 309**
lat. *Donaueschinger Psalter* – bald nach 1235
– dt. Gebetsanweisungen
R. KROOS, "Stichw. Donaueschinger Psalter", in: *Die Zeit der Staufer. Geschichte – Kunst – Kultur. Katalog der Ausstellung Stuttgart 1977, Bd. 1: Katalog*, hg. v. R. HAUSSHERR, Bd. 2: *Abbildungen*, hg. v. C. VÄTERLEIN unter Mitarb. v. U. SCHNEIDER und H. KLAIBER, Württembergisches Landesmuseum Stuttgart (Stuttgart, 1977), hier Bd.1 S. 601-602 Nr. 769 + Abb. 564; KROOS, "Die Miniaturen" (wie Anm. 60), S. 57, 59 und Abb. 10, 31.

79 **Trier, StB, Cod. 1149/451**
lat. *Gebetbuch moselfränkischer Zisterzienserinnen* – 1298/1302
– dt. Interpolationen
Die deutschen und niederländischen Handschriften der Stadtbibliothek Trier bis 1600, neu beschr. v. B.C. BUSHEY (Wiesbaden, 1996: *Beschreibendes Verzeichnis der Handschriften der Stadtbibliothek zu Trier. Neue Serie* 1), S. 324-326.

80 **Uppsala, UB, Frgm. germ. 1 + Wien, ÖNB, Cod. Ser. nova 4242**
lat. *Wien-Uppsalaer Frauengebetbuch* – 1. Viertel 13. Jh.
– dt. 'Uppsalaer Frauengebete'
– dt. Gebet
H.A. BURMEISTER und J. WOLF, "Marburger Fund- und Reiseberichte. Miszellen aus dem 'Repertorium deutschsprachiger Handschriften des 13. Jahrhunderts'", *ZfdA* 127 (1998), S. 45-68, hier S. 63-68 u. Abb. 8.

81 **Wien, Erzbischöfliche Bibl. , Hs. 136**
lat. Psalter – 1. Viertel 13. Jh.
– dt. Gebetsanweisungen
Abbildungen und Beschreibung in: http://www.oeaw.ac.at/ksbm/stb/index. htm.

82 **Wien, ÖNB, Cod. 1869**
lat. Psalter – Mitte 13. Jh.
– dt. Gebetsanweisungen
HELLGARDT, "Deutsche Gebetsanweisungen", S. 403.

83 **Wilhering, SfB, Cod. IX, 120**
lat. Psalter – 13. Jh.
– dt. Gebet
– dt. Gebetsanweisungen (marginal)
P.O. GRILLNBERGER, *Die Handschriften der Stiftsbibliothek zu Wilhering* (Wien, 1891: *Xenia Bernardina* II,2), Nr. 120.

84 **Wolfenbüttel, HAB, Cod. 1265 Helmst.**
lat.-dt. Frauengebetbuch – Ende 13. Jh.
C. BORCHLING, "Mittelniederdeutsche Handschriften in Wolfenbüttel und einigen benachbarten Bibliotheken. Dritter Reisebericht", in: *Nachrichten von der Königl. Gesellschaft der Wiss. zu Göttingen, philol.-hist. Klasse aus dem Jahre 1902* (Göttingen, 1902: Beiheft), S. 62.

85 **Wolfenbüttel, HAB, Cod. 1319 Helmst.**
lat.-dt. Frauengebetbuch – um/nach 1300
BORCHLING, "Mittelniederdeutsche Handschriften", S. 89.

86 **Wolfenbüttel, HAB, Cod. 1321 Helmst.**
lat.-dt. Frauengebetbuch – um 1300
BORCHLING, "Mittelniederdeutsche Handschriften", S. 62, 89.

87 **Wolfenbüttel, HAB, Cod. 1399 Helmst.**
lat. Frauengebetbuch – Ende 13. Jh.
– dt.: Andachten und Gebete, z.T. gereimt [Bl. 98r-109v]
BORCHLING, "Mittelniederdeutsche Handschriften", S. 92.

88 **Wolfenbüttel, HAB, Cod. 1417 Helmst.**
lat.-dt. Gebetbuch – Ende 13. Jh.
BORCHLING, "Mittelniederdeutsche Handschriften", S. 62, 93-94.

89 **Wolfenbüttel, HAB, Cod. 1430 Helmst.**
lat.-dt. Frauengebetbuch – 4. Viertel 13. Jh.
BORCHLING, "Mittelniederdeutsche Handschriften", S. 62 Anm. 1, 94.

90 **Würzburg, UB, M. p. th. f. 52**
lat. Psalter – 2. Drittel 13. Jh.
– dt . Gebetsanweisungen
H. THURN und W. WEGSTEIN, "Ein Psalterium aus dem Prämonstatenserkloster Oberzell mit mhd. Gebetsanweisungen", *Mfrk. Jahrbuch* 38 (1986), S. 25-35; HELLGARDT, "Deutsche Gebetsanweisungen", S. 403.

91 **Zürich, ZB, Cod. C 171**
lat. Gebetbuch/Psalter – Ende 12. Jh.
– dt. 'Zürcher Gebets- und Almosenanweisung' [Bl. 106v]
L.C. MOHLBERG, *Mittelalterliche Handschriften* (Zürich, 1932-1952: *Katalog der Handschriften der Zentralbibliothek Zürich* 1), S. 74-75; HELLGARDT, "Handschriften im 11. und 12. Jahrhundert", S. 69 Nr. 195

92 **Zürich, ZB, Cod. Z XIV 18**
lat. (Dominikaner-)Psalter – Mitte 13. Jh.
– dt. Gebetsanweisung zu Psalm 72 (Anfang 14. Jh.)
WALLACH-FALLER, *Alemannischer Psalter*, S. 145.

93 **Privatbesitz Antiquariat Hartung und Karl, München**
lat. Psalter – 13. Jh.
– dt. Rubriken
Manuskripte, Autographen, wertvolle Bücher, Antiquariat Hartung und Karl, Katalog 24 (1978), S. 13-14 Nr. 13a.

94 **Weimar, Hauptstaatsarchiv, Ernest. Gesamtarchiv, Reg. V. ohne Sign. (früher Einband von Bb 1461)**
lat. Missale – 13./14. Jh.
– dt. neumiertes Kirchenlied
Handschriftenarchiv der Berlin-Brandenburgischen Akademie der Wissenschaften, Archivbeschr. v. K. VOGTHERR, http://dtm.bbaw.de/HSA/Weimar_700445060000.html.

95 **Stockholm, Königliche Bibliothek, Cod. Huseby 25 (Teil 1)**
lat. Psalter und Hymnar – vor 1297
– dt. Rubriken
L. KURRAS, *Deutsche und niederländische Handschriften in der königlichen Bibliothek Stockholm* (Stockholm, 2001: *Acta Bibliothecae Regiae Stockholmensis* LXVII), S. 117-118 u. Abb. 75; A. LÖFFLER, “Swester und Oberste – ein Brevier für einen Schwesterkonvent des Deutschen Ordens”, *Quellen und Studien zur Geschichte des Deutschen Ordens* 54 (im Druck).
Für den Hinweis auf die Stockholmer Handschrift danke ich Frau Dr. A. Löffler, Leipzig, ganz herzlich.

Orality, Literacy, and/or Ekphrasis? Narrative Techniques of Visualization and the Poetics of Late Medieval Romance: Johann von Würzburg's *Wilhelm von Österreich*

MONIKA SCHAUSTEN

In Ovid's *Metamorphoses*, the tragic love story of Pyramus and Thisbe draws the attention of the modern reader to the immense impact that various modes of communication have on the fatal development of the couple. The status the story has as one important paradigm of European love literature does not exclusively result from the well-known ingredients many literary love narrations share, such as the connection of love and death, the idea of an indissoluble spiritual unity of the lovers,[1] or the friction between the feelings of the lovers and the pressure that society puts on them. Ovid emphasizes as well the immense importance that bodily presence has for the fulfilment of love, and he stresses that the fatality of the story told results from a series of miscommunications and misperceptions which ultimately lead the lovers to wrong assumptions about each other's whereabouts. Thus the story poses the question of the void that a secret love creates for the persons involved, and it seems to imply that no means of communication, be it oral communication through a crack in a wall, or a material visual sign such as Thisbe's coat, can in the end substitute for the bodily presence of the two lovers. This presence seems to be the essential condition for the experience that love promises, and love cannot be substituted by

[1] On the adoption of this prominent story in the Middle Ages see H. BRINKMANN, *Mittelalterliche Hermeneutik* (Tübingen, 1980), pp. 206-214, who stresses the impact that the idea of a spiritual unity of the lovers in the ancient text had on medieval literature, most prominently on the *Tristan* romances.

oral or visual representations of the persons involved. The tale of Pyramus who immediately takes Thisbe's coat as visual proof of her death points to the fact that it is a mistake to confuse the piece of clothing, i.e. the representation of a person, with the actual person it belongs to. At the same time, however, the story conveys that secret love in particular desperately needs such representations.[2]

Vernacular epics and romances of the Middle Ages are also largely concerned with the discourse on love and its various modes of representation. A brief glance at the numerous ways in which the texts narrate the initiation of love, as well as the absences lovers have to endure, draws our attention to the important impact that material, bodily, and imaginary signs of representation have for the telling of the stories. Be it that a future lover sees her beloved represented as an animal in a dream, as in the *Nibelungenlied*,[3] or that a golden hair represents the bride to be as in Eilhart von Oberg's *Tristrant*,[4] or again that the texts narrate how the absences of the lovers are bridged through material signs, such as the ring Laudine hands to Iwein in Hartmann von Aue's romance,[5] the little dog, Petitcrieu, that Tristan presents to Isolde and the ring Isolde presents to Tristan in Gottfried's version of the story,[6] or the statues Tristan creates of his lover in Thomas' fragment:[7] all these modes of representing the bodily presence of lovers or the lack thereof seem to emphasize the immense importance of visual bodily presentation and its material representations in medieval vernacular literature.

Literary criticism has for the most part commented on the significance of these different modes of visualization in medieval texts by considering them from the perspective of media history:[8] in view of the specific position between

[2] Ovid, *Metamorphoses*, trans. M.M. INNES (London, 1955), pp. 95-98.

[3] *Das Nibelungenlied*, I, ed. and trans. H. BRACKERT (Frankfurt am Main, 1970), strophe 13.

[4] Eilhart von Oberge, *Tristrant*, ed. F. LICHTENSTEIN (Strassburg and London, 1877: *Quellen und Forschungen zur Sprach- und Culturgeschichte der germanischen Völker* 19), ll. 1381-89.

[5] Hartmann von Aue, *Iwein*, ed. G.F. BENECKE, K. LACHMANN, L. WOLFF, trans. T. CRAMER (Berlin and New York, 1981), ll. 2945-46.

[6] Gottfried von Strassburg, *Tristan*, ed. F. RANKE, trans. R. KROHN (Stuttgart, 1980, ll. 16274-89; 18307.

[7] Thomas, *Tristan*, ed. and trans. G. BONATH (Munich, 1985: *Klassische Texte des Romanischen Mittelalters in zweisprachigen Ausgaben* 21), pp. 139-143.

[8] See for example H. WENZEL, "Schrift und Bild. Zur Repräsentation der audiovisuellen Wahrnehmung im Mittelalter", in: *Methodenkonkurrenz in der germanistischen Praxis*, ed. J. JANOTA (Tübingen, 1991), pp. 101-121, at pp. 103-104. For a summary of the research history with regard to this topic, see M. SCHAUSTEN, *Erzählwelten der Tristangeschichte im hohen*

orality and literacy in which all medieval literature is situated, depicted bodies as well as their material, and thus visual, representations in medieval literature until now mostly have been interpreted as evidence of the fact that even written texts still preserved the importance that direct face-to-face communication had for oral cultures. Thus medieval writing is not regarded as a form of communication based on completely different principles from oral modes of communicating, but rather as a new medium that preserves the more traditional form of direct, body-centred communication in writing and yet at the same time transforms distinctive characteristics of oral cultures into written texts.[9] The idea that literacy is still dependent on conditions specific to a memorial culture of direct communication is crucial to many studies concerned with the culture of the Middle Ages.[10] Horst Wenzel refers to Niklas Luhmann, when he states that each new medium, when it is first introduced to a culture, is assimilated to the pre-existing mode of communication.[11] Accordingly, for a long time writing had one dominant function in medieval times: to support memory and its capacity to secure important cultural information. In this context, audio-visual modes of perception are crucial for the purpose memory serves in oral and bi-medial cultures. Therefore, the significance of non-verbal signs depicted in written texts can, according to Wenzel, still be related to the demand of a collective memory characteristic of oral cultures.[12] The historian Gerd Althoff has extensively investigated the significance that the public staging of the bodies of those in power had for the political stability of medieval bi-medial culture. For him, the public presentation of the body was arranged for the dominant receptive organs of the eyes and the ears, securing the information conveyed through the bodies in order to shape a collective memory. However, the information about the importance of bodily forms of communication in the Middle Ages mostly

Mittelalter. Untersuchungen zu den deutschsprachigen Tristanfassungen des 12. und 13. Jahrhunderts (Munich, 1999: *Forschungen zur Geschichte der älteren deutschen Literatur* 24), pp. 91-106.

9 See for example H. WENZEL,"Medien- und Kommunikationstheorie. Ältere deutsche Literatur", in: *Germanistik als Kulturwissenschaft*, ed. C. BENTHIEN and H.R. VELTEN (Reinbek bei Hamburg, 2002), pp. 125-151, at p. 132.

10 See for example H. VOLLRATH, "Das Mittelalter in der Typik oraler Gesellschaften", *Historische Zeitschrift* 233 (1981), pp. 571-594; J. BUMKE, "Höfische Kultur. Versuch einer kritischen Bestandsaufnahme", *PBB* 114 (1992), pp. 414-492, at p. 470; U. SCHAEFER, "Zum Problem der Mündlichkeit", in: *Modernes Mittelalter. Neue Bilder einer populären Epoche*, ed. J. HEINZLE (Frankfurt am Main and Leipzig, 1994), pp. 357-375; and C.S. JAEGER, *The Envy of Angels. Cathedral Schools and Social Ideals in Medieval Europe 950-1200* (Philadelphia, 1994).

11 H. WENZEL, "Audiovisualität im Mittelalter", in: *Literatur im Informationszeitalter*, ed. D. MAJETOVSKI and F. KITTLER (Frankfurt and New York, 1996), pp. 50-70, at p. 51.

12 WENZEL, "Audiovisualität", p. 56.

derives from written texts. According to Althoff, the visible staging of political bodies was accompanied by verbally articulated agreements. Moreover, the information about these stagings was secured by historiographical modes of writing.[13] Accordingly, medieval culture produced a collective memory of its own by making use of both orality and literacy.

Strategies of visualization in medieval epics have thus mostly been treated as sources that prove the specific significance that oral forms of communication had in the Middle Ages. Within this context, literary critics have read prominent texts of the High Middle Ages mostly in order to demonstrate the position they took up in a culture that was, at least in part, more centred on the performance of literary texts than on their silent reading.[14] To medievalists, the use of specific formulas within the epics, such as *hoeren und lesen*, indicates various forms of reception by their audiences. Moreover, to them, the texts serve as appropriate historical sources for identifying the principles of visualization on which oral cultures were based. Thus the discovery of the textual principle called 'fictive orality', in which vernacular literature largely participates, commonly served to support a perspective dominated by questions that were posed by media history.[15] Rarely has the discourse on the prominent media, which all literary texts contain, been acknowledged with regard to the poetological, rhetorical, and semiotic significance it has in relation to the specific shape of vernacular epics,[16] and until now scholars have not often investigated the connections between this discourse and other prominent topics, such as the discourse on love.

Taking the late medieval romance of *Wilhelm von Österreich* as an example, I propose to explore the functional strategies of narrative visualization as

[13] G. ALTHOFF, *Spielregeln der Politik im Mittelalter. Kommunikation in Frieden und Fehde* (Darmstadt, 1997), at pp. 229-257.

[14] See M.G. SCHOLZ, *Hören und Lesen. Studien zur primären Rezeption der Literatur im 12. und 13. Jahrhundert* (Wiesbaden, 1980). With regard to the ongoing debate concerning the impact that the usage of the double formula *hoeren oder lesen* has on the dominant forms of the texts' reception, see D.H. GREEN, "Fictive Orality: A Restriction on the Use of the Concept", in: *Blütezeit. Festschrift für L.P. Johnson zum 70. Geburtstag*, ed. M. CHINCA, J. HEINZLE and C. YOUNG (Tübingen, 2000), pp. 161-174.

[15] Mostly with regard to minnesang, scholars have pointed to the performative aspect which shapes the poetology of the texts. See for example: *'Aufführung' und 'Schrift' in Mittelalter und Früher Neuzeit*, ed. J.-D. MÜLLER (Stuttgart and Weimar, 1996: *Germanistische Symposien. Berichtsbände* XVII).

[16] See for example G. BUTZER, "Das Gedächtnis des epischen Textes. Mündliches und schriftliches Erzählen im höfischen Roman des Mittelalters", *Euphorion* 89 (1995), pp. 151-188, and lately J.-D. MÜLLER, *Spielregeln für den Untergang. Die Welt des Nibelungenliedes* (Tübingen, 1998), at pp. 55-102.

well as references to modes of writing in the depiction of the love relationship between the protagonist and his lover, Aglye. More precisely, I shall focus on *ekphrasis* as an example of one important technique this text uses to fill the narrative void that the lack of a direct bodily presence of the two lovers creates at the beginning of the narration. It is my impression that the writing of difficult and extraordinary love stories is always dependent on references to media, which are depicted in the romances as necessary modes of representation that function as substitutes for the lover's bodily presence. The key questions are: what modes of representation and communication the late medieval text uses to fill these voids, whether these modes differ from the usage of media references in earlier romances (to which the later romances are intertextually linked), and whether or not the literary depiction of these representational forms can be easily traced back to a bi-medial cultural context that is still dominated by oral forms of communication.

By and large, the perspective generated by media history has so far been applied to romances and epics of the High Middle Ages.[17] As is well known, the production of these texts is already fundamentally related to a tradition of vernacular writing, which links German romances to their French predecessors. And although some of the new texts that emerged in the Late Middle Ages emancipated themselves from courtly romances of earlier times in that they no longer adopted the famous stories that had dominated the literary market for a long period of time, these texts are nevertheless strongly linked to the literature of the High Middle Ages. According to the recent monographs of Armin Schulz and Klaus Ridder, romances such as Johann von Würzburg's *Wilhelm von Österreich* embarked on plots that are concerned with a discourse of genealogy and thus introduced fictitious characters who could be associated with existing noble families of their times. However, the refusal of the later authors to base their romances on famous stories such as the legend of King Arthur did not result in the invention of completely new plots. Rather, it brought about works that consist of a dense network of intertextual references linking the late medieval texts to an established tradition of vernacular romance writing. Thus, intertextuality is their most important poetic paradigm.[18]

[17] See in particular H. WANDHOFF, *Der epische Blick. Eine mediengeschichtliche Studie zur höfischen Literatur* (Berlin, 1996: *PhStQu* 141).

[18] K. RIDDER, *Mittelhochdeutsche Minne- und Aventiureromane. Fiktion, Geschichte und literarische Tradition im späthöfischen Roman: 'Reinfried von Braunschweig', 'Wilhelm von Österreich', 'Friedrich von Schwaben'* (Berlin and New York, 1998: *Quellen und Forschungen zur Literatur- und Kulturgeschichte* 12 [246]), p. 14; and A. SCHULZ, *Poetik des Hybriden: Schema, Variation und intertextuelle Kombinatorik in der Minne- und Aventiureepik: Willehalm von Orlens – Partonopier und Meliur – Wilhelm von Österreich – Die schöne Magelone* (Berlin,

Among medievalists, Johann's *Wilhelm von Österreich*, a romance written at the beginning of the fourteenth century, in particular has earned a reputation for its multitude of intertextual references to various literary genres of the High Middle Ages.[19] Thus the narration that contains the story of the life, love, and death of a founding father of a fictitious Austrian noble lineage draws from a diverse set of genres such as Arthurian romances, heroic epics, and historiographic as well as hagiographic works. The integration of these different modes of writing in the romance helped construct what Armin Schulz has called a hybrid protagonist, i.e. a protagonist whose narrated public identity is dominated by fundamental ambivalences. In particular, the assimilation of the courtly romance to hagiographic modes of writing creates Wildhelm as a character who on the one hand comes across as an active knight and on the other hand as passive saint.[20]

But despite the multitude of intertextual references within Johann's romance, it seems evident that the relationship the text establishes to Gottfried von Strassburg's *Tristan* is one of the dominating intertextual links between the later text and its predecessors. This linkage to Gottfried's text in *Wilhelm von Österreich* is, however, not restricted to the depiction of the love discourse.[21] Both texts have a common biographical approach to the construction of the romance;[22] in both the birth and death of the protagonists frame the stories told; both works narrate the initiation of their heroes' lives as a result of rather complicated and strange circumstances; in both, the names given to the protagonists preserve the extraordinary situations preceding their birth.[23] Within the sequences that recount the initiation of the heroes' lives, both authors establish a disposition of their main characters, which makes them suitable for the story of love they are about to experience within the further course of the narration. In

2000: *PhStQu* 161), p. 9.

[19] E. MAYSER, *Studien zur Dichtung Johanns von Würzburg* (Berlin, 1931: *Germanistische Studien* 101); M.G. SCHOLZ, *Zum Verhältnis von Mäzen, Autor und Publikum im 14. und 15. Jahrhundert: 'Wilhelm von Österreich' – 'Rappoltsteiner Parzifal' – Michel Beheim* (Darmstadt, 1987), p. 83; G. VOLLMAN-PROFE, "Johann von Würzburg 'Wilhelm von Österreich' ", in: *Positionen des Romans im späten Mittelalter*, ed. W. HAUG and B. WACHINGER (Tübingen, 1991), pp. 123-135.

[20] SCHULZ, *Poetik des Hybriden*, pp. 64-66.

[21] See MAYSER, *Studien zur Dichtung Johanns von Würzburg*, pp. 31-33.

[22] With regard to the significance of biographical and autobiographical modes of writing for the construction of Gottfried's *Tristan* see M. SCHAUSTEN, "ich bin, alse ich hân vernomen, ze wunderlîchen maeren komen. Zur Funktion biographischer und autobiographischer Figurenrede für die narrative Konstitution von Identität in Gottfrieds von Straßburg 'Tristan'", *PBB* 123 (2001), pp. 24-48.

[23] See MAYSER, *Studien zur Dichtung Johanns von Würzburg*, p. 31.

Gottfried's case, it is the precarious public status of the relationship between Tristan's parents as well as their sad love story and their sudden deaths that form the hero's name and leave him an insufficient foundation for his future public status; in *Wilhelm von Österreich* it is the Austrian count Leopold who names his son Wildhelm, claiming that he himself had to travel through numerous strange (*wilde*) countries on his pilgrimage to Ephesus in order to be granted a child.[24] Tristan's status as a stranger who never reaches a final topographical and social destination makes him suitable for the experience of an illicit love, which ultimately prevents him from ever being able to gain a secure space in his life. It seems as if Johann adopted this idea of spatial instability, which Gottfried's text claims to be a condition for the experience of extraordinary love, by having the hero's father call him "Wildhelm", a name that is equivalent to the meaning of 'stranger'. Several other motifs clearly attach both texts to one another, but it is the account of the initiation of the love story that also marks fundamental differences between the two works.

As is well known, Gottfried sets his story apart from the older tradition of *Tristan* narratives by having the future lovers meet personally within a teacher-student relationship and later on accidentally drink a love potion that ties them together forever. Contrary to his predecessor, Johann already integrates the potential for a love-relationship between Wildhelm and his future lover Aglye into the narration about the protagonist's father's pilgrimage. In *Wilhelm von Österreich*, the pagan king Agrant accompanies Leopold to Ephesus and thus the two men are joined in their efforts to be granted an heir to their kingdoms. After the journey, both their children are born within the same hour under the sign of Venus and they are hence destined for each other. Thus the initiation of love in Johann's text is not dependent on the bodily presence of the lovers, but is narrated as result of the circumstances of their birth. Set within the *chanson de geste*'s "preoccupation with the defense of Christendom and feudal warfare",[25] the love relationship between the Christian hero and the pagan noble princess in Johann's text does not remain the only focus of the subsequent narrative. Rather, Johann's protagonist is not only destined to love Aglye but the Christian hero is also destined to acquire and christianize pagan territory. Thus, his story results in the marriage of the lovers. Whereas in Gottfried's case love is constructed as the result of a fatal development and thus remains the fate of the characters throughout the romance, the later text imagines the love of the

[24] See Johann von Würzburg, *Wilhelm von Österreich. Aus der Gothaer Handschrift*, ed. E. REGEL (Berlin, 1906), ll. 555-561.

[25] L.M. CLEMENTE, *Literary objets d'art. Ekphrasis in Medieval French Romance 1150-1210* (New York *et al.*, 1992: *American University Studies* II/166), at p. 12.

protagonist for the pagan king's daughter as destiny, i.e. love literally determines the spatial destination of the hero's biography caused by Wildhelm's reaction to the image of Aglye.

Therefore, the text carefully outlines the initiation of this love by using the motif of the children's birth under the sign of Venus as the key motivation which at first explains the occurrence of an attachment that both Wildhelm and Aglye experience while still children. The fact that they had never seen each other in person and that they do not even know about each other's existence is crucial to the motivation of the love story. As in many medieval texts, their love is depicted as *Fernminne*, i.e. love from a distance that precedes the actual personal meeting of the future lovers. In Johann's case, however, this *minne* is explicitly set off by Venus and her son Amor[26] who, according to the narrator, are assigned the power to initiate the love of Wildhelm and Aglye by creating an image for each of the other that haunts the lovers constantly.[27] The narrator describes this in great detail:

> *si* [Venus, M.S.] *gab im sunder laugen*
> *des nahtes für diu augen*
> *Aglyen bilde;*
> *des wolt im werden wilde*
> *sin hertze von der angesiht:*
> *diu Minne het mit ir phliht*
> *zesamen si gepflihtet,*
> *ir netze im für gerihtet,*
> *ir suezze im für gebrocket;*
> *Amor ir sun im locket,*
> *biz daz ez anders niht ergie*
> *wan daz si siu beidiu gevie*
> *und nam si in ir vancnuste*
> *also daz ir baider luste*
> *wart nach ein ander grozen.*
> *diu sueften wurden stozen*
> *diu jungen kint ie baz und baz:*
> *si minten und westen waz!* (ll. 675-692)

In the night, she [Venus, M.S.] put without denial the image of Aglye before his eyes; because of her face, his heart wanted to beat wildly. Because of her special mode of protection, Minne tied them together; she threw her net around him, she forced him with her sweetness; Amor, her son, lured him until it was inevitable that

[26] Johann von Würzburg, *Wilhelm von Österreich*, l. 662.
[27] Johann von Würzburg, *Wilhelm von Österreich*, ll. 693-697.

she would capture both of them and took them into her prison in such a way that their desire for each other was strong. They heaved heavy sighs, the young children, more and more: they were in love and did not know why!

According to the intertextual paradigm dominating the poetics of this romance, this description of the many ways in which *minne* takes possession of the hero and his lover draws on a strong literary tradition. Recently, Joachim Bumke has once again pointed to the wide range of literary, theological and scientific works which are all concerned with how love affects the persons struck by it.[28] According to Bumke, seeing the beloved lady before the inner eye is a motif which is frequently used in love poetry and usually goes along with a description of a state of mental absence that the lover experiences.[29] Both theological texts and medical treatises also portray the effects love has on persons as a loss of mental sanity, as a condition that cannot be avoided, as a feeling that takes hold of the whole person, makes him or her a prisoner and evokes a desire for the beloved which cannot be ignored.[30] In his description of the initiation of the protagonist's love, Johann applies all of these aspects of love to his text. The narrator stresses that the condition of love in this case affects children and he again explicitly points to the fact that they do not even know whom they love.

The fact that both children fall for an inner pictorial representation of a person unknown to them, for an image of the beloved before their inner eye, does not, according to Johann's narrative, weaken the threatening effects this love has on the societies to which the main characters belong. With regard to Wildhelm in particular, the condition of being in love very quickly turns out to be a potential danger to the social identity already established for him. Whereas in Gottfried's *Tristan* the protagonist's secret meetings with Isolde constantly put the hero's public position at Mark's court at risk, in Johann's case it is the image of Aglye that threatens the hero's public identity. In an inner monologue, Johann has the hero himself reflect upon the impact that the image might have for him and the noble lineage he is supposed to sustain:

er gedaht: 'uf min triwe!
min muot hat des vereinet sich,
soelt daz lant ze Osterrich
mir ymmer wesen wilde,

[28] J. BUMKE, *Die Blutstropfen im Schnee. Über Wahrnehmung und Erkenntnis im "Parzival" Wolframs von Eschenbach* (Tübingen, 2001: *Hermaea* 94), pp. 29-34.

[29] BUMKE, *Die Blutstropfen*, pp. 29-30.

[30] BUMKE, *Die Blutstropfen*, pp. 30-34.

> *ich kum do min bilde*
> *ist also schone lebende*
> *als ez mir vor ist swebende*
> *mit liehtem anblicke:*
> *mir ist reht als ein wicke*
> *baidiu erbe und aigen'*. (ll. 790-799)

> He thought: "Indeed! I have made up my mind that, even if the country of Austria should always remain foreign to me: if I cannot get to the place where the image really exists in the beautiful way that I have constantly before my eyes with its clear complexion, I shall neither care about my inheritance nor about my possessions."

Thus, the hero recognizes that distancing himself from his own country could be the result of his desire to pursue the image that haunts his mind. In fact, it is this image that the text makes responsible for the hero's ultimate estrangement from his public destiny, an estrangement which is already implicit in his name.

Johann further emphasizes the immense consequences that Wildhelm's love has for Austrian society by having the protagonist confide in his father, whom he tells about the beautiful image occupying his mind. The Austrian count Leopold immediately acknowledges the danger that his son's love for the image in his mind poses for the future of his noble family.[31] He tries to comply with Wildhelm's request to give him the image with which he is so preoccupied. Wildhelm even confronts his father with a distinct condition: if Leopold is unable to produce the picture, then Wildhelm will no longer be his son.[32] In Johann's text, this request is taken literally by the protagonist's father: whether or not he can provide his son with the pictorial representation of his future lover is politically decisive with regard to Wildhelm's future status within the family.

The fact that in Johann's text other characters participate in the knowledge of the love that the protagonist experiences, a knowledge which in other works is usually depicted as a secret of the character involved in love, leads to a dis-

[31] Johann von Würzburg, *Wilhelm von Österreich*, ll. 716-719. Here the Austrian count addresses St. John the Evangelist, to whose grave he went on a pilgrimage in order to be granted an heir: " *'Sant Johannes, herre min!/ wilt du mit laide gelten mir/ vraeude groz, die ich von dir/ und von dem rainen Got habe?'* " ("St. John, my lord! Do you want to cause me pain as payment for the joy you and the almighty God have given me?").

[32] Johann von Würzburg, *Wilhelm von Österreich*, ll. 720-725: " *'lieber vater', sprach der knabe,/ 'wilt du mich haben ze kinde,/ so hilf du mir geswinde/ daz mir werde daz bilde,/ oder dir wirt wilde min gebarn vroelich!'* " (" 'Dear father', said the boy, 'if you want me to be your child, you have to help me find the object of this image quickly, or else my good conduct will change and will appear strange to you' ").

tinct modification of the narrative motif of the beginning of love. On different levels of the narrative, the initiation of Wildhelm's love by Venus seems to be in need of further narrative investigations. That is, the text is more intensively concerned than its intertexts with the void brought about by the lack of bodily presence or personal knowledge of the characters involved in this love. In order to emphasize the immense importance that the protagonist's love has for the further course of the narrative, Johann draws in a very specific way from the poetical device of *ekphrasis* which, according to medieval poetics, is one mode of description.[33] The author has his narrator tell how Leopold, eager to resolve the problem that love is causing him, engages painters to draw portraits of beautiful women:

do wart maler vil besant,
die im do bilde entwurfen für,
ob er iender keines kuer
daz sinem bilde waer gelich;
do wart entworfen maisterlich
daz beste an alle gevaerde:
sunderbar gebaerde
ieglich bilde hat. (ll. 734-741)

Many painters were ordered to come and they sketched out paintings; the question was, whether anybody could create a painting that fully represented his [Wildhelm's, M.S.] mental image; very artistic sketches were made, the very best without any bad intentions: each of the paintings showed excellent looks.

However, the attempt to render Wildhelm's inner image visual in a concrete painting fails. The protagonist informs his father that none of the paintings created represent the beauty that is accessible to him only before his inner eye:

do sprach der knab an der stat:
'ir habt schoeniu bilde gemalt
und habt ser doch gevalt,
daz keines sich gelichen muege
dem schoenen bilde des gehuege
mir vor den augen wunnet.
ob niht min hertze kuennet

[33] See H. BRINKMANN, *Zu Wesen und Form mittelalterlicher Dichtung* (Tübingen, ^{2}1979), pp. 115-116; and N. HENKEL, "Descriptio", in: *Reallexikon der deutschen Literaturwissenschaft. Neubearbeitung des Reallexikons der deutschen Literaturgeschichte* I, ed. K. WEIMAR *et al.* (Berlin and New York 1997), pp. 337-339.

die vraeude als ez den augen git,
sus muoz ich haben laide zit,
die wil mir ist daz leben bi'. (ll. 742-751)

Immediately the young man said: "You have created beautiful images and yet you have to acknowledge that none of the paintings is able to express the beauty of the image that delights my inner eye. If my heart cannot experience the joy that my eyes receive from this image, I shall always be in pain as long as I live."

At this point, the text alludes to what in accordance with modern scholarship shall be defined here as 'imaginary *ekphrasis*',[34] a term that implies "any sought-for equivalent in words of any visual image, inside or outside art".[35] More precisely, Johann's evocation of *ekphrasis* should rather be called an ekphrastic episode, because it only vaguely contains a verbal description of an artwork but instead refers to the process of its making, which is true for many other prominent *ekphraseis* as well.[36] Homer's prominent portrayal of Achilles' shield for example not only contains a description of the artwork itself but is also concerned with the process of its making.[37] Likewise, the medieval *Tristan* romance by Thomas of Britain puts emphasis on the description of the creative process that eventually leads to the making of sculptures strongly resembling Isolde and Brangaene.[38] Moreover, the passage in Johann's romance shares some prominent features with the insertions of *ekphraseis*, as they have frequently appeared in Western literary history since the famous description of Achilles' shield in the eighteenth book of Homer's *Iliad*.[39] The term itself,

[34] In modern scholarship on *ekphrasis*, broad definitions of this literary concept dominate the discussion. See for example: *Pictures into Words. Theoretical and Descriptive Approaches to Ekphrasis*, ed. V. ROBILLARD and E. JONGENEEL (Amsterdam 1998), p. IX: The concept of *ekphrasis* "refers to the manner in which literary works evoke existing or imagined works of art".

[35] Definition taken from M. KRIEGER, "The Problem of *Ekphrasis*: Image and Words, Space and Time – and the Literary Work", in: *Pictures into Words*, ed. V. ROBILLARD and E. JONGENEEL, pp. 3-20, here p. 4.

[36] See p. 14. On the narration of the creative process crucial to every ekphrastic passage, see: J.A.W. HEFFERNAN, *Museum of Words. The Poetics of Ekphrasis from Homer to Ashbery* (Chicago and London, 1993), p. 9.

[37] CLEMENTE, *Literary objet's art*, at p. 7. Homer recounts in detail how Hephaestus wrought Achilles' shield (Homer, *Ilias*, ed. and trans. R. HAMPE [Stuttgart, 1979], c. 18, ll. 468-477.)

[38] See n. 7.

[39] On the Greek origin of *ekphrasis* as rhetorical and literary principle as well as on its first appearance in Homer's *Iliad,* see in particular: HEFFERNAN, *Museum of Words*, pp. 9-10: on *ekphrasis* and its place in ancient rhetoric, see R.C. BRISS, "'Imaginary Work': The Functions of Ekphrasis in Narrative Poetry" (Ph.D. diss. Ann Arbor, 1977), pp. 1-59; with regard to Virgil's

which in Greek means 'to describe exhaustively (*ekphrazein*)', goes back to the Greek schools of the third to fifth centuries, where it was an important rhetorical technique used by orators, and later by writers as well, to bring an artwork before the eyes of their audiences as vividly as possible.[40] From the time when they first appeared in the eighth century B.C., about the time that writing originated in Greece, *ekphraseis*, i.e. verbal descriptions of works of art that only exist as they are invented in the texts,[41] interrupt the course of the narrated events in epic texts; they bring the succession of reported actions and narrated time to a momentary standstill. Such *ekphraseis* within literary works thus seem to be detachable fragments, "descriptive detour[s] from the high road of epic narrative[s]", which could at first sight easily have been taken out of the epics without doing any harm to the motivation and continuation of the narration.[42] This is also true for Johann's romance. Ultimately, the recipients of *Wilhelm von Österreich* already know that love will drive the protagonist away from his home country, that the image before the hero's eye will set the narrative off, and that it functions to initiate a rather complicated set of adventures, which will finally result in the marriage of the couple and the protagonist's acquisition of pagan territory. So what purposes, then, does the ekphrastic passage serve within this particular romance?

Already set within a dense network of intertextual references that inform the narrative of the initiation of love, Johann's text at this point turns to the device of *ekphrasis* in order to add even more reflexive levels to the romance. One of the meta-narrative dimensions established by this allusion to *ekphrasis* serves to make the recipients of the text reflect upon the motivational aspects that the initial motif of the romance implies. In the Middle Ages, *ekphrasis* was widely known as a poetical device prescribing the verbal visualization not only of objects, but also of persons, landscapes, and cities, and as such was adopted from the ancient rhetoric books by medieval poetic literature as part of its most innovative passages concerning multiple modes of description.[43] However, as

use of *ekphrasis* in the *Aeneid* see M.C.J. PUTNAM, *Virgil's Epic Designs. Ekphrasis in the Aeneid* (New Haven and London, 1998); and P. DUBOIS, *History, Rhetorical Description and the Epic. From Homer to Spencer* (Cambridge, 1982), pp. 28-51.

[40] See ROBILLARD and JONGENEEL, *Pictures into Words*, p. IX.

[41] See M. KRIEGER, *Ekphrasis. The Illusion of the Natural Sign* (Baltimore and London 1992), p.17.

[42] HEFFERNAN, *Museum of Words*, p. 5. See also the negative comment on the insertion of *ekphraseis* into literature by C.S. BALDWIN, *Medieval Rhetoric and Poetic (to 1400): Interpreted from Representative Works* (New York, 1928), p. 19. Here Baldwin suggested that "decorative dilation in oratory confirmed a decadent habit of literature".

[43] See for example E.R. CURTIUS, *Europäische Literatur und lateinisches Mittelalter*, 11th

mentioned above, Johann's text remains vague and abstract as far as the actual descriptions of the paintings are concerned, emphasizing instead the process of creation in which the painters get involved.

The ekphrastic passage seems to be more concerned with the motivation that causes the creation of the artworks. The fact that Leopold gives explicit orders to paint images of beautiful women strongly relates this segment of the narrative to the motif which initiates the romance as a whole, namely, the inner image of a woman that haunts the hero and threatens to drive him away from his space of origin. Thus the episode stresses the threat that Wildhelm's inner vision poses to Austrian society: recounting the attempts to fix that image within an artistic representation of it is one means of addressing issues of control within the romance.[44] On the level of the narrative that Gérard Genette calls *histoire*,[45] the ekphrastic episode helps to signify a father's desperate attempt to control the dangerous impact that the image of a beautiful woman has on his son. Here, the narrative playfully conveys the possibility that an artwork could eliminate the endangering consequences that the protagonist's mental image holds for Austrian society. According to the narrative, this aspect is the factor of the unknown, the void that the lack of bodily presence, and with it Aglye's unknown identity, creates for the Austrian lineage. The passage thus helps to develop the idea that the making of a concrete image representing the hero's love could actually weaken his desire to look for the woman whose image occupies his mind. Thus the reference to *ekphrasis* introduces to the narration the possibility of gaining power over the alluring and threatening effects the female image has for the male protagonist.[46] Within this context, Johann's modification of *ekphrasis* as a rhetorical technique and the function attributed to it within the romance also insinuates a more abstract level of reflection, which is concerned with the narrative conditions of the romance itself. In this sense, using *ekphra-*

edn. (Tübingen and Basel, 1993), p. 78: "Zur stilistischen Technik der Neusophistik gehörte auch die kunstvolle 'Ausmalung' (... *descriptio*, Beschreibung) von Menschen, Örtlichkeiten, Bauten, Kunstwerken. Die spätantike und die mittelalterliche Dichtung haben damit großen Aufwand getrieben". On the origins of *descriptio* and the important status it gained within the medieval poetics, see in particular H. BRINKMANN, *Zu Wesen und Form mittelalterlicher Dichtung*, pp. 61-63; M. WEHRLI, *Literatur im deutschen Mittelalter. Eine poetologische Einführung* (Stuttgart, 1984), p. 137; and C. HANNICK and F. QUADLBAUER, "*Ekphrasis*", *LMA* 3 (1999), cols. 1770-1771.

44 With regard to the relationship between *ekphrasis* and gender, see HEFFERNAN, *Museum of Words*, p. 1.

45 G. GENETTE, *Die Erzählung* (Munich, 1994), pp. 11-20. Genette distinguishes three aspects, which, in his view, are constitutive for all narratives: *Geschichte* (*histoire*), *Diskurs* (*discours*), and *Narration* (*narration*), at p. 16.

46 See HEFFERNAN, *Museum of Words*, p. 1.

sis, which Murray Krieger defined as a "vain representational attempt of words"[47] to capture both space and the visual within the temporal sequence of the narration, makes the recipients reflect upon the formal principles that keep the narration going. Johann's insertion of the ekphrastic passage thus makes the reader ponder certain options that could put an end to the narration itself. The meaning that this poetological dimension of the text conveys is clear: if the painters succeeded in creating Aglye's image, the narrative would loose its most decisive motivation. The verbal description of the spatial, "the atemporality of art itself",[48] would then cut off the expected temporal flow of the narration and would hence be able to end the story at this point.

Here it becomes obvious that the ekphrastic segment within the romance is not limited to serving the purpose of rhetorically strengthening the motif that initiates the whole narration. Moreover, like any other *ekphrasis* in literary texts, it is used to address fundamental semiotic issues which derive from the general friction that informs them, namely the confrontation that any verbal representation of the visual signifies between language and the pictorial arts.[49] Wildhelm's monologue (above), which introduces the reference to *ekphrasis* to the romance, already implies what seems to be the fundamental semiotic desire for the natural sign, which, according to Krieger, is the source of *ekphrasis*.[50] When the protagonist expresses his desire to find the referent to the image of the woman occupying his mind, this image is perceived by the character as a natural sign, i.e. a sign that resembles its referent and is "indeed a visual substitute for its referent".[51] Based on a theory of representation that is at this point essentially mimetic, Johann addresses the friction between the verbal and visual arts in a very specific way.[52] Instead of simply using the verbal representation

[47] M. KRIEGER, "The Problem of *Ekphrasis*", p. 4.

[48] PUTNAM, *Virgil's Epic Design*, p. 2.

[49] Whilst for WENZEL, "Audiovisualität im Mittelalter", p. 61, such allusions to *ekphrasis* in vernacular romances indicate an interdependency of the visual and verbal arts, I argue that these allusions to the pictorial arts in language derive from a history of poetological literature, which for a long time favoured the capacities of the visual arts in comparison to those of the verbal arts. On the comparison of poetry with painting, which is based on Simonides of Ceos in pre-socratic times, see in particular F.A. YATES, *The Art of Memory* (Chicago, 1966), p. 28: "The theory of the equation of poetry and painting also rests on the supremacy of the visual sense".

[50] KRIEGER, "The Problem of *Ekphrasis*", p. 5.

[51] KRIEGER, "The Problem of *Ekphrasis*", p. 5.

[52] On *ekphrasis* as an important tool used to bridge the friction between the visual and the language arts see M. MOOG-GRÜNEWALD, "Der Sänger im Schild – oder: Über den Grund ekphrastischen Schreibens", in: *Behext von Bildern? Ursachen, Funktionen und Perspektiven der textuellen Faszination durch Bilder*, ed. H.J. DRÜGH, M. MOOG-GRÜNEWALD (Heidelberg, 2001), pp. 1-19, at p. 2.

of the visual in its capacity to serve as a substitute for a natural sign, the text seems fundamentally to question the visual art's abilities to fix and therefore mimetically represent Wildhelm's object of desire. In doing so, the romance takes an important stance with regard to an ongoing debate that accompanied the emergence of *ekphrasis*. Ever since Plato's *Cratylus*,[53] where, within a metaphysic based on the doctrine of mimesis, natural signs are differentiated from arbitrary signs, "the language arts have had a lengthy struggle to free themselves, because of their visually disadvantaged medium, from the secondariness assigned to them in their non-naturalness of representation".[54] The construction of the initiation of love in the late medieval text, the fact that Aglye is not yet personally known to the people struggling with her image, is taken as an incentive to negotiate again the capacities of the visual and verbal arts. The narration of the rather peculiar attempt to fixate a mental image, whose referent is neither known nor described to the painters, must eventually lead to a failure to perform the task given to the artists within the narrative. By never even mentioning any attempt by the protagonist to describe his mental image verbally, a description that would have been needed in order successfully to transform his vision into a painting, the romance explicitly points out the distinct limitations of *ekphrasis*. Thus the refusal to provide an *ekphrasis*, i.e. a verbal account of Wildhelm's image, ultimately results in the failure to create an adequate painting of Aglye. Johann's text critically reflects upon the possibilities of ekphrastic speech, in order to point to the fact that it is ultimately

[53] Plato, *Kratylos*, in: *Sämtliche Werke* 3, ed. U. WOLF, trans. F. SCHLEIERMACHER, H. und F. MÜLLER (Reinbek bei Hamburg, 1994), at pp. 69-70. See also Aristotle, *Poetik*, ed. and trans. M. FUHRMANN (Stuttgart, 1984), 1460b. Here, Aristotle claims that a poet is an imitator of reality, such as a painter or any sculptor: "Da der Dichter ein Nachahmer ist, wie ein Maler oder ein anderer bildender Künstler, muß er von drei Nachahmungsweisen, die es gibt, stets eine befolgen".

[54] KRIEGER, "The Problem of *Ekphrasis*", p. 7. The doctrine of "*ut pictura poesis*" established by Horace also seems to reflect a hierarchy of the visual and the verbal arts. Essentially, Horace favours a perspective that views poetry and paintings as aesthetically analogous. In his view, both arts can be judged according to the same criteria and points of view. It seems obvious, however, that this doctrine is nevertheless informed by the supremacy of the visual arts. With regard to Horace, see CLEMENTE, *Literary objets d'art*, p. 6. On "*ut pictura poesis*", see also J.H. HAGSTRUM, *The Sister Arts. The Tradition of Literary Pictorialism and English Poetry from Dryden to Gray* (Chicago and London, 1958), p. 37. Hagstrum also points to the anticlassical spirit of early Christian writers such as Isidore of Seville to whom painting (*pictura*) was a mode of representation that possessed "nothing of credibility or truth" (pp. 38-39). According to Hagstrum, however, the Middle Ages nevertheless retained many of the most essential elements of classical pictorialism: "when classical scholarship was active, classical pictorialism was present" (p. 40); "The Middle Ages may not have broken with the past so sharply as the early Christian apologists would have wished" (p. 44).

language that is able at least to refer to the intelligible source of the image that haunts the protagonist's mind. By systematically refusing to give its recipients a verbal account of a visual image, the episode constructs a case in which the visual arts can be denied their capacity to function as a natural sign able on its own to depict the referent of Wildhelm's image within the romance. The protagonist's inner vision remains exclusively his own.

At the same time, after the failure of representing this vision, which is what the ekphrastic episode signifies, the text shifts to questions such as where the mental image of the hero actually originated and why it is impossible to transform it into either a verbal account or an artistic representation. Here, the text draws from the topos of nature which in late ancient and medieval literature was often used to explain the cause of human beauty.[55] In Johann's romance, the topos helps to express the auratic quality which the image of Aglye has for the protagonist alone. The narrator states that it was "nature" that shaped the beautiful and perfect image of Aglye.[56] In accordance with the medieval discourse on beauty, the romance thus suggests that beauty produced by nature in general far exceeds any beauty which can be created by art and that it can as such neither be imitated by visual artistic techniques nor be sufficiently depicted by language.[57] Furthermore, the narrator also relates Wildhelm's inner vision to God, who is referred to as one of the major causes responsible for the formation of the image and for the hero's love for it.[58] This reference to God is linked to the earlier episode of the pilgrimage undertaken by the Austrian count and the pagan king. In compliance with the poetics of intertextuality, this reference to the biblical and hagiographical genres informing the initial episodes of the romance reveals, within the context of the ekphrastic episode, that language and linguistic works of art are not limited to "the sensed world about us" but can actually take "advantage of their intelligibility to claim a realm beyond".[59] Even though the beauty of Wildhelm's image of Aglye is depicted as being

[55] See for example CURTIUS, *Europäische Literatur und lateinisches Mittelalter*, p. 187.

[56] Johann von Würzburg, *Wilhelm von Österreich*, ll. 602-604: "*der Wunsch und diu Natur/ gewuerket hant so meisterlich/ sin werdes bilde*" ("Desire and nature together perfectly created his wonderful image").

[57] See M. WEHRLI, *Literatur im deutschen Mittelalter*, pp. 143-144: "Das Schöne als absolute Qualität, als Vollkommenheit, Form oder wie immer seine Namen sind, betrifft keineswegs zuerst die Kunst, das Kunstwerk oder den Kunstgenuß, vielmehr die Natur, die Schöpfung und noch eigentlicher den Schöpfer selbst. Diesem gegenüber kann der Künstler höchstens als Nachahmer, oder metaphorisch und analogisch, als Nachschöpfer und bestenfalls als Vollender im einzelnen verstanden werden".

[58] Johann von Würzburg, *Wilhelm von Österreich*, ll. 762-770.

[59] KRIEGER, "The Problem of *Ekphrasis*", p. 13.

beyond words as well as beyond any means of visualization, it is still language that is at least capable of conveying this fact by using the widely known topos that addresses the non-expressible (*Unsagbarkeitstopos*).[60] Linda Clemente's definition of *ekphrasis* in medieval literature, which in her eyes "provides an external equivalent to an inner emotional reality which translates into an objective entity that expresses a subjective state",[61] sheds light on the reason why in Johann's text this technique of visualization proves to be ineffective. It is precisely this ineffectiveness that helps to express the inner emotional reality of the protagonist as being inaccessible to those around him.

Finally, the insertion of this truly unique segment into the text seems also to elucidate the poetological concept on which the romance is based in general.[62] The rather unusual construction that imagines painters sketching out their art without even knowing whom to draw seems only to make sense precisely when taking into account the intertextual paradigm upon which the romance as a whole relies. The account of the doomed efforts of the painters seems to evoke strong similarities with those reflections made in the prologue that concern the making of the romance itself: here, like the painters in the episode, the implied author states that he does not rely on a single existing text, a source, clearly identifiable by the recipients of the story: "*ich sitze/in getihtes sinne./ tugende, aventuer, minne, daz sint cleinode driu, / swer si minnet .../ bescheidenlich, daz ist ein sit/ dem aelliu saelde volget mit*" (ll. 132-138).[63] Instead, without any concrete prototype, his story draws from multiple sources and thus creates something new: "*ich muoz von geschihten/ ein aventuer getihten*" (ll. 171-172).[64] Like the paintings sketched out by the artists, the narrative has a beauty of its own, but it does not simply represent only one already existing romance of the past. In this respect, the insertion of the ekphrastic passage gives one important hint in that it implies a poetological self-reflection, which helps to explain the innovative and rather complicated structure and content of the text as a whole.

All in all, apart from its comical implications, the description of the failed attempt to capture the image of Wildhelm's beloved in a painting thus points to the problem mentioned above, namely whether "the repertoire of representa-

[60] On what is referred to as the *Unsagbarkeitstopos*, see for example CURTIUS, *Europäische Literatur und lateinisches Mittelalter*, p. 166.

[61] CLEMENTE, *Literary objets d'art*, p. 9.

[62] See BRISS, "'Imaginary Work'", p. 37: "By representing artistic form within the poem, by representing itself and creating its own poetic, the poem transcends itself in *ekphrasis*".

[63] "I am sitting within the meaning of the poem. / Virtue, adventure, and *minne* are three ingredients, whoever loves them dearly (and this is a rule) will be favoured by complete joy".

[64] "Drawing from various stories, I have to invent an adventure".

tional techniques at the writer's disposal"[65] is suitable to signify the bodily presence of the characters involved in a love relationship. The answer seems to be clear: verbal as well as artistic attempts at visualization in this case fail truly to represent the image and beauty of the beloved woman. All in all, Johann's text refers extensively to a tradition of written texts as well as to poetic devices in order to investigate the motif of the initiation of love, which occupies the beginning of the narrative. The efforts that the text undertakes to motivate the story seem to derive from the fact that the love relation is initiated by a representation and not by a direct bodily encounter of the characters of Wildhelm and Aglye. Thereby, Johann's text differs from his important intertexts like the *Tristan* tradition or Arthurian romances. Both of these traditions make use of several narrative techniques which help to render the bodily presence of the lovers visual and as such help to motivate the initiation of love and the further development of the protagonist convincingly. In Hartmann's *Iwein* for example, the description of the direct male gaze on the female body sufficiently motivates the beginning of love.[66] In Johann's case it is the representation of the body in an imagined vision of the protagonist – an image, however, that no technique of representation can access – that dictates the course of the narrative. Thus, in this narrative, the question of how to motivate and describe love's initiation by literary means almost seems to exceed the interest in the actual telling of the love story itself.

The integration of this distinctive episode into the romance together with the intertextual paradigm that informs the poetics of this late medieval text demonstrate that when it comes to the narration of the initiation of love, the text makes a point of not seeking the verbal creation of an accessible artistic representation of Wildhelm's inner vision. Instead, it implements a sequence in the text that is explicitly concerned with denying the capacities that verbal as well as artistic techniques of visualization have to offer, in order to shift the recipients' attention to a fundamental issue, namely to the limits of representation itself. In order to point to the uniqueness of the protagonist's experience, which precisely characterizes his inner vision of Aglye, the text attributes an auratic quality to the image haunting Wildhelm's mind. It does so by linking the negotiations concerning the origin of Wildhelm's vision to the intertexts which the author used to construct the beginning of the romance in the first place, especially references to medieval love poetry, to courtly romances and epics and to hagiographic and biblical sources. Thus, the text develops multiple causes for the presence of the image, such as references to Venus and God. However, by

[65] ROBILLARD and JONGENEEL, *Pictures into Words*, p. IX.
[66] Hartmann von Aue, *Iwein*, ll. 1307-1339.

pointing to language's capacity to allude to the inexpressible qualities of the beauty revealed in this image as well as to the intelligible reasons responsible for the formation of the vision the protagonist experiences, the text consequently denies the recipients any access to what the protagonist actually sees. Thus, the romance at this point makes its recipients reflect upon a hierarchy of the different modes of representation at its disposal and clearly seems to favour the capacity of the linguistic works of art over those of the visual arts with regard to the narration of the initiation of love.

By refusing to create an initial pictorial effect that would put the experience of love before the eyes of the recipients, Johann's very specific allusion to the tradition of *ekphrasis* rather provokes thoughts about the poetics of the romance itself.[67] In so doing, Johann seems not only to reject making use of the visual effects which are supposedly crucial to the making of literary texts in the bimedial context of the Middle Ages, but the text also implies that it is impossible to narrate the experience of falling in love by turning to any techniques of visualization. Consequently, he stresses the artistic capacity of the linguistic works of art and supports a poetics of intertextuality that not only provides the readers and listeners of the text with a story but simultaneously makes the recipients reflect upon the making of the story. As far as the love story is concerned, a strategy of inversion remains at work as the narration continues: contrary to Ovid's tale, for example, where the lack of bodily presence proves the impossibility of even bringing the experience of love into its fictitious existence, Johann's romance continues to narrate long sequences of absences, in which the love of Wildhelm and Aglye is exclusively expressed and experienced within an extensive exchange of letters.[68] Again, the narration of writing within writing (art within art) is suitable to convey love's experience; and seen from this

[67] See HEFFERNAN, *Museum of Words*, p. 4: "*ekphrasis* differs from both iconicity and pictorialism because it explicitly represents representation itself".

[68] See C. DIETL, *Minne, Roman und 'historia'. Der 'Wilhelm von Österreich' Johanns von Würzburg* (Tübingen, 1999: *Hermaea* N.F. 87), p. 85: "Die realitätsstiftende Funktion des Worts wird in den ersten beiden Briefen deutlich: Die Briefe vermögen nicht nur, den Schmerz der Trennung zu lindern, sondern sie eröffnen auch einen Raum, in dem die Liebe Ryals und Aglies weiterexistieren kann". See also W. RÖCKE, "Liebe und Schrift: Deutungsmuster sozialer und literarischer Kommunikation im deutschen Liebes- und Reiseroman des 13. Jahrhunderts. (Konrad Fleck: 'Florio und Blanscheflur'; Johann von Würzburg: 'Wilhelm von Österreich')", in: *Mündlichkeit – Schriftlichkeit – Weltbildwandel: literarische Kommunikation und Deutungsschemata von Wirklichkeit in der Literatur des Mittelalters und der frühen Neuzeit*, ed. W. RÖCKE and U. SCHAEFER (Tübingen, 1996: *ScriptOralia* 71), pp. 85-108, at p. 97: "Wir sehen auch in Johanns von Würzburg *Wilhelm von Österreich* eine auffällige Konzentration des Romans auf Formen der Verbildlichung und Verschriftlichung der Liebesbeziehung zwischen Wilhelm und Aglye".

perspective it is not strange that as soon as the couple does get united, the narrator loses all interest in further elaborating on this love story.

The integration of the ekphrastic episode into Johann's text can without doubt be taken as one example of the fact that late medieval romances are not only intensively informed by an already existing tradition of vernacular writing but also make extensive use of this tradition in order to create various levels of reflection that raise important poetological concerns. However, a close examination of the ekphrastic episodes that frequently appear in medieval romances of the High Middle Ages also shows that, even in those cases where the descriptions of works of art are actually given, the poetical implications of these passages cannot easily be overlooked. Taking the hall of statues as described in Thomas of Britain's *Tristan* romance as one prominent example,[69] it is evident that the impact such passages have on the construction of the romances cannot be sufficiently explained by simply pointing to the important function that strategies of narrative visualization have for the demands of a collective, or in this case rather personal, memory that is still crucial to the bi-medial context of the High Middle Ages. Thomas' text also seems to demonstrate the capacity of the written word to simulate the art of a sculptor verbally.[70] Thus it already participates in the tradition of all *ekphraseis*, namely to emphasize the possibilities of the linguistic works of art compared to those of the visual arts. Moreover, the episode seems to be related to other important poetic dimensions of the text, such as the biographical paradigm crucial to its genesis.[71] *Ekphrasis*, as one important strategy of visualization in literary texts, cannot thus be reduced to the status of a relic and cannot simply be taken as evidence that written vernacular romances are still informed by oral modes of communication. And although *ekphrasis* originates from ancient rhetorical devices and is thus linked to the demands of a concept of memory that was imagined as a spatial and pictorial tool to preserve important information,[72] medieval poetics incorporated this technique of visualization and, as a mode of description, made *ekphrasis* part of its prescriptions aimed at the construction of written texts.[73] Being a vivid part

[69] See n. 7.

[70] See CLEMENTE, *Literary objets d'art*, p. 5: "As discrete elements of the narrative, *ekphraseis* are further statements of ... the hyper-conscious creation of art within art".

[71] See SCHAUSTEN, "Ich bin, alse ich hân vernomen, ze wunderlîchen maeren komen", p. 47.

[72] See YATES, *The Art of Memory*, p. 28: "The elusive relations with other arts which run all through the history of the art of memory are thus already present in the legendary source, in the stories about Simonides who saw poetry, painting and mnemonics in terms of intense visualization."

[73] See CURTIUS, *Europäische Literatur und lateinisches Mittelalter*, p. 79: "Das bedeutet

of the tradition of vernacular romance writing, *ekphraseis* always exceed the mimetic function originally assigned to them. The method of verbally describing an art work in literature thus is never only mimetic, but always also poetic.[74] Thus literary criticism needs to turn to such strategies of visualization in medieval epic literature and not only elaborate on them from the perspective of media history, but also examine their poetological implications within a tradition of written linguistic works of art.[75]

nichts anderes, als daß die Rhetorik ihren ursprünglichen Sinn und Daseinszweck verlor. Dafür drang sie in alle Literaturgattungen ein. Ihr kunstvoll ausgebautes System wurde Generalnenner, Formenlehre und Formenschatz der Literatur überhaupt."

[74] CLEMENTE, *Literary objets d'art*, p. 11; and MOOG-GRÜNEWALD, "Der Sänger im Schild", p. 3.

[75] See T. REUVEKAMP-FELBER, "Briefe als Kommunikations- und Strukturelemente in der 'Virginal': Reflexionen mittelalterlicher Schriftkultur in der Dietrichepik", *PBB* 125 (2003), pp. 57-81, at pp. 80-81.

Polytextual Reading:
The Meditative Reading of Real and Metaphorical Books

SYLVIA HUOT

This essay examines a medieval practice that we might call 'polytextual reading'. By this I mean a type of reading taught in devotional manuals for the laity, fostered by the presence in Books of Hours and other devotional manuscripts of vivid marginal illustrations, and encouraged through more learned techniques of exegesis, glossing, and meditative reading. Through all of these means, the reading of one text becomes a process of reading multiple 'virtual' texts. These supplemental texts may be produced through intellectual and imaginative processes of memory and association, whereby a single text becomes a springboard for the recollection and reconsideration of many others.[1] They may also be generated from the different perspectives taken on the text at hand, as when allegorical exegesis offers multiple interpretations of a given passage. Evidence for these practices is plentiful, in the form of glosses, marginal annotations noting analogous passages in other texts, and compendia like

[1] I have discussed these meditative and associative reading practices with regard to Old French devotional anthologies in "A Book Made for a Queen: The Shaping of a Late Medieval Anthology Manuscript (B.N. fr. 24429)", in: *The Whole Book: Cultural Perspectives on the Medieval Miscellany*, ed. S.G. NICHOLS and S. WENZEL (Ann Arbor, 1996), pp. 123-143. On the relevance of these techniques to prayer, see my "Inventional Mnemonics, Reading and Prayer: A Reply to Mary Carruthers", *Connotations* 3.2 (1993/94), pp. 1-8. Marginal annotations in *Roman de la Rose* manuscripts show that readers of that poem frequently linked it in their minds with other familiar texts, particularly those of Ovid but also other Latin poets and even canon law; see my *The Romance of the Rose and its Medieval Readers: Interpretation, Reception, Manuscript Transmission* (Cambridge, 1993: *Cambridge Studies in Medieval Literature* 16), pp. 47-84.

the *Ovide moralisé* in which the various interpretations provided for a given tale end up producing many different stories from each narrative unit.[2]

This kind of associative and free-wheeling approach to the text as a gateway to literary proliferation accords well with the cultivation of reading as a spiritual exercise. A succinct account of this aspect of reading appears in *Li Livres des enfans Israel*, found in a late fourteenth-century manuscript which once belonged to the aristocratic poet Charles d'Orléans.[3] The text opens with the following account of reading:

> *Trois manieres sont d'esperituel exercite. C'est leçons, meditations, et oroisons. Ces trois sont si conjointes que l'une ne puet valoir sans l'autre. Car leçons sans meditations tourne a negligence et a ociosité. Meditations sans leçons maine en erreur. Et meditations sans oroison engendre vanité. Et oroisons sanz meditation est sans lumiere et sans fervour. Pour ce convient premiers le cuer enfourmer par leçon, et fermer par meditation, et puis refourmer par oroison.*[4]
>
> There are three kinds of spiritual exercise: reading, meditation, and prayer. These three are so interconnected that no one of them is worth anything without the others. For reading without meditation turns to negligence and idleness. Meditation without reading leads to error, and meditation without prayer engenders vanity. And prayer without meditation is lacking light and fervour. Therefore one must first inform the heart through reading, and firm it up through meditation, and then reform it through prayer.

In this formulation, based on the monastic tradition of *lectio*, *meditatio*, and *oratio*, reading is the necessary foundation for all further spiritual progress, neither an end in itself nor an avoidable part of the overall process of spiritual formation and development. As an example of this technique in the context of lay piety, we might think of texts such as the explications of the 'Pater noster' or 'Ave maria', in which each line of the prayer in question is examined, amplified, considered in different contexts, and associated with other scriptural pas-

[2] On the *Ovide moralisé* see R. BLUMENFELD-KOSINSKI, *Reading Myth: Classical Mythology and Its Interpretations in Medieval French Literature* (Stanford, 1997). These examples are well known. For example the story of Orpheus can be simply about a man who grieved for his wife and turned to pederasty, or about the soul's descent into sin, or about Christ's passion, harrowing of hell, and selection of a new bride (Ecclesia) after being spurned by his former bride, Synagoga.

[3] The manuscript is Paris, BN fr. 1802. On Charles' ownership, see L. DELISLE, *Le Cabinet des manuscrits de la Bibliothèque Nationale* 1 (Paris, 1881), pp. 110, 148.

[4] BN fr. 1802, f. 201v.

sages.[5] The point of these treatises is not really to explain the meaning of the text under scrutiny, since these simple and deeply familiar prayers would not have required such elaborate exegesis. Rather, these texts provide a model of how the prayer, in conjunction with meditative reflection informed by reading, can be the occasion for a potentially endless review of religious dogma, sacred history, and individual morality.

This 'polytextual' reading also figures in the visionary accounts of prayerful meditation. The thirteenth-century Carthusian prioress Marguerite d'Oingt describes her devotions in terms of a visionary book in her treatise entitled *Speculum*.[6] Speaking of herself in the third person, Marguerite explains that "*Citi creatura, per la graci de Nostre Seignor, aveit excrit en son cor la seinti via que Deus Jhesu Criz menet en terra ... E ... li eret semblanz alcuna veis que il li fut presenz e que il tenit un livro clos en sa mayn per liey ensennier*" ("By the grace of our Lord, this creature had written into her heart the holy life that Jesus Christ had led on earth ... [and] it sometimes seemed to her that He was present and that He held a closed book in His hand in order to teach from it").[7] The outside of this book was covered all over with writing in letters of white, black, and red, while the clasps were covered with letters of gold. The colour-coding corresponded to the different texts recording the life of Christ:

> *En les lettres blanches eret escrita li sancta conversations al beneit fil Deu ... En les neyres erant escrit li col et les tenplees et les ordures que li Jue li gitavont en sa sainti faci ... En les vremelles erant escrite les plaes et li pretious sans qui fut espanchies per nos.*
>
> In the white letters was written the saintly life of the blessed Son of God ... In the black letters were written the blows and the slaps and the filthy things that the Jews

[5] See my discussion of the 'Pater noster' in "A Book Made for a Queen". Mary Carruthers also discusses medieval meditative reading, commenting that the reader's memory "is freed to roam its memorial symphony, 'gathering up' harmonies and antitheses in the compositional activity which Hugh of St. Victor described as 'meditation', the highest kind of study ... Interpretation can then become a form of prayer'": *The Craft of Thought: Meditation , Rhetoric, and the Making of Images, 400-1200* (Cambridge, 1998: *Cambridge Studies in Medieval Literature* 34), pp. 147-148.

[6] Marguerite d'Oingt, *Speculum*, in: *Les Oeuvres de Marguerite d'Oingt*, ed. A. DURAFFOUR, P. GARDETTE and P. DURDILLY (Paris, 1965: *Publications de l'Institut de Linguistique Romane de Lyon* 21), pp. 89-103. Quotations are taken from this edition and the English translation as *Mirror*, in: R. BLUMENFELD-KOSINSKI, *The Writings of Margaret of Oingt, Medieval Prioress and Mystic* (Newburyport, MA, 1990), pp. 41-47.

[7] *Speculum*, p. 90; *Mirror*, p. 42.

> had thrown at His saintly face ... In the red letters were written the wounds and the precious blood that was shed for us.[8]

On the clasps, golden letters proclaimed that "*Deus erit omnia in omnibus*" ("God will be everything to everyone") and "*Mirabilis Deus in sanctis suis*" ("God is marvellous in His saints").[9]

Marguerite then explains that she would read the different coloured texts of this book during her meditations, comparing the white account of Christ's holy acts to what she read in the book of her conscience ("*el livro de sa concienci*") and thereby learning to correct her own faults; moving on to the black letters, she learned to have patience in adversity; from the red letters, she learned to enjoy ("*deleitier*") her tribulations; and finally the gold letters taught her to "*desirrar les choses celestiaux*" ("desire the things of heaven").[10] These meditations culminated in a vision one day of the book suddenly opening up and revealing "*uns lues delicious*" with "*una tres gloriosa lumeri, que se devisavet en tres parties*" ("a delightful place ... a glorious light which divided itself into three parts").[11] Through an orderly reading of the three visionary texts along with the book of her conscience, then, Marguerite moved between self-scrutiny and meditation on the Incarnation and Passion of Christ and advanced from a consideration of earthly life to contemplation of Heaven.

Marguerite was writing in a monastic context, but treatises on lay devotions also portray pious meditation as a process of reading books accessed within the self. I draw my next examples from another fourteenth-century devotional anthology, associated with the court of Saint-Pol, and bearing a colophon stating that it was compiled for the education and entertainment of both the children and the adults at court. This anthology includes two texts that explicate the human psyche as an aggregate of three books. One of these texts, called *Le Dit des trois chevaliers et des trois livres*, is quite simple in its presentation and generous in its illustration, and was probably among the texts intended for the education of children. *Le dit des trois chevaliers* tells the story of three companions, all of them knights, who undergo a collective religious conversion while riding through the forest on the way home from a tournament and promptly join a nearby monastery. When the two younger companions tire of this existence and complain that since they are illiterate, they are unable to participate properly in monastic life, the older member of the trio tells them that he knows of

8 IBID.
9 IBID.
10 *Speculum*, p. 92; *Mirror*, p. 43.
11 *Speculum*, p. 94; *Mirror*, p. 44.

three books that can and should be read every day even by the totally unlettered. These books, he explains, are "*le livre de la conscience*" ("the book of the conscience"), "*le livre de science*" ("the book of knowledge"), and "*le livre de sapience*" ("the book of wisdom"). He then goes on to describe these books in visual and material terms. The book of the conscience is "*escript de lettres occures et noires*" ("written in obscure, black letters"), and records the sins of the individual.[12] The book of knowledge records the Passion of Christ:

> *Le parchemin est blanc comme noif, et la leittre est vermeille comme sanc. Car le parchemin dont fu fait cest livre fu nostre humanité, que le saint esperit purefia et saintefia en la beneoite virge Marie ... Je regarde ensement la rougeur et les leittres vermeilles de sa trés angoisseuse passion.*[13]
>
> The parchment is as white as snow, and the writing is as red as blood. For the parchment from which this book was made was our humanity, which the Holy Spirit purified and sanctified in the Blessed Virgin Mary ... Thus I gaze upon the redness and the crimson letters of his most agonizing passion.

The book of wisdom, finally, is revealed by the Holy Spirit and "*escript de leittres d'or*" ("written in letters of gold");[14] it records sacred mysteries and the joys of paradise. These three books can be identified with the three non-literal levels of Biblical exegesis – the moral or tropological, the allegorical, and the anagogical – and suggest a programme of pious reflection, self-scrutiny, and spiritual progress that is very similar to that of Marguerite d'Oingt.

Another text in the same collection, the *Livre de vie et aguillon de vraie amour* opens with a miniature depicting a woman in prayer before a gigantic open book whose spine is formed by the Crucifixion (fig. 1). This text explains that the "*livre de vie*" ("book of life") is Christ himself, and that other metaphorical books derive from him:

> *Et de cest benoit livre de vie sunt extrez .iii. petiz livres, qui nous sunt donnez pour nous enformer en vie espirituele par quoi nous puissons venir a vie pardurable. Et de ces .iii. livres, le premier est appelé le livre de la conscience ... Le secont livre est de la devine congnoissance a qui l'en ne puet riens celer ... Et le tiers est le livre de la souveraine et de la pardurable sapience.*[15]

[12] Paris, BN nouv. ac. fr. 4338, f. 141r.
[13] BN nouv. ac. fr. 4338, ff. 141v-142r.
[14] BN nouv. ac. fr. 4338, f. 142v.
[15] BN nouv. ac. fr. 4338, f. 160r.

Fig. 1 The opening miniature from the *Livre de Vie*, showing the crucified Christ as a book. Paris, Bibliothèque Nationale, nouv. ac. fr. 4338, f. 143v. Photo: Bibliothèque Nationale de France.

> And from this blessed book of life are extracted three little books, which are given to us in order to instruct us in the spiritual life so that we can pass into eternal life. And of these three books, the first is called the book of conscience ... The second book is that of divine knowledge, from which nothing can be hidden ... And the third is the book of sovereign and eternal wisdom.

The *Livre de vie* also recommends reading the book of one's conscience in tandem with the book of Christ, so as to ensure that all of one's sins are properly expunged and replaced with suitably pious text. The author warns, in fact, that the devil will endeavour to corrupt the text of one's conscience:

> *Et lors le faus notaire – c'est le deable, nostre adversaire – escript en celle meisme conscience escripture de toute vilté et de toute fausseté: c'est l'escripture de pechié.*[16]
>
> And then the false notary – that is, the devil, our adversary – writes in this same conscience a script of complete vileness and falsity: that is the script of sin.

To counteract the devil's scribal activities, daily proofreading and corrections of the book of the conscience are needed.[17]

The average medieval lay reader did not experience visions, nor were they trained in scriptural exegesis or mythography. But I would argue that the experience of reading polytextually was available, at least to the wealthy, through the existence of profusely illustrated psalters and Books of Hours. As is well known, many of the images that fill the margins of such books have little or no direct bearing on the texts. In many cases these marginal images seem hardly more than distractions from the pious content of the page, as though placed there to tempt the reader away from his or her devotions. But while that may, of course, have been an effect welcomed by some readers, it would be reductive – if not downright bizarre – to see such books as simply a device for the avoidance of prayer. It is true that in one sense, the pictures do compete with the text, seeming to lure the reader away from the devout words that fill the page and the suitably devotional subjects depicted in the main miniatures. But for someone trained in the art of reading multiple texts simultaneously, constantly making links between the text on the page and the myriad of texts in his or her mind

[16] BN nouv. ac. fr. 4338, f. 163v.

[17] On these texts see my discussion in "The Writer's Mirror: Watriquet de Couvin and the Development of the Author-Centered Book", in: *Across Boundaries: The Book in Culture and Commerce*, ed. B. BELL, P. BENNETT and J. BEVAN (Winchester and New Castle, DE, 2000), pp. 29-35.

and attending to the oppositions and intersections between them, such a book could be a powerful stimulation to prayerful meditation and creative reading. Such readings could be both edifying and entertaining, free-wheeling or strictly orthodox, according to the inclinations and mood of the reader.

A typical manuscript of this type – one of a great many possible examples – is the Flemish psalter, dated ca. 1320-30, that is preserved today in two volumes as Douce MSS 5 and 6 in the Bodleian Library, Oxford. Surrounding the text of the psalms are marginal images depicting hybrids, apes, fanciful vignettes, and scenes from daily life, none of which can be seen as simple illustrations of the psalms. As a case in point we may take f. 83v of Douce 6, which contains the ending of Psalm 111 ("*Beatus vir qui timet Dominum*" ["Blessed is the man that feareth the Lord"], Ps. 112) and the beginning of Psalm 112 ("*Laudate, pueri, Dominum*" ["Praise ye the Lord"], Ps. 113).[18] In the lower margin a woman is trapping a sleeping man in an elaborate snare (fig. 2). Clearly, this unfortunate fellow is the opposite of the upright man lauded in the psalm that is just ending. We might in fact identify him with the sinner evoked in its closing lines, whose fate will be to gnash his teeth over the good fortunes of the virtuous man: "*Peccator videbit, et irascetur ... Desiderium peccatorum peribit*" (Ps. 111: 10) ("The wicked shall see it, and be grieved ... the desire of the wicked shall perish", Ps. 112: 10). The pious reading, certainly, is that this man, lulled into spiritual lethargy, is about to be seduced into the sin of lechery. At the same time, the possibility exists for a wittier, if somewhat irreverent, association of this erotic fantasy with the psalm's comment on the virtuous man's triumph: "*Cornu eius exaltabitur in gloria*" (Ps. 111: 9) ("his horn shall be exalted with honour", Ps. 112: 9). A well-established clerical tradition of scriptural parody, whereby Biblical verses taken out of context are invested with sexual innuendo or other humorous implications, had not failed to note the potential for a sexual *double entendre* in this image, which recurs several times in the psalms, of the 'exalted horn'. The rhetorician Boncompagno da Signa (ca. 1170-ca. 1240) employed this very phrase in a scurrilous context in his *Rhetorica novissima*: "*Quidam qui cognoverat monialem dixit: 'Non violavi thorum divinum, sed quia me in sua factura Dominus delectavit, cornu eius studui exaltare'*" ("A certain man who had had carnal knowledge of a nun said: 'I did not violate the divine marriage bed, but since God had favoured me in his

[18] I quote from the Vulgate Bible, with translations from the King James Bible, giving the appropriate numbering in each case.

Fig. 2 Marginal illustrations at the end of Psalm 111. Oxford, Bodleian Library, Douce 6, f. 83v. By permission of the Bodleian Library, University of Oxford.

works, I sought to exalt his horn'").[19] For a reader in search more of amusement than of stern morality, this image might then be a humorous pun, playing on the opposition between exaltations of the spirit and those of the flesh.

In effect, the reader is being given a choice of two possible models. On the one hand, the inattentive reader who allows himself to be seduced by the lurid image and to ignore the text can expect to meet the same fate as the sleeper – for better or for worse, depending on his perspective – but the reader who draws the appropriate moral lesson will be saved and indeed reinforced in his determination to emulate the upright man. The page thus allows for several different 'readings' to emerge: pleasurable indulgence in sensual fantasies ('Oh, to fall into her snares ... '), narrative elaboration ('And then after the man woke up ...'), self-scrutiny ('Am I guilty of this?'), or moral reflection ('Such are the perils of this sinful world'). Having completed Psalm 111 and drawn the appropriate moral lesson, secure in pious vigilance or refreshed by his contemplation of potential sin, the reader can then proceed to join in with the joyful praise of God in Psalm 112. Nor is this image unique; various studies have shown that such seemingly fanciful and frivolous marginalia as people riding backwards on beasts or children playing games can serve not only as aesthetically pleasing ornamentation and delightful distraction from the serious business of prayer, but also as moral or allegorical glosses that reinforce the main text.[20]

With this in mind I propose to look at two Books of Hours, both richly illustrated, to see how they foster this kind of meditative and polytextual reading. The examples that I have chosen are perhaps somewhat unusual in the extent and the coherence of their marginalia, but they are by no means anomalous among medieval Books of Hours.

[19] Boncompagno da Signa, *Rhetorica novissima*, ed. A. GAUDENZI (Bologna, 1892; reprint Turin, 1962), p. 284. On Boncompagno's propensity for incorporating Biblical verses into erotic contexts, see J. PURKART, "Rhetoric in Later Latin: Boncompagno of Signa and the Rhetoric of Love", in: *Medieval Eloquence: Studies in the Theory and Practice of Medieval Rhetoric*, ed. J.J. MURPHY (Berkeley, 1978), pp. 319-331.

[20] See, for example, R. MELLENKOFF, "Riding Backwards: Theme of Humiliation and Symbol of Evil", *Viator* 4 (1973), pp. 153-176; L. RANDALL, "Games and the Passion in Pucelle's Hours of Jeanne d'Evreux", *Speculum* 47 (1972), pp. 246-257; L. FREEMAN SANDLER, "A Bawdy Betrothal in the Ormesby Psalter", in: *A Tribute to Lotte Brand Philip, Art Historian and Detective*, ed. W.W. CLARK *et al.* (New York, 1985), pp. 155-159. Mary Carruthers discusses the possible significance, both serious and playful, of decorative marginalia in *The Book of Memory: A Study of Memory in Medieval Culture* (Cambridge, 1990: *Cambridge Studies in Medieval Literature* 10), pp. 242-248, and *The Craft of Thought*, pp. 161-165. As she notes, this "verbal-pictorial play ... is witty fun, it gets attention, it gets one started, perhaps off to heavenly things" (*Craft*, p. 165).

My first example is a book of hours dating from the mid-fifteenth century and known today as the Hours of Isabella Stuart, although it was actually made for the Duchess Yolande of Anjou (Cambridge, Fitzwilliam Museum, MS 62).[21] Books of Hours vary somewhat in their contents, but Duchess Yolande's book follows a very typical format. It begins with a calendar indicating holy days; then follow readings from each of the four Gospels, providing narrative relevant to the four important Feast Days of Christmas, Epiphany, the Annunciation, and Ascension. Next is the Hours of the Virgin, which consist of appropriate prayers, hymns, and Biblical readings for each of the canonical hours of the day, selected so as to pertain to the Virgin Mary, her life, and her role in the Incarnation and the Redemption of humanity. There then follow the seven penitential psalms, the litany, the Hours of the Cross and the Hours of the Holy Spirit, a series of prayers, the Office of the Dead, and more prayers directed to the Virgin, Christ, and a series of saints.

A Book of Hours is a compilation of diverse materials and not a single, integrated text designed for continuous, cover-to-cover reading. The Hours of the Virgin, for example, consist of prayers, psalms, and snippets of Biblical text that have been cut and pasted into a textual pastiche that celebrates the Virgin as Bride of God, Queen of Heaven, Intercessor on behalf of humankind, and so on. As one reads in a Book of Hours, then, one is constantly proceeding through little blocks of text, alternating between verse and prose, and moving through cycles of new and repeated passages. Some degree of continuity is imposed by the miniatures. In the Hours of the Virgin, for example, the section for each new Hour is headed by a full-page miniature, and the series of miniatures takes us through the key events in the Virgin's life. Thus the text fragments this underlying narrative and alludes erratically to diverse moments within it, sometimes explicitly and often much more obliquely, by citing Biblical passages that medieval exegetes understood as pertaining allegorically to some aspect of the Virgin's life or her theological function. The illustrations, on the other hand, present a narrative that moves in an orderly, linear fashion. In this way the book already invites at least two different kinds of reading. The visual reading ignores the divisions into hours and moves through the episodes of the Virgin's life; each miniature in turn offers a visual spectacle that is fuel for meditation, for recalling texts previously read, and so on. The textual reading in effect uses the visual narrative as a springboard for more exploratory movement through a series of texts and passages; the reader must ruminate on each bit in turn, endeavouring to work out its relevance to the life of the Virgin.

[21] See M. MEISS, *French Painting at the Time of Jean de Berry: The Limbourgs and Their Contemporaries* (New York, 1974), pp. 263-266.

Both the visual and the textual reading, in other words, require the active participation of the reader, who needs to bring his or her prior knowledge of the Gospel story to bear on the material offered by the book.

Like so many Books of Hours, however, Yolande's Hours are embellished with additional illustration beyond the main miniatures. In this particular manuscript, the supplementary material takes the form of small rectangular images located in the side margin of every page except those that have full-page miniatures. These rectangular images form several cycles, which are disposed so as to correspond to major divisions of the book. In brief: the opening series of lessons from the Gospels and the prayers attached to these are illustrated with a narrative sequence of the life of Christ; the Hours of the Virgin are illustrated with a sequence representing the Apocalypse; the penitential psalms, litany, and Hours of the Holy Spirit and the Cross are illustrated with a narrative sequence outlining the progress of the human soul as it is assailed by the seven deadly sins and aided by both Reason and Divine Grace; the Office of the Dead is adorned with another narrative series chronicling the journey of the soul after death, as it views the pains of both hell and Purgatory and meets its Judgment; and the other prayers are decorated with images of Christ, the Virgin, or the appropriate saints.

Another detail must be explained if this manuscript is to be understood. The marginal images form four primary narrative cycles: the life of Christ, the Apocalypse, the journey of the soul in life, and the journey of the soul in death. All of these are based on written texts. The Apocalypse is of course Biblical. The others, as is clearly indicated in rubrication, are based directly on a three-part narrative cycle in Old French, composed in the late fourteenth century by a Cistercian monk, Guillaume de Deguilleville, and titled respectively the *Pelerinage Jesus Christ*, the *Pelerinage de la vie humaine*, and the *Pelerinage de l'ame*.[22] The *Pelerinage de la vie humaine*, in particular, was an immensely popular text that circulated widely both in French and in English translation. It offers an allegorical account of life as a struggle against temptation, recounted in the form of a dream-vision, and features bizarre allegorical personifications of numerous virtues and vices, described in great detail with their clothing and other attributes (figs. 3a and 3b). These allegorical figures are always illustrated in equally minute detail in manuscripts of the poem, and must accordingly have acquired a certain currency with late medieval readers. Aside from the title

[22] These images are briefly discussed by S. HAGEN, *Allegorical Remembrance: A Study of the 'Pilgrimage of the Life of Man' as a Medieval Treatise on Seeing and Remembering* (Atlanta, 1990), pp. 126-127 and figs. 60-64. Hagen notes that the use of these images "offers vivid proof of the images' ability to elicit the substance of the written poem" (p. 126).

Fig. 3a The Hours of Isabella Stuart. Cambridge, Fitzwilliam Museum, MS 62, f. 127r: the opening page of the Hours of the Holy Spirit, showing Pentecost in the main miniature; in the margin, a scene from the *Pelerinage de la vie humaine* in which the pilgrim is attacked by Envy. By permission of the Syndics of the Fitzwilliam Museum.

rubrics at the start and finish of each narrative cycle of illustrations, the images appear without any caption or explanation. Clearly the reader was meant to follow the sequence of images and to recognize the striking figures depicted there from a knowledge of the texts in question.

These marginal images thus allow for yet another way of reading the book. In the opening section, the text offers a fragmentary account of Christ's appearance on earth and his return to Heaven, crystallized in a series of just a few key moments; the visual sequence counters with a much more complete representation of his birth, life, death, and resurrection. The Hours of the Virgin offer a visual representation of the key events in the Virgin's life along with a multitude of texts that comment upon or allude to that life and its cosmic significance; the marginal images expand the scope of the text to include the Second Coming of Christ, the end of time and history, the final cataclysmic event that all else leads up to. It was in preparation for this day that Christ came to earth; it is in preparation for this day that each individual must organize his or her life. Even more than the miniatures representing the life of the Virgin, the marginal representation of the Apocalypse imposes a linear progression and narrative unity on the pages of the book, overriding the textual transitions and the subdivisions into the hours of the day. As one reads through the Hours of the Virgin, various different temporal frames are superimposed: the hours of a single day in the life of the individual reader, the succession of events in the entire life of the Virgin, the pivotal historical moment of the Incarnation of God on earth, the unravelling of human temporality itself and its embedding in eternity. The reader can follow these various implied narratives simultaneously, meditating upon the relevance of each for his or her life.

The other two narrative cycles, in turn, more explicitly invite this kind of introspective focus on the self. In the pilgrimage of life and the pilgrimage of the soul, the individual reader can see his or her own moral and spiritual journey mirrored. The striking allegorical images demand deciphering, forcing the reader to recall Deguilleville's text, which is thus, in effect, read in the mind, in tandem with the Book of Hours itself. Faced with the dangers, temptations, and spiritual victories of the 'pilgrimage of life', the reader is invited to examine the 'book' of his or her own conscience, comparing the 'text' inscribed therein with what is depicted in the images and also evaluating it in the light of the sacred texts that fill the pages. At regular intervals, a full-page miniature presents a scene from sacred history or a vision of God in majesty. As it happens, the effect is not unlike the visions described by Marguerite d'Oingt, who read comparatively in the book of her conscience and the book of Christ's life before being rewarded with a full-page image of Heaven.

Fig. 3b The Hours of Isabella Stuart, Cambridge, Fitzwilliam Museum, MS 62, f. 138v: marginal illustration and accompanying *explicit* for the *Pelerinage de la vie humaine*, here called the *Pelerinage du corps*. By permission of the Syndics of the Fitzwilliam Museum.

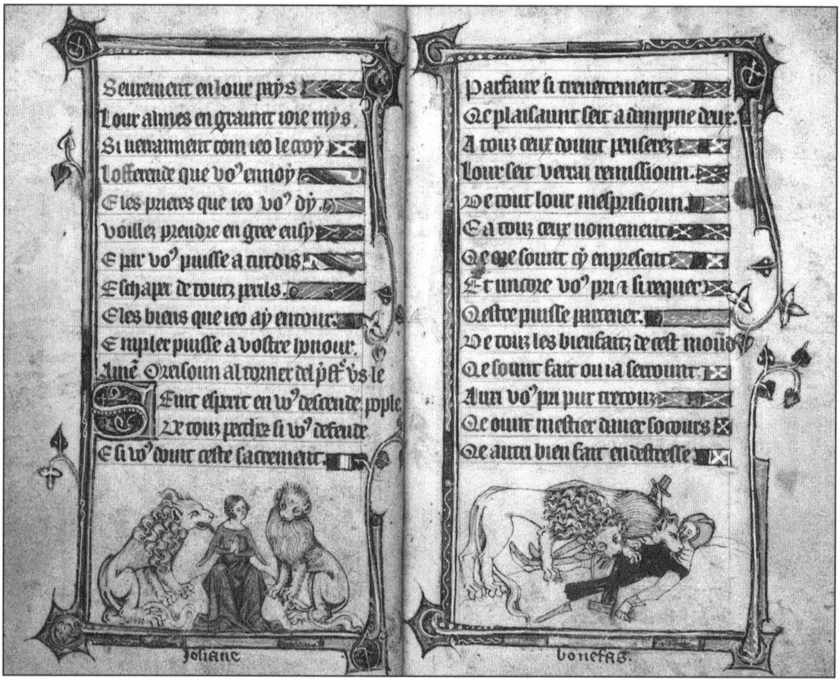

Fig. 4 The Taymouth Hours, with marginal images illustrating scenes from *Beuves de Hantone*. London, British Library, Yates Thompson 13, ff. 8v-9r. By permission of the British Library.

In short, as Duchess Yolande or any subsequent owner paged through this book, she would meet with interlocking textual and visual sequences whose temporal scope varied from a single hour of the day to a human life to all of eternity, and whose focus shifted between the moral life of the individual, the spiritual afterlife, the life of Christ, the expanse of history. Here, truly, is a book that affords a multi-faceted reading in the book of the conscience, the book of Christ, and the book of Holy Wisdom, encompassing a consideration of the moral, allegorical, and anagogical levels of meaning contained within the texts.

My other example is the British Book of Hours known as the Taymouth Hours (BL, Yates Thompson MS 13), which can be dated ca. 1325-35 and which was probably made for the unidentified aristocratic lady whose image appears repeatedly throughout the manuscript. It is decorated with an impressive series of illustrations occupying the lower half of every page, some of which feature hagiographic or Biblical themes while others form narrative sequences completely unrelated to the accompanying texts. One finds here an episode from the epic *Beuves de Hantone*, two episodes from *Gui de Warwick*, the tale of a lady rescued from a wildman by a knight, and a sequence in which noble ladies go hunting in the forest (fig. 4). All of these scenes are identified with captions in Anglo-Norman.[23] In these sections, then, the reader is confronted with two entirely different texts, one verbal and one primarily visual, that pull in different directions. And while some medieval readers might well have been happy to stray from the tedium of repetitive prayer into the glamorous world of epic and romance, it is equally possible that these familiar stories would have been viewed through the lens of prayer. The picture-stories provide an intermittent chronicle of feudal life, the history 'we' are part of, as a continuum with sacred history; and the devotional context invites a moral or allegorical reading of the narratives that are threaded through the prayers.

The most salient motif to emerge from these marginal narratives is that of heroic men who slay wild creatures. In an opening sequence of Biblical images, we have already encountered Samson slaying the lion.[24] A few pages later, Beuves de Hantone kills two lions that are harassing the virgin queen Josiane, whom Beuves has rescued from an unwanted marriage, after having already killed her chamberlain Boneface; Josiane assists by attempting to block the lions from attacking Beuves.[25] In a development familiar from various vernacular texts, Gui of Warwick kills a dragon that was attacking a lion, thereby winning the lion's gratitude and friendship; he then pursues a wild boar that has killed numerous hunting dogs, inadvertently trespassing onto the lands of a nobleman whose young son accosts Gui and is slain in the resulting fracas.[26] Later, following another series of Biblical images, comes the story of a woman saved from a wild man by an elderly knight; she later chooses to go off with a younger knight who appears, thereby proving her ingratitude and ultimately finding herself abandoned in the forest after the older knight has killed his young rival.[27]

[23] For a discussion of the *Beuves* and *Gui* images, including reproductions of the *Beuves* sequence and quotations of the relevant passages from the Middle English *Beves of Hampton*, see L. BROWNRIGG, "The Taymouth Hours and the Romance of *Beves of Hampton*", *English Manuscript Studies 1100-1700* 1 (1989), pp. 222-241.

[24] BL, Yates Thompson MS 13, f. 7v.

[25] BL, Yates Thompson MS 13, ff. 8v-12r.

[26] BL, Yates Thompson MS 13, ff. 12v-17v.

[27] BL, Yates Thompson MS 13, ff. 60v-67r. On the various known versions of this story, see R.S. LOOMIS, "A Phantom Tale of Female Ingratitude", *Modern Philology* 14 (1917), pp. 751-755. Loomis prints the Anglo-Norman captions for the illustrations in the Taymouth Hours (p. 753).

Since the first scene of beast-slaying is Biblical, and a standard allegory for Christ vanquishing the devil, the possibility is raised that the others might be susceptible to similar interpretations. Such associations could be made with the images in the Taymouth Hours. The most famous dragon-slayer, after all, was Saint George, while Christ himself is the amorous Bridegroom whose heroic suffering saved the lady that he loved – the individual human soul or, collectively, Ecclesia – from the persecution of the devil. In the *Beuves* vignette, Josiane's status as royal virgin, which protects her from being harmed by the otherwise vicious lions and enables her to assist in their destruction, is particularly suggestive of possible allegorical readings. The depiction of the Gospel story in allegories of feudal intrigue was certainly not unknown in medieval vernacular literature, appearing, for example, in the tale transmitted variously as *Vertus* or *Le Dit des .IIII. Serurs*.[28] In this little poem, a king is wronged by his seneschal whom he imprisons; but after the intervention of the king's four daughters, Truth, Mercy, Justice, and Peace, the king's son offers himself as hostage for the seneschal, willingly undergoing the punishment that would have been meted out to the latter. The poem includes an explication of the story as an allegory of Christ's Passion. While I do not wish to posit a connection between that poem and the Taymouth Hours, such texts show the limitless possibilities for the allegorization of scenarios drawn from feudal politics and court life.

It is obvious that neither Beuves nor Gui is an allegory of Christ as such. They belong to secular, not sacred, history. But their actions, taken out of the context of their stories and implanted into the Book of Hours, can become emblematic of the larger themes of salvation, struggle, victory, gratitude and love. The picture-story can be read simply as a heroic struggle of good against evil, a moral exemplum of cultural importance, but it can also trigger associations that lead back to the sacred content of the book. The various grateful and ungrateful ladies provide role models, both good and bad, to whom the reader could compare herself. One can easily speculate about other possible lessons that could be drawn from these visual narratives. Gui's altercation with the young nobleman, for example, might illustrate the dangers of anger, the ever-present threat of death, or even the unfortunate consequences of the blood sport of hunting, which was often criticized by the Church. The aristocratic huntresses might be interpreted as seeking the fruits of knowledge or as indulging

[28] Various versions of this text have come down to us. See my "Book Made for a Queen", p. 137; A. LÅNGFORS, "Notice des manuscrits 535 de Metz et 10.047 des nouvelles acquisitions françaises de la Bibliothèque Nationale, suivie de cinq poèmes français sur la parabole des quatre filles de Dieu", *Notices et extraits des manuscrits de la Bibliothèque Nationale et autres bibliothèques* 42 (Paris, 1933), pp. 212-428.

in frivolous pleasures, with appropriate morals to be drawn in either case. The bas-de-page scenes, whether Biblical, hagiographic, or feudal, represent the world of experience, the world in which the reader lives and in which the cycle of temptation, sin, penance, and salvation takes place: in short, the fraught world of human life through which we are guided by the teachings and the prayers that appear on the pages of the book.

These two examples show that the supplementary 'books' coded into the prayer book might be moral or devotional in nature; or they might treat historical, feudal, or fanciful themes. It was not so much the content of the images that mattered, for these were subject to enormous variation. What mattered was creating a visual text that ran alongside the text of the Hours, providing a set of links to virtual books held in the memory. In this way the endless repetition of prayers and readings, the unending cycle of the Hours, need not be tedious at all: each encounter could provide the basis for a new imaginative journey through books, oral tales, or personal memories, all of which were in turn grist for the mill of meditation, interpretation, penitential reflections, and prayer.

In closing, an inevitable question arises: were these images planned with precisely this effect in mind? In most cases, we will probably never know who planned them or just why this was done. But clearly considerable expense and effort went into executing these illustrated prayer books, which must in turn have been valued, and presumably examined with pleasure and curiosity, by their owners. Vernacular poets writing for the aristocracy, such as Baudouin and Jean de Condé or Watriquet de Couvin, delighted in describing images that resemble marginal drolleries and vignettes – hybrid creatures, beasts, insects, household objects – and elaborating their moral or allegorical significance.[29] This does not necessarily mean that the artists who painted these images conceived of them that way. We do not know whether those artists would have been familiar with such poetry, or to what extent they concerned themselves with the textual content of the pages they were decorating; nor do we know how the visual decoration of a manuscript was designed or how much conscious planning went into each book. Most likely the answer is that some books were carefully planned while others were not, and that some artists thought about the relationship of verbal and visual elements while others chose images at random from pattern books or amused themselves by painting whatever came to mind.[30] Clearly, a narrative sequence of images with captions, planned so

[29] For some examples, see my "Book Made for a Queen", p. 137; "Writer's Mirror", pp. 38-43.

[30] For the case against seeing illuminators as interpreters of the texts they illustrated, see R.H. and M.A. ROUSE, *Manuscripts and Their Makers: Commercial Book Producers in*

that each episode would cover exactly one quire and corresponding to subdivisions within the overall book, such as one finds in the Taymouth Hours, would require planning of some kind. But whether these plans included consideration of the visual text as a gloss on the main text – and if so, in what sense – must remain a matter for speculation.

But however the books came into being, they were always susceptible of interpretation by clever readers. One could invoke here the 'Theory of Accidental Meaning in Illumination' offered by Alcuin Blamires and Gail C. Holian in their study of *Roman de la Rose* manuscripts.[31] Noting that artists were unlikely to have had the luxury of researching their illustrative programmes but that these illustrations could certainly have been scrutinized by readers, Blamires and Holian suggest ways that a detail of illumination "accidentally galvanizes the viewer into quite fresh speculation about, say, large gender issues in the narrative" and argue that the illustrations should be seen as "a series of pleasurable *ad hoc* visual stimuli whose generation of interpretative questions was substantially a matter of choice".[32] The same argument can be made regarding Books of Hours. Whatever the intentions of the scribe, artist, or planner may or may not have been, a lavishly illustrated manuscript would have had a powerful impact on a sensitive and attentive reader. The training that came with even a basic aristocratic education would have encouraged active and inventive readings of these pages – some perhaps even more adventuresome than anything we can imagine today.

Medieval Paris 1200-1500, 2 vols. (Turnhout, 2000), I, pp. 252-260. The Rouses' study is a comprehensive survey of Parisian book production that provides a wealth of information about the artisans themselves and the conditions of their work; as they note, pressures of time and the sharing of work would commonly have worked against any possibility for the careful and systematic planning even of miniatures, much less marginalia. The Rouses do acknowledge, however, that there is a distinction between creation and reception, and that the presence of illustrations or marginalia, even if they resulted from an artist's misinterpretation of the text, would surely have affected the reader's experience of the text.

[31] A. BLAMIRES and G.C. HOLIAN, *The Romance of the Rose Illuminated: Manuscripts at the National Library of Wales, Aberystwyth* (Tempe, AZ, 2002), pp. XXXVI-XXXVIII.

[32] *The Romance of the Rose Illuminated*, p. XXXVII.

Aural Illumination: Books and Aurality in the Frontispieces to Bishop Chevrot's *Cité de Dieu*

JOYCE COLEMAN

Pictures in books are meant to be looked at.[1] Even if the text refers to an audience of hearers, such references are likely to be dismissed as conventional or archaic, since only by holding the book oneself could one really see and appreciate the illustrations. Thus, a century or so of medieval scholarship has operated happily with the unspoken assumption that illuminated manuscripts were meant, chiefly or even solely, for private reading and viewing. The more recent scholarly interest in medieval orality, aurality, and literacy has done little to challenge this assumption.[2] Once a text is written down, it has begun moving into a literate environment. By the time we are dealing with, say, patristic texts translated into the vernacular by royal commission and handsomely presented in a series of elaborately illustrated exemplars – then, surely, we are well past any serious engagement with orality in any form.

[1] The research for and writing of this article began with the help of an American Philosophical Society summer grant in 1994, and was continued under the auspices of a National Endowment for the Humanities Summer Seminar in July-August 2000. I am very grateful to Claire R. Sherman for her comments on a previous draft, and to the librarians of the Bibliothèque Royale Albert Ier for permission to view MSS. 9005-6 and 9015-16.

[2] 'Aurality' and 'aural' refer to the public reading of written texts. Aurality combines aspects of 'orality' (when defined as 'the hearing of texts') and of 'literacy' (when defined as 'the reading of written texts'). For further discussion of this terminology, and of the many ambiguities inherent in the current vocabulary of orality and literacy, see J. COLEMAN, *Public Reading and the Reading Public in Late Medieval England and France* (Cambridge, 1996: *Cambridge Studies in Medieval Literature* 26), pp. 34-51.

Only very recently, beginning with the pioneering research of D.H. Green, have some scholars begun to consider the intersections of public reading with written texts. Green's and my own work have found considerable evidence that elite medieval audiences often preferred to have their books – even their beautifully illuminated copies of prestigious works – read aloud to them.[3] One source of support for this contention is the manuscript illuminations themselves. Derek Pearsall and Elizabeth Salter have noted that some later medieval literary texts begin with an illumination that shows the author reading his or her book to an audience[4] (what I will call a 'prelection picture'[5]). Pearsall and Salter's main interest, however, was in analysing these images in relation to the famous *Troilus and Criseyde* frontispiece that shows Chaucer standing in a pulpit before a courtly group.[6] They do not discuss the pictures as evidence for modes of reading, or examine the contradictions they seem to pose. My own research has turned up similar scenes functioning as frontispieces or internal illustrations for numerous other literary, and non-literary, texts. I have reproduced a few of these in an earlier work,[7] but did not have space to discuss them at any length.

Typically, prelection pictures show the author at a lectern that holds an open book; the left hand may lie on the book while the right hand is often ex-

[3] D.H. GREEN, "On the Primary Reception of Narrative Literature in Medieval Germany", *Forum for Modern Language Studies* 20 (1984), pp. 289-308; ID., "Orality and Reading: The State of Research in Medieval Studies", *Speculum* 65 (1990), pp. 267-280; ID., *Medieval Listening and Reading: The Primary Reception of German Literature 800-1300* (Cambridge, 1994); COLEMAN, *Public Reading*; EAD., "The Text Recontextualized in Performance: Deschamps' Prelection of Machaut's *Voir Dit* to the Count of Flanders", *Viator* 31 (2000), pp. 233-248; EAD., "Lay Readers and Hard Latin: How Gower May Have Intended the *Confessio Amantis* to Be Read", *Studies in the Age of Chaucer* 24 (2002), pp. 209-235.

[4] D. PEARSALL, "The *Troilus* Frontispiece and Chaucer's Audience", *Yearbook of English Studies* 7 (1977), pp. 68-74; E. SALTER, "The 'Troilus Frontispiece'", in: *Troilus and Criseyde: A Facsimile of Corpus Christi College Cambridge MS 61* (Cambridge, 1978), pp. 15-23; E. SALTER and D. PEARSALL, "Pictorial Illustration of Late Medieval Poetic Texts: The Role of the Frontispiece or Prefatory Picture", in: *Medieval Iconography and Narrative*, ed. F.G. ANDERSEN *et al.* (Odense, 1980), pp. 100-123. Salter prints a miniature of Guillaume de Machaut reading his work aloud (Pl. 11); the same prelection picture reappears in the Salter and Pearsall article, joined by one of Jean Froissart (pp. 122, 112).

[5] I use the word 'prelection' to mean 'reading aloud to one or more listeners', and 'prelector' to mean the person doing that reading. These terms help distinguish public reading, as a social event, from private, individual reading – whether the private reader is reading aloud or silently. See COLEMAN, *Public Reading*, pp. 35-37.

[6] Corpus Christi Cambridge MS 61, f. 1.

[7] The frontispiece and plates 1, 3, 5-6, and 8-9 to COLEMAN, *Public Reading*, depict prelections by, respectively, a servitor to Philip the Good and court, Vitruvius to masons, a monk in a refectory, a woman to Mary, Avicenna to medical students, Sappho to three men, and Flavius Vegetius to an emperor and knights.

tended, sometimes pointed, towards one or more clusters of people placed directly in front and, perhaps, also to one side. Often the iconography of prelection evokes or elides with that of academic lecturing; ancient authors like Cicero may be posthumously appointed to a Sorbonne chair, while even love-poets like Froissart sport academic robes. The audience may be shown sitting on benches, like students in teaching pictures, perhaps holding books themselves; or they may stand or sit more freely – though usually in clusters that reflect, I think, the bonding achieved in group listening.[8] The number of late medieval frontispieces showing the recipient of the book reading it privately are comparatively very few.

How are we to understand the self-contradictory yet widespread iconography of aurality? Prelection pictures certainly should not be interpreted simplistically, as portrayals of actual reading events; too many of them incorporate improbable or impossible elements, such as a massive chair deposited in a garden, or Avicenna lecturing in a fifteenth-century classroom. Rather than reflecting modern ideas of verisimilitude, these illuminations must be read as richly symbolic statements about the relationships among text, author, translator (if any), and audiences past and present, real and ideal. The first and most striking feature of this iconography is that it presents public reading as the ground for all other literary relationships. For this reason, prelection pictures occur particularly as frontispieces, offering a précis of the text's origins, interest, and target audience.

But if the book was to be read aloud, who was going to see the prelection picture, or any other illumination? The present article offers a first foray into the complex question of the meaning and function of prelection pictures, through a study of another well-known frontispiece: the picture of St. Augustine and Clovis in Brussels, Bibl. Royale Albert I[er] 9015, a dual-language version of Augustine's *Civitas Dei* (see fig. 1).

In this unique variation on a somewhat standardized iconography, Augustine sits high in his bishop's chair, reading aloud, from a book on a lectern, to two rows of men who sit perpendicular to him. Some of this group hold their own books. Meanwhile, in front of and below Augustine, a Benedictine monk sits on a low seat, reading to two men. All of this takes place on a tiled floor that sits unexpectedly on an expanse of green grass. In the background is a

[8] See COLEMAN, *Public Reading*, pp. 91, 119-120.

Fig. 1: The opening page of Bishop Jean Chevrot's *Cité de Dieu*. Brussels, Bibliothèque Royale Albert Ier 9015, f. 1; ca. 1445. Copyright Bibliothèque Royale de Belgique.

walled city with a large cathedral, while to the right Clovis, the first king of the Franks, stands amidst various symbolic paraphernalia.

In themselves, the text and the manuscript bespeak a highly literate and textual culture. Everyone associated with it was of high status. The *City of God*, one of the paradigmatic texts of medieval Christianity, is presented in its Latin original, along with the annotated French translation prepared in 1375, at the command of King Charles V, by Raoul de Presles, a layman who served as *avocat du roi*. BR 9015 itself was created around 1445 for Jean Chevrot (ca. 1380-1460),[9] bishop of Tournai and a close advisor of Philip the Good, Duke of Burgundy. None of these men could possibly have needed the work read aloud, in the sense that they were illiterate or even non-latinate. And the two-volume, bilingual text, with its 21 other illustrations, clearly invited close visual inspection.

Yet Bishop Chevrot chose to launch potential readers or hearers into this canonical work not with a presentation picture, or a picture of the author writing, but with a scene of concatenated public readings and disputations. We have noted above that prelection pictures establish public reading as the means or metaphor around which other literary relations are configured. As the complicated story within and behind the Chevrot frontispiece unfolds, we will discover how prelection of a key theological text becomes a metaphor for Chevrot's own pointed statements about the relative powers of church and state. Explication of this one complex example will help give us insight into the nature and status of 'aural illumination' in the late Middle Ages.

Such an investigation will take us into a deep intersection of codicology, art, history, and politics. Scholars in each discipline have mentioned Chevrot or his *City of God*, but none has reached across disciplinary boundaries to assemble the complete story of the commission and the illustration programme of BR 9015.

Raoul de Presles' Translation of the Civitas Dei

The story begins with Charles V's original commission to Raoul de Presles. As fig. 2 shows, the kingship of France had reverted to the Valois line in

[9] J. BARTIER, *Légistes et gens de finances au XVe siècle: Les Conseillers des ducs de Bourgogne Philippe le Bon et Charles le Téméraire* (Brussels, 1955: *Mémoires de l'Académie Royale de Belgique* 50, fasc. 2), pp. 310 n. 1, 321.

Charles, count of Valois and Anjou, d. 1325

7 PHILIP VI, r. 1328-50

8 JOHN II, r. 1350-54

Philip the Bold
duke of Burgundy
r. 1363-1404

John the Fearless
duke of Burgundy
r. 1404-19

Philip the Good
duke of Burgundy
r. 1419-67

Charles the Bold
duke of Burgundy
r. 1467-77

9 CHARLES V
r. 1364-80

CHARLES VI
r. 1380-1422

CHARLES VII
r. 1422-61

LOUIS XI
r. 1461-83

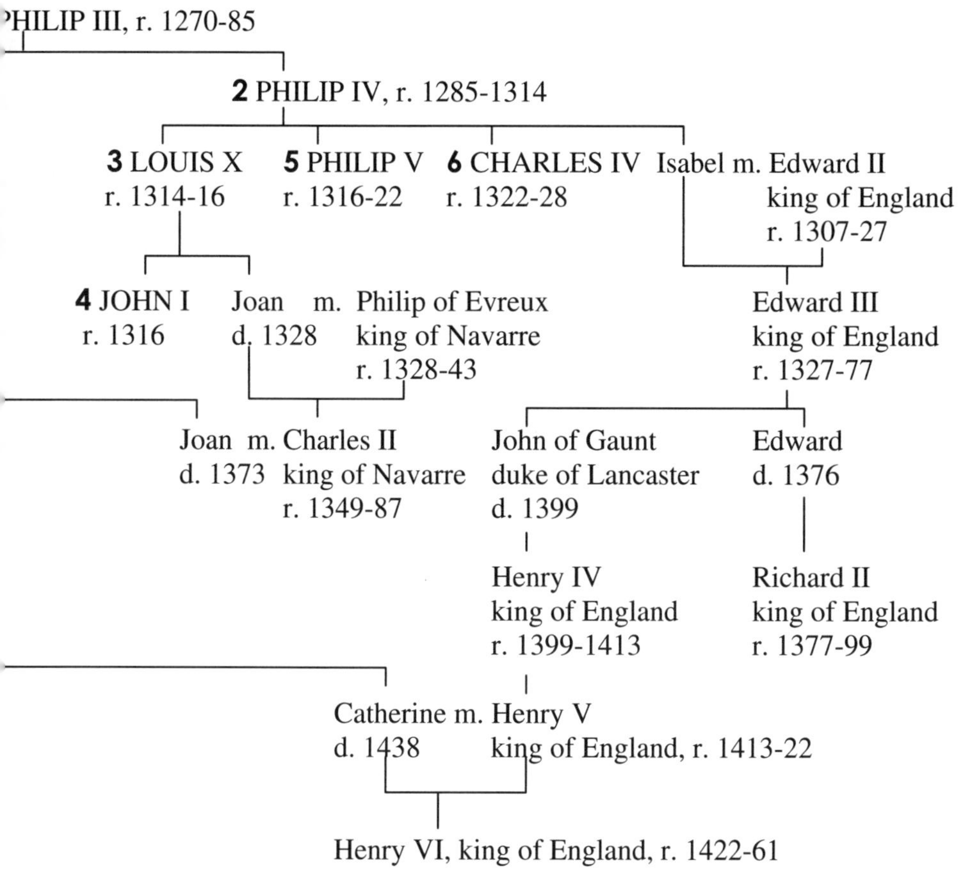

Fig. 2: Genealogy of French and English kings and nobles. Kings of France are in capital letters; the order of the French succession from Philip III through Charles V is indicated with boldface numbers. The chart is based on W.M. HINKLE, *The Fleurs de Lis of the Kings of France, 1285-1488* (Carbondale, 1991), fig. 2, and B. TOMPSETT, "Directory of Royal Genealogical Data", www.dcs.hull.ac.uk/public/genealogy/royal.

1328, after the failure of male heirs in Philip IV's line. The Hundred Years' War commenced soon after, based upon Edward III of England's claim to France through his mother, who was Philip's daughter. The reign of Charles V (r. 1364-80) was haunted by the constant pressure of English ambition, as well as by the pretensions of Charles II of Navarre, son of Louis X of France's daughter (see fig. 2). To bolster his line's claim to France's shaky throne, Charles V established what has been called "a kind of propaganda bureau",[10] a collection of on-staff intellectuals whom he commissioned either to create or to translate a series of works on government, history, and religion. The serious content and the prestige of these texts gave stature to his kingship, and their vernacularity promoted a sense of national identity. Most importantly for our purposes, these authoritative texts often featured prologues full of praise for Charles, his dynasty, and the concept of French monarchy.

One of the most significant of these propagandistic prologues was that provided by Raoul de Presles for his translation of the *City of God*.[11] Raoul relates three miracle stories. As St. Rémi was baptizing Clovis (r. 481-511) in Reims Cathedral, Raoul begins, the Holy Spirit flew down from heaven in the form of a dove, bearing the chrism in a vial, and placed it in the saint's hand. Next, Raoul recounts the story of Clovis' conversion. Eager to convert Clovis, and with him the Franks, God sent a device of three fleurs-de-lys to a venerable hermit to whom Clovis' Christian wife regularly brought food. The hermit gave her the device, explaining it would bring Clovis victory in his forthcoming battle, and she accordingly replaced the crescents on her husband's shield with the lilies. Victory duly followed, as Clovis fought upwards from a valley to the hill of Montjoie. In honour of the great day, the king founded the abbey of Joyenval. The final legend concerns the royal banner known as the *oriflamme*. According to the tale, the Emperor Constantine, beleaguered by Saracens, dreamed he saw an armed and mounted knight by his bed, holding a shining lance with a banner of flame. Who else could this great warrior be but Charle-

[10] C.R. SHERMAN, "Representations of Charles V of France (1338-1380) as a Wise Ruler", *Medievalia et Humanistica* n.s., 2 (1971), pp. 83-96.

[11] S. LUSIGNAN, *Parler vulgairement: Les Intellectuels et la langue française aux XIIIe et XIVe siècles* (Montreal, 1986), pp. 129-137; C.R. SHERMAN, *Imaging Aristotle: Verbal and Visual Representation in Fourteenth-Century France* (Berkeley, 1995), pp. 6-12. Raoul's prologue is given in full (from BNF fr. 170) in A. DE LABORDE, *Les Manuscrits à peintures de la 'Cité de Dieu' de Saint Augustin*, 3 vols. (Paris, 1909: *Société des Bibliophiles François*), I, pp. 63-67; and (from BNF fr. 22912, with an English translation) in J. BEER, "Patronage and the Translator: Raoul de Presles's *La Cité de Dieu* and Calvin's *Institution de la religion Chrestienne* and *Institutio religionis Christianae*", in: *Translation and the Transmission of Culture Between 1300 and 1600*, ed. J. BEER and K. LLOYD-JONES (Kalamazoo, 1995), pp. 121-131.

magne? Summoned by the emperor, Charlemagne collected the *oriflamme* from St. Denis and set off to liberate both Constantinople and Jerusalem.[12]

As scholars have shown, this body of legend had been evolving since the late thirteenth century, with the patronage of various kings and of the religious establishments involved.[13] Under Charles V's aegis, however, Raoul de Presles adapted and embellished the stories into a coherent body of propaganda clearly designed to demonstrate God's personal endorsement of the French monarchy.[14] Raoul's tales took root quickly, reappearing in many other forms and even generating debate in another treatise before he had finished the translation.[15]

The cooptation of divine sanction as support for Charles' monarchy appears quite clearly in the frontispiece of the presentation manuscript, Paris, Bibl. Nat. de France fr. 22912-13, dated to 1375 (see fig. 3). Although the figures, in the *retardataire* style of the painting, seem charmingly naive, the syncretized iconography is stunningly bold. As in conventional scenes of book-presentation, Raoul kneels to offer his completed work to the king, who sits on a faldstool before a cloth of honour. The presence of Augustine supporting Raoul, however, recalls the iconography of religious patronage, in which a patron saint would be shown introducing a kneeling supplicant to Mary or God. Here, Charles V takes the place of divinity, a semiotic enhanced by the angels who hold up the cloth of honour behind him.[16]

Charles' choice of a lay translator indicates that he was aiming at a general audience. Raoul calls attention to the fact himself, as Jeanette Beer has astutely remarked, by marvelling, with a "somewhat ostentatious humility", that with so many "*souverains clers*" ("sovereign clerks") available, the king selected him

[12] Quoted in DE LABORDE, *Manuscrits*, I, pp. 64-65.

[13] R. BOSSUAT, "Poème latin sur l'origine des fleurs de lis", *Bibliothèque de l'Ecole des Chartes* 101 (1940), pp. 80-101; W.M. HINKLE, *The Fleurs de Lis of the Kings of France, 1285-1488* (Carbondale, 1991), pp. 1-31.

[14] See J. KRYNEN, *Idéal du prince et pouvoir royal en France à la fin du Moyen Age (1380-1440): Etude de la littérature politique du temps* (Paris: 1981), pp. 220-228; HINKLE, *Fleurs de Lis*, pp. 32-46. Hinkle points out that Raoul also seeded his commentary on Augustine with pro-Valois propaganda; e.g. a defence of the Salic law that forbade inheritance of the throne by descendants through the female line, such as Edward III (p. 34); see also S.O. DUNLAP SMITH, "Illustrations of Raoul de Praelles' Translation of St. Augustine's *City of God* between 1375 and 1420" (Ph.D. dissertation, New York University, 1974), pp. 38-39; BEER, "Patronage", pp. 105-109.

[15] HINKLE, *Fleurs de Lis*, p. 37.

[16] See C.R. SHERMAN, *The Portraits of Charles V of France (1338-1380)* (New York, 1969), pp. 22-24; for other examples of Charles' willingness to hybridize iconographies, see SHERMAN, "Representations", p. 89.

Fig. 3 Raoul de Presles presenting his *Cité de Dieu* to King Charles V. Paris, Bibliothèque Nationale, fr. 22912 (presentation copy), f. 3r; 1375. Photo: Bibliothèque Nationale de France.

to translate the great doctor.[17] Charles must have feared that a clerical translator taking on St. Augustine would produce a long-winded, pedantically annotated work, instead of the clearly written, well-commentated version that could serve "the King and his nobility as an encyclopedia on Rome and her culture".[18]

Burgundian Copies of Raoul's Cité*: 'Family 4'*

Throughout the vicissitudes that affected Charles V's heirs, copies continued to be made of Raoul's *Cité de Dieu*: over five hundred, by Alexandre de Laborde's count.[19] Bishop Chevrot's copy, however, with its striking frontispiece, is related to a particular cluster of *Cité* manuscripts that emerged in the second quarter of the fifteenth century. Dubbed 'Family 4' by de Laborde,[20] this series of exemplars begins with a copy (Brussels, Bibl. Royale Albert Ier 9005-6) commissioned by Gui Guilbaut between 1420 and 1440.[21] Chevrot's exemplar (Brussels, Bibl. Royale Albert Ier 9015-16), although its French half was copied directly from Guilbaut's around 1445, is a variant member of the family. The next full-fledged member is Turin, Bibl. Naz. L.I.6, created in 1466, and after it London, Brit. Lib. Royal 14.D.i, dated to between 1470 and 1480.[22]

[17] BEER, "Patronage", p. 97.

[18] DUNLAP SMITH, "Illustrations", pp. 9-28 (quote from p. 37); see also C.C. WILLARD, "Raoul de Presles's Translation of Saint Augustine's *De civitate dei*", in: *Medieval Translators and Their Craft*, ed. J. BEER (Kalamazoo, 1989), pp. 329-346; BEER, "Patronage", pp. 101-109.

[19] DE LABORDE, *Manuscrits*, I, p. 73; see also DUNLAP SMITH, "Illustrations".

[20] DE LABORDE, *Manuscrits*, I, pp. 198-199.

[21] Gaspar and Lyna date the manuscript to between 1420 and 1435, basing the *terminus ab quo* on the acanthus-leaf decoration in the border. They refer to unspecified details of clothing and coiffure as confirming their dating, but it's not clear if the date being confirmed is the earlier or the later one. No other evidence is offered for the 1435 *terminus ad quem*: C. GASPAR and F. LYNA, *Les Principaux Manuscrits à peintures de la Bibliothèque Royale de Belgique*, vol. 2 (Brussels, 1945; rpt. 1987), p. 43. HINKLE, *Fleurs de Lis*, p. 79, offers the date "sometime in the 1430s". The recent Bousmanne-van Hoorebeeck catalogue simply repeats Gaspar and Lyna's date-range, without comment: *La Librairie des ducs de Bourgogne: Manuscrits conservés à la Bibliothèque royale de Belgique*, ed. B. BOUSMANNE and C. VAN HOOREBEECK, vol. 1: *Textes liturgiques, ascétiques, théologiques, philosophiques, et moraux* (Turnhout, 2000), p. 58. De Laborde's date of ca. 1410 (*Manuscrits*, II, pp. 319-320) is based on now-superseded information.

[22] **BR 9005-6**: de Laborde's exemplar No. 30 (*Manuscrits*, II, pp. 318-323); see also J. VAN DEN GHEYN, *Catalogue des manuscrits de la Bibliothèque Royale de Belgique*, vol. 2: *Patrologie* (Brussels, 1902), p. 179; GASPAR and LYNA, *Les Principaux Manuscrits*, pp. 40-45; DUNLAP SMITH, "Illustrations", pp. 170-172; HINKLE, *Fleurs de Lis*, pp. 79-80; BOUSMANNE and VAN HOOREBEECK, *La Librairie des ducs de Bourgogne*, pp. 56-73 (catalogue description written by

Both the Turin and Royal manuscripts follow Guilbaut's copy in featuring a frontispiece that precisely illustrates the content of Raoul's prologue (see figs. 4-6). Attributed to the Master of Guillebert de Mets or an associate,[23] the Guilbaut frontispiece shows the eagle that, like Augustine and Charles, soars above all, able to contemplate the sun (that is, God) directly. On the right, Clovis appears with his hill, his valley, an angel bearing the fleurs-de-lys shield, and a dove carrying the vial of holy oil. Charlemagne's *oriflamme* stands to Clovis' right, and in the background is a religious structure – probably either Joyenval or St.-Denis.[24] On the left, St. Augustine is presented in a conventional writing scene, at his desk scribing earnestly away as an angel hovers overhead, raining inspiration. As figures 5 and 6 show, the Turin and the British Library copies follow this schema closely, albeit in different artistic styles.

Sophie Somers). **BR 9015-16**: exemplar No. 38 (DE LABORDE, *Manuscrits*, II, pp. 341-345); see also VAN DEN GHEYN, *Catalogue*, p. 180; F. LYNA, *Les Principaux Manuscrits à peintures de la Bibliothèque Royale de Belgique*, vol. 3, pt. 1 (Brussels, 1989), pp. 25-31; HINKLE, *Fleurs de Lis*, pp. 80-81; BOUSMANNE and VAN HOOREBEECK, *La Librairie des ducs de Bourgogne*, pp. 74-86 (catalogue description written by Dominique Vanwijnsberghe); D. VANWIJNSBERGHE, *'De fin or et d'azur': Les Commanditaires de livres et le métier de l'enluminure à Tournai à la fin du Moyen Age (XIVe-XVe siècles)* (Leuven, 2001), pp. 40-44. **Turin, Bibl. Naz. L.I.6**: exemplar No. 49 (DE LABORDE, *Manuscrits*, II, pp. 371-387); see also HINKLE, *Fleurs de Lis*, pp. 82-83. **BL Royal 14.D.i**: exemplar No. 47 (DE LABORDE, *Manuscrits*, II, pp. 365-368); see also G.F. WARNER and J.P. GILSON, *Catalogue of Western Manuscripts in the Old Royal and King's Collections* 2 (London, 1921), p. 138; HINKLE, *Fleurs de Lis*, pp. 82-83. (I omit mention of two Family 4 manuscripts that do not include the Augustine-Clovis frontispiece; see DE LABORDE, *Manuscrits*, I, pp. 198-199.) There was also an early print, issued by Pierre Gérard and Jehan du Pré, 2 vols. (Abbeville, 1486-87), which was based on the Turin manuscript (DE LABORDE, *Manuscrits*, I, p. 199; II, pp. 481-490; WILLARD, "Raoul de Presles's Translation", p. 346). In her dissertation, written under the direction of Millard Meiss, Sharon Off Dunlap Smith somewhat revises de Laborde's datings and categorization. Since she ends her survey of *Cité de Dieu* manuscripts in 1420, however, her comments do not cover the later Burgundian copies.

[23] GASPAR and LYNA, *Les Principaux Manuscrits*, p. 44; BOUSMANNE and VAN HOOREBEECK, *La Librairie des ducs de Bourgogne*, pp. 69-72.

[24] Art historians differ on their identification of this structure; cf., e.g. HINKLE, *Fleurs de Lis*, p. 80 (Joyenval) and BOUSMANNE and VAN HOOREBEECK, *La Librairie des ducs de Bourgogne*, p. 59 (St.-Denis). Although the hill to Clovis' left is labelled "*monioye s^o denys*" in the Guilbaut frontispiece, the building itself is not labelled. The prologue mentions the foundation of Joyenval as one of the results of Clovis' victory, and then gives a detailed description of the ceremony at St.-Denis by which the oriflamme is claimed for use in battle (ff. 3v-4 in Guilbaut's copy). Perhaps one could say that the building in the frontispiece represents either or both royal abbeys, or, generally, the idea of a royal abbey sustained by dynastic miracles.

Fig. 4 Augustine and Clovis: the Guilbaut *Cité*. Brussels, Bibliothèque Royale Albert Ier 9005, f. 3r; 1435-40? Copyright Bibliothèque Royale de Belgique.

Fig. 5 Augustine and Clovis: the Turin *Cité*. Turin, Biblioteca Nazionale, MS L.I.6, f. 1r; 1466. By permission of the Biblioteca Nazionale Universitaria di Torino.

Fig. 6 Augustine and Clovis: the British Library *Cité*. London, British Library, Royal 14.D.i, f. 1r; 1470-80. By permission of the British Library.

If what unites these manuscripts artistically is their employment of the Augustine-Clovis iconography, what unites them politically is that each one was commissioned by a person close to the enormously powerful duke of Burgundy, Philip the Good. Guilbaut was Philip's treasurer; the Turin copy was owned by Philip's natural son, Antoine le Bâtard; and the British Library exemplar bears the arms of an important Burgundian family, Saulx de Tavannes.[25] Chevrot, commissioner of the variant Family 4 manuscript, was the head of Philip's council. Why would the satellites of Philip the Good – whose alliance with the English was only the most noticeable of his constant struggles with the kings of France – embrace a text whose prologue had become the *locus classicus* underwriting the legitimacy of France's kings? Not only that – why would they want a frontispiece that spelled out, in painstaking detail, every miracle arranged by God to authorize the kings upon whose power Philip was constantly encroaching? And, finally and most relevantly for us, why is the frontispiece in Chevrot's copy the only one that shows Augustine not writing, but presiding over an extended sequence of public readings and disputations?

The gestation of Family 4 may be traceable to historic events. After his father's assassination in 1419, Philip had allied himself with the English pretenders to the French throne. In 1435, however, Philip signed the Treaty of Arras with Charles VII, thus deserting the English to re-ally with his Valois kindred.[26] Is it too far-fetched to relate Guilbaut's commission directly to this event? In fact, Gui Guilbaut was one of the men delegated by Philip to negotiate the terms of the treaty, and shared with the group a substantial reward (or bribe) from the king.[27] Philip's historian Georges Chastellain presumably spoke for most of his peers in claiming that the house of France was the "*mère maison*" ("mother-house") of the Burgundians.[28] Happy to be back on the 'right' side, one can imagine, Philip's treasurer may not only have wanted a copy of the book whose prologue epitomized Valois self-promotion, but may also have conceived of a frontispiece that spelled out each monarchical miracle in detail – especially after the grateful Charles VII ennobled him, in November 1436.[29]

[25] WARNER and GILSON, *Catalogue of Western Manuscripts*, p. 138.

[26] L. FOUREZ, "L'Evêque Chevrot de Tournai et sa *Cité de Dieu*", *Revue belge d'archéologie et d'histoire de l'art* 23 (1954), pp. 73-110, at p. 87.

[27] M.-R. THIELEMANS, *Bourgogne et Angleterre: Relations politiques et économiques entre les Pays-Bas bourguignons et l'Angleterre, 1435-1467* (Brussels, 1966), pp. 54-55, 79 n. 79; M.T. CARON, *La Noblesse dans le duché de Bourgogne, 1315-1477* (Lille, 1987), p. 317.

[28] Cited in J.-C. DELCLOS, *Le Témoignage de Georges Chastellain, historiographe de Philippe le Bon et de Charles le Téméraire* (Geneva, 1980), p. 205.

[29] H. FREMAUX, "Anoblissements et légitimations donnés par les rois de France, en vertu de leurs droits de suzeraineté royale, en Flandre, Artois, et Tournaisis depuis 1315 jusqu'en

The speed with which Family 4 commissions succeeded each other within Philip's circle may suggest a similar eagerness to re-assert French identity and loyalty.

Bishop Chevrot Commissions his Cité de Dieu

Bishop Chevrot, however, had a more complicated eagerness. There is no doubt that the French text of Chevrot's manuscript, and its first frontispiece, was based on Guilbaut's. He had access to it both through Guilbaut himself, Chevrot's colleague in Philip's inner circle, and through Guilbaut's son-in-law, Baudouin d'Ongnies, a "*bon ami*" of Chevrot's who inherited the manuscript upon Guilbaut's death in 1447.[30] Not only did Chevrot add the original Latin text to Raoul's French, however; he retained only about a third of Guilbaut's chapter-frontispieces, most of these in volume 2. For volume 1 (books 1-10), he replaced Guilbaut's historical and mythological illustrations with pictures devoted to abstractions, such as Justice, and disputations. In volume 2 (books 11-22), he prefaced Raoul's second prologue with a presentation scene, rather than 'Nembroth talking to the descendants of Cain', and, eliminating more Guilbaut 'story pictures', created instead a series of typological scenes illustrating the course of sacred history.[31] Even when he retained a subject, such as Cain and Abel (9006, f. 70; 9016, f. 116v), he slanted the iconography towards his sacerdotal concerns: in this case, featuring the brothers' respective sacrifices, an element ignored in the Guilbaut picture.

Chevrot's taste for Latin, abstractions, and disputations seems appropriate in an ecclesiast. But then, why did he depart from Guilbaut's arduously writing Augustine to design a miniature brimming with aurality? In Chevrot's volume 1 frontispiece (see fig. 7), Clovis still has angel and shield, dove and vial, valley and hill; and the *oriflamme* stands noticeably to his right. The eagle duly

1525", *Bulletin de la Commission Historique du Département du Nord* 28 (1911), pp. 117-154, at p. 139.

[30] G.H. DE LOO, "Gui Guilbaut", *Bulletin de la Société d'Histoire de d'Archéologie de Gand* 19 (1911), pp. 329-341, at p. 337; FOUREZ, "L'Evêque Chevrot", pp. 79, 83, quote from Chevrot's will, p. 109; H.T. DE MOREMBERT, "Jean Chevrot, évêque de Tournay et de Toul vers 1395-1460", *Mémoires de l'Académie nationale de Metz* 145th year, 5th ser. (1963-64), pp. 171-220, at p. 184.

[31] GASPAR and LYNA, *Les Principaux Manuscrits*, pp. 41-43; DE LABORDE, *Manuscrits*, II, pp. 341, 344-345.

Fig. 7 Augustine and Clovis: the Chevrot *Cité*. Brussels, Bibliothèque Royale Albert Ier 9015, f. 1r; c. 1445. Copyright Bibliothèque Royale de Belgique.

soars above. However, along with his regulation angel, Augustine now sits in cathedra, with a lectern, the two rows of men perpendicular to him, and the little reader before him with his own small auditory. The men on the benches, who seem to be either listening to Augustine or engaging in their own lively discussions, presumably represent later scholars, who have read (or, literally, heard)[32] Augustine's classic work and have derived from it their own argu-

[32] According to the statutes of the University of Paris, a theology student had to 'hear' (*audire*) texts (i.e. hear them read aloud in lectures) for a set number of years before he himself could 'read' (*legere*) them (i.e. become the master prelecting them in class): H. RASHDALL, *The*

ments. The man who sits at the bishop's feet would be the lay translator, Raoul – here depicted, inaccurately, as a monk. This misidentification, regarded by Delaissé as an error,[33] has the no doubt deliberate effect of purging the *Cité*, and its contemporary transmission, of lay connections. The monastery, associated with Clovis in the other pictures, has now become the City of God – a walled city dominated by a cathedral.

Where Guilbaut and later followers were content to locate, and limit, Augustine's authority in his act of writing alone, Chevrot here gives us an extended exposition of authority and its transmission. From the fifth century, Augustine's aural publication of his *Civitas* echoes down the ages in the work – read aloud and disputed in turn – of scholarly commentators and thinkers. Vernacularity picks up the chain in a scaled-down but still legitimate and legitimizing format that carries Augustine's voice forward into the present day, in the person of the two men listening to 'Raoul' read his *Cité*. Compared to this ever-widening ripple of sound and influence, Clovis' sceptre, angel, and shield seem like consolation prizes. Moreover, unlike his counterparts in other manuscripts, Chevrot's Clovis has only a corner of hill; even the *oriflamme* and the dove are, respectively, blowing and flying away from him, towards Augustine. The composition is balanced by the weight of the city behind the king, but it's no longer 'his' – not an abbey he founded or patronized, but the City of God itself. Clovis seems isolated in time and place, a static, off-centre centre. Meanwhile, Augustine sits higher than Clovis, and has an indefinitely extending influence, in time and in the picture space.[34]

What motivated this assertive reconfiguration? Given that Chevrot was a bishop, a natural first assumption is that he augmented Augustine's role in the frontispiece out of piety, bolstered perhaps by episcopal solidarity. But Chevrot was not particularly known for piety; his true career was as one of Philip the Good's closest advisors and president of his council. Philip rewarded Chevrot

Universities of Europe in the Middle Ages, revised edition by F.M. POWICKE and A.B. EMDEN, vol. 1: *Salerno, Bologna, Paris* (London, 1936), pp. 472 and 472 n. 1.

[33] L.M.J. DELAISSÉ, *Miniatures médiévales de la librairie de Bourgogne au Cabinet des Manuscrits de la Bibliothèque Royale de Belgique* (Geneva, 1959), p. 118.

[34] "The Seven Sacraments", a triptych commissioned by Chevrot from Rogier van der Weyden (painted ca. 1453-55), also offers a unique iconography that compresses time and space to communicate the ancient and quotidian power of the church; see E. PANOFSKY, *Early Netherlandish Painting: Its Origins and Character*, 2 vols. (Cambridge, 1953), I, pp. 282-284; J. SNYDER, *Northern Renaissance Art: Painting, Sculpture, the Graphic Arts from 1350 to 1575* (New York, 1985), p. 129.

Fig. 8 Jean Wauquelin presents the *Chroniques de Hainaut* to Philip the Good, duke of Burgundy. The man directly to Philip's right is Nicholas Rolin; to Rolin's right is Jean Chevrot. The man behind them may be Gui Guilbaut. Brussels, Bibliothèque Royale Albert Ier 9242, f. 1; 1448. Copyright Bibliothèque Royale de Belgique.

not only with a salary and large bonuses, but with a string of canonries and archdeaconships that together made him a very rich man, if a less than dutiful priest.[35] The bishopric of Tournai was only the last and biggest of these political plums. Chevrot can be seen in his natural place, standing to Philip's right, in the famous presentation scene that opens volume 1 of the *Chroniques de Hainaut* (Brussels, Bibl. Royale Albert Ier 9242, f. 1; see fig. 8); Panofsky notes "his amiably skeptical, horse-lipped face".[36] On Chevrot's left is Nicholas Rolin, Philip's chancellor and the bishop's close friend.[37]

[35] FOUREZ, "L'Evêque Chevrot", pp. 74-75; BARTIER, *Légistes*, p. 119; see IBID., pp. 310-324, for a detailed account of Chevrot's political career.

[36] PANOFSKY, *Early Netherlandish Painting*, I, p. 282.

[37] FOUREZ, "L'Evêque Chevrot", p. 74. Jeffrey Chipps Smith has suggested that the man standing behind Rolin and Chevrot might be Gui Guilbaut: "The Artistic Patronage of Philip the

The explanation, again, may lie in politics. When the see of Tournai fell vacant in 1433, Philip wanted to gain control of the diocese by installing Chevrot. But the appointment was in the gift of the king of France, then Charles VII. Charles nominated his councillor Jean d'Harcourt, who immediately set out to Rome to seek confirmation from Pope Eugene IV. There began a shoving match between Philip and Charles, with the pope, the Council of Basle, the two nominees, and various Tournai dignitaries all taking part. Chevrot's feelings about the king were reflected in his support of an Anglophile policy at the Arras negotiations of 1435 – although he found it advisable to ally himself afterwards with the official policy of rapprochement with France.[38]

In 1436, Philip's diplomacy succeeded in winning the pope's approval of Chevrot's appointment to the see of Tournai, but the city itself continued to support the king. When Chevrot sent a proxy to be installed as bishop, the people pulled him off the cathedra and tore off his surplice. In retaliation, Philip declared a boycott of Tournai, and the pope threatened excommunication. At last, the Tournaisiens agreed reluctantly to accept Chevrot as their bishop, and he was installed in November 1438.[39]

Chevrot must have issued his *Cité* commission within a few years of 1438, since the 449-folio first volume was completed in 1445.[40] The implication is that Chevrot conceived the iconography of his frontispiece in the aftermath of the controversy over his appointment. In its shift of emphasis from king to bishop, it communicates his conviction that the power of the state, though worth respect, is far outweighed by that of the church. It's a face-off between the sceptre and the book, and clearly it is the book – especially the book made audible – that wins.

The Volume 2 Frontispiece

The meditation on the power of books, and the polite devaluation of the monarchy, do not stop with the frontispiece to volume 1. The much less famous frontispiece to the second volume of Chevrot's *Cité* opens with a presentation

Good, Duke of Burgundy (1419-1467)" (Ph.D. dissertation, Columbia University, 1979), p. 189.

[38] Antoine de la Taverne, *Journal de la paix d'Arras, 1435*, ed. A. BOSSUAT (Arras, 1936), pp. XVIII, 85-86; BARTIER, *Légistes*, pp. 312, 315; DE MOREMBERT, "Jean Chevrot", pp. 176-180; THIELEMANS, *Bourgogne et Angleterre*, p. 78 n. 77.

[39] FOUREZ, "L'Evêque Chevrot", pp. 75-78; BARTIER, *Légistes*, pp. 312-315; VANWIJNSBERGHE, *'De fin or et d'azur'*, pp. 32-33.

[40] VAN DEN GHEYN, *Catalogue*, p. 180.

Fig. 9 Presentation frontispiece, volume 2 of Chevrot's *Cité de Dieu*. Brussels, Bibliothèque Royale Albert Ier 9016, f. 1; ca. 1445. Copyright Bibliothèque Royale de Belgique.

scene that has no precedent in the Guilbaut manuscript (see fig. 9).[41] The very displacement of this scene to second rank suggests a deliberately deflected hierarchy of value; every other *Cité de Dieu* with a presentation scene puts it at the beginning of the first volume.[42]

Comparing the two Chevrot frontispieces, we can see that the presentation scene represents a great contraction of spatial, temporal, and philosophical scale: from eternal verity in the sky and in the City, a fifth-century Father of the Church presiding over a thousand years of transmitted authority and a king founding a great dynasty with enduring miraculous phenomena, to – a reception room with some people standing around in it. Most scholars identify the scene as Raoul de Presles presenting the book to Charles V, i.e., as a recreation of the 'original' presentation of the translation. Alternatively, it could be Charles VII imagined as receiving the new exemplar from its scribe. The important thing in either case is the kingship, emphasized by the fact that behind this king hangs a cloth of honour woven in the same brocade as that worn by Clovis in the first volume's frontispiece. The king resembles Clovis facially, while his robe is covered with the fleurs-de-lys given to Clovis in the first frontispiece, and he holds (in his left hand, pointing right) a sceptre very similar to the one that Clovis holds prominently (in his right hand, pointing left) in the first frontispiece. Several other pictorial elements link this presentation scene to the first frontispiece. The kneeling presenter wears the same black robe as the falsely clergified Raoul from the first frontispiece. The bishop standing to the left strongly recalls Augustine, both facially and in his mitre and blue robe. Finally, the blue-and-grey checkerboard pattern on the cathedral floor, in the first frontispiece, is echoed in the floor of the second frontispiece.

However, while the king's authority is visible in the traditional iconography of elevated position, cloth of honour, and kneeling book-presenter, other factors contribute to offset him. On either side stands a crowd of witnesses. On the left, a cardinal and the bishop also hold books, like the men on the benches in the first volume's frontispiece. A Benedictine abbot and four canons stand behind.[43] The king is receiving one book, as we watch (or, he is gesturing down to it, at some distance from his throne), but these ecclesiasts have more books among them, implying more knowledge and wisdom, upon which the king will need to rely. Meanwhile, the king, though high, seems young and small, dwarfed by the large chair he sits on (Charles VII would have been 42 in 1445);

[41] See also L.M.J. DELAISSÉ, *La Miniature flamande: Le Mécénat de Philippe le Bon* (Brussels, 1959), pp. 35-36 and Pl. 9.

[42] Cf. FOUREZ, "L'Evêque Chevrot", p. 90.

[43] FOUREZ, "L'Evêque Chevrot", p. 86.

the ecclesiasts seem quite comfortable and unawed by his presence. In the original presentation illumination, Augustine was shown encouraging Raoul to approach the great king; in this distant ancestor, the ecclesiasts stand by pleasantly while the lowest-ranking of them does the honours.

On the right of the picture, the laymen crowd in; they seem less like royal attendants than *bourgeois de la ville*, eager to advise or influence the king. Just as the cardinal on the left recalls Chevrot's depiction in the Hainault frontispiece, and may be intended to represent him, so does one particular figure stand out among the bourgeois. His square face and slightly stooped attitude, as well as his chaperon and pleated, fur-bordered gown, recall the depiction of Nicholas Rolin in the Hainault presentation.[44] But unlike that scene, which is dominated by the intelligent, autocratic figure of Philip the Good, Chevrot's frontispiece gives us a little king on a too-big throne, surrounded, or bolstered, or intimidated by the accumulated wisdom and political experience of a crowd of book-wielding advisors, chief among them Philip the Good's two main councillors.

The shields in the back windows go even further in displacing the king: we see France and Chevrot on the left, Burgundy and Flanders on the right.[45] Such elements are not necessarily meant to be read realistically, i.e. to imply that the king is a visitor in Burgundian territory – specifically at Chevrot's residence – rather than presiding in his own palace.[46] On the other hand, the rest of the page further emphasizes Chevrot's shield: not only does it appear on a banner held by a man-beast, in the upper right-hand corner of the border, but it features prominently, supported on a crozier, in the eight-line initial C that begins the text. The brightest element on the page, the gold-decorated initial sends the eye up to the shield in the picture above it. Moving back down, the eye catches the two croziers held by the bishop and the abbot in the picture, which return one to the crozier behind Chevrot's arms in the initial below – recalling, through them, Augustine and the apostolic authority.[47] The effect is to offset the king's

[44] The Hainault frontispiece is dated to 1448 (P. COCKSHAW, *Les Miniatures des 'Chroniques de Hainaut' (15ème siècle)* [Mons, 1979], p. 7), a few years after the date of 1445 usually attached to Chevrot's *Cité*. However, the 1445 date is actually derived from Cotin's colophon to volume 1 of the Chevrot manuscript; the 519-folio second volume (LYNA, *Les Principaux Manuscrits*, p. 25) could easily have taken another couple of years to write, and may only then have gone to the illuminator.

[45] FOUREZ, "L'Evêque Chevrot", pp. 79, 87.

[46] If the scene is set in Chevrot's residence, this would presumably be his *hôtel* at Lille (see FOUREZ, "L'Evêque Chevrot", pp. 79, 87; VANWIJNSBERGHE, *'De fin or et d'azur'*, pp. 34-35).

[47] By contrast, Chevrot's shield in the historiated initial of the first frontispiece is much smaller and less noticeable.

eminence still further, reducing him from king in his castle, like Charles V in the presentation copy, to the guest of a powerful ecclesiast.

Aurality and Illumination

The habit of medievalists, in discussions of texts and illuminations, has been to talk of authors, artists, sources, patrons – and only finally, and minimally, of reception. Chevrot's volume 1 frontispiece has attracted a good deal of attention, for example – almost all of it from art historians, for whom the compelling question has been: how close is it to Jan van Eyck? Although most agree that the frontispiece is by another artist, its quality and a number of its pictorial elements recall other manuscript and panel paintings possibly or definitely painted by Jan.[48] If all such problems are or can be resolved, one sup-

[48] Jan van Eyck was in Philip the Good's service from May 1425 to his death in July 1441, and often took commissions from the duke's associates. See P. LORENTZ, "Les Rolin et les 'primitifs flamands'", in: *La Bonne Etoile des Rolin: Mécénat et efflorescence artistique dans la Bourgogne du XVe siècle*, ed. B. MAURICE-CHABARD (Autun, 1994), p. 23; E. DHANENS, *Hubert and Jan van Eyck* (London, 1980), p. 55.

L.M.J. Delaissé remarks that the style of the Chevrot frontispiece "poses one of the most complex problems in the history of the Flemish miniature" (*Miniatures médiévales*, p. 116). Very briefly: the Chevrot frontispiece is usually considered in relation to two other works of art: (1) "The Virgin with Two Saints and Donor" (otherwise called "The Virgin and Child with Saints Barbara and Elizabeth and Jan Vos" or the "Vierge au chartreux"), a panel painting in the Frick Museum; and (2) several miniatures in the Turin-Milan Hours attributed, in Georges Hulin de Loo's classification, to Hands G and H (*Heures de Milan* [Brussels, 1911], pp. 27-38) and associated more recently by Anne van Buren with Hand I-J (whom she calls the Chevrot Master) ("The Genesis of the Eyckian Book of Prayers and Masses", in: *Heures de Turin-Milan*, vol. 2 [Lucerne, 1996], pp. 332-333). The Chevrot City of God recurs as the city in the background of the Frick Madonna, while art historians have equated various details in the Chevrot volume 1 frontispiece with corresponding elements in the Turin-Milan miniatures. Other similarities have been noted between this set of material and verifiable works by Jan van Eyck – especially the painting some consider his masterpiece, the Louvre's "Vierge du Chancelier Rolin".

Based on these relationships, and on the quality of the painting, some earlier experts attributed one or both Chevrot frontispieces, the Frick Madonna, and/or the Turin-Milan miniatures to Jan van Eyck. The modern consensus, however, is that this material is merely 'Eyckian', attributing the reappearing pictorial elements to the common use of workshop sketches. One of the most recent hypotheses about the Chevrot frontispiece posits that its background was copied directly from the Frick Madonna (T. TOLLEY, "Jan van Eyck and the English", in: *England and the Continent in the Middle Ages*, ed. J. MITCHELL [Stamford: 2000], pp. 267-297, at pp. 283-284 n. 61). (Besides the sources already named, this discussion has drawn on PANOFSKY, *Early Netherlandish Painting*, I, pp. 232-246; FOUREZ, "L'Evêque Chevrot", pp. 90-99; F. LYNA, "Les van Eyck et les 'Heures de Turin et de Milan' ", *Bulletin des* poses, the manuscript would be returned to its metaphorical shelf, to sit there radiant but passive. Even studies of illustration, marginal or not, of 'bad manuscripts', of glossing, and of other in-written commentary seek to elucidate only the reading of one illuminator, one scribe, one glossator, one private, scribbling reader.

The idea of aurality opens that closed world out, and sets the manuscripts dancing on their shelves. Syntax, authorial topoi, characterization, and even illumination may be viewed not (or, not only) as the idiosyncratic result of writers and artists struggling with, or against, their sources and models, but also as features meant to enhance the audience's comprehension or enjoyment, meant to take form in performance in ways we are only beginning to explore.

One particular use of this aurality, as we have seen, is propaganda. A myriad of prologues, introducing the commissioned texts and translations of magnates from Charles V to Philip the Good and beyond, establish not only that the lord liked to have such books read to him, but that the book was full of noble deeds and wise action, meant as a model to the courtly world.[49] It hardly takes deep cynicism to perceive that all these models came larded with heavy doses of the politically desirable message of the day. For the message to get out, the book must be given voice. The lord brought in his household, as owners of later copies brought in theirs, to learn from the authoritative text that the kings of France ruled by divine decree, or that the dukes of Burgundy were the rightful and beloved lords of Hainault. Nor was this listening a chore; aural propaganda exploited not the listeners, but the listeners' long-standing love of hearing books together, in social groups. Literacy, in the sense of private reading, did not negate but interacted with this practice, the private reader's study of a work informing his or her further aural experience (and vice versa).

As D.H. Green has argued, the growing literacy of the later Middle Ages led not to the extinction of orality but to a 'bimodality', or what he calls "the intermediate mode of reception ... in which a work was composed with an eye

Musées Royaux des Beaux-Arts: Miscellanea Erwin Panofsky [Brussels, 1955], pp. 7-20; O. PÄCHT, *Van Eyck and the Founders of Early Netherlandish Painting*, trans. D. BRITT [London, 1994], pp. 177-210; BOUSMANNE and VAN HOOREBEECK, *La Librairie des ducs de Bourgogne*, pp. 78-79; S. JONES, "The Use of Workshop Drawings by Jan van Eyck and His Followers", in: *Investigating Jan van Eyck*, ed. S. FOISTER, S. JONES and D. COOL [Turnhout, 2000], pp. 197-207. For an overview of the arguments, see M. SMEYERS, *Flemish Miniatures from the 8th to the Mid-16th Centuries*, trans. K. BOWEN and D. IMHOF [Leuven, 1999], pp. 257-260.)

49 COLEMAN, *Public Reading*, pp. 23-26; cf. A. DUBOIS, "La Scène de présentation des *Chroniques de Hainaut*: Idéologie et politique à la cour de Bourgogne", in: *Les Chroniques de Hainaut, ou les ambitions d'un prince bourgignon*, ed. P. COCKSHAW and C. VAN DEN BERGEN (Turnhout, 2000), pp. 119-124.

to public recital from a written text, but also for the occasional private reader".[50] The fact that words can be read aloud while pictures cannot is thus a trivial problem for the study of 'aural illumination'. If there were only one or two listeners, they could sit beside the prelector and look at the pictures – and, indeed, pause to discuss them and their relation to the text. If the listeners were sitting (or standing) before the reader – as in the Chevrot frontispiece and most other prelection illuminations – the prelector might perhaps describe the picture. Listeners might stroll over to look as the reading progressed, or might come to examine the book once it had ceased.

Intersecting with this usage, individuals could also take up the manuscript privately, or in small groups, to page over and read, or to admire or even study the illustrations. Over time, people resident in a given household who had an interest in books would no doubt become familiar with the text and pictures of the books within that household. Private viewing could fill in the gaps of the public reading, or past private viewings would inform any later public reading, so that the auditor had a mental image of the picture to refer to as the reading progressed. Thus the viewing of pictures flowed into and out of different forms of reading: images could be described, seen, discussed, remembered, and seen again, as circumstance and tastes demanded. Like the texts themselves, the pictures could be described as 'bimodal', experienced alternately or conjointly through private and public modes.

Thus Gui Guilbaut's frontispiece of Augustine and Clovis, though it does not depict public reading, was surely meant to attract public viewing – meant for more than the patron's eyes. We may be sure that Philip the Good had a look at it; he later bought the manuscript from Guilbaut's grandson – one of the few books Philip is known to have purchased.[51] Clearly, so did Jean Chevrot and the other important Burgundians who had copies made. If Guilbaut did commission his exemplar in celebration of the Treaty of Arras, the frontispiece is as much a political statement, and thus as much public property, as the prologue on which it draws. Thus, illuminations can create 'viewing communities' who share and further propagate their message. They are another form of what Jeffrey Chipps Smith calls (speaking of tapestries) 'portable propaganda'.[52]

The famous Hainault presentation frontispiece obviously had a similar intent, and even more impact. The skill of a very gifted artist – Rogier van der

[50] GREEN, "Orality and Reading", p. 277.

[51] G. DOUTREPONT, *La Littérature française à la court des ducs de Bourgogne* (Paris, 1909), p. 209; DE LOO, "Gui Guilbaut", pp. 330-331.

[52] J. CHIPPS SMITH, "Portable Propaganda – Tapestries as Princely Metaphors at the Courts of Philip the Good and Charles the Bold", *Art Journal* 48 (1989), pp. 123-129, at p. 123.

Weyden or an associate – imbued such authority into the image of Philip (backed by his church-state consultation team of Chevrot and Rolin) that the scene was recreated in numerous later manuscripts.[53] From this point of view, even the talent of the artist employed becomes a strategy of self-promotion by the patron. Not only will eyes be constantly drawn to the picture, and tongues consequently set wagging, but other patrons will request copies, and other artists imitate the scene, spreading its impacted messages in ever-widening ripples. Anne Dubois describes the Hainault presentation scene as one of the best examples of the "vast propaganda effort" Philip conducted by means of commissioned manuscripts.[54]

We may suppose that Jean Chevrot had a similar ambition, when he selected a gifted artist for his *Cité de Dieu* frontispiece, and when he designed a unique iconography sure to appeal to fellow ecclesiasts. Indeed, his *Cité* was being copied by another bishop in 1458, when Chevrot wrote his will,[55] and Willem Vrelant imitated the reading/teaching scene in a later *City of God.*[56] But Chevrot's frontispiece takes the phenomenon to another level, not only illustrating a text that relies on aurality, but employing that aurality to make an elaborate statement about the nature of the text and its relationship to secular authority. Chevrot takes us back to the older sense of 'propaganda', of doctrine to be propagated by the highest religious authorities. The illustrated prologue to Raoul's translation now becomes an essay on translation, specifically on *translatio auctoritatis*. On one side, the *translatio imperii* is implied by the eagle that recalls the Roman emperor's standard. On the other side, far more impressively, the many-levelled, multilingual flow of public reading, private reading, writing, translation, and more public reading encodes a thousand-year-long *translatio studii*.[57]

Frontispieces that show the book being presented to a patron communicate chiefly that the text is prestigious, associated with royalty or nobility. Prelection frontispieces go further, in suggesting to viewers both who created the text and for whom it was created. Chevrot rekeyed Raoul's layman's *Cité* towards

[53] DUBOIS, "La Scène de présentation".

[54] DUBOIS, "La Scène de présentation", p. 122.

[55] FOUREZ, "L'Evêque Chevrot", p. 106.

[56] Bruges, Stadsbibliotheek 106, f. 22 (a Latin-only copy, hence presumably for a clerical owner); see B. BOUSMANNE, *'Item a Guillaume Wyelant aussi enlumineur': Willem Vrelant, Un aspect de l'enluminure dans les Pays-Bas méridionaux sous le mécénat des ducs de Bourgogne Philippe le Bon et Charles le Téméraire* (Turnhout, 1997), pp. 72, 73 (Pl. 26), 227.

[57] See A.G. JONGKEES, "*Translatio studii*: Les Avatars d'un thème médiéval", in: *Miscellanea Mediaevalia in Memoriam Jan Frederik Niermeyer* (Groningen, 1967), pp. 41-51; LUSIGNAN, *Parler vulgairement*, pp. 154-171.

an ecclesiastical audience not only by having Raoul portrayed as a monk, but also by presenting only male auditors. Other *Cité* frontispieces show Raoul reading or propounding to mixed groups of laymen and women,[58] suggesting the work's potential interest as recreational reading. In depicting only male auditors, within a hierarchical ecclesiastical framework, Chevrot emphasizes instead a more scholarly or religious aurality.[59]

Even within the ecclesiastical framework, moreover, audiences and auralities are distinguished by language. The advanced latinity of one audience corresponds to their generally higher rank – as indicated by their robes of office – and to their own stature as contributors to the intellectual and theological tradition inaugurated by Augustine – as indicated by the books they hold. Their Latin skills equip them, as it were, to listen directly to the great doctor himself. The vernacular audience – perhaps a friar and a secular cleric or canon – are clearly of humbler status. The fact that they apparently require a translated *City of God* suggests that their Latin would have been sufficient for administrative or pastoral purposes, but not enough to equip them to understand patristic writings. Perhaps they represent the lower strata of clerical functionaries within episcopal households such as Chevrot's. They are denied direct access to Augustine's voice, but hear it closely echoed from the translator, positioned at the foot of the saint's throne. Each in their way suggests the Christian community, and ecclesiastical lines of authority, created across time and space, and within any given time and space, by shared reading, hearing – and viewing – of Augustine's seminal work.

The volume 1 frontispiece even links, through one last subtle piece of iconography, the primacy of the spoken word in the constitution of authority with the foundational authority of the spoken word in Christianity. In a panel at the base of Augustine's cathedra has been 'carved' (i.e. painted in grisaille) the core event of Christianity – the Annunciation (see fig. 7). The breath-blown scroll bearing Gabriel's words seems to float upwards towards Augustine above – underwriting, as it were, the power of the Logos carried on by the saint and incarnated in the City of God behind.

The first hearers and viewers of Chevrot's *Cité* would have found no contradiction in a picture about reading aloud. As they gathered to admire the

[58] Paris, Bibl. Nat. de France fr. 19, f. 1 (bet. 1469-73) and Nantes, Bibl. Mun. fr. 8, f. 1 (ca. 1478). The complete Paris manuscript is BNF fr. 18-19, de Laborde's exemplar No. 54 (*Manuscrits*, II, pp. 397-416); the Nantes manuscript is volume 2 of a *Cité* whose first volume is The Hague, Museum Meermanno-Westreenianum MS 11; together these form de Laborde's exemplar No. 56 (*Manuscrits*, II, pp. 423-448).

[59] See COLEMAN, *Public Reading*, pp. 140-147, for a discussion of different forms of aurality.

beautiful, complex miniature, they would have seen their quotidian reality of textual reception given vast significance, as one link among the innumerable links in the millennium-long transmission of core Christian beliefs. That thought, and picture, in mind, they could then have settled onto their benches as a prelector undertook Raoul de Presles' role in leading them through the many-tongued text.

Index

1. Manuscripts

Note: This index does not include the appendices on pp. 92-102 and 168-179. Where the manuscript signature does not appear in the text, the short title of the work it contains has been given, so that the reference can be identified.

2. Names and sources